European Union and its Neighbours in a Globalized World

Volume 25

The series publishes monographs and edited volumes in the field of European and international law and policy. A special focus is put on the European neighbourhood policy, current problems in European and international law and policy as well as the role of the European Union as a global actor. The series supports the publishing and distribution of research results of cross-border research consortia. Besides renowned scientists the series is also open for publication projects of young academics. The series emphasizes the interplay of the European Union and its neighbouring countries as well as the important role of the European Union as a key player in the international context of law, economics and politics.

Rita Remeikienė • Ligita Gasparėnienė
Editors

Work and Legal Guidelines in the Age of Digitalisation and Green Transition

Platform Labour Across the EU and its Neighbours

Springer

Editors
Rita Remeikienė
Faculty of Law
Vilnius University
Vilnius, Lithuania

Ligita Gasparėnienė
Faculty of Law
Vilnius University
Vilnius, Lithuania

ISSN 2524-8928 ISSN 2524-8936 (electronic)
European Union and its Neighbours in a Globalized World
ISBN 978-3-032-03510-3 ISBN 978-3-032-03511-0 (eBook)
https://doi.org/10.1007/978-3-032-03511-0

This scientific study was funded by the European Union under Grant Agreement No. 101126470 (JWCPW — SOCPL-2022-IND-REL) within the framework of the Directorate-General for Employment, Social Affairs, and Inclusion (EMPL.C – Working Conditions and Social Dialogue). Views and opinions expressed are those of the authors only and do not necessarily reflect those of the European Union or the European Commission. Neither the European Union nor the granting authority can be held responsible for them.

This Springer imprint is published by the registered company Springer Nature Switzerland AG
The registered company address is: Gewerbestrasse 11, 6330 Cham, Switzerland

Acknowledgements

Funded by the European Union. Views and opinions expressed are however those of the author(s) only and do not necessarily reflect those of the European Union or Vilnius university. Neither the European Union nor the granting authority can be held responsible for them.

This monograph was published under the Project 101126470 — JWCPW — SOCPL-2022-IND-REL EU Directorate-General for Employment, Social Affairs and Inclusion foundation (Grant Agreement Project 101126470 — JWCPW).

Funded by the European Union

Co-funded by the European Union

Contents

Chapter 1
Introduction

Rita Remeikienė and Ligita Gasparėnienė

In the twenty-first century, structural transformations in the economy and labour markets have been primarily driven by two converging forces: digitalisation and the green transition. These megatrends—fostered by technological innovation, environmental imperatives, and new forms of economic organisation—are reshaping how work is structured, how employment relations are formed, and how labour is regulated. Across the European Union (EU) and its Eastern and Southeastern neighbours, these developments challenge existing legal frameworks and compel new approaches to social protection, employment governance, and sustainable development.

This book explores the intersection of digitalisation, the green economy, and labour market regulation within the emerging platform economy. Through an interdisciplinary lens that integrates legal, economic, and policy analysis, it examines how labour relations are evolving in response to technological innovation and ecological transformation. Special attention is devoted to platform work, its legal status, working conditions, and the European Union's efforts to ensure a fair and inclusive digital labour market. Comparative insights from post-Soviet and Balkan countries highlight regional disparities and legal fragmentation in adapting to these shifts.

The second chapter investigates the dual effects of digitalisation and greening on the labour market. It explores how robotisation, automation, and platformisation are transforming employment structures, skill demands, and power dynamics between workers and employers. Simultaneously, the green transition—driven by the European Green Deal—introduces new industrial logics, fosters environmental innovation, and redefines job creation. This chapter concludes by analysing the

R. Remeikienė (✉) · L. Gasparėnienė
Faculty of Law, Vilnius University, Vilnius, Lithuania
e-mail: rita.remeikiene@tf.vu.lt; ligita.gaspareniene@tf.vu.lt

R. Remeikienė, L. Gasparėnienė (eds.), *Work and Legal Guidelines in the Age of Digitalisation and Green Transition*, European Union and its Neighbours in a Globalized World 25, https://doi.org/10.1007/978-3-032-03511-0_1

combined impact of these transformations, highlighting their synergetic potential and risks of labour market polarisation.

The third chapter delves into the conceptual and practical specificities of platform work. It defines the phenomenon, traces its emergence in the digital economy, and examines the conditions under which digital labour is performed. Key themes include the role of trade unions, the contractual status of platform workers, and the challenges of informality and precarity, particularly in post-Soviet contexts.

The fourth chapter addresses European Union policy responses, focusing on strategies aimed at regulating digital platform work while promoting sustainable economic growth. It examines instruments such as the Digital Agenda, the European Green Deal, and recent EU Platform work Directive, assessing how the EU is attempting to reconcile innovation with social protection in a rapidly evolving labour environment.

The fifth chapter offers a comparative legal analysis of Eastern and Southeastern European countries, including Moldova, Ukraine, Bosnia and Herzegovina, Serbia, Montenegro, and Albania. These case studies reveal the challenges of adapting national legal systems to the realities of the platform economy, uncovering issues such as enforcement deficits, legal uncertainty, and socio-economic inequality.

The sixth chapter presents empirical findings from a field survey conducted among digital platform workers in Moldova. The data provide grounded insight into workers' income levels, skill usage, employment classification, and access to social protection. These findings serve to validate and enrich the book's earlier theoretical and normative discussions. Moldova was selected as a case study due to its illustrative regulatory, economic, and social context, the limited availability of existing research, and the quality and relevance of the newly collected empirical data. Maintaining this chapter as a distinct section is methodologically justified and contributes to the overall coherence and applied value of the book.

Overall, this book seeks to contribute to ongoing academic and policy debates by offering an interdisciplinary synthesis of law, economics, and social policy that provides a comprehensive understanding of the digital-green-labour nexus. By linking macro-level regulatory and policy transformations with micro-level labour and employment realities, it delivers a multidimensional perspective on how digitalisation and ecological imperatives are reshaping the future of work and law. The study is intended for scholars, policymakers, and practitioners working at the intersection of labour regulation, digital economy governance, and sustainability. It advocates for equitable, adaptive, and coherent regulatory strategies that respond effectively to structural change while promoting social inclusion and decent work in a rapidly evolving European economy shaped by the digital-green transition.

Chapter 2
Digitalisation, Greening and the Labour Market

Rita Remeikienė and Ligita Gasparėnienė

Abstract This chapter explores the dual impact of digitalisation and the green transition on the labour market, highlighting how these transformations reshape work structures, employment relations, and skill demands. It first examines digitalisation through the lenses of automation, robotisation, and digital labour platforms. While these developments boost productivity, they also pose risks such as job displacement and labour market polarisation, especially for low- and medium-skilled workers. Additionally, new forms of platform-based, non-standard work challenge traditional legal definitions and weaken social protections. The green transition is discussed as a major industrial shift influenced by EU policies, particularly the European Green Deal. The chapter outlines how innovation, energy efficiency, and sustainable production alter employment patterns. It identifies key mechanisms of change—such as resource efficiency and process innovation—and evaluates their implications for job creation and transformation. By integrating technological and environmental perspectives, the chapter proposes a framework to assess how these twin transitions interact and shape labour dynamics. It also points to policy measures that can mitigate associated risks and support inclusive, sustainable employment growth.

The past decade has seen unprecedented structural changes, including business automation, digitalisation of systems, and the shift toward the green economy to mitigate climate change. These changes reflect the profound phenomena which take place in the economy and society due to the use of digital technologies (Majchrzak et al. 2016; Agrawal et al. 2022) and popularisation of sustainable economic systems (Razminienė and Tvaronavičienė 2018; Baldassarre et al. 2019). Thus, they

R. Remeikienė (✉) · L. Gasparėnienė
Faculty of Law, Vilnius University, Vilnius, Lithuania
e-mail: rita.remeikiene@tf.vu.lt; ligita.gaspareniene@tf.vu.lt

R. Remeikienė, L. Gasparėnienė (eds.), *Work and Legal Guidelines in the Age of Digitalisation and Green Transition*, European Union and its Neighbours in a Globalized World 25, https://doi.org/10.1007/978-3-032-03511-0_2

indisputably have a significant impact on the labour market, affecting the balance of labour demand and supply, the skills of the labour force required by the market, and the forms of work that emerge in the modern economy. Perception of the links between the phenomena mentioned above and the analysis of their effects on the labour market can help to assess the potential of the long-term sustainable development of the labour market and identify the major risk factors which can be purposefully managed both at the national and the EU levels. This section analyses various aspects of the impact of digitalisation and green transformation on the labour market and presents a model for assessing their combined impact.

2.1 Effects of Digitalisation on the Labour Market

Digitalisation is widely recognised as one of the most significant drivers of structural economic transformation in contemporary societies. Its importance has been emphasized in the World Economic Forum in Davos, Digital Innovation Hubs Day in Stuttgart, Mobile World Congress in Barcelona and many other conferences and debates. Although digitalisation is considered one of the key factors in the green transformation of economic and social life, it will undoubtedly lead to significant structural changes in social life and the labour market.

The digital transformation of business activities is a response to the rapid development of digital technologies. Digital transformation in business refers to the organisational transformations which are related to the changes in internal business processes, sectoral changes, and transformations of supply chains (Hetmanczyk 2023). In contrast to the traditional approach, where the labour market focused on job functions and characteristics, digitalisation requires competency-based human resource management. In the process of digitalisation, we are moving towards attention to diversity, openness, knowledge, willingness to accept changes, the use of various distribution channels and more efficient organisation of work. Technologies are becoming a source of comparative advantage which can be exploited by technologically literate individuals as an advantage in the labour market, and employers can exploit this advantage to achieve desired business outcomes.

Digitalisation also alters the distribution and quality of jobs, intensifies the need for re-skilling, and reshapes the nature of work relations (Vasilescu et al. 2020). When analysing the impact of digitalisation on the labour market, it is important to answer the questions of how digitalisation changes the distribution of jobs, which jobs are newly created and which are likely to disappear, how work processes are organised and relations between workers and employers are formed, and whether there is a risk of polarisation in the labour market (Buhrer and Hagist 2016).

Based on the literature, the main dimensions through which digitalisation affects the labour market can be summarised as follows (Macias 2018; Vasilescu et al. 2020):

1) robotisation and automation of work;
2) work organising through digital platforms;
3) organising the relations between workers and employers;
4) polarisation in the labour market.

These aspects are examined in the following subsections. However, while prior research provides a solid foundation, there remains a need to distinguish how these transformations manifest differently across employment categories and national contexts. The analysis that follows addresses this gap by exploring digitalisation in relation to emerging forms of employment regulation and labour market policies, with a particular focus on platform work.

2.1.1 *Effects of Robotisation and Automation of Work*

This section outlines how automation and robotisation—key drivers of the digital economy—are reshaping employment structures across sectors, with potential long-term implications for platform-based labour models.

In the next decade, digitalisation may lead to changes in how businesses generate profits: advanced robotics and artificial intelligence solutions will be increasingly used to generate profits. Experts believe the number of robots to increase not only in factories, but also in the environment near people—in workplaces, at home, in streets. 5G technologies will allow digital devices to be connected to a single network. The development of the modern industry and the improvement of the quality of life will require the management of big data and the development of business algorithms (Raczko 2015). Today's cloud computing solutions will make service delivery processes digital, and at the same time will transform service business models (Raczko 2015).

Industrial robotics is gaining momentum, and the market share of industrial robotics is growing rapidly.

Figure 2.1 indicates that the global market share of industrial robotics was estimated at \$18.31 billion in 2022; it is expected to reach \$23.44 billion in 2024, and

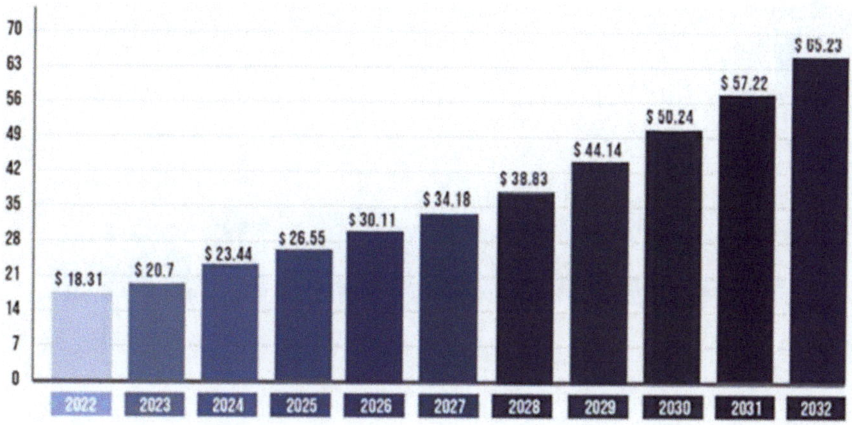

Fig. 2.1 Dynamics of the industrial robotics market share between 2022 and 2023 (USD billion). Source: "Precedence Research", 2023

$65.23 billion by 2032, i.e. it is forecast to grow more than 3.5 times in 10 years. Robots are increasingly being used in different industries, most notably in manufacturing. If initially large robotic arms were used to handle heavy objects (e.g. car parts), with the advent technologies, such as visual recognition, machine learning, failure prediction, and collaborative robots (co-bots), the potential of robots has increased significantly.

There were 3.9 million operational robots at the global level in 2022 (the World Robotics 2023 Report, presented by the International Federation of Robotics (2023)). The global robot density (the number of industrial robots per 10,000 workers) was 151 in 2022.

Figure 2.2 shows that the leading positions in terms of robot density in 2022 were held by the Republic of Korea (1012 robots per 10,000 employees), Singapore (730 robots per 10,000 employees) and Germany (415 robots per 10,000 employees). The average robot density in Europe is 136, in the EU—208, with Germany being the clear leader with a 5 percent compound annual growth rate (CAGR) increase in robot density since 2017 (Bachmann et al. 2022).

Robots have become an integral part of many industries. The illustration of the top industries, where robots are most widely used, is presented in Fig. 2.3.

The automotive industry was the largest user of robots in 2020. About 28 percent of industrial robots are used in this industry (Fairchild 2021). The electrical/electronics industry uses robots because the processes in this industry are characterised by repetitive production and standardization of parts. However, compared to the automotive industry, electronic parts are much smaller than heavy metal car parts. Thus, robots used in electronics tend to be smaller, lighter and faster. The metalworking sector uses robots which can work at high temperatures and rotate at high speeds. In the plastics and chemical industries, they help protect workers from exposure to harmful substances. Although the construction sector is still

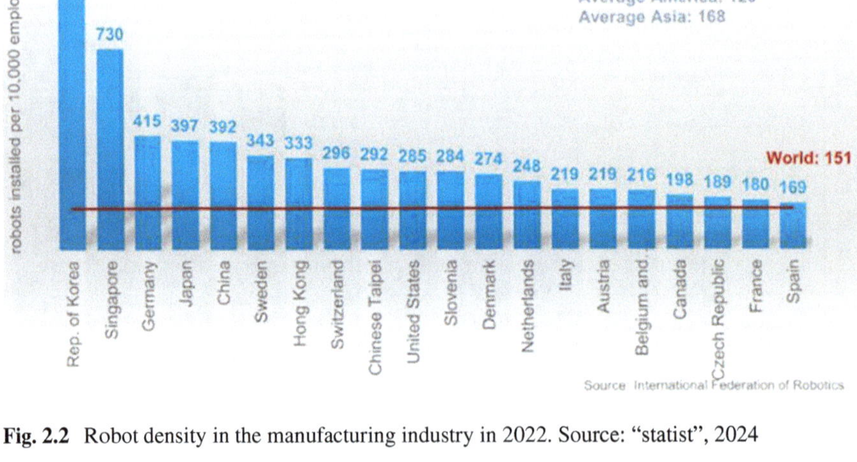

Fig. 2.2 Robot density in the manufacturing industry in 2022. Source: "statist", 2024

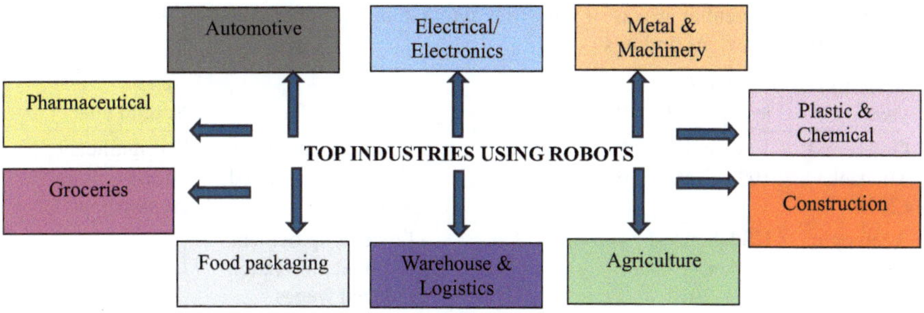

Fig. 2.3 Top 10 robot using industries. Source: compiled by the authors with reference to Fairchild (2021)

labour-intensive, robots are increasingly used here for lifting cement blocks and tying reinforcing metal bars. The agricultural sector uses self-driven vehicles, weeding and harvest picking robots, thus reducing high labour costs. The higher operational productivity and lower labour costs generated by robots can also be seen in the warehouse and logistics sector, where box loading, labelling, and sorting processes have been automated. The packaging of food products by robots is already in its commercial stage, and automated storage and retrieval systems (AS/RS) can be fit into the back of many grocery stores. In the pharmaceutical industry, robots place tablets into blister packs and dispense precise amounts of liquid into testing vials (Fairchild 2021).

According to Goos (2018), robotisation and automation are the structural components of business transformation which will lead to changes in the labour market in the near future. "The Future of Jobs Report", provided by the World Economic Forum (2018), indicates that 28 percent of business companies worldwide expect to increase their work productivity by 2022, and more than a quarter expect that automation will help create new jobs in their companies. Businesses are intending to expand the use of outsourcing contractors for specialised work, also to decentralise operations, and employ workers on flexible terms for remote work. In general, the report points out that the format, location, quality, and duration of new job functions will change significantly. Previous studies suggest that the effects of robotisation and automation on the labour market can be mixed (see Table 2.1).

After conducting a study in Germany in the period 1994–2014, Dauth et al. (2021) found that automation can be associated with stable employment for incumbent workers because they can learn to perform new types of tasks in their old company, and the new jobs are often of better quality than the old ones. Robots also help reduce workload, thus freeing managers and technical workers from additional tasks. Nevertheless, robotisation can cause the displacement effect in the manufacturing sector, but this effect is likely to be offset by the increase in the number of jobs in the service sector. These findings are slightly different from the results of the German labour market research, presented by Damelang and Otto (2023): having researched the German manufacturing industry, Damelang and Otto (2023) found a considerably lower unemployment risk for high-skilled workers, but did not find

Table 2.1 The potential effects of industrial automation and robotisation on the labour market: review of some previous findings

Author(s), year	Country(-ies), period	Positive effects	Negative effects	Neutral effects
Graetz and Michaels (2018)	17 countries, 1993–2007	Higher labour productivity	Reduced employment share of low-skilled workers	No significant effects on total employment
Acemoglu and Restrepo (2020)	US labour market, 1993–2014	–	Lower employment-to-population ratio, reduced wages	–
Dauth et al. (2021)	Germany, 1994–2014	New jobs in old companies tend to be of higher quality; fewer additional tasks for managers and technical workers	Displacement effect in the manufacturing sector	Stable employment for incumbent workers; displacement can be offset by new jobs in the service sector
Damelang and Otto (2023)	Germany, not indicated	A considerably lower unemployment risk for high-skilled workers	–	No higher unemployment risk for low- and medium-skilled workers is observed
De Vries et al. (2020)	37 countries, 2005–2015	–	Decrease in the number of manual-intensive jobs in high-income economies	No decrease in the number of manual-intensive jobs in developing economies
Gregory et al. (2021)	European countries, 1999–2010	Higher labour productivity creates demand and thus employment in other sectors of the economy	Loss of workplaces due to replacement of human labour by robots	–
Koch et al. (2021)	Spain, 1990–2016	10 percent higher net job creation rate	–	–
Klenert et al. (2022)	European countries (EU-28), 1993–2017	An increase in aggregate employment	–	No evidence of robots reducing the share of low-skilled workers
Anton et al. (2022)	European regional labour markets, 1995–2015	–	Robotisation of industry tends to slightly increase unemployment; robotisation can lead to polarisation in the labour market	–

(continued)

Table 2.1 (continued)

Author(s), year	Country(-ies), period	Positive effects	Negative effects	Neutral effects
Bachmann et al. (2022)	16 European countries, 1998–2017	Beneficial effect on the labour transition of young and old workers in the countries with low labour costs	Insignificant negative effect on job separation and job finding	No significant effects on aggregate employment
Chinoracky and Čorejova (2019)	28 countries, 2013–2019	Rapid growth of labour productivity, easier work; increasing demand for technology control	Difficulties for the low-skilled labour force to adapt to the new environment; declining demand for manual labour	–

Source: compiled by the authors

any greater robotisation-caused risks for low- and medium-skilled workers. The study by Klenert et al. (2022) also did not find any evidence of robots reducing the share of low-skilled workers in Europe; their study implies that the use of robots is associated with an increase in aggregate employment. These contrasting findings suggest that the employment effects of robotisation cannot be generalised across economies and labour categories. The policy environment, sectoral structure, and adaptability of the workforce are all crucial mediators of automation outcomes.

After conducting a study of the impact of the use of industrial robots on European regional labour markets (in particular, on jobs and employment structures) in the period 1995–2015, Anton et al. (2022) found that the impact of industrial robotisation on employment was negative, but insignificant between 1995 and 2005, and positive between 2005 and 2015. Their research also implies that that robotisation may lead to a slight polarisation in the labour market. Bachmann et al.'s (2022) research, focused on the effects of robotisation on worker flows in 16 European countries in the period 1998–2017, revealed a slight negative effect on job separations and a slight positive effect on finding a job. Their research also found that robotisation has a beneficial effect on the labour transition of young and old workers in the countries with low labour costs.

Having combined country-industry data for robot adoption and occupations, de Vries et al. (2020) found that robotisation tends to reduce the number of manual-task intensive jobs, and this tendency is more pronounced in high-income countries compared to developing economies, i.e. the results of the study imply that the impact of robotisation on the labour market may depend on a country's level of development: a decrease in jobs is observed in the areas where work functions are associated with intensive routine manual tasks in high-income countries, but this correlation was not found in emerging and transition economies. The authors explain this tendency by invoking the fact that labour costs affect the economic incentives of companies since the higher are the labour costs, the greater is the probability that human labour will be replaced with robotic labour, other conditions being equal. Thus, robotisation is likely to have less significant impact on the economies with low labour costs than the economies with higher labour costs.

Gregory et al.'s (2021) study revealed both positive and negative aspects of the impact of automation and robotisation on the labour market. The authors found that automation and robotisation primarily threaten employment in European countries since robots replace a significant part of the human workforce (a direct effect). The indirect positive effect manifests itself as follows: robotic technologies allow for increased labour productivity, which, in its turn, creates greater value added and generates higher income for the companies and sectors which are most automated and robotized. The effect of higher income spills over into other sectors: the demand for products/services in other sectors is growing, and the number of workplaces is increasing respectively. This results in an indirect positive effect of automation and robotisation on total employment. Similar findings were provided by Bachmann et al. (2022) and Klenert et al. (2022).

Having researched the economic impact of modern industrial robots which are flexible, versatile and autonomous, Graetz and Michaels (2018) found that robots can provide a comparative advantage in performing specific tasks. The authors estimated that the robots increase labour productivity by approximately 0.36 percentage points, and also contribute to the total factor productivity and reduce output prices, thereby reducing the employment share of low-skilled workers, but do not significantly reduce total employment. Koch et al.'s (2021) study of the Spanish manufacturing sector revealed that robots are likely to be installed in *ex ante* more productive (measured though output and labour productivity) companies; they are expected to increase the output gains by 20–25 percent, reduce labour costs by 5–7 percentage points, and raise net job creation rate by 10 percent within 4 years.

Nevertheless, these results contradict the findings presented by Acemoglu and Restrepo (2020). After researching the potential effects of robots on employment and wages, Acemoglu and Restrepo (2020) noticed that the effects of robots on the economy differ from the effects of types of capital and technology and found that one additional robot per 1000 workers tends to reduce the employment-to-population ratio by approximately 0.2 percentage points, and lessens wages by 0.42 percent. According to Chinoracky and Čorejova (2019), the increasing use of industrial robots will lead to faster labour productivity growth. Some workers will even benefit from it, as the nature of their work will become more pleasant (job functions will be limited to robot maintenance) and they will likely earn higher wages (robot maintenance will require specific skills rare in the labour market, so these skills will be well paid). Meanwhile, other workers will find it difficult to adapt to the new environment, they will face the risk of losing their jobs since the demand for robot maintenance and management will gradually increase, whereas the demand for manual labour will decrease accordingly. The statistical data portal "Statista" (2024) provides the forecasts (based on the estimations by "PwC", "Frey and Osborne" and OECD), which indicate that the share of jobs at high risk of automation is such developed economies as the USA, the United Kingdom, Germany and Japan, is significant.

According to "Statista" (2024) the share of jobs at high risk of automation can exceed 30 percent (according to the data from different assessment institutions), i.e. nearly a third of the workforce may face the problem of job loss due to automation. While much of the current research and data relate to traditional industries, the observed automation trends are gradually spilling over into platform-mediated work environments, where algorithmic management and autonomous systems increasingly shape task distribution and working conditions.

According to the U.S. Government Accountability Office (2022), workers with lower education and performing routine tasks (e.g. cashiers, case managers, data loggers, accountants) are going to face the greatest risk of losing their jobs. Workers at risk of losing their jobs to automation will need to develop new skills to adapt to changing job demands or to get a new job. The U.S. Government Accountability Office (2022) indicates that the following skills will see the greatest growth in demand over the next 10 years:

a) soft skills, i.e. communication skills for successful communication with people;
b) process skills, i.e. the skills which help to quickly acquire knowledge (e.g. active learning, critical thinking);
c) specific technical expertise skills, i.e. the skills which are required for the management and maintenance of certain equipment (e.g. robot management).

Thus, worker training and retraining programs should be directed to help workers to build the skills which are expected to be in-demand for getting a high-quality job.

Overall The findings presented in this section reveal that the effects of robotisation on employment are complex and context-dependent. Although automation can displace low-skilled labour, its aggregate impact on employment varies across countries and sectors, influenced by wage levels, institutional capacity, and complementary policies such as reskilling programmes. Importantly, this raises questions about whether similar patterns may emerge within the platform economy—where automation is embedded not only in machines but in algorithmic management itself.

2.1.2 Work Organising Through Digital Platforms

Historically, work was geographically and institutionally bounded (Hudson 2001). However, the global expansion of internet connectivity has fundamentally transformed the organisation and coordination of labour. Digital labour platforms emerged in the mid-2000s as a modern phenomenon of the digital economy. In fact, it was part of the evolution of the digital economy, when the shift from online digital services towards institutional and technological drivers occurred between 2000 and 2001. This shift allowed the development of digital platforms as an emerging flexible model of work (Valenduc 2021). Digital labour platforms facilitate new forms of work organisation and restructure traditional labour processes (Rani and Furrer 2021; Collins 2021; Torrent-Sellens et al. 2021; Cruz and Gameiro 2023; Leong et al. 2023, etc.). They are not only technological tools but also social institutions that reshape labour relations, control mechanisms, and income generation models.

Digital platforms operate as intermediaries, linking service users with providers (Berg et al. 2018; ILO 2018c; OECD 2019b; Dunn 2020; Rivera and Lee 2021; Kalamatiev and Murdzev 2022, etc.) (see Fig. 2.4). Working through platforms, workers see various tasks posted by clients to a crowd and can choose to complete these tasks (ILO 2018a). Gawer (2021) notes that digital platforms facilitate direct interaction between two or more economic agents. Basically, it is the interaction within a group participants carried out through technological means (computing and network resources (the Internet, data centres, open standards, and consumer devices) which collect and store digital data) (Evans and Gawer 2016; Constantinides et al. 2018; Jacobides et al. 2018), where either a customer or a platform owner/manager can be treated as an employer, while a product supplier or service provider acts as a worker (Kilhoffer et al. 2017; Graham et al. 2017). These digital infrastructures not only mediate transactions but also embed algorithmic control systems that determine access to work, monitor performance, and enforce discipline. This concept of digital platforms shows that digital platform labour is not based on the traditional concept of 'firm plus employee', but uses the model 'platform plus individual' (sharing model via crowdsourcing, referred to as C2C) (Zhou 2020). Nevertheless, as noted by Kassi and Lehdonvirta (2016), though being flexible and short-term, digital platform labour (or crowdwork) must be recognised as a model of employment.

Coordination of work through digital platforms is essential to ensure that participants are aware of their specific tasks and interdependencies (Van Alstyne et al. 2016). Nevertheless, practical coordination of work poses many challenges since the activities of interrelated, but at the same time independent actors are legally autonomous. In contrast to the coordination of employee activities in a traditional organisation based on a hierarchical structure, where actors are bound by the ties of legal employment, digital platforms do not have any formal authority over participating agents (Leong et al. 2023). Moreover, digital platforms are even expected to help workers bypass intermediaries (represented by employers in the traditional

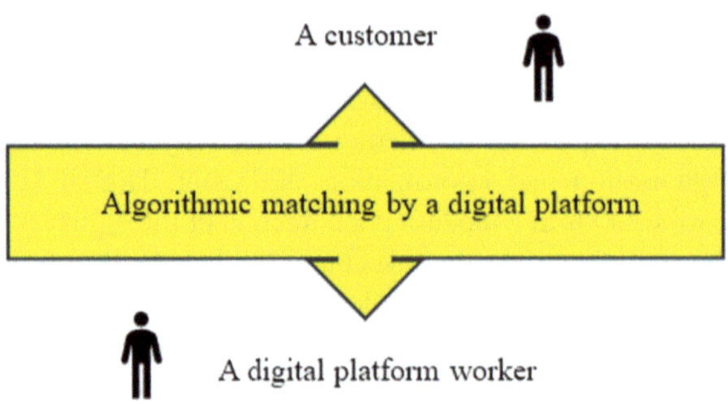

Fig. 2.4 Illustration of the principle of operation of digital platforms. Source: compiled by the authors, based on the data by the Council of Europe (2024)

employment model) and gain direct access to domestic or international digital labour markets in response to the demand for certain skills (Graham et al. 2017).

European Commission's (2021) Proposal for a Directive of the European Parliament and of the Council on Improving Working Conditions in Platform Work defines digital platform work as a work performed "by an individual on the basis of a contractual relationship between the digital labour platform and the individual, irrespective of whether a contractual relationship exists between the individual and the recipient of the service" (p. 33). This definition indicates that the relationship between a person who acts through a digital platform as a service provider and the platform itself is contractual, but the relationship between a service provider and a recipient does not have to be formalised. In any case, the contractual nature of the relationship between a digital platform and a worker is one of the central elements of digital platform work, although there is much debate as to whether this contract can be equated to an employment contract. Even if not, it has many characteristics of an employment contract: it accumulates certain skills, knowledge and expertise which are used to accomplish particular tasks (Idowu and Elbanna 2020), a salary is paid for the performance of tasks, which is one of the central elements of the employment relations (Drugau-Constantin 2018; Berg et al. 2018). Considering the fact that digital platform work is recognised as a flexible modern mode of employment, whether temporary or permanent, it can be stated that digitalisation has made digital platforms an integral part of the global labour market.

When analysing the global market of digital platform work, researchers find that the demand for digital platform work is the greatest in the United States (47 percent of the total global demand), and most of the supply is generated by developing countries, notably India, Bangladesh, Pakistan, the Philippines, and Ukraine (Rani and Dhir 2020). According to the estimates provided by the Council of Europe (2024), there were 28.2 million digital platform workers in the European Union in 2022, and this number is expected to grow to 43 million in 2025. This quantitative growth not only indicates market expansion but also underscores the urgency to address regulatory asymmetries between supply and demand regions. These estimations show that the market for digital platform work in Europe has a large growth potential.

Digital labour platforms are penetrating more and more sectors of the economy. According to the ILO (2021a, b), digital platform work is carried out in such key areas as service provision to individual users, work mediation, and exchange facilitation and mediation.

Figure 2.5 illustrates that with the mediation of digital platforms; work can be carried out on the web or in locations. Such remote services as microtasking, competitive programming, medical consulting and various other freelanced work are provided via the web. The main services provided at a customer's place include taxi, carriers, delivery, various home services and domestic work, care services (care for children, elderly people). Services provided to individual customers may cover news, media, entertainment, advertising, search, reviews, rental goods and assets, communication, application and marketplace, while exchange facilitation and mediation services, typically used by businesses, cover retail and wholesale,

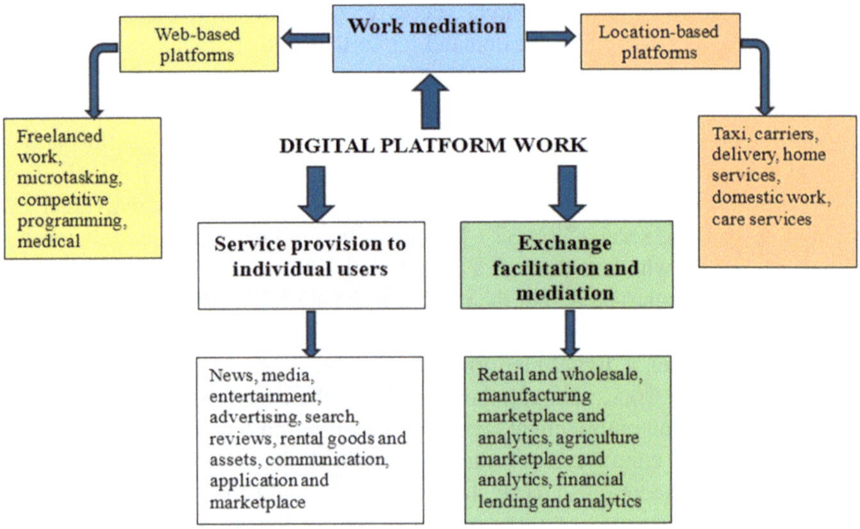

Fig. 2.5 Work areas and services on digital platforms. Source: compiled by the authors, based on the report by the ILO (2021a, b)

manufacturing marketplace and analytics, agriculture marketplace and analytics, financial lending and analytics. This fragmentation of work modalities highlights the hybrid nature of platform labour, which blurs the lines between online and offline service provision, as well as between economic sectors.

The Council of Europe (2024) provides a statistics on the distribution of the most popular services available through digital platforms.

The most common services provided through digital platforms in the EU are taxi and transportation services and food and grocery delivery services, home services (such as cleaning and craft) being third. All of them are the services, provided on location, while web-based services occupy a relatively small share in the market of digital platform services in the EU. This predominance of location-based services reflects the current demand structure and implies that, despite the digital nature of platforms, much of the work remains physically embedded and reliant on human presence.

However, according to the statistics, the payment for working through digital platforms is not high. For instance, Berg (2016), De Stefano (2016) and Berg et al. (2018) found that a statistically significant proportion of digital platform workers work for a salary that is lower than the average in their professional category, or is lower than the established minimum monthly salary or an hourly wage rate. According to the ILO (2017), a digital platform worker earned an average of $4.43 per hour in 2017 when calculating paid working time only (part of the time that digital platform workers spend searching for tasks, participating in forums, responding to requests, leaving responses is not paid), and with consideration of the balance between total paid and unpaid hours, the average hourly wage drops to $3.29. The payment for digital platform work is often lower than national minimum rates. For instance, Forde et al. (2017a, b) provide the estimations which show that the median pay for digital platform work in France is 54.1 percent, in the UK—46.8 percent, in Germany—29.3 percent, and in Spain—9.1 percent lower than the national hourly minimum wage. When analysing this situation from an economic point of view, Forde et al. (2017a, b) explain that the relatively low wages for digital platform work are determined by two main reasons: first, shorter paid work time (task search and communication time is not paid); second, the global competition (residents from developed countries compete on digital platforms with cheaper labour force from developing countries, which reduces the average wage level) (the latter argument was confirmed by the results of the study conducted by Forde et al. (2017a, b) not only in France, but also in the UK and Bulgaria). These wage dynamics highlight a fundamental tension within platform work: while it expands opportunities for income generation, it simultaneously weakens the bargaining power of workers, especially in transnational labour markets lacking coordinated wage-setting mechanisms.

One of the main personal motivations why individuals choose to work through digital platforms despite relatively low wages is flexibility and autonomy. For instance, Tusinska (2023) conducted a survey, the results of which revealed that the flexibility and autonomy of working through digital platforms is important for 50 percent of the respondents. The importance of this factor was also confirmed in the studies by Barnes et al. (2015) and Torrent-Sellens et al. (2021). Tomlinson and Corlett's (2017) study in the United Kingdom revealed an increasing number of mid-professionals who give up their permanent full-time employment and accept a modest decrease in income in exchange for greater flexibility, which is characteristic of digital platform work (flexibility is understood as the ability to freely choose working time, duration, location, means, etc. (Woodcock and Graham 2019), and also the freedom to optimise available resources (e.g. time, technological means, other assets) (Burtch et al. 2018)). The survey, conducted by the European Institute for Gender Equality (EIGE) and the European Foundation for the Improvement of Living and Working Conditions (Eurofound) (2023), shows that work flexibility is the desired work characteristic that does not depend on the age or education of a working person, i.e. work flexibility motivates whether younger or older, lower- or higher-skilled workforce. This suggests that platform work aligns with evolving worker expectations regarding autonomy, indicating a broader shift away from rigid employment models and towards task-based, self-directed economic activity.

As for the skill level required for work through digital platforms, it should be noted that theoretically the skill level of a person should serve as the basis for the nature, scale and complexity of the tasks a person can be hired for (i.e. higher competence should raise the potential of a person to perform more complex and better-paid works). Nevertheless, the concept of "crowdwork" is based on the idea that digital platform work is open to anyone and does not require high qualifications, i.e. the assumption that task performers are interchangeable is followed (Schmidt 2017). The Council of Europe (2024) provides the information which shows that digital platform work generally requires low skills (see Fig. 2.6):

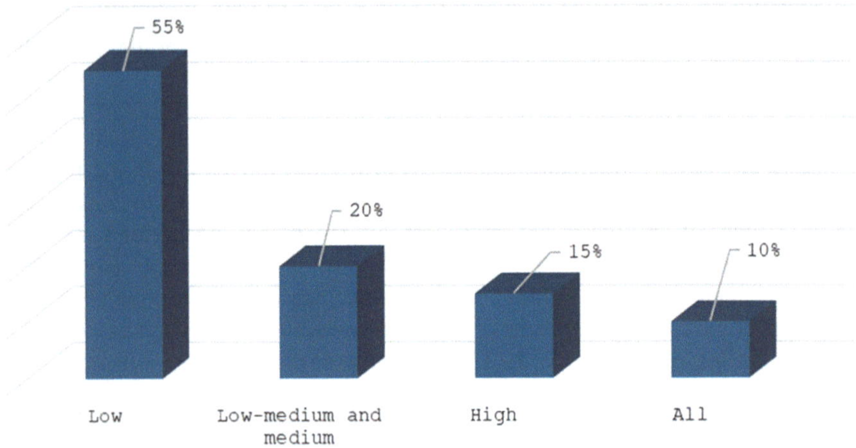

Fig. 2.6 Qualification required for digital platform work in the EU. Source: compiled by the authors, based on the data by the Council of Europe (2024)

Thus, most digital platform workers are over-qualified for the work they do. In this way, the potential of the workforce is not fully utilized (e.g. a qualified engineer can work as a food delivery person), and the requirements formally set on a platform to perform a certain task are not related to a person's education and qualification, which leads to the so-called "skill mismatch" in the digital labour market ("Cedefop" 2020). This pattern illustrates a structural inefficiency in labour allocation, where accessible platform work can paradoxically result in the underuse of human capital, particularly among the highly educated segments of the workforce.

When analysing the advantages and disadvantages of digital platform work in the economic context, it should be noted that this type of work contributes to simple and faster labour market transactions, it promotes unusual forms of work, such as self-employment and multiple employment (combining platform work with traditional work, work across multiple platforms, etc.) (Torrent-Sellens et al. 2021). Aleksynska et al. (2019) note that digital platform work helps to match labour supply and demand and go beyond the boundaries of local labour markets, thus eliminating their geographical limitation. In addition, the process of matching labour demand and supply is short (a worker is quickly found to perform a specific task). This allows to minimise the frictions inherent in labour markets and reduce transaction costs (De Stefano 2016). By using digital labour platforms, businesses can relatively quickly find workers with the necessary skills and competencies that would be expensive to hire on a permanent basis (Marvit 2014; Aleksynska et al. 2019). It can be observed that these advantages are particularly attractive to employers and platform owners, while the benefits to workers are often limited by precarious conditions, income instability and weak access to social protection.

When analysing digital platform labour from the point of view of labour supply, it can be observed that digital labour platforms help to use the skills of the labour supply in the most efficient way (Graham et al. 2017). According to Sundararajan

(2016a, b), digital labour platforms provide innovative income earning opportunities, can expand the market for individuals creating intellectual property, allow service providers to set their own prices, manage customer relationships and create long-term customer relationships based on growing reputation, thus promoting public entrepreneurship.

Summarising The model of work organising through digital platforms shows that digitalisation is accelerating structural transformations in the labour market and promoting more flexible forms of employment. Alongside the traditional model based on an employment contract, digitally mediated work arrangements—such as service-based contracts, freelancing, and multi-platform work—are increasingly taking root (Eichhorst and Rinne 2017). Digital labour platforms help to match labour supply and demand more efficiently and expand access to cross-border opportunities. However, the analysed data confirm that the market remains segmented: platform work is mostly concentrated in a limited number of service sectors and frequently relies on low-skilled or overqualified workers, raising concerns about skill mismatch. Furthermore, the reviewed evidence highlights that the benefits of platform work are not equally distributed—while platform owners and clients profit from flexibility and reduced transaction costs, workers often face income insecurity, weak social protection, and limited opportunities for career advancement. These asymmetries suggest that without adequate policy responses, platformisation may reinforce rather than reduce labour market inequalities.

2.1.3 Organising the Relations Between Workers and Employers

According to Acquier (2017), not having real estate and devoting the majority of their budgets to the development of search engines and marketing, digital labour platforms are difficult to define in both legal and institutional sense, and the attempt to minimize the external regulation of the relations between workers and employers is a distinct characteristic of digital labour platforms (Lehdonvirta 2016). Forde et al. (2017a, b) argue that the relationship between/among different subjects on digital platforms are regulated by establishing agreements, and various combinations of the agreements between different actors (platform managers, workers, customers, intermediaries) can also be concluded. Since the legal implications of such agreements are not fully understood, the rights and obligations of the parties to an agreement can be interpreted in different ways. This legal uncertainty has direct implications for social protection frameworks and the enforceability of labour rights. It also highlights the need for a renewed regulatory approach capable of capturing the specificities of platform-mediated interactions.

Having analysed the conditions for organising and managing the labour relations on digital platforms, Dieuaide and Azais (2020) argue that the relations between workers and employers on digital platforms are of disruptive nature. Digitalisation is replacing standard employment contracts, and the relations are no longer bilateral, but tripartite—"worker-platform-customer" relations. Under such conditions, labour relations become unclear and undefined, subordination between entities disappears at the organisational level, and the institutional visibility is lost (i.e. a worker and an employer do not see each other). In the legal context, the norms of commercial law gain supremacy over the norms of labour law. Dieuaide and Azais (2020) introduce the term "employment grey zone" which, in their opinion, allows focusing on "intermediate spaces of regulation", i.e. concentrating on the labour relations which are relatively autonomous and characterised by their own dynamics. This conceptualisation is particularly relevant in the context of platform work, where hybrid organisational arrangements challenge traditional legal classifications and call for nuanced regulatory approaches.

Macrostructures used in digital platforms (e.g. the modular technological architecture) are not able to consider the competitive interactions between agreement parties. Thus, although the parties perceive that they have mutual interests, tensions are inevitable (Van Alstyne et al. 2016), and they usually arise between platform owners/managers and workers rather than in more complex web interactions (Leong et al. 2023). Tiwana et al. (2010) and Li and Kettinger (2021) note that the management of digital platforms is usually analysed through the lens of control, authority, and regulation rather than the mutual interests and actions of agreement parties, especially in terms of cooperation when pursuing predetermined goals. Such asymmetry reinforces managerial dominance, despite platforms' portrayal as neutral facilitators, and illustrates the structural imbalance embedded in digital labour ecosystems.

According to Gawer (2021), despite the use of coordination mechanisms, such factors as the nature, role and choice of an individual side are ignored in the relations between the agents on digital platforms; the major focus falls on the architectural coordination mechanism. The coordination mechanisms, possessed by platform owners, position platforms as market actors, while platform owners remain behind the legal boundaries of traditional business owners, i.e. the economic perspective created by a platform becomes the central element, and the relationships between actors as well as their interdependence are treated as external elements, though they are technologically coordinated at arm's length (Ghazawneh and Henfridsson 2013; Gawer 2014). This structural distancing enables platforms to externalise responsibility while retaining strategic control, thereby complicating accountability mechanisms and weakening protections traditionally afforded through direct employment relationships.

As noted by Stewart and Stanford (2017), Graham et al. (2017), Pesole et al. (2018), Berg et al. (2018) and other researchers, regulating the relations between workers and employers on digital platforms is difficult, primarily because the status of workers is not clearly defined. According to Forde et al. (2017a, b), the problem is that the traditional features, according to which the status of a person is identified, no longer correspond to the new reality, when innovative, technology-based forms of work organising and algorithmic system management are used. Many digital platforms categorise workers as self-employed, freelancers or independent contractors even when the nature of work organising and subordination within a platform are similar to those underlying work organising in traditional employee-employer models (Wood et al. 2016; Graham et al. 2017; Remeikienė et al. 2022). Since digital platforms are considered intermediaries between a customer of the service and its provider rather than an employer, digital platform workers are not categorised as employees, but as self-employed, autonomous workers or independent contractors, who themselves assume all the risks associated with independent work (for instance, the risk of accidents at work, an illness, unemployment, etc.) (Aloisi 2016; Berg et al. 2018; Torrent-Sellens et al. 2021). This framing allows platforms to avoid employer obligations while placing full economic vulnerability on workers, revealing a systemic misalignment between legal categorisation and the functional realities of digital labour. According to Davulis (2020), until the law provides otherwise, platform workers are considered self-employed persons as long as their degree of subordination to an ordering company is not similar or close to subordination of an employee working under an employment contract.

The Council of Europe (2024) provides the data which show that 19 percent of all digital platform workers are likely to be incorrectly classified (see Fig. 2.7).

93 percent of digital platform workers in the EU are categorised as the self-employed. It has been argued that, whether formally recognised as the self-employed or possessing an incorrect employment status, digital platform workers often fall outside of the scope of labour and social protection law, which increases their vulnerability and limits their access to such social protection (Berg et al. 2018; the Council of Europe 2024). This claim is based on the observation that such workers typically do not benefit from the protections afforded by traditional employment contracts, including minimum wages, regulation of working hours, paid holidays, maternity and paternity leave, health and unemployment insurance (Rogers 2015;

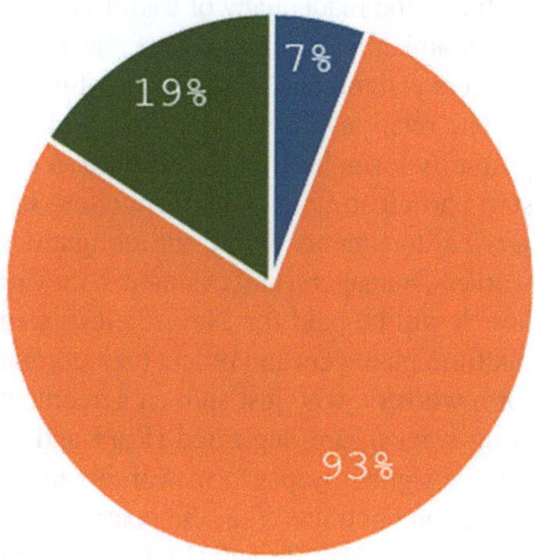

Fig. 2.7 Classification of the employment status of digital platform workers in the EU. Source: compiled by the authors, based on the data by the Council of Europe (2024)

Risak and Warter 2015; Van Doorn 2017; Rani and Dhir 2020). This reveals a systemic gap in the design of social protection systems, which remain institutionally dependent on binary employment classifications and are ill-equipped to respond to hybrid or ambiguous work forms prevalent in platform-based economies. However, it should be acknowledged that the legal classification of platform workers and their entitlements under social protection law vary across countries. In some jurisdictions, such workers may be covered either as self-employed persons or under a third, intermediate category.

When assessing whether a certain person working on digital platforms can be considered an employee, it should be noted that the EU Directive 2003/88 (the European Parliament and the Council 2003) does not provide the concept of an employee. According to the Court of Justice of the European Union (CJEU), national courts must decide in each case whether the concept of "an employee" is applicable. The decision must be made after assessing the circumstances indicated by all parties involved and based on objective criteria. To determine whether a person carries out activities under the management of another person, a judge must assess whether there is a hierarchical relationship between an employee and an employer (judgments of the CJEU of 10 September 2015, C-47/14, and of 20 November 2018, C-147/17), whether a person can be considered an "independent contractor", whether this independence is real or imaginary, or perhaps disguised.

If an agreement between the parties allows a person: 1) to use subcontractors or other persons for the services the person has undertaken to provide, 2) to accept or not accept various tasks proposed by a purported employer or unilaterally determine the maximum number of those tasks, 3) to provide services to any third party, including direct competitors of a purported employer, 4) to set working hours within certain parameters and tailor working time to one's own personal needs, not just the interests of a purported employer, such relationship does not qualify a person as an employee, since it is impossible to establish the existence of a subordinate relationship between the person and a platform (Naumowicz 2021). These legal criteria highlight the inadequacy of traditional tests for employment status when applied to algorithmically mediated work, where managerial control is exercised without direct oversight, and autonomy is often only nominal.

The relationships of platform workers with platform managers and clients are primarily formalised in *terms of service* documents which workers sign when they start participating in a platform (Berg et al. 2018; Rani and Dhir 2020). *Terms of service* documents define the obligations, responsibilities and rights of platform workers, managers, and customers, they provide how the work will be evaluated and how it will be paid for. Nevertheless, terms of service are often unilaterally set by platform managers and reflect their commercial interests, while the interests of platform workers, who just sign an agreement without negotiating it (including negotiating wages), are neglected (Rani and Dhir 2020). For this reason, the terms of service signed by platform workers are referred to not as labour contracts, but as 'adhesion contracts' (i.e. the contracts written by only one of the contract parties) (Berg et al. 2018; ILO 2021a, b). This shows that platform managers have a significant power-advantage over digital platform workers (Muldoon and Apostolidis

2023). This structural imbalance suggests that formal contractual autonomy often masks underlying power asymmetries, where platform workers operate in a legally permissive environment that limits their ability to contest unfavourable terms. This view is supported by Bucher et al. (2021b) who found that the 'Amazon MTurk' platform uses the technologies which allow selecting workers according to established criteria, while no selection mechanisms are available to workers. Goloventchik (2023) emphasizes the asymmetry of the relationship between platform managers/owners and workers actually subordinate to them, and notes that this relationship falls out of the scope of the national labour legislation.

According to Aleksynska et al. (2019), considering the fact that the share of the digital economy in the general economy is gradually increasing, the fact that digital platform workers do not have a clearly defined legal status and often even work informally is an obstacle to the creation of sustainable labour relations and sustainable social protection schemes. Goloventchik (2023) argues that platform workers must be able to exercise their legal and social rights regardless of their employment status. Choudary (2018) notes that the well-being of digital platform workers can be improved by measures that would allow for an increase in the degree of representation of the interests of these workers (for example, it is necessary to create the conditions and encourage the establishment of worker agencies) and would help reduce the control of workers exercised by digital platform managers/owners. This highlights that the absence of legal clarity not only weakens the enforcement of workers' rights but also hinders the broader policy objective of building resilient and inclusive social protection systems in the digital age. If these measures were implemented, digital platform workers would gain more bargaining power with respect to each transaction.

Some authors (Karanovic et al. 2020; Malgonde et al. 2020; Sandberg et al. 2020, etc.), however, argue that agreement parties on digital platforms do not always blindly obey owners' power, and their influence and power are growing with the evolution of digital platforms. As knowledge about the working principles of digital platforms is deepening, opportunities for workers to follow logic, operate in a pluralistic environment, make autonomous decisions, and take autonomous actions are increasing. Such dynamics suggest that the distribution of power on platforms may gradually shift, particularly where collective action, platform transparency, or supportive regulation strengthens workers' strategic position.

Summarising The attempt to minimise the external regulation of the relations between workers and employers is one of the key characteristics of digital labour platforms. Macrostructures used in digital platforms (e.g. the modular technological architecture) are not able to consider either the competitive interactions between agreement parties or the nature, role, and choice of an individual side. Therefore, the relations between workers and employers on digital platforms are of disruptive nature, they become unclear and undefined, subordination between actors disappears at the organizational level, and institutional visibility is lost. Many digital platforms categorise workers as self-employed persons or workers possess an incorrect employment status, which violates their rights and raises the risk of social vulnerability. Terms of service is the main document formalizing the relationship between workers and employers on digital platforms. But they reflect the commercial interests of platform owners, while the interests of platform workers are neglected. This shows that platform owners have a significant power-advantage over digital platform workers. Nevertheless, with the evolution of digital platforms and deepening knowledge about the principles of their operation, the opportunities for workers to make autonomous decisions are increasing. This evolving balance between managerial control and worker autonomy indicates that digital labour platforms are not static structures, but adaptive systems where power dynamics may shift in response to legal, technological, and social developments.

2.1.4 Polarisation in the Labour Market

Digitalisation leads to the transformations in work processes and operating procedures, i.e. the ways and methods to perform certain tasks and jobs are changing. As noted by Dachs (2017), the use of technologies can increase inequality through the differences in skills and tasks performed by the labour force. Following the 'task-based approach' proposed by Autor et al. (2003), Levy and Murnane (2005) note that digitalisation leads to a new division of labour between humans and machines: machines replace human labour in performing routine tasks, but human labour is still irreplaceable in performing non-routine tasks, such as creativity and problem solving. In this way, digitalisation tends to increase polarisation in the labour market since it leads to the division of the workforce into two sharply contrasting groups: manual workers who previously performed routine tasks, whose jobs are likely to be lost due to digitalisation, and educated workers who are creative and able to make decisions, and whose risk of losing a job due to digitalisation is low. This emerging division challenges the cohesion of the labour market and highlights the growing importance of targeted upskilling policies that prioritise adaptability and digital competence across all worker groups.

Having assessed the risk of polarisation in the UK's labour market, Goos et al. (2010) provide evidence that digitalisation leads to polarisation in the labour market, and the greatest risk of losing a job is for workers with medium skills, who will have to upgrade their qualifications or be retrained to be able to fall into the category of decision-making workers. Having researched the situation in the USA, Frey and Osborne (2013) confirm the risk of polarisation in the labour market posed by digitalisation; they estimate that 47 percent of jobs of various profiles will be lost due to digitalisation. According to Dachs (2017), it can be expected that digitalisation will lead to uneven distribution of costs between lower- and higher-skilled workers because the former are going to face higher risks of displacement in their jobs. This analysis reveals that medium-skilled workers occupy a particularly vulnerable position, as their functions are too complex to be easily automated but too standardised to stand out through creative or strategic competencies. Therefore, greater attention should be paid to upskilling strategies targeted specifically at this group.

Helmrich et al.'s (2017) research in Germany, however, reveals the accelerated structural changes in the labour market due to digitalisation and the trends in employee qualification improvement, which at least partially reduce the risk of polarisation in the labour market. According to the authors, the intensive use of digital work tools (the use of work tools directly determines how workers perform their work) will raise the digital literacy of workers, and thus, will lead to their higher qualifications, which will reduce the problem of polarisation. Weller et al.'s (2020) study confirms these findings and shows that digital technologies as work tools will be used by both groups of workers—the ones performing routine and non-routine tasks. In the first case, workers will make more extensive use of machines and installations as well as measurement devices and diagnostic tools, while in the second case, various types of software will be used more widely. Nevertheless, higher skill requirements will be imposed on workers in both cases. Domini et al. (2021) found that job automation in the French manufacturing sector correlates with a lower separation rate and a higher worker hiring rate. These findings imply that the adverse effects of polarisation can be mitigated through targeted investments in digital skill development and broader access to upskilling pathways. By aligning digital tool use with systematic training, polarisation risks may be reduced not only in high-skill but also in medium-skill sectors.

The above-discussed findings of previous studies indicate that the risk of polarisation in the labour market due to digitalisation vary from country to country. Bachmann et al. (2022) attempted to elucidate the reasons for these differences. Bachmann et al.'s (2022) study, focused on the effects of robotisation on worker flows in 16 European countries in the period 1998–2017, revealed that cross-country differences in the strength of the impact of digitalisation are largely determined by country-specific labour costs: a greater positive impact of digitalisation is noticeable in the countries with low or average labour costs, while it is much milder in the countries with high labour costs, i.e. the results of the research imply that robotisation tends to raise employment in the countries with low or average labour costs. The research also revealed that the groups of workers whose functions are characterised by intensive manual work or routine cognitive tasks are more sensitive. This suggests that labour cost structures not only mediate the speed of automation adoption but also shape the degree of worker vulnerability across skill levels. Policy responses should therefore be calibrated to national wage dynamics and the relative exposure of routine task occupations.

Blix (2017) argues that the effects of digitalisation are not critical in the short run (e.g. they are not as critical as the effects of a fiscal or financial crisis, where GDP can fall dramatically, and many jobs can be lost when economic growth stops or even a recession starts). According to the author, there is still no convincing evidence that the unemployment rate in the OECD countries is decreasing due to digitalisation. The author believes that the modern labour market is characterised by the huge potential for change and the constant creation of new jobs, especially in the service sector. Nevertheless, it is recognised that digitalisation will inevitably lead to tensions in the labour market in the medium to long run. Technological advancement is expected to increase polarisation and is likely to negatively affect middle-level workers, whose income will become volatile and uncertainty about job retention will increase (Goos et al. 2014; Vasilescu et al. 2020). These observations imply that while digitalisation may not immediately destabilise employment figures, it gradually shifts labour market dynamics in ways that weaken the position of mid-skilled workers. In anticipation of these shifts, forward-looking reskilling policies and transitional support measures are critical for maintaining social and economic cohesion.

According to Blix (2017), digitalisation directly and indirectly affects 3 poles of the welfare state:

a) social protection costs financed by federal transfers (benefits, education, health care);
b) social inclusion through education and employment;
c) worker-employer power balance when negotiating working conditions, salary, and resolving conflicts.

Dachs (2017) notes that the power of states to allocate sufficient funds for social protection can reduce the reap of economic benefits from innovation. The author highlights the tendency that only a few companies, mostly large ones, can implement innovations without state support in the modern economy, so the tendency "the winner takes all markets" becomes dominant. The benefit from innovation is not distributed equally to business; it is appropriated by a small number of companies which can gain monopolistic positions, while small businesses are affected negatively. In the absence of equal distribution of benefits, less funds are accumulated by state budgets, so less funds remain for social protection expenses. This reveals a structural tension between innovation-driven economic concentration and the fiscal sustainability of welfare states, suggesting that inclusive digital transformation must also address the redistribution mechanisms that underpin long-term social resilience.

Technological advancement and digitalisation tend to increase polarisation, which affects middle-aged workers whose income is becoming more volatile and social inclusion is decreasing (Goos et al. 2014). The Gini coefficient is a common measure of income inequality. This coefficient tends to rise in many developing countries (Blix 2017). Although trade and globalisation have reduced income inequality in the world, it can still vary from country to country. In the future, the problem of income inequality is likely to be fuelled by the rapidly aging population and new technologies which will compete with human labour in many areas, especially in modern services. With increasing competition between human and technologies, wages are expected to stagnate. This points to the need for proactive policy measures that not only mitigate wage stagnation, but also address generational and sectoral vulnerabilities emerging from this labour–technology competition. Digitalisation-driven changes in the labour market are more gradual than the changes in consumption (the surge in e-commerce and online orders), but the gradualness of the changes depends on the pace at which young people enter the labour market and older people change jobs or retire (OECD 2017a).

Digitalisation in the labour market is likely to reduce the bargaining power of workers. A middle manager will become a function under pressure from robots in many areas of work. This pressure is already visible in the banking and retail sectors (technological progress allows to reduce staff and automate part of the services provided). With a limited attachment to a particular workplace, workers' awareness of their bargaining power will decrease (Cazes et al. 2019). This dynamic raises structural concerns, as diminished bargaining power may not only exacerbate income inequality but also hinder collective responses to precarity in increasingly fragmented labour markets.

Considering the potential risks of polarisation in the labour market caused by digitalisation, Blix (2017) nevertheless believes that modern welfare states are sufficiently resistant to market changes, so there is no need to create new institutions or safety nets in response to the changes in the labour market driven by digitalisation. With incremental changes, welfare states should have enough time to adapt and reform. However, the reforms can be too slow or not initiated at all. It is often difficult for national political systems to implement reforms when the costs of action are incurred immediately, but the potential economic benefits are gained much later. In addition, when implementing reforms, authorities often face opposition from specific interest groups and employers' organizations since any transformations usually mean the changes in the levers of power. This indicates a need for more agile and anticipatory governance mechanisms, capable of responding to gradual structural shifts before labour market imbalances become entrenched. Since digitalisation affects some fundamental elements of a welfare state (e.g. employment), the existing institutions need to be reformed in order not to undermine the social contract between society and the state. Welfare states must provide protection to their population in response to disruptive economic/market changes so that innovation is promoted, and its benefits and harms are properly balanced.

Summarising Although digitalisation-driven changes in the labour market are more gradual than the changes in consumption, technology work competing with human labour may lead to the division of the workforce into two sharply contrasting groups: manual workers who previously performed routine tasks and whose jobs are likely to be lost, and educated workers who are creative and able to make decisions, and whose risk of losing a job due to digitalisation is low. With a limited attachment to a particular workplace, workers' awareness of their bargaining power is likely to decrease. With increasing competition between human and technologies, wages are expected to stagnate. Cross-country differences in the strength of the effects of digitalisation are largely determined by labour costs specific to a particular country: greater positive effects of digitalisation are observed in the countries with low or average labour costs, while the effects are much milder in the countries with high labour costs. Polarisation in the labour market is reduced by rising worker qualifications, in particular, the wider use of machines, installations, measurement devices and diagnostic tool for routine tasks, and the use of software for non-routine tasks. This suggests that proactive investment in digital upskilling across occupational categories could serve as a key mechanism for buffering labour markets against structural polarisation trends. Since digitalisation affects some fundamental elements of a welfare state (e.g. employment, declining bargaining power of workers), protections must be provided to the population in welfare states in response to the disruptive economic/market changes so that innovation is promoted, and its benefits and harms are properly balanced.

2.2 The Green Transition and Its Effects on Industrial Transformation and Employment

The understanding of conventional economics, i.e. people's relationship to the natural world, the purpose of economies, the sources of wealth and the function of markets, is changing in the twenty-first century. If the researchers of conventional economics (e.g. Adam Smith and David Ricardo) treated nature as a huge inexhaustible source of economic resources, and the government was considered the main institution for solving environmental problems through the mechanisms of taxes, prices and financial incentives and penalties, sustainable economics treats traditional natural resources as exhaustible, promotes the use of renewable energy sources, reduction in the amount of industrial waste, and considers all economic agents responsible for environmental protection. With different understanding of the major dimensions and agents of the economy, the modern fair and sustainable economy is expected to save the natural environment and provide decent, well-paid jobs. This conceptual shift also reshapes the role of the industry in contemporary economies, positioning industrial transformation not only as an environmental necessity, but also as a social and labour market imperative.

The effects of the green transition on industry are primarily related to the European Green Deal and the Paris Agreement. The European Green Deal, approved in 2020, is a set of policy initiatives by the European Commission with the main objective of making the European Union climate neutral by 2050 (Tamma et al. 2019; Simon 2019). Climate neutrality can be achieved by decarbonising the EU's energy system and achieving zero greenhouse gas emissions (by 2050, according to the plan) (Simon 2019). The European Green Deal aims to show that countries can develop economically without increasing the use of resources. The main objectives of the Paris Agreement are as follows: to ensure that the increase in the global average temperature is less than 2 °C compared to the temperature of the pre-industrial period, and to make efforts to keep the global average temperature from increasing by more than 1.5 °C. Although the Paris Agreement does not provide for any binding emission limits, it indicates that the policies for reducing carbon emissions must be implemented in the economy as a whole (Kuh 2018). These agreements create a regulatory framework that indirectly influences digital platform activities, particularly in energy-intensive sectors, thereby linking green policy objectives with transformations across employment models, including platform-based forms.

Since the industry is a fundamental driver of the economy, it will have to go through significant changes in the direction of reducing carbon emissions. In the industrial transition, a balance between electrification, energy efficiency and the use of renewable energy should be achieved. In addition, industrial sectors are expected to cooperate to utilize the excess heat (Mathiesen et al. 2023). These industrial transformations will have an impact on employment since the structure of the industry and the rate of its transformation significantly affect the structure and dynamics of employment. While the discussion in this section focuses on industry-level transformation, the implications extend to platform-mediated labour as well. As the demand for green skills rises and sustainability standards reshape market dynamics, platform-based services are also expected to adapt, particularly in areas like logistics, energy efficiency consultancy, and circular economy-related tasks. This subsection analyses how and through which channels the green transition affects the industry as an important source of employment, and what effects can be expected in the labour market.

2.2.1 The Impact of the Green Transformation on the Industry as a Source of Employment

Conventional, or the brown, economy relies on non-sustainable energy resources. It is characterized by high consumption of materials, the reliance on fossil fuels, low energy efficiency and great damage to the environment and climate, which is caused by ignoring the negative consequences of economic production (World Bank 2013). It is said that the current brown economy is experiencing the so-called three "F" crisis, i.e. the crisis of finance, food and fuel (United Nations Environment Program (UNEP) 2008; Atlama and Ozsoy 2011; the World Bank Group 2022). The crisis of finance is related to investment because an unreasonable amount of investment goes to finance cheap credits, financial derivatives and housing bubbles, but this investment does not create decent jobs (Atlama and Ozsoy 2011). The fuel crisis is related to excessive costs on carbon emitting fossil fuels: a significantly larger share of investments and subsidies go to carbon emitting fossil fuels than the use of renewable energy. The recent estimates by the International Institute for Sustainable Development (IISD) (2023) show that G20 countries have reached an all-time high of $1.4 trillion in public funds to support and maintain the fossil fuel industry in 2022. This amount includes $1 trillion subsidies for the fossil fuel sector, $322 investment in this sector by state-owned enterprises, and $50 billion allocations in the form of loans, provided by public financial institutions. The International Monetary Fund (2023) reports $7 trillion subsidies for the fossil fuel industry (the report of 24 August 2023). The differences between the investment in fossil fuel supply and low-emission fuel supply are depicted in Fig. 2.8.

The figure illustrates that the share of funds allocated for fossil fuel supply is still significantly higher than the share of funds allocated for the supply of low-emission fuels.

Finally, food crisis is related to the dependence of the agricultural sector on subsidies, and when the subsidies are decreasing, the productivity of the agricultural sector is also decreasing. The report by the Institute for European Environmental Policy (2022) suggests that that CO_2, temperature changes, ozone concentration, extreme weather events and the increased incidence of pests and diseases have the negative effects on crop yields, yield stability and the quality of crops. The most severe negative effects are observed in Eastern, Western and Southern Europe, where the significant changes in temperature and precipitation have a negative impact on the yields of wheat, barley, maize and sugar beet, leading to the recent yield stagnation. The data provided by the "Eurostat" (2023) indicate that agricultural labour productivity in the EU decreased by 6.6 percent from 2019 to 2022. This decline was caused by a 7.9 percent decrease in the real value of the income generated by economic units (factor income) and a 1.4 percent decrease in the volume of agricultural labour. 19 EU Member States recorded lower agricultural labour productivity in 2023, with the steepest decline observed in Estonia (−57.9 percent), Sweden (−31.7 percent), Ireland (−30.3 percent), Lithuania (−30.2 percent) and Bulgaria (−28.6 percent). This triple crisis—finance, food, and fuel—demonstrates the unsustainability of the brown economy model and highlights the need to redirect capital towards sectors that promote resilience, sustainability, and inclusive employment. Such reallocation is especially relevant for digital platform-based activities, which are increasingly interfacing with sectors influenced by the green transition,

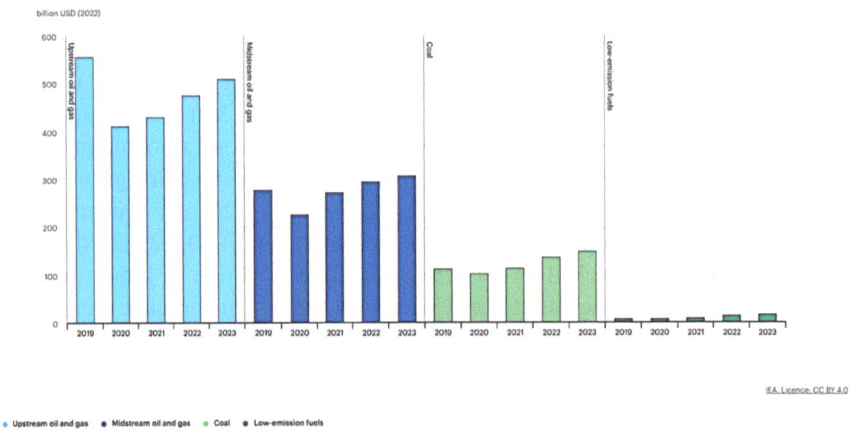

Fig. 2.8 Investment in fuel supply in the period 2019–2023. Source: International Energy Agency (2023)

including sustainable food delivery chains, renewable energy installation services, and climate-related data collection tasks.

The general result of the aforementioned three crises (finance, food and fuel) is the gross misallocation of capital. This means that too much capital is poured into property, fossil fuels and structured financial assets with embedded derivatives, which no longer stimulates the economy and job creation. In contrast to the brown economy, the green economy is based on the use of renewable energy sources and cleaner technologies, economic activity minimises damage to the environment, and cleaner products and services are provided to the market. This paradigm shift calls for investment patterns that not only support environmental goals but also foster sustainable forms of work. Notably, platform-mediated labour may become a vehicle for delivering green services, such as shared mobility, last-mile delivery via low-emission transport, and remote energy audits, expanding the role of digital platforms in achieving climate-neutral objectives.

The challenges of the European Green Deal are related to the transformation of various sectors of the economy, including construction, biodiversity, energy, transport and food. The main policy areas of the European Green Deal are depicted in Fig. 2.9. These sectoral transitions are not isolated from changes in labour market structures; on the contrary, they increasingly involve platform-mediated services, especially in logistics, energy diagnostics, sustainable mobility, and urban service delivery. The integration of environmental goals into economic policy indirectly reshapes the platform economy by generating demand for digitally mediated green services.

Clean Energy The main principles which are expected to be followed during the transition to the use of clean energy are prioritising energy efficiency, developing an energy sector based mainly on the use of renewable resources, ensuring affordable energy supply to the population, and creating a fully integrated, interconnected, digitalised EU energy market (European Commission 2019b). The EU Strategy for Energy System Integration, which provides measures for the shift towards the circular economy, will also help the energy transformation. These transformations are already generating new forms of digitally mediated work, such as remote energy

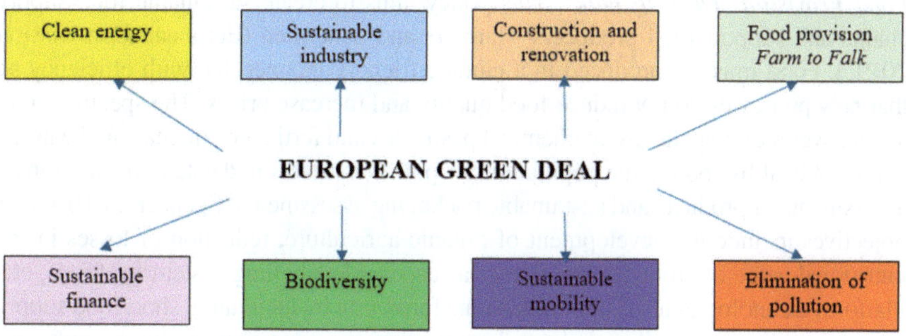

Fig. 2.9 The main policy areas the European Green Deal. Source: compiled by the authors

audits, virtual consultancy on energy efficiency, and data-driven energy consumption optimisation, often performed via specialised digital platforms. This demonstrates a growing convergence between green and digital transitions.

Sustainable Industry The foundations for the creation of sustainable industry were laid after the approval of the EU's Circular Economy Industrial Policy. In March 2020, the EU approved the industrial strategy (European Commission 2020c) aimed at empowering citizens, revitalizing regions and having the best technologies. The key policy aspects in this area include the development of the modern industry, the exploration and development of climate-neutral and circular economy-friendly markets, industrial decarbonisation and the modernization of energy-intensive industries, such as steel and cement production. To reduce the generation of material waste, the Sustainable Products Policy, when the final products will be reused or recycled, will be implemented. These industrial changes increasingly rely on digital monitoring and reporting tools, with emerging opportunities for platform-based labour in areas such as material flow analysis, sustainability reporting, and real-time emissions tracking.

Construction and Renovation This policy area aims to reform the unsustainable methods of construction and renovation of buildings and reduce the use of non-renewable resources in these processes. In this context, the main focus falls on the application of energy-efficient construction methods (construction of climate-resistant buildings, digitalisation of buildings, compliance with requirements for energy efficiency of buildings). Renovations of council housing will aim to reduce energy bills for the most sensitive groups of society (European Commission 2019a). One of the objectives is to triple the rate of renovation of all buildings in order to reduce pollution (Simon 2019). Applied properly, modern digital technologies can play a significant role in solving environmental problems. Smart urban mobility, precision agriculture, sustainable supply chains, environmental monitoring and disaster forecast are just a few examples of applications of digital technologies (European Investment Bank 2022). This suggests that platform workers involved in building maintenance, energy audits, or remote monitoring services will need to develop digital and green skills simultaneously.

Food Provision 'Farm to Falk' This policy aims to create sustainable food supply chains and support food producers—farmers and fishermen (European Commission 2019c). Food must be produced in a climate-friendly manner, but with efficiency so that new processes do not reduce food quality and increase prices. The specific target areas cover reducing the use of chemical pesticides and fertilizers, increasing the availability of healthy food to the population, helping consumers understand health impact assessments of products and sustainable packaging assessments (Spencer 2020). Other objectives include the development of organic agriculture, reduction of losses in the nutritional value of products, creation of a sustainable labelling system for foods, etc. Platform technologies also support this transformation by facilitating short food supply chains, enabling traceability tools, and connecting eco-conscious producers with consumers directly through digital marketplaces.

Elimination of Pollution The "Zero Pollution Action Plan", which was approved by the European Commission in 2021 (European Commission 2021), aims that there would be no air, water and soil pollution from any sources by 2050 (Schaible 2020). Environmental quality standards must be fully respected, and all industrial activities must be carried out in an environment free of toxic substances. Agricultural and urban industrial water management systems shall be revised to comply with the principles of the pollution elimination policies. To achieve this goal, harmful resources, such as microplastics and chemicals, must be replaced. It is believed that providing food from farms to the population will also help to reduce the level of pollution since less harmful substances will be used in the processes of food production and transportation. In parallel, the implementation of pollution control standards is expected to influence service models in the platform economy, particularly those involved in urban logistics, food delivery, and household services, which increasingly rely on platform-mediated labour.

Sustainable Mobility Another target area of the European Green Deal policy is the reduction of vehicle emissions. For this purpose, the Sustainable and Smart Mobility Strategy was approved. The use of sustainable and alternative fuels in road, sea and air transport will be promoted, and the emission standards will be set for vehicles with internal combustion engines ("Green Facts" 2022). Sustainable alternative solutions are expected to be available to business and society. The intelligent traffic management systems and programs, as well as the methods of cargo delivery via land or waterways are intended to be developed. The implementation of public transport reforms will aim to reduce traffic congestion and pollution, expand the infrastructure of charging stations for electric cars, and promote the purchase of low-emission vehicles (European Commission 2019d). These transformations in mobility systems are likely to reshape the working environment of ride-hailing, courier, and goods delivery platforms, potentially altering task organisation, emission standards for service providers, and the algorithmic parameters used to assign rides or deliveries.

Biodiversity The target areas of this European Green Deal policy are the management of forests and marine areas, environmental protection, and solution of the problems of the loss of plant and animal species and ecosystems ("Green Facts" 2022). The negatively affected ecosystems are expected to be restored by applying the methods of organic farming, helping plant pollination processes, restoring free-flowing rivers, reducing pesticides which harm wildlife, and reforesting. The Biodiversity Strategy is one of the essential parts of the European Union's climate change mitigation strategy. Of the 25 percent of the EU's total budget for combating climate change, a large part will be allocated for restoring biodiversity and implementing nature-based solutions (European Commission 2020a). The growing demand for environmental monitoring and restoration projects also creates opportunities for platform-based microtasking services, especially those involving geospatial data collection, drone-assisted monitoring, or citizen science platforms.

Sustainable Finance Sustainable, or green, finance refers to a set of financial regulations, standards, norms and products which aim to achieve environmental goals and, in particular, to facilitate the energy shift towards the use of renewable energy sources. Sustainable finance is expected to enable the EU's financial system to connect with the economy and population, and fund economic actors while sustaining economic growth. This long-term concept began to be implemented with the approval of the United Nations Paris Climate Agreement which stipulates that countries must ensure that financial flows are directed to the reduction of greenhouse gas emissions and the promotion of climate-friendly development (United Nations 2015). Increased investment in green sectors may indirectly stimulate the growth of platform-based labour in sustainability-focused industries, as funding for climate action and environmental entrepreneurship encourages new models of decentralised and flexible service delivery.

The literature analysis revealed that the impact of the green transformation on industry is likely to manifest itself through five major channels: resource and innovation efficiency, transformations in production processes, changes in the demand structure, changes in aggregate income and macroeconomic conditions, and changes in trade and competitiveness (see Fig. 2.10).

Resource and Innovation Efficiency The European Green Deal includes the measures to ensure that countries which are dependent on fossil fuels are not left alone in their transition to renewable energy (Geden et al. 2020). National public and private investment should play an important role here. The European Commission is intending to support research and innovation in the areas of transport technologies (in particular, vehicle batteries), clean hydrogen, low-carbon steel production, circular biotechnology and the built environment (European Commission 2019b). A special investment plan—the so-called "InvestEU" plan—is intended to finance the implementation of the European Green Deal policy measures. According to this plan, the estimated amount of investment is nearly €1 trillion. The approximate

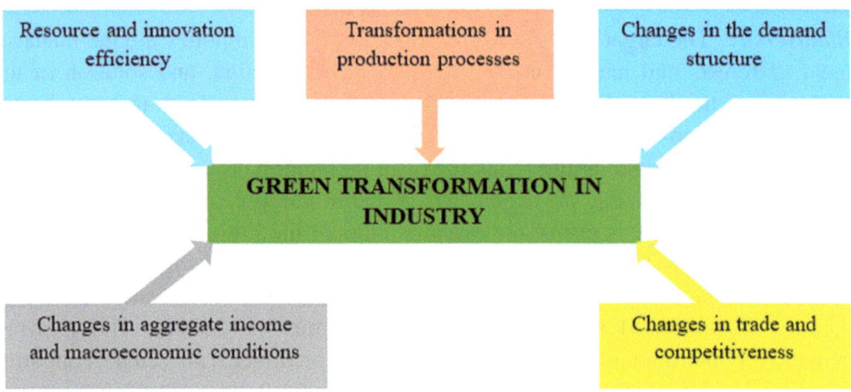

Fig. 2.10 Channels of the impact of green transformation on industry. Source: compiled by the authors

estimations indicate that around €260 billion of investment will be needed annually to achieve the goals set out in the European Green Deal until 2030 (European Commission 2020b). This shift in innovation priorities is likely to affect labour demand across multiple sectors, including digital platform-mediated services, especially in areas supporting clean technology deployment, resource monitoring, and the maintenance of decentralised energy solutions.

The growth of green innovation is associated not only with the replacement of traditional technologies with green technologies, but also with the growth of innovation overall because green innovation often requires additional complementary innovation (Hasna et al. 2023). According to the European Commission (2022a), eco-innovation reduces business costs, allows expanding growth opportunities and strengthens business reputation among consumers. Hasna et al. (2023) note that the economic benefits of green innovations can be manifested already in the first year with an increase in investments. Economic growth in the long term is stimulated by cheaper energy and more energy efficient production processes. Nosheen et al.'s (2021) study in Eastern and Western European countries, the purpose of which was to assess the cross-sectional dependency and heterogeneity promoted by technological innovation between 2000 and 2017 (the research was based on Westerlund cointegration approach and the fully modified ordinary least square (FMOLS) method), revealed that the use of renewable energy promotes the growth of industries. Therefore, this type of investment should be actively promoted through public-private partnership and the exemptions in taxes for the economic agents that use environmentally friendly technologies. The authors admit that renewable energy innovations are expensive to implement, but they ensure an improved return on green growth. In this context, platform-based services could become enablers of innovation diffusion, for instance, through digital marketplaces for green technologies, on-demand energy audits, or app-mediated maintenance of eco-efficient equipment.

It can be stated that the transformation to a low carbon industry and the development of the green economy are expected to achieve resource and innovation efficiency, thus maintaining not only the industrial *status quo*, but promoting growth, which, in its turn, stimulates the creation of new jobs. Hasna et al.'s (2023) calculations show that doubling green patent fillings can increase GDP by 1.7 percent in the period of five years. Sun et al.'s (2023) GMM (Generalized Method of Moments) technique-based research of the effects of green innovation on resource efficiency and sustainability in E7 (China, Indonesia, Mexico, Russian Federation, Turkey, Brazil, and India) in the period 2010–2021 revealed that green innovation positively and significantly affects the growth of the green economy in the target countries. The emission-trading schemes, which allow to minimize prices for producers of renewable energy, government spending on R&D and global policy synchronization are considered the effective means to stimulate green innovations (local innovators will have more incentives to develop low-carbon technologies if they know that they can sell these technologies in global markets (the market size effect)) (Hasna et al. 2023). Such developments may also indirectly influence platform-mediated labour markets by expanding demand for specialised services, such as installation and remote diagnostics of low-emission systems, data-driven environmental compliance solutions, or sustainability-focused freelance consultancy. The major sectors with the highest growth in green innovation are presented in Table 2.2.

Table 2.2 indicates that most green innovations are implemented in the renewable energy industry, followed by transport, electricity access and telecommunication innovations. Water provision and sanitation industry as well as health and education sectors remain important green innovation sectors (judging by the increase in the percentage of innovative projects in the period 2015–2022). Meanwhile, the volumes of green innovation in the agrifood industry are declining. This trend suggests that platform work related to green transition may increasingly concentrate in sectors showing high innovation intensity, particularly renewable energy and smart infrastructure, whereas areas like agrifood may offer fewer opportunities unless complementary digital or sustainability solutions are introduced.

According to the United Nations Conference on Trade and Development (UNCTAD) (2023), global investment in industries related to the implementation of

Table 2.2 Sectors with the highest growth in green innovation

Industry	Sector	Examples of technologies	Change in the number of innovation projects in the period 2015–2022
Infrastructure	Transport	Bus rapid transit, low-emission vehicles and fuels, biogas, hybrid and plug-in electric vehicles	+16
	Electricity access	Smart power grids, stoves using renewable energy, off-grid technologies (e.g. wind turbines)	
	Telecommunication	Wireless communications, cooperative communications, interference alignment, cognitive radio technologies, real time pricing	
Climate change	Renewable energy	Smart power grids, renewable energy technologies	+21
	Building/Construction energy efficiency	Smart power grids, smart meters, thermal insulation, energy efficient lightning, energy recovering stoves, building envelopes, heat pumps	No data
WASH (provision of water and sanitation)	Water management	Desalinization plants, wastewater treatment plants, non-sewered, off-grid urban green sanitation, wastewater reuse and disposal technologies	+13

(continued)

Table 2.2 (continued)

Industry	Sector	Examples of technologies	Change in the number of innovation projects in the period 2015–2022
Agrifood systems	Agricultural production and processes	Genetically modified crops, mechanical irrigation and farming techniques, higher-yield seeds, drought resistant crops and cultivation practices	−19
	Fertilisers, pesticides and other chemicals	Nitrate-based mineral fertilisers with extracted hydrogen, green ammonia, low-carbon fertilisers, pesticides derived from organic sources	
	Technologies	Zero tillage, vertical farming, drones, fleet management, digital sensors	
Health and education	Healthcare	Energy efficiency, waste management, digitalisation of medical records, improvement of electrical infrastructure	+11
	Education	LED lighting systems, solar panels, green roofs, rainwater harvesting systems, energy-efficient windows, low-flow faucets	

Sources: Hultman et al. (2016), p. 34; UNCTAD (2023); authors' own elaboration

sustainable development growth (SDG) increased in 2022. However, the estimations show that the annual investment gap is still significant.

According to UNCTAD (2023) the biggest gaps between targeted and implemented investments are observed in energy, water and sanitation, infrastructure, agrifood and biodiversity industries. This means that the volume of green investments in these sectors will have to grow, so it is likely that more jobs will be created. This investment gap is also likely to shape the geography and nature of platform-mediated work, as emerging employment niches may form around infrastructure maintenance, renewable energy services, and biodiversity monitoring, especially in regions receiving targeted funding.

Transformations in Production Processes According to Mallik (2023), production processes refer to the preliminary production of tangible products which are later stored in inventory. Production processes have little contact with a user. They are characterised by a longer reaction time to changes and implementation of changes, and they are highly capital intensive. However, their main purpose is to support a company's competitive priorities and create a competitive advantage. Green transformation and the implementation of digital technologies will allow at least partially mitigating the instabilities inherent in production processes and improving the performance of their main purpose. This transformation is also expected to affect the structure of platform-based work, as the shift towards digitalised and automated production creates demand for new forms of remote supervision, algorithm-based diagnostics, and digital systems maintenance.

The literature (OECD 2019a; Mauksch et al. 2020; Bocker and Silva 2022; Vandeplas et al. 2022; Mallik 2023; Cheba et al. 2023; "EIT Manufacturing" 2023) analysis helped to identify the following potential directions for the changes in production processes:

1) competence-enhancing and competence destroying technological changes (destruction of the resources and capabilities of traditional mechanical products; efficiency enhancing technologies);
2) implementation of disruptive technologies (disruptive technologies add attributes to existing technologies, raise production potential);
3) the use of advanced materials (the use of substitutes (e.g. CVD diamond instead of natural diamond) which will lower costs, add value to products and facilitate recycling);
4) implementation of forecasting technologies (allows to predict successful technological trends, set standards for an industry).

The study by "EIT Manufacturing" (2023), co-funded by the European Union, proposes that production processes should be transformed through the use of artificial intelligence (AI), the effectiveness of which could be improved by balancing technical knowledge and industry know-how. The innovative ecosystem of production processes, represented by the Internet of Things, artificial intelligence, and digital twins, is expected to develop along the entire value chain. Artificial Intelligence (AI), blockchain technologies and the Industrial Internet of Things (IIoT) will allow to digitalise production processes, thus reducing labour costs, economic input and machine downtime and increasing production speed (OECD 2019a). Machine Learning (ML) methods (a subset of Artificial Intelligence (AI)) will allow the use of computer algorithms in production processes. The algorithms will initially use the available data, but will eventually improve and be able to make decisions automatically, using their experience, i.e. smart technologies will no longer require preprogramming. ML methods in production processes will allow identification of bottlenecks, and will ensure production safety and quality control (Mallik 2023). These technological shifts are likely to create new opportunities for specialised freelance workers, such as algorithm trainers, predictive maintenance operators, and AI-data auditors, many of whom may be contracted through digital labour platforms.

According to "EIT Manufacturing" (2023), the effects of smart technologies on production processes will manifest themselves as a reduction in the resources used, which will allow an increase in production output, an increase in efficiency, an increase in quality by reducing costs, and reimaging employee engagement. Nevertheless, as noted by Mallik (2023), technological changes in production processes will not occur suddenly or according to one specific plan, but will have to be implemented sequentially. In parallel, platform-mediated work is expected to play a role in facilitating this transition, particularly in tasks that involve remote machine diagnostics, virtual commissioning, and just-in-time support services for manufacturing systems. This signals a gradual convergence between industrial modernisation and digital labour markets.

Another source of changes in production processes is business activity in compliance with the principles of environmental protection and climate change awareness. The report by the OECD (2017a, b, c) proposes that the green transformation, which aims for less pollution and more efficient use of resources, will lead to significant structural changes in demand and production processes. By adapting to the principles of the green economy and green growth regulations, business enterprises will use fewer polluting inputs, and their production processes will become less pollution intensive. According to Dai and Yang (2023), significant transformations of production processes in the context of the green transition can be caused by digital empowerment, the impact of which is manifested through scale and technology effects. The authors believe that transformations caused by digital empowerment (for example, digitalisation can empower pollution monitoring technologies) are heterogeneous and can take place in industries with different energy consumption intensities (OECD 2019a; Dai and Yang 2023). Moreover, digital empowerment is expected to provide a positive spillover effect along all industrial chain (i.e. in upstream and downstream enterprises) (Naghshineh and Carvalho 2021; Mallik 2023). To achieve tangible results, it is necessary to align productivity, sustainability and resilience (resilience will be developed through non-linear distributed production) ("EIT Manufacturing" 2023). This emerging industrial ecosystem may increasingly rely on external talent pools accessed through online platforms for environmental auditing, carbon reporting, and lifecycle assessment—functions that require a blend of technical knowledge and digital mobility.

When assessing the impact of the green economy on employment in this context, it is important to note that after the transformation of production processes, workplaces will be maintained, but it will be especially important for the workforce to quickly reorient from the work in traditional production processes to the work in production processes which use different energy and raw materials. It should also be noted that if the traditional "brown" industry (e.g. metallurgical industry) is capital intensive, then the green transformation will stimulate a shift towards more labour-intensive industries. On the other hand, even green sectors will not be able to create many new jobs if they are capital intensive (OECD 2017b). These workforce shifts may also reshape labour platforms, as the demand for technicians, consultants and skilled freelancers with green economy competences is likely to rise. This highlights the importance of equipping platform workers with relevant upskilling opportunities and aligning platform governance with broader green policy goals.

Changes in the Demand Structure According to the OECD (2019a, b), the substitution of polluting products with non-polluting ones will change the demand structure in the long term, but the total economic output, as well as the aggregate demand, will not decrease. The demand growth is expected for the products delivered by the low-carbon intensity sectors, in particular, electric vehicles and renewable energy.

Mallik (2023) in his analysis of the prospects and challenges of the technology-based manufacturing in the EU indicates that the consumer demand will be stimulated by rapid prototyping (the strategy used for product development), which will allow creating 3-dimensional prototypes of potential products, testing and optimising such product characteristics as size, shape and overall usability. This way a product will be tested in the development process, its prototype will look realistic, and potential users will be able to interact with it. All this will make it possible to better match a product to the needs of consumers and shorten the time of a product's entry into the market, thus stimulating the demand.

Anti-pollution policies will induce a shift towards the use of renewable energy, while implementation of the principles of circular economy will reduce the efficiency of the use of traditional resources in production processes. Therefore, there will be noticeable changes in the demand for energy and production resources: the demand for fossil fuels will decrease, while the demand for wind, solar, ocean, geothermal, bioenergy and hydropower will increase. Green policies will lead to a reduction of the prices of clean products and services relative to the prices of polluting products and services. Reduced prices will lead to an increase in demand for clean products and services, which, in its turn, will stimulate the growth of the sectors that produce clean products/services and thus an increase in the number of jobs in these sectors (OECD 2019a). The restructuring of demand patterns will also have implications for platform-based commerce and service provision, as digital platforms may become key intermediaries for green products and services. Therefore, ensuring platform transparency and environmental labelling of offerings could be important policy considerations.

Changes in Aggregate Income and Macroeconomic Conditions According to the OECD (2019a, b), indirect macroeconomic benefits will be obtained through technological and non-technological knowledge spillovers, R&D, which will become the public knowledge, and productivity improvement. The OECD (2019a, b) provides the estimates which show that the marginal social rates of return from R&D and knowledge spillovers can reach from 30 to 50 percent.

The implementation of the principles of the green economy can cause changes in state budgets due to the changes in tax obligations for economic actors: national governments can increase their budget revenues by selling pollution permits, and the reduction of harmful labour market taxation will result in improved well-being of citizens. This means that the aggregate income is likely to increase, which will stimulate the aggregate demand. In response to the growing aggregate demand, business enterprises will increase the volume of production/service provision, and thus the number of jobs will also increase (OECD 2017b). The OECD (2017c) report for the G20 emphasizes that many G20 countries can achieve substantial improvements in their GDP in case they permanently increase the investment in the low-carbon transition. Businesses can also receive support from national governments or targeted funds for green transformation or/and staff training, which will reduce the negative transformational impacts (OECD 2017b).

Nevertheless, as noted by Victor (2022), the impact of green investment on macroeconomic objectives (GDP, unemployment, public debt, private sector (household) debt, income inequality) remains a major concern in the EU and the USA. Having applied the LowGrow SFC simulation model (the model was calibrated to Canada and the United Kingdom) to research the modest and ambitious green transformation scenarios between 2022 and 2072, the author found that the changes induced by the green transformation would lead to an increase in GDP at an average annual rate of 1.5 percent in the modest scenario and 0.5 percent in the ambitious scenario, while GDP in the base case (without the green transformation) would increase by 2.1 percent annually. A slower GDP growth in the conditions of the green transformation under both modest and ambitious scenario would be caused by the diversion of some investment to non-productive capital, and this diversion would be more pronounced in the case of the ambitious scenario. The unemployment rate in all cases fluctuates around 6 percent, which shows that the green transition tends not to lead to any dramatic changes in the labour market. The ratio of government debt to GDP would be very similar under the base and modest scenarios, but it would be significantly higher in the case of the ambitious scenario. This is believed to be due to lower tax revenues and increased government support to households to reduce income inequality. When analysing the indebtedness of the private sector (households), the author found that it would remain stable under the modest scenario, would increase under the base scenario, and would decrease under the ambitious scenario. The latter decrease is explained by the likelihood that consumers would borrow less with the declining levels of consumption. Thus, the results of the study propose that national economies can grow in the conditions of the green transformation, but the growth rates will be slower than in the conditions of the traditional economic environment. The financing of the green transformation will require huge government incentives and direct government investment, so it will be focused not on economic, but on environmental and social benefits as the main goal. In this context, digital labour platforms may play an important role in mediating temporary or project-based green employment, offering flexible access to work opportunities aligned with green transition investments. However, such roles are currently underexamined in macroeconomic modelling, revealing a gap for further research.

Changes in Trade and Competitiveness Fankhauser et al. (2013) believe that competitiveness in the conditions of the green transition will depend on 3 factors:

1) the speed at which businesses will be able to transform traditional products and processes into green ones (the rate of green innovation);
2) the ability of businesses to maintain and increase their market share (comparative advantage);
3) a favourable starting point (current output).

The greatest increase in competitiveness is expected in the sectors which have the current comparative advantage and implement substantial green innovation, which shows that their transition to low-carbon products and production processes should be comparatively smooth. These sectors are the competitive strength of national economies. For example, if measuring by the Green Innovation Index, the heavy industry sector is considered the competitive strength in Germany, and the light industry sector—in France. The competitive potential in the future is represented by the sectors where the current comparative advantage is low (i.e. they export less than the global average of the sector). By actively implementing green innovation, these sectors will be able to gain an advantage from innovative low-carbon products and processes, and will become the basis of the national economic strength. For example, this is expected from the heavy industry sector in France and partly from the light industry sector in Germany (as measured by the Green Innovation Index) (OECD 2019a).

A special investment plan—the so-called "InvestEU" plan—is intended to finance the implementation of the European Green Deal policy measures. The plan includes the carbon dioxide emission tariffs for the countries which cannot reduce greenhouse gas emissions at the same pace as the EU (Valatsas 2019). A special mechanism called the Carbon Border Adjustment Mechanism (CBAM) is provided for this. Under this mechanism, a carbon tax would be applied to imports of certain goods from third countries. Additional taxes would be levied on the products made in the countries with less stringent environmental requirements than in the EU. This would help ensure that goods imported from third countries are not cheaper than an equivalent product produced in the EU (European Parliament 2021). According to the European Parliament (2021), the abovementioned mechanism should comply with the rules of the World Trade Organization and become part of the EU industrial strategy in the future. The mechanism should cover the entire energy sector and energy-intensive industries by 2030. It is noted that the mechanism is intended only to implement the objectives of combating climate change and reduce the risk of carbon dioxide leakage (emissions) (European Parliament 2021).

The study by "EIT Manufacturing" (2023), co-funded by the European Union, proposes that business competitiveness can be promoted through cooperation with reliable partners to maintain uninterrupted and smoothly functioning trade chains. This strategy will allow businesses to achieve strategic autonomy and maintain global competitiveness. In addition, since the principles of value creation are changing, businesses should move from a competitive to a more collaborative mindset: to exchange knowledge and expertise within a certain branch or local industry by following some pre-agreed criteria and standards. This type of ecosystem will enable more efficient use of valuable resources and information along the entire supply chain, thus creating a competitive advantage.

The green transformation is often seen as regressive due to the high costs to industry. However, according to the European Parliament (2022), if countries manage to reach the objective of 1.5 °C, established in the Paris Agreement, which entered into force on 4 November 2016, the output of energy-intensive industries will be less affected. Industrial competitiveness can be increased by free allocation of emissions trading system (ETS) allowances and the targeted use of carbon revenue.

Nevertheless, the failure to meet climate policy goals would make business less competitive. In jurisdictions where the legal regulation of business will be based on the principles of the green economy, pollution-intensive products will become relatively more expensive than similar products in the jurisdictions which will not consider the principles of the green economy. Therefore, pollution-intensive products produced in green economy jurisdictions will be less competitive, and the export income of the companies which make these products will decrease (OECD 2017a). On the other hand, compliance with environmental standards promotes innovation, which provides companies with a competitive advantage (OECD 2019a). In the context of platform economy, the trade and competitiveness dynamics can also influence platform-mediated services that contribute to green transformation goals. Cross-border freelance and gig workers—especially those involved in sustainability consulting, digital circular economy services, or remote design of green technologies—may become increasingly important for maintaining national competitiveness in low-carbon sectors.

It should be noted that not all green transformations have a positive impact on industrial growth. For example, Nosheen et al.'s (2021) study in Eastern and Western Europe showed that the technological innovations in the areas of transport and production-related climate change technologies tend to have a negative impact on green growth. The report by the OECD (2017a, b, c) suggests that not all business enterprises and industries can reorient so quickly due to the high costs, time and organisational factors, so they will be considered technologically backward from the point of view of the green economy, although their productivity will remain the same when working with old technologies. According to Mathiesen et al. (2023), some scenarios of the European Commission, for instance, the EU 1.5 TECH in "A Clean Planet for all", do not provide measures to prevent the risks posed by the green transformation to industry, such as overinvestment, blind investment, general pan-industrial investment and unrealistic implementation rates. In addition, excessive protectionism of green innovations on the part of governments (lowering tariffs on low-carbon technologies) can have a negative impact since it will hinder the wider spread of these innovations in the market and there will be a risk of duplication of efforts across countries (Hasna et al. 2023). Also, as noted by Kozluk and Zipperer (2013), Victor (2022), Mallik (2023) and other researchers, the increase in the investment in the green transformation essentially means only the redistribution of investment: investments and innovations are directed to green sectors, but reduced in traditional sectors, but this does not lead to more investment and innovation *per se*. According to Hasna et al. (2023), the momentum of green innovation in developed countries reached its peak in 2010 (measuring by 10 percent of total patent filings in 2010), but has been slowly decreasing since then. This decrease is determined by various factors, for example, hydraulic fracking, which caused the price of oil to decrease, and technological maturity of some initial technologies (e.g. renewables). Sun et al.'s (2023) research found the negative impact of the workforce on the growth of the green economy. In the case of the latter incompatibility, the authors recommend promoting employment by developing green FDI, activating green financing tools and launching green job creation schemes through SMEs. Li et al.'s (2022) observations of 687 listed companies in China in the period 2016–2020 disclosed that green innovation may significantly reduce the economic efficiency of business enterprises, especially in the cases when innovation achievements are not sufficiently protected, when companies have accumulated limited knowledge and technology. The authors argue that the efficiency of companies in the latter case can be improved by high market competition, upgrading of production processes and freedom of technology selection.

Summarising The joint effects of finance, food and fuel crises on industry in the conditions of the "brown" economy manifest themselves as the gross misallocation of capital, which no longer stimulates the economy and job creation. In contrast to the "brown" economy, the green economy is expected to promote economic growth in the long term due to cheaper energy, more efficient production processes and socially responsible consumption. The literature analysis revealed that the impact of the green transition on industry is likely to manifest itself through resource and innovation efficiency, transformations in production processes, changes in the demand structure, changes in aggregate income and macroeconomic conditions, and changes in trade and competitiveness. The growth of the green innovation is associated with the growth of innovation overall because the green innovation often requires additional complementary innovation. The biggest gaps between targeted and implemented investments are currently observed in the energy, water and sanitation, infrastructure, agrifood and biodiversity industries. This means that the volume of green investments in these sectors will have to grow, so it is likely that more jobs will be created. The main expected directions of the transformations in production processes are destruction of the resources and capabilities of the traditional mechanical products and the use of efficiency enhancing technologies, implementation of disruptive technologies which increase production potential, the use of advanced materials which lower costs, add value to products and facilitate recycling, and implementation of forecasting technologies. Demand growth is expected for products which are produced in low-carbon intensity sectors, in particular, electric vehicles and renewable energy. The reduced price will lead to an increase in demand for clean products and services, which, in its turn, will stimulate the growth of the sectors which produce these products/services, and thus will increase employment in these sectors. Indirect macroeconomic benefits will be obtained through technological and non-technological knowledge spillovers, R&D, which will become the public knowledge, and productivity improvement. The greatest increase in competitiveness is expected in the sectors which have the current comparative advantage and implement substantial green innovation, which shows that their transition to low-carbon products and production processes should be comparatively smooth. These sectors are the national competitive strength and employment accelerators. In addition, platform-based labour models may support this transition by offering flexible access to highly specialised services, especially in domains related to eco-design, digitalisation of sustainability reporting, and decentralised project work on green infrastructure. This functional flexibility may contribute to industrial resilience in the face of green transformation.

Nevertheless, the existing evidence regarding the positive impact of the green economy on industrial growth is not yet conclusive, and so far the impact of the environmental policy on macroeconomic indicators (in particular, GDP growth) has been relatively small. Researchers note that not all business companies and industries can quickly reorient due to the high costs, time, organisational factors, and some scenarios of the European Commission (for instance, the EU 1.5 TECH in "A Clean Planet for all") do not provide the measures to prevent the risks posed by the green transformation to industry, such as overinvestment, blind investment, general pan-industrial investment and unrealistic implementation rates. In addition, excessive protectionism of the green innovation on the part of governments (lowering tariffs on low-carbon technologies) can have a negative impact. Therefore, it should be noted that the modeling of business activities for the shift towards the green economy must be carried out in the way so that the transformation would allow to boost economic growth not only through permanent, but also through temporary increases in investment.

2.2.2 The Effects of the Green Transition on the Labour Market

According to the European Parliament (2022), the green transformation policies will significantly transform the labour market, which will face both new opportunities and risks, and certain industries and groups of workers will be disproportionately affected. During the green transition, most occupations will be indirectly affected by energy supply and energy-intensive industries, as well as by changing energy prices and new work practices. This transformation is also expected to reshape the nature of work in platform-mediated environments, especially where on-demand services intersect with green economy goals, such as in sustainable mobility, repair services, and energy efficiency tasks.

The shift from the brown to the green economy is inevitably associated with huge costs, for example, the investment in renewable energy sources, pollution control equipment, pesticide level measurements, waste sorting and recycling systems, etc. On the one hand, this investment helps create new jobs (green jobs) since the operation, monitoring and maintenance of the equipment and systems mentioned in the example require human labour. On the other hand, products and services produced in the green economy are more expensive, and the costs fall on the shoulders of consumers. As a result, the aggregate demand as well as previous production and consumption volumes may decrease, and companies which have not transformed quickly enough may become uncompetitive. There is a risk that the green economy could increase unemployment. This duality of effects underscores the need for policy mechanisms that not only stimulate green investment, but also support labour market adaptability—particularly in flexible employment models such as platform work, where job stability and access to social protection may be insufficient in the face of transition shocks.

According to Atlama and Ozsoy (2011), the effects of green jobs can manifest themselves in two different ways: on the one hand, green jobs reduce unemployment and help solve social problems, such as poverty and inequality; on the other hand, since green jobs are related to raising marginal costs and decreasing sales, these effects can lead to higher unemployment. This two-sided dynamic is particularly relevant in the context of digital platforms, where the creation of new green tasks (e.g. remote energy audits, sustainability consulting) may be offset by job insecurity or lack of upskilling opportunities. The literature analysis allowed to identify the main positive, negative and neutral potential effects of the green transition on the labour market (see Table 2.3).

The framework for characterising green jobs was provided by the United Nations Environment Program (UNEP) in collaboration with the International Labour Organisation (ILO), the International Trade Union Council (ITUC), the International Organisation of Employers (IOE) and the World Health Organisation (WHO) (2008). In their report, green jobs are defined as "work in agriculture, manufacturing, research and development, administrative and service activities that contributes substantially to preserving and restoring environmental quality". The report also notes that green jobs include the jobs which help to protect ecosystems and biodiversity, reduce energy, materials and water consumption through high-efficiency strategies, de-carbonize the economy, and minimize and altogether avoid generation of all forms of waste and pollution (2008, p. 3). In addition, the UNEP (2008)

Table 2.3 The major positive, negative and neutral potential effects of the green transition on the labour market

Direction of the effect	Manifestation	Author(s), year
Positive effects	Creation of green jobs and green collar jobs	The U.S. Department of Energy (2001); Bezdek et al. (2008); UNEP, ILO, ITUC, IOE and WHO (2008); Popp et al. (2020); Vandeplas et al. (2022)
	Creation of new jobs in technologically advanced industries	OECD (2017b)
	Net increase in jobs due to the changes in the structure of the economy	OECD (2017b); Vandeplas et al. (2022)
	Increase in the share of low- and medium-skilled labour force in total employment	The European Parliament (2022)
	Creation of jobs which are less prone to geographical concentration of the population	Terzi (2022); Bircan et al. (2023)
	Job creation online	McCarthy et al. (2018)

(continued)

Table 2.3 (continued)

Direction of the effect	Manifestation	Author(s), year
Negative effects	Stringent environmental regulation can raise marginal costs and reduce sales, which will lead to higher unemployment	Atlama and Ozsoy (2011); OECD (2017b)
	The decrease in the number of jobs in industries characterised by large environmental footprints	OECD (2017b); Chateau et al. (2018); ILO (2018b); the European Parliament (2022); Vandeplas et al. (2022)
	Limited productivity growth in less agile companies that have not yet exhausted the potential of old investments will prevent the creation of new jobs	OECD (2017b)
	Declining share of high-skilled labour force in total employment	The European Parliament (2022)
	Rapid obsolescence of technologies can lead to obsolescence in some jobs, large additional investment in retraining human capital	The U.S. Department of Energy (2001); Adao et al. (2022); Vandeplas et al. (2022); the European Parliament (2022)
	Slightly greater inequality and polarisation of labour markets	Alexandri et al. (2024)
Neutral effects	The limited impact on the service sector will not lead to significant changes in employment in this sector	The European Parliament (2022)
	The negatively affected industries will constitute a relatively small share of total employment, which will lead to a moderate general effect	Chateau et al. (2018); Vandeplas et al. (2022); the European Parliament (2022)
	Only 9 percent of jobs are at risk of being automated	Arntz et al. (2016)
	Jobs may not be lost, but shifted across sectors	OECD (2019a); Niggli and Rutzer (2021); Vandeplas et al. (2022)

Source: compiled by the authors

emphasises that green jobs need to be decent. i.e. they must offer adequate wages, safe working conditions, job security, reasonable carrier prospects and exercise workers' rights. This emphasis on decent work is particularly relevant in the platform economy context, where task-based jobs often lack social protection and stability. Ensuring that green platform-based work meets these decency criteria is essential for a truly sustainable labour transformation. Referring to the new 2030 Agenda for Sustainable Development, proposed by the UN General Assembly in September 2015, the ILO (2015) notes that decent work must be based on the four pillars: employment creation, social protection, rights at work and social dialogue, i.e. decent works must be productive and secure, respect labour rights, provide adequate income and social protection, and offer union freedom, social dialogue, collective bargaining and worker participation. These principles are particularly important for guiding labour market reforms in response to both digitalisation and the green transition, as both trends challenge conventional employment models and demand new approaches to ensuring work decency and inclusiveness.

The report, provided by the United Nations Environment Program (UNEP) (2008), concludes that the global transition from the conventional brown to a low-carbon sustainable economy will promote economic development and add a large number of green jobs across many sectors of the innovative green economy. The green economy, i.e. the use of environmentally friendly technologies, products and services not only minimizes pollution and reduces the negative impact of industry on the environment, but also stimulates the creation of green jobs in the major industries, such as construction, transportation, energy, agriculture and forestry. This suggests that the employment potential of the green economy lies not only in emerging sectors but also in the transformation of traditional industries, especially when these sectors embrace technological upgrades aligned with sustainability goals.

One of the main industries growing due to the promotion of the green economy is the renewable energy (wind, solar, photovoltaic and biomass energy) industry. The delivery of products related to this industry, for instance, hydro-small and large geothermal systems, fuel cells, hydrogen, energy conservation and energy efficient products, as well as hybrid vehicles, passive, solar/green, sustainable buildings, energy-smart design and day lighting, is developing rapidly (Bezdek et al. 2008, p. 21). Thus, there is a noticeable correlation between the development of the above-mentioned industries and technologies and the growth of the number of jobs, i.e. the expanding use of renewable energy has a positive impact on employment. The pace and scale of this transformation indicate that renewable energy sectors could become central not only to energy policy but also to long-term employment strategies, particularly in regions seeking to replace declining brown economy sectors. With the conduct of air, water, land pollution control, waste management, environmental monitoring, analysis and assessment, as well as environmental research, development and engineering, many new jobs are created in the aforementioned areas (Atlama and Ozsoy 2011). These areas represent an expanding segment of the labour market, which is likely to absorb a growing share of the workforce displaced by traditional sectors, provided that adequate training and upskilling mechanisms are in place.

Popp et al. (2020) found that the number of green jobs in the US increased due to the subsidies provided under the American Recovery and Reinvestment Act (ARRA) of 2009. A significant increase in the number of green jobs is observed in the construction and waste management sectors. This suggests that strategic public investment plays a pivotal role in accelerating the green transition, particularly in labour-intensive sectors, and highlights the importance of coordinated policy support to ensure equitable employment outcomes. Bircan et al. (2023) analysed the "LinkedIn Economic Graph" statistics and found that the demand for workers with "green" skills is so high that a wage premium of 4 percent is paid to these workers. This shows that the demand for the workers with "green" skills exceeds their supply in the labour market. This growing skill premium underscores the urgency of aligning education and training systems with the needs of a green economy to avoid bottlenecks in labour supply and to maximise the employment potential of the green transition. In the region of the European Bank for Reconstruction and Development (EBRD), advertisements for green jobs on the "LinkedIn" platform accounted for 14 percent of total paid job postings at the beginning of 2023 (for comparison, this percentage did not exceed 9 percent in 2018). In developed countries (France, Germany, Italy, the UK, the USA), this number increased from 10 to 21 percent from 2018 to 2023. This growing share of green job postings highlights a structural transformation in labour demand that is not limited to traditional industries. It suggests an expanding role for digital platforms as intermediaries in the green labour market, especially for specialised, location-flexible tasks.

The concept of green jobs is distinguished from the concept of green collar jobs. In general, green collar jobs can be interpreted as traditional blue-collar jobs, but those in green businesses whose products and services directly contribute to improving environmental quality and energy efficiency (Pinderhughes 2007). As noted by Atlama and Ozsoy (2011), these jobs usually require less than a four-year university or college degree, but often are a stepping stone to high-skill professional green jobs and green entrepreneurship. More specifically, green collar jobs are defined as vocational jobs in an ecologically responsible trade (e.g. constructing and maintaining wind farms, practicing organic agriculture, recycling materials, etc.). For instance, the industry of renewable energy offers a wide variety of jobs, and although it can be difficult to find a personal professional niche, persons with different types and degrees of education can improve their qualifications or retrain and get involved in this industry. The analysis provided by the U.S. Department of Energy (2001) proposes that the industry of renewable energy offers many green collar jobs in the areas of communication, sales, marketing, business support (e.g. corporate planning, finance, human resource management, law, information technologies), community outreach. Other jobs are specific to the operation and management of the major renewable energy power sources—wind, solar, bio-, geothermal and hydropower.

Bircan et al. (2023), indicate that a higher proportion of workers moved into green industries than moved out of them in different economies between 2015 and 2023.

"Brown" industries are characterised by a net outflow of the labour force, while "green" industries experience a net inflow. Greater job transitions into "brown" industries are observed in economies outside the EBRD region, whereas EBRD economies see more significant shifts into "green" industries. While this section primarily focuses on traditional industrial labour market changes, platform-mediated work is also starting to contribute to the green transition—particularly in specialised, location-independent roles such as renewable energy consultancy, environmental data analysis, and circular economy services.

According to the OECD (2017a, b, c), the impact of the green economy on the labour market will manifest itself in four following directions:

1) more jobs will be created in the "green" sectors which will make products/provide services reducing environmental pressure;
2) the number of jobs will decrease in the sectors/industries characterised by large environmental footprints;
3) there will be a noticeable net increase in the number of jobs stimulated by the changes in the structure of the economy (the largest increase in the number of jobs is expected in labour-intensive sectors);
4) there will be a noticeable net decrease in the number of jobs determined by the decrease in business profitability due to extremely high environmental requirements and stringent regulation.

Any of these directions can be both short-term (i.e. related to the transition towards the green economy of a specific business) and long-term (i.e. typical of the green economy in general).

The report by the OECD (2017a, b, c) suggests that environmental policies promote specialisation and the development of "clean" industries, but at the same time mean stringent environmental regulation, the effects of which on industrial productivity may vary across business companies and industries. This means that technologically advanced business companies and industries can expect to grow and create new jobs, but less nimble, larger companies and industries, especially those that have already invested in the most effective operational strategies and technologies, will not be in a hurry to switch to new technologies (for example, because the potential of the old technologies has not been fully utilized, because the transformation may require significant business interruptions which cause losses, because a firm or an industry is essentially not agile, etc.). Therefore, their productivity growth will be very limited from the point of view of sustainability, and no new jobs will be created without productivity growth. Given the accelerated technological changes associated with the green transition, continuous skills development and retraining are critical to prevent labour market mismatches and to enable workers to seize new opportunities in emerging green sectors.

The green transition is expected to cause significant changes in the sectoral composition of employment. For example, the number of jobs in the coal sector is expected to decrease by about 50 percent by 2023. A large decrease in jobs is also expected in other fossil fuel sectors. Chateau et al. (2018) estimated a decrease of approximately 8 percent of jobs in mining and fossil fuels supply and fossil-fuel electricity generation sectors. The ILO (2018) believes that the reduction of the labour force in the gas and petroleum extraction sector may amount to about 11 percent, and in the coal-powered electricity generation sector—about 19 percent by 2023.

The dynamics of the number of jobs in energy-intensive industries should be closely related to the impact of the transition on output in these industries. A large increase in the number of jobs is expected in the electricity supply and construction sectors, and the implementation of climate neutrality measures should increase employment in the industries such as production of renewable energy and building renovation. The services sector, which currently provides the largest number of jobs in the EU, will be affected to a relatively limited extent (European Parliament 2022).

The high-skilled labour force will be more negatively affected than the low- and medium-skilled labour force because a large part of the newly created jobs will be intended for low- and medium-skilled workers; thus, the negative impact of digitalisation on these categories of workers will be offset at least partially. Nevertheless, if carbon revenues are used to reduce labour taxation, aggregate employment will increase, so the negative impact of the green transformation on high-skilled labour force will be partially mitigated (European Parliament 2022).

Many workers will undoubtedly need to be retrained and adapt to innovative production methods, which will require significant investment in human capital to ensure that labour demand matches labour supply in the labour market (European Parliament 2022). Vandeplas et al. (2022) explain that technological progress in the conditions of the green transformation will mean the accelerated obsolescence of technologies, which, in its turn, will result in the obsolescence of human capital, i.e. the obsolescence of some jobs. If the demand for certain skills decreases, workers will be forced to retrain at their own expense, at the expense of the state or a potential new employer. How quickly the skills of the labour force will again meet the requirements of the labour market will depend on the speed with which countries will be able to roll out green technologies. According to Adao et al. (2022), the ICT technology adaptation process showed that skill mismatches tend to persist, especially in local markets, which adapt relatively slowly. The authors argue that the transition to jobs with strong skill specificity will be more difficult. Having applied a three-sector macro-econometric analysis model, Alexandri et al. (2024) researched the impact of the industrial climate change mitigation on the European labour markets. The results of their study show that the climate change mitigation policies will affect the structure of the European labour markets, and will also lead to a small increase in inequality and polarisation in the labour market till 2023. The authors believe that greater manifestations of inequality and polarisation in the labour market will be characteristic of those European countries where industry will be more severely affected by the green transition. However, the uneven regional and sectoral impacts of the green transition underscore the need for targeted social policies to mitigate inequality and support vulnerable groups disproportionately affected by structural shifts in employment.

Nevertheless, as stated by the European Parliament (2022), the assessment of both positive and negative aspects of the green transition implies that the overall impact of the green transition on the labour market should be moderate since the negatively affected industries are expected to constitute a relatively small share of total employment, and the strength of the impact will depend on the use of carbon revenues. Chateau et al.'s (2018) estimations suggest that the aggregate impact of the green transformation on employment should be limited. When analysing the structural changes in the labour market which could be caused by decarbonisation policies by 2035, the authors performed the simulations which revealed that the overall reallocation of jobs (i.e. the sum of destructed and created jobs) will be around 0.3 percent in the OECD countries and around 0.8 percent in non-OECD countries. For comparison, job reallocation rates averaged at 20 percent in the OECD countries between 1995 and 2005. On the other hand, the authors admit that the relatively small job allocation rates obtained during the simulation may be determined by a small share of total employment in energy sectors which will experience the greatest consequences of the green transition, but due to the small share of jobs in total employment, the overall labour market will experience relatively small changes due to employment transformations in the energy sector. Vandeplas et al. (2022) provide the statistical data which indicate that the sectors of electricity production, transport, manufacturing, agriculture and mining, which together produce about 90 percent of all CO_2 emissions in the EU, employ only about 25 percent of the total workforce. More than 75 percent of the workforce is employed in the construction, wholesale, retail and other service sectors, but the overall impact of the green transformation on the latter sectors is likely to be less significant because they together produce only about 12 percent of all CO_2 emissions in the EU. Alexandri et al. (2024) found that the reduction in the use of fossil fuels in the road transport and electricity supply sectors may even have a modest, but positive impact on GDP and total employment in the European labour markets (in more than half EU Member States, especially those with such industries as mining and quarrying, utilities and manufacturing of coke and refined petroleum products) by 2023.

Arntz et al. (2016) employed the task-based approach in their research of 21 OECD countries and found that only about 9 percent of jobs are at risk of being automated. These findings lead to the conclusion that the green transition poses a greater risk to technological progress than to employment, thus, the effects of the green transition are manageable.

The OECD (2019a, b) argues that the process of the green transformation can shift some jobs to other sub-sectors, but jobs will not be lost. For instance, the expected decrease in the number of jobs in the fossil fuels sector can be offset by the increase in the number of jobs in the renewable energy sector, so the overall effect on employment will be neutral. A similar opinion is held by Vandeplas et al. (2022) who observe that the structural economic changes, brought about by the green transformation, will equalize the proportions of people leaving the labour market and people entering the labour market. Niggli and Rutzer (2021) who conducted an employment study in 19 EU Member States in the period 1992–2010, when environmental requirements were tightened almost three times, found that the impact of this policy on aggregate employment was insignificant because the tightened requirements caused a shift from the sectors characterised by low green potential to the sectors characterised by high green potential. Terzi (2022) notes that the green transition can stimulate the creation of jobs which are less prone to geographical concentration of the population, promote delocalisation and dehumanise repetitive tasks by automation. McCarthy et al. (2018) add that in the circular economy, part of the jobs will be created online, which will at least partially compensate for the reduction of jobs in physical companies.

The standard model, provided by the European Parliament (2022) (the JRC-GEM-E3 model is based on the presumption that wages are fully flexible, allocation in industries is free, business companies cannot incorporate the opportunity costs, generated by free allocation, and cannot optimise their market share, the power, buildings and road transport sectors are characterised by auctioning, and unemployment rate is close to the baseline level), suggests that the negative effects of the green transition on employment should reach about –0.26 percent (i.e. negatively affect about 494,000 jobs) by 2023. However, after using carbon revenues to reduce labour taxation, the positive impact on employment should reach about 0.06 percent (i.e. affect about 110,000 jobs). If carbon revenue is directed to support energy efficient investment and reduce VAT, consumption and GDP growth will be stimulated, which, in their turn, are likely to increase employment by 0.20 percent (i.e. to contribute to creating nearly 412,000 jobs). Finally, if carbon revenue is used to reduce labour taxation for low-skilled labour force, net wages for lower-skilled workers will increase and labour costs for business will decrease, which is likely to increase employment by 0.45 percent (European Parliament 2022).

According to Vandeplas et al. (2022), the major labour market intervention measures, which can mitigate the shock caused by the green transition, can be categorized as pre-transition and transition measures. The pre-transition measures include identifying which groups of workers will be most affected, conducting an audit of their skills, reviewing the current labour regulations, setting up institutions and partnerships to manage the labour market transition, and providing early job search assistance. The transition (during and after) measures include providing temporary income support, implementing active labour market policies and providing access to vital social services, such as healthcare, childcare, social services. The above-mentioned measures are believed to cushion the loss of income for workers who have lost their jobs due to the changes in the economic structure caused by the green transformation, and to help them reintegrate into the labour market. It should be emphasized that, given the uneven regional and sectoral impacts of the green transition, targeted and flexible social policies will be necessary to support workers and communities disproportionately affected by these changes, ensuring an inclusive and just labour market transition.

Summarising The green transformation policies will significantly transform the labour market which will face both new opportunities and risks. The literature analysis revealed that the impact of the green transition on the labour market can be assessed as positive, negative and neutral. The positive effect is expected to manifest itself through the creation of green and green collar jobs in transforming industries, especially construction, transportation, energy, agriculture and forestry, the creation of new jobs in technologically advanced industries (for instance, waste management, environmental monitoring, analysis and assessment, environmental research, development and engineering), net increase in the number of jobs due to the changes in the structure of the economy, the increase in the share of low- and medium-skilled labour force in total employment, the creation of jobs which are less prone to geographical concentration of the population, and creation of jobs online. The negative impact of the green transformation on the labour market is likely to manifest itself through rising marginal costs and decreasing sales, which can lead to a reduction of jobs, especially in industries characterised by large environmental footprints, limited productivity growth in less agile companies that have not yet exploited the potential of their old investments, the decrease in the share of high-skilled labour force in total employment, the rapid obsolescence of technologies and large additional investments in retraining of human capital, and slightly higher inequality and polarisation in labour markets. Nevertheless, after assessing the aspects of both positive and negative effects, the overall impact of the green transition on the labour market is believed to be moderate since the negatively affected industries are expected to form a relatively small share of total employment, the limited impact on the service sector will not cause significant changes in employment in this sector, only 9 percent of jobs are expected to be automated, and many jobs may not be lost, but shifted across sectors. How quickly the current skills of workers can be adapted to the demand for new skills in the labour market will depend to a large extent on the speed with which countries develop green technologies. The experience of ICT implementation has shown that greater mismatches between labour supply and demand can be expected in local labour markets which are characterised by slower reorientation in response to global and national changes.

2.3 The Joint Impact of Digitalisation and Green Transformation on the Labour Market in the Context of the European Green Deal

Digital transformations in Europe are taking place in parallel with the implementation of the Green Deal policy. Although at first glance digitalisation and the Green Deal may appear to be separate things, they are in fact closely interrelated since the success of neither is possible without the other. This interdependence underscores the necessity of integrated policy approaches that simultaneously foster digital innovation and green investments, ensuring that neither transformation hampers but rather accelerates the other's progress. Moreover, both of them are extremely important for the future of Europe (European Commission 2022b). Digitalisation can help reduce carbon emissions, people can join video conferences instead of traveling to meetings, monitor how much energy they use at home, and even make farming more sustainable. The dual role of digitalisation as both an enabler of sustainability and a sector with its own carbon footprint calls for balanced strategies that maximise environmental benefits while minimising digital sector emissions.

As noted by Wolf et al. (2021), the Green Deal is much more than climate neutrality. It also covers the measures for reducing regional and social exclusion, job creation and price stability since the changes in the climate strategy are only possible after moving the economy in the direction of digitalisation. The European Union is exploring the potential of integrating digital technologies into the industry and economy without deviating from the objectives of the Green Deal. This underinvestment highlights a strategic gap that needs urgent attention to leverage digital technologies for climate goals effectively.

The Communication 'Shaping Europe's Digital Future' by the European Commission (2020d) provides the vision of the role of digitalisation in achieving climate and sustainable development goals. The Communication emphasises that positive social changes are expected due to the synergy between digitalisation and sustainability. The European Commission (2020d) highlights the need for more sustainable, energy- and resource-saving digital infrastructures and technologies and introduces Digital Product Passports. A Digital Product Passport should enable sharing the key product-related information which is essential for sustainability and circularity of a product. It is expected to provide new business opportunities through circular value retention and optimisation, and at the same time provide greater transparency and accountability in monitoring the resources used for production (European Commission 2023). Also, it is a significant proposal for digitalisation in the area of production. In addition, the European Commission expects to implement digital solutions which could help reduce greenhouse gas emissions and the use of pesticides in agriculture, and promote the use of transport technologies which can reduce the sector's impact on the environment (Institute for European Environmental Policy 2021).

The interrelations between the European Green Deal and digitalisation were also revealed by many scientific studies. For instance, Fetting (2020) believes that digitalisation is a key enabler of the Green Deal policies which will contribute to expanding sustainable and labour-intensive economic activities. Digitalisation can help make the industry more mobile, improve the availability of information on the new standards for construction, energy efficiency in buildings and insulation. The food production industry could digitalise labelling the products which were made with consideration of the principles of the Green Deal. The transportation sector could associate digitalisation with intelligent traffic management systems, development of multimodal transport (when goods are transported under one contract, but with the use of at least two different modes of transport), reduction of pollution, and traffic congestion in cities.

According to Wolf et al. (2021), although the information and communication technology (IT) sector itself is characterised by carbon dioxide emissions, digitalisation can help to significantly reduce emissions by saving energy in buildings, the transport sector, industry, households, agriculture, etc. With the exception of some specialised niches, the IT sector in the EU is lagging behind its main global competitors. The investment in R&D activities in the IT sector amounted to only about 0.2 percent of GDP in 2019, and the investment financed by federal budgets was less than 0.05 percent of GDP (Wolf et al. 2021).

Gailhofer et al. (2021) found that digital technologies can help fight against the negative environmental effects since digital technologies are capable of accumulating huge amounts of data, the analysis of which can help to make informed decisions. Data analysis performed by artificial intelligence can help to more accurately forecast the potential impact on the environment, and intelligent systems allow monitoring of ongoing processes. Automatic mechanisms and technologies allow to optimise the security of the operations performed. With artificial intelligence monitoring energy consumption, it is easier to integrate renewable energy sources into common energy networks. In the agricultural sector, digital technologies will make it possible to use water more efficiently and reduce the negative impact of pesticides and fertilizers on the environment, They will help to better plan transport and infrastructure systems, increase the efficiency of engines, optimise the charging process of electric cars, control and manage railway systems, and coordinate various modes of transport in the transport sector. Digital technologies will help to inspect, sort, separate and disassemble materials for reuse in circular processes in the manufacturing sector.

Bertoncelj (2022) argues that the Internet of Things and other interconnected cyber-physical systems can completely take control of production and eliminate the need for human intelligence to monitor/intervene task execution. The author expects the greatest efficiency in waste reduction and recycling systems, the transport and logistics sectors. Smart technologies are believed to have the potential to exponentially increase market value and scale.

Marvin et al. (2022) researched the effects of digitalisation and artificial intelligence on sustainable food systems and found that creating a sustainable food system, as envisioned in the European Green Deal strategy, requires a strategic approach which would cover all economic, environmental (climate, ecosystems) and social aspects related to the production and consumption of sufficient and healthy food. The researchers conclude that artificial intelligence and digitalisation have great potential to change the roles and interactions of economic actors throughout the value chain when products travel from farmers to consumers, and thus accelerate the shift towards a sustainable food system. They emphasise that data availability and processing are the critical factors at all stages of the value chain. Such technological advancements should be accompanied by policies to manage workforce transitions, ensuring reskilling and protection against displacement.

Thus, both the European Commission's communication "Shaping Europe's Digital Future" (2020d) and previous scientific studies show that the European Green Deal can help create value for consumers through more sustainable production processes and final products/services. Increasing sustainability is expected to bring greater economic and social benefits to society. When implementing the Green Deal strategy, the main factors which are necessary for transforming traditional business models in the modern economy are *digitalisation* and *green transformation*.

The purpose of digitalisation is to create a significant competitive advantage that customers/consumers are willing to pay for ("Innolytics" 2022). Thus, digitalisation helps create the value which is based on the development of customer/user benefits through digital technologies. Development of digital business models is an important task for businesses when dealing with the challenges of digital transformation. Merely extending an existing analog business model with a certain digital component (for example, ordering goods online from a brick-and-mortar retailer) is a preliminary stage in the implementation of a digital business model, but it is not yet a digital business model. Digital business models are characterised by different features, but the main ones are as follows:

- *The use of digital technologies.* Creating value added would not be possible without the use of digital technologies. For example, companies, such as 'Amazon', 'Uber' or 'Airbnb', could not operate without Internet technologies.
- *Digital business innovations.* Digital business models are based on providing services that are new to the market.
- *Customer attraction and distribution of products/services are based on digital channels.* Companies which develop and promote digital business models often reach potential customers through digital technologies. Sales are characterised by such trends as sales automation and early onboarding.
- *Customers are willing and agree to pay for digital services.* Digital business models help create unique customer value which can be monetised.

Consumer willingness to pay and independent value creation are the most prominent features of a digital business model. However, it should be noted that the mere provision of digital services (e.g. the ability for consumers to monitor the amount of electricity consumed through a special app can be treated as a digital offer to consumers, but it is not yet a digital business model ("Innolytics" 2022).

The concept of green business transformation refers to innovative and environmentally friendly ways of doing business ("Force technology" 2014). A greater focus on green business models can ensure that a business is ready for potential legal requirements, customer demands, energy supply, limited resources, waste management systems, etc.

Green business models typically cover one or more of the following elements: product and material recycling, exchange economies, and replacing unwanted or toxic materials with more environmentally friendly ones ("Force technology" 2014).

Green business models are associated with product orientation (e.g. clean technology companies which use renewable wind and/or solar energy, make resource-efficient products), service orientation (e.g. environmental consulting), and process-oriented initiatives in the value chain (e.g. environmental ISO standards, corporate social responsibility, "green" reports, etc.). Adopting these innovative business models requires both organisational agility and supportive regulatory frameworks to thrive within evolving market and environmental demands.

The previous subsections revealed the specific aspects of the effects of digitalisation and green transformation on the labour market. On the basis of the literature analysis, the model of the joint impact of these two factors on the labour market in the context of the European Green Deal can be developed.

Figure 2.11 shows that digitalisation-driven automation and robotisation can directly reduce employment because smart devices replace the human workforce. Nevertheless, since technologically advanced sectors create more added value, demand for labour in those sectors is likely to increase, which will have a positive impact on total employment. As the management of automated and robotic systems requires higher human resource expertise, skilled labour will be better paid. Digital platform work creates a potentially growing digital labour market which is part of the total labour market, so digital platform work tends to increase total employment. Nevertheless, due to the shorter actual paid working time compared to the paid

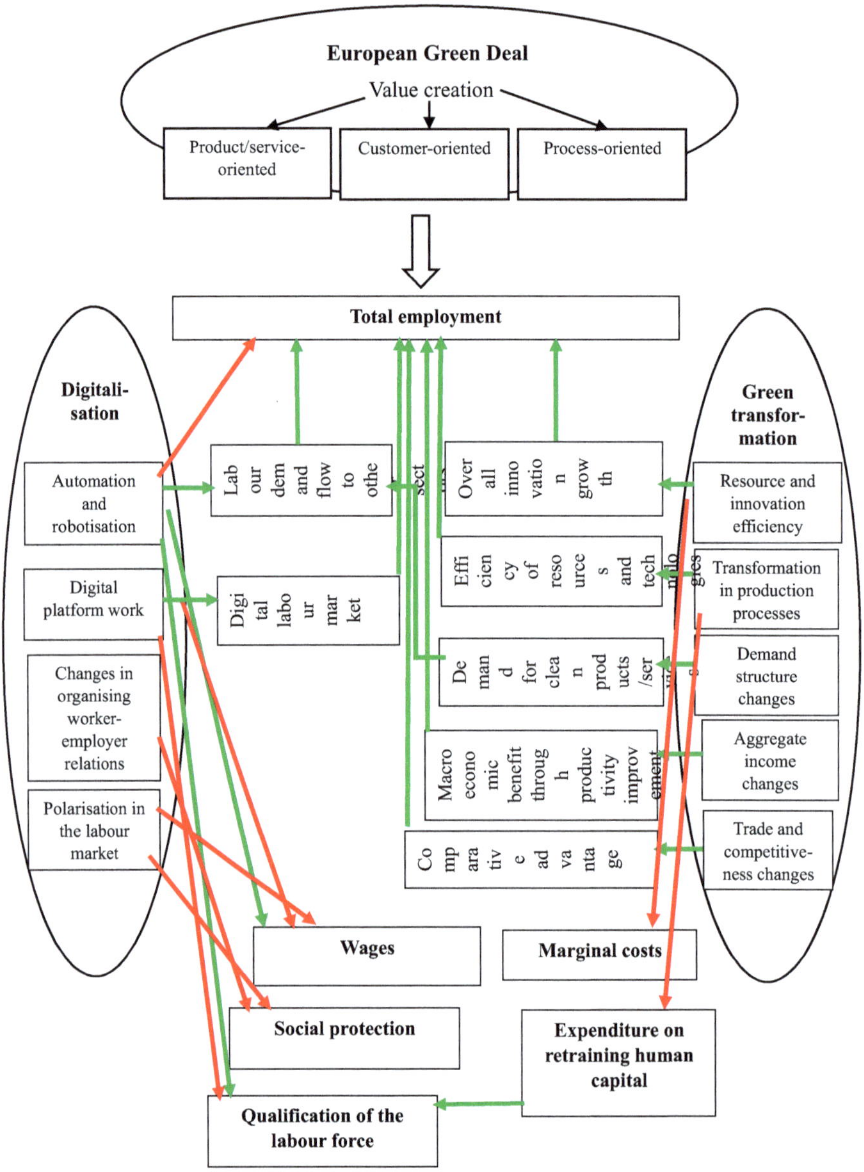

Fig. 2.11 The model of the joint impact of digitalisation and green transformation on the labour market in the context of the European Green Deal. Source: compiled by the authors. *Positive effects are represented by green arrows, negative effects—by red arrows

working time under traditional employment contracts, as well as the high competition on digital platforms (competition not only in domestic, but also in international markets, when lower-paid workers from developing economies compete with higher-paid workers from advanced economies), average wages are decreasing. Digital platform work does not require a highly qualified workforce. Digital organising of the worker-employer relations leads to the disruptive nature of this relation, as well as uncertainty and unclear subordination between parties, which violates workers' rights and increases the risk of their social vulnerability. Polarisation between low-/medium- and high-skilled labour force in the labour market reduces workers' bargaining rights and can lead to wage stagnation, which in turn increases workers' social risk and income inequality.

Resource and innovation efficiency promoted by the green transformation is expected to stimulate economic growth in the long term, so it should lead to higher total employment rate. Production, focused on resource and technology efficiency, is likely to increase production potential, lower production costs and add value to products, which should also stimulate economic growth, the aggregate income, and thus employment. Greater demand for clean products/services will stimulate the growth of the sectors which produce/provide these products/service; the green sectors will be characterised by a higher comparative advantage, which will allow to expect an increase in employment in these sectors. The negative impact of green transformation on the labour market is likely to manifest itself through rising marginal costs of investment and high costs for retraining workers, which can lead to reduction of jobs, especially in the industries characterised by large environmental footprints and small businesses which do not have funds for large investment.

After comparing the most important directions of the impact of digitalisation and green transformation on the labour market, it can be stated that digitalisation directly (positively or negatively) affects the major elements of the labour market—the structure of the market, wages, worker qualifications and social protection. Meanwhile, the impact of green transformation is indirect: it manifests itself through the changes in the structure of the economy, influence on macroeconomic indicators (GDP reflecting economic growth, aggregate income growth, competitiveness, etc.). Thus, the impact of digitalisation on the labour market is felt in the short run, while the impact of the green transformation is felt in the long run.

The report by the World Economic Forum (2023) suggests that big data analytics, climate change, environmental management technologies, encryption and cybersecurity will be the biggest drivers of job growth, while agricultural technologies, digital platforms and applications, e-commerce, digital commerce and artificial intelligence will cause the most significant disruptions to the labour market in the next five years. Employers expect that the structural decline of the labour market will amount to 23 percent in the next five years.

Nevertheless After assessing various aspects of the impact of digitalisation and ther green transformation on the labour market, it can be stated that the overall impact should be moderate in the long run since the most negatively affected industries are expected to constitute a relatively small share of total employment, and many jobs may not be lost, but shifted across sectors. Complex impacts of digitalisation and green transition require continuous research and policy monitoring. The biggest questions arise regarding the changes in the workers' qualifications, their social protection and wage dynamics since the results of previous studies on these issues are very contradictory.

References

Acemoglu D, Restrepo P (2020) Robots and Jobs: Evidence from US Labor Markets. Retrieved from: https://shapingwork.mit.edu/wp-content/uploads/2023/10/Robots-and-Jobs-Evidence-from-US-Labor-Markets.p.pdf

Acquier A (2017) Retour vers le futur ? Le capitalisme de plateforme ou le retour vers le ≪domestic system≫. Dossier Évolutions du Travail, Plates-Formes et Digital, Le Libellio d'AEGIS 13:87–100

Adao R, Beraja M, Pandalai-Nayar N (2022) Fast and slow technological transitions. Mimeo. Retrieved from: https://economics.mit.edu/sites/default/files/2022-09/transitions_website.pdf

Agrawal R, Wankhede VA, Kumar A, Upadhyay A, Garza-Reyes JA (2022) Nexus of circular economy and sustainable business performance in the era of digitalization. Int J Product Perform Manag 71(3):748–774. https://doi.org/10.1108/IJPPM-12-2020-0676

Aleksynska M, Bastrakova A, Kharchenko N (2019) Working Conditions on Digital Labour Platforms: Evidence from a Leading Labour Supply Economy. IZA Discussion Paper No. 12245. Retrieved from: https://docs.iza.org/dp12245.pdf

Alexandri E, Anton J-I, Lewney R (2024) The impact of climate change mitigation policies on European labour markets. Ecol Econ 216(108022). https://doi.org/10.1016/j.ecolecon.2023.108022

Aloisi A (2016) Commoditized workers. Case study research on labour law issues arising from a set of "on-demand/gig economy" platforms. Comp Labor Law Policy J 37(3):620–653

Anton JI, Klenert D, Alaveras G, Fernandez-Macias E, Urzi Brancati MC (2022) The labour market impact of robotisation in Europe. Eur J Ind Relat 28(3). https://doi.org/10.1177/0959680121107080

Arntz M, Gregory T, Zierahn U (2016) The risk of automation for jobs in OECD countries. OECD social, employment and migration working papers, no. 189. OECD, Paris. Retrieved from: https://www.oecd-ilibrary.org/social-issues-migration-health/the-risk-of-automation-for-jobs-in-oecd-countries_5jlz9h56dvq7-en

Atlama S, Ozsoy S (2011) The possible effects of green economy on employment. Paper presented at EconAnadolu 2011: Anadolu International Conference in Economics II. Retrieved from: https://www.researchgate.net/publication/368780634_The_Possible_Effects_of_Green_Economy_on_Employment

Autor DH, Levy F, Murnane RJ (2003) The skill content of recent technological change: an empirical exploration. Q J Econ 118(4):1279–1333

Bachmann R, Gonschor M, Lewandowski P, Madon K (2022) The impact of robots on labour market transitions in Europe. IZA DP No. 15303. Retrieved from: https://docs.iza.org/dp15303.pdf

Baldassarre B, Schepers M, Bocken N, Cuppen E, Korevaar G, Calabretta G (2019) Industrial Symbiosis: towards a design process for eco-industrial clusters by integrating circular economy and industrial ecology perspectives. J Clean Prod 2016:446–460. https://doi.org/10.1016/j.jclepro.2019.01.091

Barnes S-A, Green A, de Hoyos M (2015) Crowdsourcing and work: individual factors and circumstances influencing employability. N Technol Work Employ 30(1):16–31. https://doi.org/10.1111/ntwe.12043

Berg J (2016) Income security in the on-demand economy: findings and policy lessons from a survey of Crowdworkers (March 1, 2016). Comp Labor Law Policy J 37(3):2016. Available at SSRN: https://ssrn.com/abstract=2740940

Berg J, Furrer M, Harmon E, Rani U, Silberman MS (2018) Digital labour platforms and the future of work: Towards decent work in the online world. International Labour Organization (September 20, 2018). (1) (PDF) Digital labour platforms and the future of work: Towards decent work in the online world. Retrieved from: https://www.ilo.org/publications/digital-labour-platforms-and-future-work-towards-decent-work-online-world

Bertoncelj A (2022) Digital transformation in the context of European Union's Green Deal. Amfiteatru Economic 24(59):5–7

Bezdek RH, Wendling RM, DiPerna P (2008) Environmental protection, the economy, and jobs: national and regional analysis. J Environ Manag 86:63–79

Bircan C, Kitzmuller L, Noor S, Satish N (2023) Labour markets in the green economy. Retrieved from: https://cepr.org/voxeu/columns/labour-markets-green-economy

Blix M (2017) *The effects of digitalisation on labour market polarisation and tax revenue.* CESifo forum, ISSN 2190-717X. ifo Institut - Leibniz-Institut für Wirtschaftsforschung an der Universität München, München 18(4):9–14

Bocker R, Silva EK (2022) Innovative technologies for manufacturing plant-based non-dairy alternative milk and their impact on nutritional, sensory and safety aspects. Future Foods 5(100098). https://doi.org/10.1016/j.fufo.2021.100098

Bucher E, Fieseler C, Lutz C, Buhmann A (2021b) Professionals, purpose-seekers and passers-through: how microworkers reconcile alienation and platform commitment through identity work. New Media Soc. Retrieved from: https://journals.sagepub.com/doi/full/10.1177/14614448211056863#tab-contributors

Buhrer C, Hagist C (2016) The Effect of Digitalization on the Labor Market. The Palgrave Handbook of Managing Continuous Business Transformation, pp. 115–137

Burtch G, Carnahan S, Greenwood BN (2018) Can you gig it? An empirical examination of the gig economy and entrepreneurial activity. Manag Sci 64(12). https://doi.org/10.1287/mnsc.2017.2916

Cazes S, Garnero A, Martin S, Touzet C (2019) Facing the future of work: How to make the most of collective bargaining. OECD iLibrary. Retrieved from: https://www.oecd-ilibrary.org/sites/f312cb04-en/index.html?itemId=/content/component/f312cb04-en

Cedefop (2020) Developing and matching skills in the online platform economy: findings on new forms of digital work and learning from Cedefop's CrowdLearn study. Retrieved from: https://www.cedefop.europa.eu/en/publications-and-resources/publications/3085

Chateau J, Bibas R, Lanzi E (2018) Impacts of green growth policies on labour markets and wage income distribution. No. ENV/WKP(2018)333. OECD, Paris. Retrieved from: https://www.oecd-ilibrary.org/environment/impacts-of-green-growth-policies-on-labour-markets-and-wage-income-distribution_ea3696f4-en

Cheba K, Bak I, Pietrzak MB (2023) Conditions of the green transformation. The case of the European Union. Technol Econ Dev Econ 29(2):438–467. https://doi.org/10.3846/tede.2022.17993

Chinoracky R, Čorejova T (2019) Impact of digital technologies on labor market and the transport sector. Transportation Res Procedia 40:994–101

Choudary SP (2018) The architecture of digital labour platforms: Policy recommendations on platform design for worker well-being. ILO Research Paper. Retrieved from: https://socialprotection-humanrights.org/wp-content/uploads/2018/07/wcms_630603.pdf

Collins P (2021) The sharing economy: definition, examples and advantages. Retrieved from: https://climate.selectra.com/en/environment/sharing-economy

Constantinides P, Henfridsson O, Parker GG (2018) Introduction-platforms and infrastructures in the digital age. Inf Syst Res 29(2):381–400

Council of Europe (2024) Infographic - Spotlight on digital platform workers in the EU. Retrieved from: https://www.consilium.europa.eu/en/infographics/digital-platform-workers/

Cruz SA, Gameiro A (2023) Digital work platform: understanding platforms, workers, clients in a service relation. Front Sociol 7(1075808). https://doi.org/10.3389/fsoc.2022.1075808

Dachs B (2017) The impact of new technologies on the labour market and the social economy. MPRA Paper No. 90519. Retrieved from: https://mpra.ub.uni-muenchen.de/90519/1/MPRA_paper_90519.pdf

Dai X, Yang S (2023) Digital empowerment, digital input source and green transformation of manufacturing industry. China Economic Transition (CET) 6(1):57

Damelang A, Otto M (2023) Who is replaced by robots? Robotization and the risk of unemployment for different types of workers. Work Occup. https://doi.org/10.1177/07308884231162953

Dauth W, Findeisen S, Suedekum J, Woessner N (2021) The adjustment of labor markets to robots. J Eur Econ Assoc 19(6):3104–3153. https://doi.org/10.1093/jeea/jvab012
Davulis T (2020) Ar legalus yra maisto išvežiotojų "streikas"? [Is the strike of food delivery people legal?] Retrieved from: https://www.teise.pro/index.php/2020/07/15/t-davulis-ar-legalus-yra-maisto-isveziotoju-streikas/
De Stefano V (2016) The rise of the "just-in-time workforce": on-demand work, crowdwork, and labour protection in the "gig-economy.". Comp Labor Law Policy J 37(3):471–504
De Vries G, Gentile E, Miroudot S, Wacker KM (2020) The rise of robots and the fall of routine jobs. Labour Econ 66(101885). https://doi.org/10.1016/j.labeco.2020.101885
Dieuaide P, Azais C (2020) Platforms of work, labour, and employment relationship: the Grey zones of a digital governance. Front Sociol 5(2) Retrieved from: https://www.ncbi.nlm.nih.gov/pmc/articles/PMC8022829/
Domini D, Grazzi M, Moschella D, Treibich T (2021) Threats and Opportunities in the Digital Era: Automation Spikes and Employment Dynamics. Research Policy 50(7) No. 104137
Drugau-Constantin AL (2018) New-employment work arrangements in digital labour marketplaces: who's fooling who? J Self-Governance Manag Econ 6(3):136–142
Dunn M (2020) Making gigs work: digital platforms, job quality and worker motivations. N Technol Work Employ 35:232–249. https://doi.org/10.1111/ntwe.12167
Eichhorst W, Rinne U (2017) Digital challenges for the welfare state. Retrieved from: https://docs.iza.org/pp134.pdf
EIT Manufacturing (2023) Future European Manufacturing System. Retrieved from: ems-future-manufacturing-system-ok.pdf (eitmanufacturing.eu)
European Commission (2019a) Building and renovating. Retrieved from: https://ec.europa.eu/commission/presscorner/detail/en/fs_19_6725
European Commission (2019b) Communication from the Commission to the European Parliament, the European Council, the Council, the European Economic and Social Committee and the Committee of the Regions. The European Green Deal. Retrieved from: https://ec.europa.eu/info/sites/default/files/european-green-deal-communication_en.pdf
European Commission (2019c) From farm to folk. Retrieved from: https://ec.europa.eu/commission/presscorner/detail/en/fs_19_6727
European Commission (2019d) Sustainable mobility. Retrieved from: https://ec.europa.eu/commission/presscorner/detail/en/fs_19_6726
European Commission (2020a) Circular economy action plan. Circular economy action plan—European Commission. Retrieved from: https://environment.ec.europa.eu/strategy/circular-economy-action-plan_en
European Commission (2020b) Biodiversity strategy for 2030. Retrieved from: https://environment.ec.europa.eu/strategy/biodiversity-strategy-2030_en#the-new-eu-wide-biodiversity-strategy-will
European Commission (2020c) Financing the Green Transition: The European Green Deal Investment Plan and Just Transition Mechanism. Retrieved from: https://ec.europa.eu/commission/presscorner/detail/en/ip_20_17
European Commission (2020d) Internal market, industry, entrepreneurship and SMEs. Retrieved from: https://ec.europa.eu/growth/industry/strategy_en
European Commission (2021) Proposal for a Directive of the European Parliament and of the Council on improving working conditions in platform work. COM/2021/762 final. Retrieved from: https://eur-lex.europa.eu/legal-content/EN/ALL/?uri=CELEX%3A52021PC0762
European Commission (2022a) Green Business. Retrieved from: https://green-business.ec.europa.eu/eco-innovation_en
European Commission (2022b) Green digital sector. Retrieved from: https://digital-strategy.ec.europa.eu/lt/node/9583
European Commission (2023) Digital Product Passport. Retrieved from: https://hadea.ec.europa.eu/calls-proposals/digital-product-passport_en

European Investment Bank (2022) Digitalisation in Europe 2021–2022. Retrieved from: https://www.eib.org/en/publications/digitalisation-in-europe-2021-2022

European Parliament (2021) Carbon leakage: EP seeks carbon tax on EU imports. Retrieved from: https://www.europarl.europa.eu/news/lt/headlines/priorities/klimato-kaita/20210303STO99110/ep-siekia-apmokestinti-es-importa-anglies-dioksido-mokesciu

European Parliament (2022) Economic impacts of the green transition. Retrieved from: https://www.europarl.europa.eu/RegData/etudes/BRIE/2022/733623/EPRS_BRI(2022)733623_EN.pdf

Evans P, Gawer A (2016) The Rise of the Platform Enterprise: a Global Survey. Retrieved from: https://www.thecge.net/wp-content/uploads/2016/01/PDF-WEB-PlatformSurvey_01_12.pdf

Fairchild M (2021) Top industries using robots. Retrieved from: https://howtorobot.com/expert-insight/top-industries-using-robots

Fankhauser S, Bowen A, Calel R, Dechezleptrete A, Grover D, Rydge J, Sato M (2013) Who will win the green race? In search of environmental competitiveness and innovation. Glob Environ Chang 23(5):902–913. https://doi.org/10.1016/j.gloenvcha.2013.05.007

Fetting C (2020) The European Green Deal. ESDN Report. Retrieved from: https://www.esdn.eu/fileadmin/ESDN_Reports/ESDN_Report_2_2020.pdf

Force technology (2014) Green business models and sustainable initiatives. Retrieved from: https://forcetechnology.com/en/services/emissions-bioenergy-resources/green-business-models

Forde C, Stuart M, Joyce S, Oliver L, Valizade D, Alberti G, Hardy K, Trappmann V, Umney C, Carson C (2017a) The Social Protection of Workers in the Platform Economy. Retrieved from: https://www.europarl.europa.eu/RegData/etudes/STUD/2017/614184/IPOL_STU(2017)614184_EN.pdf

Forde C, Stuart M, Joyce S, Oliver L, Valizade D, Alberti G, Hardy K, Trappmann V, Umney C, Carson C (2017b) The social protection of workers in the platform economy. European Parliament. The Social Protection of Workers in the Platform Economy. Retrieved from: https://www.europarl.europa.eu/thinktank/en/document/IPOL_STU(2017)614184

Frey CB, Osborne MA (2013) The future of employment. How susceptible are jobs to computerisation? Retrieved from: https://www.oxfordmartin.ox.ac.uk/downloads/academic/The_Future_of_Employment.pdf

Gailhofer P, Herold A, Schemmel JP, Scherf CS, Urrutia C, Kohler AR, Braungardt S (2021) The role of artificial intelligence in the European Green Deal. Retrieved from: https://www.researchgate.net/profile/Peter-Gailhofer/publication/351747124_The_role_of_Artificial_Intelligence_in_the_European_Green_Deal/links/60a76a8aa6fdcc6d6262ea58/The-role-of-Artificial-Intelligence-in-the-European-Green-Deal.pdf

Gawer A (2014) Bridging different perspectives on technological platforms: toward an integrative framework. Res Policy 43(7):1239–1249

Gawer A (2021) Digital platforms' boundaries: the interplay of firm scope, platform sides, and digital interfaces. Long Range Plan 54(5) No. 102045

Ghazawneh A, Henfridsson O (2013) Balancing platform control and external contribution in third-party development: the boundary resources model. Inf Syst J 23(2):173–192

Goloventchik GG (2023) The Impact of Digital Employment Platforms on the Transformation of the Labor Market in the Digital Economy. In: Big Data in Information Society and Digital Economy, pp 81–88. https://doi.org/10.1007/978-3-031-29489-1_10

Goos M (2018) The impact of technological progress on labour markets: policy challenges. Oxf Rev Econ Policy 34(3):362–375

Goos M, Manning A, Salomons A (2010) Explaining Job Polarization in Europe: The Roles of Technology, Globalization and Institutions. CEP Discussion Paper No. 1026. Retrieved from: https://cep.lse.ac.uk/pubs/download/dp1026.pdf

Goos M, Manning A, Salomons A (2014) Explaining job polarization: routine-biased technological change and offshoring. Am Econ Rev 104:2509–2526

Graetz G, Michaels G (2018) Robots at work. Rev Econ Stat 100(5):753–768. https://doi.org/10.1162/rest_a_00754

Graham M, Hjorth I, Lehdonvirta V (2017) Digital labour and development: impacts of global digital labour platforms and the gig economy on worker livelihoods. Transfer Eur Rev Labour Res 23(2). https://doi.org/10.1177/1024258916687250. Retrieved from: https://journals.sagepub.com/doi/10.1177/1024258916687250#bibr14-1024258916687250

Green facts (2022) The essentials of the "Green Deal" of the European Commission. Retrieved from: https://www.greenfacts.org/en/europe-green-deal-2019/l-2/index.htm#0

Gregory T, Salomons A, Zierahn U (2021) Racing with or against the machine? Evidence on the role of trade in Europe. J Eur Econ Assoc 20(2):869–906. https://doi.org/10.1093/jeea/jvab040

Hasna Z, Jaumotte F, Pienknagura S (2023) How green innovation can stimulate economies and curb emissions. IMF Blog. Retrieved from: How Green Innovation Can Stimulate Economies and Curb Emissions (imf.org)

Helmrich R, Tiemann M, Troltsch K, Lukowski F, Neuber-Pohl C, Lewalder AC, Güntürk-Kuhl B (2017) Digitalisation of working landscapes—no polarisation of the world of work but accelerated structural change and job switching. Bonn 2017

Hetmanczyk P (2023) Digitalization and its impact on labour market and education. Selected aspects. Open access article. Educ Inf Technol. Retrieved from: https://link.springer.com/article/10.1007/s10639-023-12203-8

Hudson R (2001) Producing places. Guilford Press, New York

Hultman N, Sierra K Shapiro A (2016) Innovation and technology for green growth. Retrieved from: https://www.brookings.edu/wp-content/uploads/2016/06/10-green-growth-hultman-sierra.pdf

Idowu A, Elbanna A (2020) Digital Platforms of Work and the Crafting of Career Path: the Crowdworkers' Perspective. Retrieved from: https://link.springer.com/article/10.1007/s10796-020-10036-1

ILO (2015) Decent work. Retrieved from: https://www.ilo.org/global/topics/decent-work/lang%2D%2Den/index.htm

ILO (2017) World Social Protection Report 2017–19: Universal Social Protection to Achieve the Sustainable Development Goals. Retrieved from: https://www.ilo.org/global/publications/books/WCMS_604882/lang%2D%2Den/index.htm

ILO (2018a) Women and men in the informal economy: a statistical picture, 3rd edn. Geneva, ILO

ILO (2018b) Care jobs and the care economy: a challenge and an opportunity for the future of decent work. Retrieved from: https://www.ilo.org/wcmsp5/groups/public/%2D%2D-dgreports/%2D%2D-dcomm/%2D%2D-publ/documents/publication/wcms_633135.pdf

ILO (2018c) Greening with Jobs - World Employment and Social Outlook 2018. Retrieved from: https://www.ilo.org/global/research/global-reports/weso/greening-with-jobs/lang%2D%2Den/index.htm

ILO (2021a) Non-standard forms of employment. Retrieved from: https://www.ilo.org/global/topics/non-standard-employment/lang%2D%2Den/index.htm

ILO (2021b) World employment and social outlook 2021: the role of digital labour platforms in transforming the world of work. International Labour Office. Retrieved from: World Employment and Social Outlook 2021: The role of digital labour platforms in transforming the world of work (ilo.org)

Innolytics (2022) What is a digital business model? Retrieved from: https://innolytics-innovation.com/digital-business-model/#

Institute for European Environmental Policy (2021) Coupling digitalisation and sustainability for an equitable and inclusive Green Deal. Retrieved from: https://ieep.eu/news/coupling-digitalisation-and-sustainability-for-an-equitable-and-inclusive-green-deal

Institute for European Environmental Policy (2022) Environmental degradation: impacts on agricultural production. Retrieved from: https://ieep.eu/wp-content/uploads/2022/12/Policy-brief_Environmental-degradation.-Impacts-on-agricultural-production_IEEP-2022.pdf

International Energy Agency (2023) World Energy Investment 2023. Overview and key findings. Retrieved from: https://www.iea.org/reports/world-energy-investment-2023/overview-and-key-findings

International Federation of Robotics (2023) World Robotics 2023 Report: Asia ahead of Europe and the Americas. Retrieved from: https://ifr.org/ifr-press-releases/news/world-robotics-2023-report-asia-ahead-of-europe-and-the-americas
International Institute for Sustainable Development (2023) Fanning the flames: G20 provides record financial support for fossil fuels. Retrieved from: https://www.iisd.org/publications/report/fanning-flames-g20-support-of-fossil-fuels
International Monetary Fund (2023) IFM Fossil fuel subsidies data: 2023 update. Retrieved from: https://www.imf.org/en/Publications/WP/Issues/2023/08/22/IMF-Fossil-Fuel-Subsidies-Data-2023-Update-537281
Jacobides M, Cennamo C, Gawer A (2018) Towards a theory of ecosystems. Strateg Manag J 39(8):2255–2276
Kalamatiev T, Murdzev N (2022) The notion of digital labour platforms and the European incentive for improvement of the working conditions of the platform workers. 2022 Harmonius J Legal Soc Stud South East Europe, 207
Karanovic J, Berends H, Engel Y (2020) Regulated dependence: platform workers' responses to new forms of organizing. J Manag Stud 58(4):1070–1106
Kassi O, Lehdonvirta V (2016) Online labour index: measuring the online gig economy for policy and research. In: The internet, policy and politics conferences proceedings. Oxford Internet Institute, University of Oxford, Oxford. Retrieved from: https://www.sciencedirect.com/science/article/abs/pii/S0040162518301331
Kilhoffer Z, Lenaerts K, Beblavy M (2017) The Platform Economy and Industrial Relations: Applying the Old Framework to the New Reality. *CEPS Research Report*, No. 2017/12, August 2017; ISBN 978-94-6138-631-1. Retrieved from: https://ssrn.com/abstract=3053826
Klenert D, Fernandez-Macias E, Anton J-I (2022) Do robots really destroy jobs? Evidence from Europe. Econ Ind Democr 44(1). https://doi.org/10.1177/0143831X2110688
Koch M, Manuylov I, Smolka M (2021) Robots and firms. Econ J 131(638):2553–2584
Kozluk T, Zipperer (2013) Environmental policies and productivity growth: a critical review of empirical findings. OECD economics department working papers, no. 1096. OECD Publishing, Paris. https://doi.org/10.1787/5k3w725lhgf6-en
Kuh KF (2018) Paris Agreement. Retrieved from: https://www.sciencedirect.com/topics/earth-and-planetary-sciences/paris-agreement
Lehdonvirta V (2016) Algorithms that divide and unite: delocalization, identity, and collective action in 'microwork'. In: Flecker J (ed) Space, place and global digital work. Palgrave Macmillan, London, pp 53–80
Leong C, Lin S, Tan F, Yu J (2023) Coordination in a digital platform organization. Information Systems Research. Retrieved from: https://pubsonline.informs.org/doi/full/10.1287/isre.2023.1226
Levy F, Murnane RJ (2005) The new division of labor: how computers are creating the next job market. Princeton University Press, New Jersey
Li H, Kettinger WBJ (2021) The building blocks of software platforms: understanding the past to forge the future. J Assoc Inf Syst 22(6):1524–1555
Li Y, Huang N, Zhao Y (2022) The impact of Green innovation on Enterprise Green economic efficiency. Int J Environ Res Public Health 19(24) No. 16464. https://doi.org/10.3390/ijerph1924164644
Macias EF (2018) Automation, digitisation and platforms: implications for work and employment. Eurofound, Publications Office of the European Union, Luxembourg. Retrieved from: https://www.eurofound.europa.eu/en/publications/2018/automation-digitisation-and-platforms-implications-work-and-employment
Majchrzak A, Markus ML, Wareham J (2016) Designing for digital transformation: lessons for information systems research from the study of ICT and societal challenges. MIS Q 40(2):267–277
Malgonde O, Zhang H, Padmanabhan B, Limayem M (2020) Taming complexity in search matching: two-sided recommender systems on digital platforms. MIS Q 44(1):49–84

Mallik AK (2023) The future of technology-based manufacturing in the European Union. Results Eng 19., No. 101356. https://doi.org/10.1016/j.rineng.2023.101356

Marvin HJP, Bouzembrak Y, van der Fels-Klerx HJ, Kempenaar C, Veerkamp R, Chauhan A, Stroosnijder S, Top J, Simsek-Senel G, Vrolijk H, Knibbe WJ, Zhang L, Boom R, Tekinerdogan B (2022) Digitalisation and artificial intelligence for sustainable food systems. Trends Food Sci Technol 120:344–348. https://doi.org/10.1016/j.tifs.2022.01.020

Marvit MZ (2014) How Crowdworkers Became the Ghosts in the Digital Machine. The Nation. Retrieved from: https://www.thenation.com/article/archive/how-crowdworkers-became-ghosts-digital-machine/

Mathiesen BV, Johannsen RM, Kermeli K, Crijns-Graus W, Lund H, Skov IR (2023) The green transition of industry—an introduction to IndustryPLAN. Smart Energy 11., No. 100111. https://doi.org/10.1016/j.segy.2023.100111

Mauksch S, von der Gracht HA, Gordon TJ (2020) Who is an expert for foresight? A review of identification methods. Technol Forecasting Soc Change 154., No. 119982. https://doi.org/10.1016/j.techfore.2020.119982

McCarthy A, Dellink R, Bibas R (2018) The macroeconomics of the circular economy transition: a critical review of modelling approaches. OECD environment working papers, no. 130. OECD, Paris. Retrieved from: https://www.oecd-ilibrary.org/environment/the-macroeconomics-of-the-circular-economy-transition_af983f9a-en

Muldoon J, Apostolidis P (2023) Neither work nor leisure': Motivations of microworkers in the United Kingdom on three digital platforms. Open access article. https://doi.org/10.1177/14614448231118394

Naghshineh B, Carvalho H (2021) The implications of additive manufacturing technology adoption for supply chain resilience: a systematic search and review. Int J Prod Econ 247., No. 108387. https://doi.org/10.1016/j.ijpe.2021.108387

Naumowicz K (2021) Some remarks to the legal status of platform workers in the light of the latest European jurisprudence. Stud Labour Law Soc Policy 28(3):183

Niggli M, Rutzer C (2021) Environmental policy and heterogeneous labor market effects: evidence from Europe. WWZ Working paper 2020/09, University of Basel. Retrieved from: https://www.econstor.eu/bitstream/10419/240418/1/2020-09.pdf

Nosheen M, Iqbal J, Abbasi MA (2021) Do technological innovations promote green growth in the European Union? Environ Sci Pollut Res 28:21717–21729. Retrieved from: https://link.springer.com/article/10.1007/s11356-020-11926-2

OECD (2017a) Collective Bargaining in a World of Changing Work. Chapter 4 in OECD Employment Outlook 2017

OECD (2017b) Employment implications of green growth: linking jobs, growth and green policies. OECD report for the G7 environment ministers. Retrieved from: https://www.oecd.org/environment/Employment-Implications-of-Green-Growth-OECD-Report-G7-Environment-Ministers.pdf

OECD (2017c) Investing in climate, investing in growth. OECD Publishing, Paris. https://doi.org/10.1787/9789264273528-en

OECD (2019a) Innovation and Business/Market Opportunities Associated with Energy Transitions and a Cleaner Global Environment. Retrieved from: https://www.oecd.org/g20/summits/osaka/OECD-G20-Paper-Innovation-and-Green-Transition.pdf

OECD (2019b) OECD employment outlook 2019: the future work. OECD Publishing, Paris. Retrieved from: https://www.oecd-ilibrary.org/employment/oecd-employment-outlook-2019_9ee00155-en

Pesole A, Urzi Brancati MC, Fernandez-Macias E, Biagi F, Gonzalez Vazquez I (2018) Platform workers in Europe. Evidence from the COLLEEM survey. EUR 29275 EN. Publications Office of the European Union, Luxembourg. https://doi.org/10.2760/742789. Retrieved from: https://publications.jrc.ec.europa.eu/repository/handle/JRC112157

Pinderhughes R (2007) Green collar jobs: an analysis of the capacity of green businesses to provide high quality jobs for people with barriers to employment. Retrieved from: http://bss.sfsu.edu/raquelrp/documents/v13ExecSummary.pdf

Popp D, Vona F, Marin G, Chen Z (2020) The Employment Impact of Green Fiscal Push: Evidence from the American Recovery Act. NBER Working Paper 27321. Retrieved from: https://www.nber.org/system/files/working_papers/w27321/w27321.pdf

Precedence Research (2023) Industrial Robotics Market. Retrieved from: https://www.precedenceresearch.com/industrial-robotics-market

Raczko R (2015) *Wykorzystanie chmur obliczeniowych w biznesie.* Roczniki Kolegium Analiz Ekonomicznych, Szkoła Główna Handlowa Warszawa, No. 36

Rani U, Dhir RK (2020) Platform work and the COVID-19 pandemic. Indian J Labour Econ 63:163–171. https://doi.org/10.1007/s41027-020-00273-y

Rani U, Furrer M (2021) Digital labour platforms and new forms of flexible work in developing countries: algorithmic management of work and workers. Compet Chang 25:212–236. https://doi.org/10.1177/1024529420905187

Razminienė K, Tvaronavičienė M (2018) Detecting the linkages between clusters and circular economy. Terra Economicus 16(4):50–65

Remeikienė R, Gasparėnienė L, Lazutka R (2022) Working conditions of platform workers in new EU member states: motives, working environment and legal regulations. Econ Soc 15(4):186–203. https://doi.org/10.14254/2071-789X.2022/15-4/9

Risak M, Warter J (2015) Legal strategies towards fair conditions in the virtual sweatshop. Paper presented at the IV Regulating for Decent Work Conference (ILO, Geneva, 8–10 July). Available at: http://www.rdw2015.org/download

Rivera VA, Lee DT (2021) I want to, but first I need to: understanding crowdworkers' career goals, challenges and tensions. ACM Human-Comp Interaction 5(CSCW1):1–22

Rogers B (2015) Employment as a Legal Concept. Temple University Legal Studies Research Paper No. 2015–33. Available at SSRN: http://ssrn.com/abstract=2641305

Sandberg J, Holmstrom J, Lyytinen K (2020) Digitization and phase transitions in platform organizing logics: evidence from the process automation industry. MIS Q 44(1):129–153

Schaible C (2020) EU industrial strategy for achieving the 'zero pollution' ambition set with the EU Green Deal (large industrial activities. Retrieved from: https://eeb.org/wp-content/uploads/2020/03/EEB-basic-elements-on-Industry-Strategy-IED-FIN-1.pdf

Schmidt FA (2017) Digital labour market in the platform economy: mapping the political challenges of crowd work and gig work. Retrieved from: https://library.fes.de/pdf-files/wiso/13164.pdf

Simon F (2019) EU Commission unveils 'European Green Deal': the key points. Retrieved from: https://www.euractiv.com/section/energy-environment/news/eu-commission-unveils-european-green-deal-the-key-points/

Spencer N (2020) EU 'farm to folk' strategy aims to feed sustainable food system. Retrieved from: https://www.foodnavigator.com/Article/2020/03/17/EU-farm-to-fork-strategy-aims-to-feed-sustainable-food-system

Statista (2024) Share of jobs at high risk of automation by early 2030 in select countries worldwide, by study, as of 2017. Retrieved from: https://www.statista.com/statistics/716847/worldwide-proportion-of-jobs-at-high-risk-of-automation/

Stewart A, Stanford J (2017) Regulating work in the gig economy: what are the options? Econ Lab Relations Rev 28:420–437. https://doi.org/10.1177/1035304617722461

Sun Y, Gao P, Tian W, Guan W (2023) Green innovation for resource efficiency and sustainability: empirical analysis and policy. Resour Policy 81., No. 103369. https://doi.org/10.1016/j.resourpol.2023.103369

Sundararajan A (2016a) The sharing economy: the end of employment and the rise of crowd-based capitalism. MIT Press, Cambridge

Sundararajan A (2016b) Crowd-based capitalism? Empowering entrepreneurs in the sharing economy. MIT Sloan Management Review. Retrieved from: https://sloanreview.mit.edu/article/crowd-based-capitalism-empowering-entrepreneurs-in-the-sharing-economy/

Tamma P, Schaart E, Gurzu A (2019) Europe's Green Deal plan unveiled. Retrieved from: https://www.politico.eu/article/the-commissions-green-deal-plan-unveiled/
Terzi A (2022) A green industrial revolution is coming. The Centre for Economic Policy Research (CEPR). Retrieved from: https://cepr.org/voxeu/columns/green-industrial-revolution-coming-0
The European Institute for Gender Equality (EIGE) and the European Foundation for the Improvement of Living and Working Conditions (Eurofound) (2023) Gender differences in motivation to engage in platform work. Retrieved from: https://eige.europa.eu/publications-resources/publications/gender-differences-motivation-engage-platform-work
The European Parliament and the Council (2003) Directive 2003/88/EC of the European Parliament and of the Council of 4 November 2003 concerning certain aspects of the organisation of working time. Retrieved from: https://eur-lex.europa.eu/eli/dir/2003/88/oj
The U.S. Department of Energy (2001) Careers in renewable energy. Retrieved from: http://www.nrel.gov/docs/fy01osti/28369.pdf
The World Bank Group (2022) The food and energy crisis: weathering the storm. Development committee paper. Retrieved from: https://www.devcommittee.org/content/dam/sites/devcommittee/doc/documents/mgr/Final%20Food%20and%20Energy%20DC2022-0005.pdf
Tiwana A, Konsynski B, Bush AA (2010) Research commentary-platform evolution: coevolution of platform architecture, governance, and environmental dynamics. Inf Syst Res 21(4):675–687
Tomlinson D, Corlett A (2017) A tough gig? The nature of self-employment in 21st century Britain and policy implications. Resolution Foundation, London. Retrieved from: https://www.resolutionfoundation.org/publications/a-tough-gig-the-nature-of-self-employment-in-21st-century-britain-and-policy-implications/
Torrent-Sellens J, Ficapal-Cusi P, Ertz M (2021) Motivations for labour provision on digital platforms in Europe. In: Handbook of research on the platform economy and the evolution of E-commerce, pp 81–103. https://doi.org/10.4018/978-1-7998-7545-1.ch004. Retrieved from: https://www.igi-global.com/viewtitle.aspx?titleid=288441
Tusinska M (2023) Motives and expectations of platform workers in Poland. Ekonomia i Prawo 22(2):385–398. https://doi.org/10.12775/EiP.2023.022
U.S. Government Accountability Office (2022) Which Workers Are the Most Affected by Automation and What Could Help Them Get New Jobs? Retrieved from: https://www.gao.gov/blog/which-workers-are-most-affected-automation-and-what-could-help-them-get-new-jobs
UNEP (2008) Green jobs: towards decent work in a sustainable, low-carbon world. Retrieved from: https://wedocs.unep.org/bitstream/handle/20.500.11822/8825/UNEPGreenJobs_report08.pdf
United Nations (2015) Paris Agreement. Retrieved from: https://unfccc.int/files/meetings/paris_nov_2015/application/pdf/paris_agreement_english_.pdf
United Nations Conference on Trade and Development (2023) World investment report 2023. Retrieved from: https://unctad.org/publication/world-investment-report-2023
United Nations Environment Program (UNEP), International Labour Organisation (ILO), International Trade Union Council (ITUC), International Organisation of Employers (IOE), World Health Organisation (WHO) (2008) Green Jobs: Towards Decent Work in a Sustainable LowCarbon World. Retrieved from: http://www.unep.org/labour_environment/PDFs/Greenjobs/UNEP-GreenJobs-Report.pdf
Valatsas D (2019) Green Deal, Greener World. Retrieved from: https://foreignpolicy.com/2019/12/17/united-states-democrats-green-new-deal-eu-europe-technically-feasible-environment-progress/
Valenduc G (2021) A historical perspective on the drivers of digital labour platforms. In: Drahokoupil J, Vandaele K (eds) A modern guide to labour and the platform economy, chapter 5. Edward Elgar Publishing, Cheltenham, pp 81–95
Van Alstyne MW, Parker GG, Choudary PS (2016) Pipelines, platforms, and the new rules of strategy. Harv Bus Rev 54–60:62. Retrieved from: https://hbr.org/2016/04/pipelines-platforms-and-the-new-rules-of-strategy
Van Doorn N (2017) Platform labor: on the gendered and racialized exploitation of low-income service work in the "on-demand" economy. Inf Commun Soc 20(6):898–914

Vandeplas A, Vanyolos I, Vigani M, Vogel L (2022) The possible implications of the green transition for the EU labour market. European Commission, discussion paper No. 176. Retrieved from: https://economy-finance.ec.europa.eu/system/files/2022-12/dp176_en_green%20transition%20labour.pdf

Vasilescu MD, Serban AC, Dimian GC, Aceleanu MI, Picatoste X (2020) Digital divide, skills and perceptions on digitalisation in the European Union—Towards a smart labour market. Retrieved from: https://journals.plos.org/plosone/article?id=10.1371/journal.pone.0232032

Victor PA (2022) The macroeconomics of a green transformation: the role of green investment. Retrieved from: https://eu.boell.org/en/macroeconomics-green-transformation

Weller S, Lukowski F, Baum M (2020) Digital work tools and tasks: firm-level evidence from Germany. In: Helmrich R, Tiemann M (eds) Defining work tools: studying effects of digitalising work tools, pp 78–93

Wolf S, Teitge J, Mielke J, Schutze F, Jaeger C (2021) The European Green Deal — more than climate neutrality. Intereconomics 56:99–107

Wood AJ, Graham M, Lehdonvirta V, Barnard H, Hjorth I (2016) Virtual production networks: fixing commodification and Disembeddedness. In: The internet, Policy & Politics Conference. Oxford Internet Institute, University of Oxford, Oxford

Woodcock J, Graham M (2019) The gig economy. A critical introduction. Polity, Cambridge. http://acdc2007.free.fr/woodcock2020.pdf

World Bank (2013) From brown to green: the economic benefits of climate action. Retrieved from: https://www.worldbank.org/en/news/feature/2013/06/25/growing-green-europe-and-central-asia

World Economic Forum (2018) The future of jobs report 2018: insight report. World Economic Forum, Geneva. Retrieved from: http://www3.weforum.org/docs/WEF_Future_of_Jobs_2018.pdf

World Economic Forum (2023) The Future of Jobs Report 2023. Retrieved from: https://www.weforum.org/publications/the-future-of-jobs-report-2023/digest/

Zhou I (2020) *Digital labour platforms and labour protection in China*. ILO Working Paper No. 11. Retrieved from: https://www.econstor.eu/bitstream/10419/263077/1/ilo-wp11.pdf

Chapter 3
The Specifics and Types of Platform Work

Rita Remeikienė and Ligita Gasparėnienė

Abstract This chapter explores the nature and diversity of digital platform work, examining its conceptual foundations, emergence, and evolution across global and post-Soviet contexts. It identifies the main drivers of platform work, including technological advancement, labour market flexibility, and economic insecurity, highlighting both the appeal and the risks associated with this employment model. The chapter presents five distinct categories of platform work, ranging from highly skilled developers to gig workers and micro-taskers, and analyses their working conditions, income levels, and challenges. A central focus is placed on the employment status of platform workers, particularly the widespread classification as self-employed contractors, which limits access to social protections and legal entitlements. The chapter analyses typical contractual provisions used by major platforms and examines the evolving role of trade unions in defending platform workers' rights. It further reviews new forms of collective organisation such as cooperatives, guilds, and quasi-unions. Finally, the chapter offers a comparative insight into the specific conditions of platform work in post-Soviet economies, where informal labour markets, weak legal enforcement, and socio-economic instability create both opportunities and vulnerabilities. It concludes that the fragmented legal and social landscape calls for adaptive and inclusive regulatory strategies.

R. Remeikienė (✉) · L. Gasparėnienė
Faculty of Law, Vilnius University, Vilnius, Lithuania
e-mail: rita.remeikiene@tf.vu.lt; ligita.gaspareniene@tf.vu.lt

R. Remeikienė, L. Gasparėnienė (eds.), *Work and Legal Guidelines in the Age of Digitalisation and Green Transition*, European Union and its Neighbours in a Globalized World 25, https://doi.org/10.1007/978-3-032-03511-0_3

3.1 The Concept and Emergence of Platform Work

The initial digital platforms for work and services appeared in the mid-1990s, but the sector truly began to flourish from the mid-2000s onwards. This growth was fuelled by increased Internet speeds and the advent of smartphones (World Economic Forum 2020). According to the World Economic Forum (2020), digital platforms are demonstrating rapid growth which confirms their value to individual consumers and business customers. Nevertheless, this business area is linked to a number of controversies, especially when it comes to platform companies which are facing legal challenges in different countries. These challenges are mostly related to the employment status of platform workers, and sometimes even question workers' right to operate. It is important to note that social security law is no longer limited to traditional employees; it now encompasses various categories of workers and self-employed persons, which has relevance for platform workers whose status may differ across legal frameworks. Digital labour platforms have transformed traditional labour relations and provided new forms of task distribution for workers (Vallas and Schor 2020; Rani and Furrer 2021; Umar et al. 2021). It is important to distinguish between labour law and social security law when discussing platform work, as social protection rights may extend beyond traditional employment relationships and apply differently across jurisdictions. This distinction will be further discussed in later sections.

Platforms allow customers to post orders which can be accessed by a large number of geographically dispersed workers who have platform accounts (Huws et al. 2016).

The World Economic Forum (2020) distinguishes between two types of digital platforms:

1. Platforms engaged in asset sharing and monetization (e.g. *Airbnb*). These platforms aim at letting property; payments and customer evaluations (comments) are conducted online.
2. Platforms where individuals can offer their skills and services (e.g. *Uber*, *Up Work*). These are platforms where individuals can offer their skills and labour to business companies and consumers; payments and customer evaluations (comments) are conducted online; tasks can be performed remotely or on-site.

The major platform companies, like *Airbnb* and *Uber*, have been operating for more than a decade. Their emergence coincided with the Great Recession, which facilitated the development of digital companies and involved workers who had recently graduated or who could not find any traditional work and who had not had time to establish themselves in the labour market. Since then, the gig economy has been growing rapidly and conducts many digitally mediated economic transactions, i.e. the exchange of goods and services (Vallas and Schor 2020). The gig economy also covers "temporary work" which is characterised by a defined or limited duration (for instance, freelance contract work and/or consulting which is not performed through digital labour/service platforms, but is provided by temporary workers offered by recruitment agencies) (World Economic Forum 2020). Thus, while digital platforms are innovative in terms of technology, the idea of intermediation services is not new. Services, like transportation, delivery and design, have been provided for a long time already. Moreover, the development of platform work is taking place in the context of the broader growth of temporary work.

What were the causes of the development of platform work? Kenney and Zysman (2016) and Srnicek (2016) provide two fundamental causes of the emergence of platform work. First, business companies in the traditional economy began to digitalise their internal operations and transactions with other companies. The origins of this trend lie in the advent of minicomputers (1980s), the popularity of personal computers (1990s), and the spread of the Internet (1990s and beyond). Business companies currently have public websites which operate together with internal information systems to perform a company's operational functions. Along with the emergence of Lean management, the internal departments of companies began to view each other as customers with whom business operations were concluded. All of this started promoting a kind of cross-platform work in traditional companies through the spread of applications and mobile devices.

Second, digital content-based businesses made the extensive use of the Internet to capture the existing markets or create entirely new markets. For example, e-commerce platforms partially displaced retail outlets, capital-based platforms were created for renting accommodation, goods or cars, platforms for ride-hailing or housekeeping services entered the service market, video streaming and content development platforms started competing with broadcast or other traditional media companies.

The World Economic Forum (2020) and Cruz and Gameiro (2023) provide the "push" and "pull" factors which tend to raise the number of digital platform workers:

- *The appeal of flexibility and autonomy*. The desire to have more flexible and autonomous working conditions is increasing. Workers can choose the amount of work and tasks they want to complete; they can also decide about their work time and place. Platforms provide an opportunity to earn additional income. Flexibility and autonomy encourage persons to work from home because they provide the advantages for those with health problems or household burdens.
- *Economic insecurity*. In developed markets where real average wages are stagnating and economic insecurity is increasing; casual platform work can help people supplement their income. In emerging markets where the size of the informal economy is large, platform work can become a safer and a more professional alternative.

Although the positive effects of flexibility in time and space are commonly treated as the major advantages of platform work (Anwar and Graham 2021), scientific studies also emphasise that platform work often means insecure working conditions (Huws et al. 2016; Kahancová et al. 2020; Vallas and Schor 2020; Tubaro and Casilli 2022). Some most obvious shortcomings are the lack of regulation of platform work and precarious working conditions for platform workers (World Economic Forum 2020).

To provide a better understanding of digital platform work, we will present the categories of platform work suggested by some previous scientific studies (Vallas and Schor 2020).

The first category of digital platform work covers highly skilled professionals who become independent contractor-developers in professions, such as platform architects and technologists. They design and maintain the digital infrastructure of platforms (Kelkar 2018). They undertake risks and long hours of work in the labour market in the hope of earning a significant amount of income through initial public offerings or acquisitions.

The second category of digital platform work, according to Drahokoupil and Piasna (2019), emerges after answering the question of whether digital platforms promote outsourcing in the traditional economy, or whether they provide a digital infrastructure for replacing temporary employment agencies. This category covers cloud computing consultants or freelancers who offer their professional services through the platforms such as *UpWork* or *Freelancer*. While these consultants, like the workers in the first category of platform work, provide professional services, they are treated more as users than developers. Christin (2018) believes that this category covers the professionals with a high level of technical skills (graphic design, computer programming and journalism). Cloud computing consultants can have a stable source of their income only if they manage to maintain a sufficient number of customers.

The third category of digital platform work covers gig workers whose services are ordered through platforms but performed offline, such as food delivery, home repair work, nursing/maintenance work. These workers get casual work, one-day assignments, and enjoy the benefits of a flexible work schedule and autonomy. Nevertheless, the challenges faced by gig workers are multifaceted and significant. Firstly, unlike traditional employees who often have their operational costs covered by their employers, gig workers must bear these costs themselves. The costs are associated with equipment, transportation and maintenance, and can vary greatly from sector to sector (Rosenblat 2018).

The fourth category of digital platform work covers the assignments which are performed online (microtasking). Workers operating through "Amazon Mechanical Turk" (AMT) or "Figure Eight" (formerly "CrowdFlower") are representatives of microtasking (Berg 2016). These workers undertake human intelligence tasks which cannot be completed by computers, and which are part of the process of machine learning. Microtasking (e.g. describing or classifying content in images, editing computer-generated text, verifying user accounts on social networks, or transcribing short audio recordings) commonly requires less training and experience than cloud computing consulting and freelance work.

The fifth category of digital platform work covers social media and podcast content creators and influencers. This type of platform work is often performed for free with the hope of achieving a sufficient level of awareness and securing a regular income in the future (Duffy 2017).

The analysis of the similarities and differences of the five major categories of digital platform work has revealed the following aspects which characterise this type of work and distinguish it from traditional work:

1. *Labour market dynamics.* Different groups of platform workers operate in different labour market conditions in terms of labour supply and demand: there is a noticeable shortage of technologists and architects, and currently there is an obvious surplus of micro-taskers and freelance content creators.
2. *Worker-platform relationship.* Worker roles and influence on the activities of a platform may vary greatly: the activities can range from active creation to passive consumption.
3. *Income levels and work attitudes.* Although the level of income earned by different groups of workers may vary greatly, many platform workers, especially content creators and influencers, have entrepreneurial qualities.
4. *Platform work transformations.* Due to the constant changes in algorithm design, market conditions and regulatory policies, platform work tends to undergo constant transformations; therefore, it is necessary to consider the peculiarities of the legal regulation of platform work and initiate the amendments if they are needed for a particular purpose.

Digital labour platforms act as intermediaries between workers and customers (Dunn 2020; Cruz and Gameiro 2023), operate on a global scale and aim to match the supply of and the demand for goods and services, thus allowing customers to find professionals who offer their services/goods. The key feature of digital labour platforms is digital performance of work without an organisational structure of a business (Vallas and Schor 2020). Platform work is coordinated, regulated and monitored through algorithms; it is distributed to stakeholders and the public without the functional authority structure typical of a traditional business. Categorisation of platform workers as the self-employed poses challenges to the traditional models of labour regulation (Stewart and Stanford 2017) because being qualified as the self-employed, platform workers are not entitled to the minimum wage, disability benefits, unemployment benefits, sick or maternity benefits or paid vacation—the social protection measures provided by labour law. It is important to note that social security law no longer applies exclusively to traditional employees. It now covers a broader range of social categories, including self-employed individuals, platform workers, and other non-standard forms of employment. Therefore, social protection systems must adapt to these evolving labour market realities. This condition is very favourable and beneficial to platforms as employers since they evade additional costs, legal or social responsibility. Customers naturally pay pays less for the services they receive (Stewart and Stanford 2017). According to Cruz and Gameiro (2023), work mediated through digital platforms necessarily requires the involvement of three parties: platform organisers, workers, and customers. Algorithmic management on digital platforms regulates worker behaviour and performance with minimal human intervention, while customers provide the data which are used for platform operations. This allows platforms to accumulate large amounts of data and to build power-based relationships with workers, customers and other platforms.

Although the algorithmic system is designed to ensure control and efficiency, workers can still show their own initiative (e.g. to communicate directly with customer and bypass a platform's mediation), which can be beneficial for both parties—workers and customers (Cruz and Gameiro 2023).

Summarising, it can be stated that a digital labour platform is a form of economic activity aimed at mediating the negotiations and exchanges between the supply (customers) and demand (workers) sides, which contributes to a new configuration of the work and consumption process. Digital algorithms serve for connecting product suppliers/service providers and customers. The biggest problem in the execution of platform work is legal regulation of labour relations, so the next subsection reviews the terms and conditions of digital platform work.

3.2 Terms and Conditions of Digital Platform Work

It is important to distinguish between labour law and social protection law in the context of platform work. While labour law traditionally regulates employment relationships, social protection law has expanded its scope beyond employees to cover a wider range of workers, including self-employed and platform workers. Consequently, social benefits such as unemployment or maternity benefits may be available to categories of workers other than traditional employees, which complicates the analysis of platform workers' entitlements.

Provisions for Self-employed Platform Workers According to De Stefano et al. (2021) platform managers unilaterally set the terms and conditions under which they interact with customers and workers. These terms usually classify platform workers as either "the self-employed" or "independent contractors". Platforms take the position that a worker-customer relationship is a self-employment relationship. De Stefano et al. (2021) present the examples of the most common provisions for self-employed platform workers:

- Amazon Mechanical Turk (2020): "Workers complete tasks for customers as independent contractors using their personal resources but not as employees of *Amazon Mechanical Turk* (or the affiliates of *Amazon Mechanical Turk*). As a worker, you agree that (i) you are responsible for compliance with all applicable laws and registration requirements, including those applicable to independent contractors and maximum working hours; (ii) this Agreement does not create an association, a joint venture, a partnership, a franchise, or an employer/employee relationship between you and Customers, or between you and *Amazon Mechanical Turk* (or the affiliates of *Amazon Mechanical Turk*); (iii) you do not advertise yourself as an employee or a representative of a Customer or *Amazon Mechanical Turk* (or the affiliates of *Amazon Mechanical Turk*). [...] As a customer, you will not engage a worker in any activities that may jeopardize the status of a worker as an independent contractor completing tasks for you."

- Doordash (2020): "A Contractor declares that he/she runs an independently established company providing delivery services and that he/she meets all legal requirements necessary to perform the services provided for in this Agreement. As an independent contractor, he/she is solely responsible for how he/she runs his/her business and how he/she provides the contracted services. [...] The parties acknowledge and confirm that this Agreement is entered into between two equal, independent business entities that are separately owned and managed. The parties intend this Agreement to create a principal-independent contractor relationship, but not an employer-employee relationship. The parties are not employees, agents, joint owners or general partners of each other for any purpose. [...]. "
- Ola (2016): "Until the end of this Agreement, the Transportation Service Provider will operate and have the status of an independent contractor but not of an agent or an employee of the *OLA*. The relationship between the parties is equal and mutually independent, and no provision of this Agreement shall be construed to create an employer-employee relationship between the Transportation Service Provider and the *OLA* at any time, under any circumstances, or for any purpose."
- Taskrabbit (2019): "Taskers[1] are independent contractors of customers but not employees, partners, representatives, agents, co-owners, independent contractors or franchisees of the *Taskrabbit*. The *Taskrabbit* does not perform tasks or hire people to perform tasks. Users hereby acknowledge that the company does not direct, control or monitor a tasker's work and expressly disclaims (to the extent permitted by law) any responsibility for the work and the tasks performed in any respect [...]."
- Handy (2020): "The Service Provider is an independent contractor and is not employed by *Handy* to perform services on *Handy's* behalf. Instead, the Service Provider has signed this Agreement in order to gain access to the *Handy* Platform, for which *Handy* is paid a fee [...]. The Service Provider declares that he or she is ordinarily engaged in an independent trade, profession or business which provides services to the general public, or the Service Provider declares that he or she maintains a principal residence of business which is related to the Service Provider's trade, profession or business and which is suitable for deductibility of business expenses for federal income tax purposes. [...]."
- Instacart (2020): "You are entering into this Agreement as an independent contractor in a business relationship between you and *Instacart*. It is understood that by agreeing to perform services under this Agreement, a Contractor shall act and at all times act as an independent contractor but not as an employee of *Instacart* for any purpose, including but not limited to taxes, payments required by law, or any other deductions or transfers to any government agency or institution. [...] You further acknowledge that this Agreement does not create any employer-

[1] The word "taskers" is used on the *Taskrabbit* platform and refers to persons who are registered on the platform to provide various services or perform specific tasks for customers. These persons act as independent contractors but not as employees of *Taskrabbit*. Taskers can provide a variety of services, such as assembling furniture, housekeeping, relocation, gardening, etc., depending on their skills and the needs of their customers.

employee relationship between the Third-Party Retailer and you, and that you are not entitled to any benefits, including but not limited to Workers' Compensation insurance, provided to any Third-Party Retailer employees."

De Stefano et al. (2021) mention other digital platforms which are trying harder than others to downplay their contribution to the overall transaction. For instance, *Care.com* does not introduce, provide, select, or recommend caregivers to careseekers. Instead, the company offers an online forum which, among other things, allows careseekers and caregivers (nurses) to communicate with each other about the potential job opportunities.

The above-cited agreements of independent contractors on *Instacart*, *Handy*, *Taskrabbit*, *Doordash*, *Ola*, and *Amazon's Mechanical Turk* share several common features which demonstrate the approach of these platforms to labour relations. Firstly, all the platforms recognise the status of independent contractors since all of them categorise workers as independent contractors but not as employees. This means that workers are responsible for their business operations, taxes, insurances and other activity expenses. Second, the contracts do not cover an employee-employer relationship, i.e. the texts of the contracts clearly state that the conclusion of the contracts does not create an employer-employee relationship. This means that the platforms do not provide workers with social guarantees, such as social or unemployment insurance, insurance against accidents at work, vacation or sick pay. However, social protection systems may offer some benefits to broader categories of workers. Access to these benefits varies significantly depending on national regulations and individual circumstances, leading to gaps in social protection for many platform workers. Third, workers declare that they act as self-employed persons providing services directly to customers or but not to a platform. A platform only provides intermediary services by connecting service providers with end customers. Fourth, the platforms waive the responsibility of an owner. The platforms clearly indicate that they do not control how the work is done, do not supervise workers and are not responsible for the quality of the work or compliance with legal regulations. Contractors themselves are responsible for quality performance of work and compliance with regulations. Finally, the agreements emphasize that the relationship between a platform and a service provider is a business relationship based on the cooperation of independent businesses, but not a traditional employment relationship. These common features reflect the characteristics of platform work which differ from the traditional employment relationship and reveal the challenges in terms of workers' rights and social protection.

Provisions for Employees Some platforms hire employees through payroll service companies or third-party staffing providers (De Stefano et al. 2021). For instance, an employee's work agreement on the Wonolo (2020) platform is categorised as the work paid through payroll services (the so-called "Payrolled Wonolo Engagement"). An employee agrees that the payroll service company (the "Payroll Company") will be considered an official employer, but only for the fulfilment of *Wonolo's* obligations—for paying wages. All other *Wonolo's* obligations will be fulfilled through an independent contractor, i.e. the Payroll Company will assign a client to the *Wonolo* worker, and this client will be responsible for supervising the worker.

The Upwork (2018) agreement includes the "Upwork Payroll" service which allows clients to use a third-party staffing provider to hire freelancers. When a client uses this service, the staffing provider officially employs a freelancer, and the client is responsible for the supervision of the freelancer. A freelancer assigned to a client becomes a salaried employee under the contract, but remains a freelancer under the terms of service. The availability of this service may depend on various factors, such as the location of a freelancer, the duration of the project, the salary, and the nature of work. An application to use the "Upwork Payroll" service can be rejected for various legal reasons.

Platform *Hilfr* allows working as an employee or a freelancer. The *Hilfr's* collective agreement regulates the working conditions of cleaning assistants who work in private households through the *Hilfr's* digital platform. This agreement applies only to assistants who work as employees but not as freelancers. The agreement stipulates that freelancers automatically acquire the status of an employee after 100 h of work through the platform and become parties in this contract. Freelancers who want to acquire the status of an employee earlier, must notify *Hilfr* prior to completing 100 hours of work. Those who wish to remain freelancers even after 100 hours of work must notify *Hilfr* of their decision in advance (the Collective Agreement between Hilfr ApS and 3F Private Service 2018).

Summarising, it can be stated that digital labour platforms can offer another option of the employment relationship—they can treat a worker as an employee but without interfering with the quality of service provided to a customer.

3.3 The Role of Trade Unions in Platform Work

The expansion of digital platform work as an innovative form of employment poses new challenges for existing institutional frameworks, including worker representation. The automation of organisational functions, which made it possible to expand the pool of workers beyond the geographical boundaries of traditional labour markets together with the use of algorithmic management and digital surveillance systems, leads to problems in maintaining social dialogue between workers and employers. To maintain well-functioning economic and labour market structures, the issues of collective interest representation and worker mobilisation are becoming extremely relevant.

The European Foundation for the Improvement of Living and Working Conditions (2024) refers to representation of workers as their right "to seek a union or individual to represent them for the purpose of negotiating with management on issues as wages, hours, benefits and working conditions". Traditionally, trade unions are considered the bodies which can help organise and represent workers. Recently, they are becoming increasingly active in representing platform workers and making efforts to equalize the bargaining power of stakeholders—workers and employers. Furthermore, trade unions play a crucial role in advocating for enhanced social protection frameworks tailored to the specific needs of platform workers, addressing gaps left by traditional labour laws and ensuring equitable access to benefits such as unemployment support, health coverage, and pension schemes. Although many authors write about social protection risks augmented by digital work management methods (European Commission 2017; European Parliament 2017; ILO 2017; Van Doorn 2017; Forde et al. 2017a, b; Berg et al. 2018; Aleksynska et al. 2019; Rani and Dhir 2020; Rivera and Lee 2021; Torrent-Sellens et al. 2021, etc.), opaque surveillance practices (Berg et al. 2018; ILO 2018a; Eurofound 2018; Jabagi et al. 2019; Geissinger et al. 2021, etc.) and unfair employee rating systems (ILO 2017; ILO, ISSA and OECD 2023, etc.), these problems could be at least partially resolved through the dialogue between the stakeholders, if such dialogue could take place on equal terms. Thus, the inequality of the bargaining power of the contract parties and the asymmetry of information should be considered the fundamental problems in platform work, since they lead to the situation when decisions are made unilaterally (from the side of a platform manager), and there are no channels to appeal unfair decisions (Wood et al. 2019; Piasna and Zwysen 2022).

According to Vandaele (2018), the very treatment of platform workers as "independent contractors" complicates the collective representation of their interests since the status of "an independent contractor" is incompatible with membership in a trade union. It is, however, believed that certain models of representation of the interests of platform workers are emerging and developing.

The basic actions through which platform workers try to empower their efforts are the unification of workers on the same platform, when *ad hoc* strikes, demonstrations or online campaigns are organised to express the protest or draw attention to certain contentious issues (Johnston and Land-Kazlauskas 2018). Being constantly connected through forums, chats and social media groups, workers can mobilise and state their demands (Piasna and Zwysen 2022). Some of the initiatives have turned into unions, allowing to further increase the bargaining power of platform workers.

Johnston and Land-Kazlauskas (2018) notice such forms of collective representation of platform workers' interests as worker-led platform cooperatives, union-affiliated guilds, grass-root unions, mainstream or longstanding unions, labour market intermediaries as labour mutuals or quasi-unions. These organisations usually represent the interests of high-skilled crowdworkers and on-demand platform workers and are based on either "a logic of membership" or "a logic of influence" (Vandaele 2018). In the first case, the main focus falls on the relationship between an organisation and the needs of its members, while in the second case, the focus is on the relationship between an organisation and interlocutors (Serrano 2014). The logic as well as the major advantages and disadvantages of the abovementioned unions established for representing platform workers are reviewed in Table 3.1.

Platform cooperatives are based on the logic of membership. This means that platform workers are platform owners and participate in the platform; they sell goods/services through websites and/or mobile apps (OECD 2023), thus directly

Table 3.1 Review of the most common forms of collective representation of digital platform workers

Form of collective representation	Logic of functioning	Advantages	Disadvantages
Platform cooperatives	Logic of membership	Prioritisation of members' needs, democratic governance, collective decision-making, favouritising value creation to communities, prevention of worker exploitation	Lack of experience in collective bargaining and social dialogue
Union-affiliated guilds	Logic of membership	Provision of services and resources to members, influence on media profiles, discursive power	Lack of bureaucratic representation structure, weak power to represent workers' interests
Grass-root unions	Logic of membership	Energy, organisational creativity, mobilisation of the young labour generation, low membership fees	Lack of experience in collective bargaining and social dialogue, acting only at the local level
Mainstream or longstanding trade unions	Logic of influence	Multisectoral activities, efficiency in collective negotiations and social dialogue, cooperation with employer organisations, conclusion of collective and cross-border agreements	Anti-trust and competition regulation, exclusion of the self-employed and freelancers
Labour market intermediaries (quasi-unions)	Logic of influence	Represent the self-employed and freelancers, help to gain legitimacy from employers and political authorities	Limited resources to provide additional services

Source: compiled by the authors, based on the literature analysis

competing with venture-capital platforms (Scholz 2016). These cooperatives are established as a counterbalance to the power of digital platform organisers in order to ensure better working conditions. Platform cooperatives prioritize the needs of members (OECD 2023), and, in contrast to traditional platforms, they are characterised by democratic ownership and control (Scholz et al. 2021). Decisions regarding platform management and working conditions are made collectively (OECD 2023). Since workers themselves are platform owners, this prevents their exploitation, and the interest in platform cooperatives is growing, although very few of them have been established so far (some examples are the *Collectif des coursier-e-s/KoeriersKollectief* in Belgium, the *Plataforma Riders X Derechos BCN* in Spain) (Vandaele 2018). Collective ownership and participatory governance help to solve the problem of the asymmetry in bargaining power, promote accountability and transparency (ILO 2021). Scholz et al. (2021) and the International Cooperative Alliance (2022) confirm such benefits yielded by platform cooperatives as enhanced worker retention, worker well-being, improved productivity, better compensation, and greater worker autonomy over labour conditions.

The logic of membership is also followed by *union-affiliated guilds*, which are set up by groups of self-organised on-demand workers (Staunton 2018). They are often supported by longstanding and independent unions that provide legal, logistic, and other resources. Guilds offer their members logistics, consulting, crowdfunding for litigation and other services and resources. They can have a positive impact on media profiles and give their members discursive power, but they lack the bureaucratic representation structure, typical of traditional trade unions (Dencik and Wilkin 2020), and collective bargaining experience, so their power to represent the interests of platform workers against employers is weak. The examples of this type of guilds are the *Collectif Livreurs Autonomes de Paris*, *the Deliverunion* in Germany, the *Deliverance Milano* in Italy, the *Riders Union* in the Netherlands (Lieman 2018).

Grass-root unions are small autonomous organisations founded by activists. They are characterised as having impressive energy and organisational creativity (Joyce and Stuart 2021). They often attract young people, for whom a union helps to go through the school-to-work transition phase more easily and learn to defend their interests at relatively low cost since the membership in such unions is free or membership fees are low. The main objectives of grass-root unions are support for members and member empowerment through mobilisation campaigns (Vandaele 2018). Staunton (2018) adds that grass-root unions succeed in organising high-profile campaigns which attract media attention through creative demonstrations. The *Independent Workers Union* in Great Britain and the *Freie Arbeiterinnen-und Arbeiter-Union (FAU)* in Germany can be presented as extremely successful examples of grass-root unions. Mainstream unions can learn from grass-root unions initiative, dynamism, determination, organisational innovation, mobilisation capacity and the ability to attract a new generation of workers, but grass-root unions will have to learn collective bargaining and social dialogue development methods from traditional mainstream unions (Staunton 2018; Joyce and Stuart 2021). A common shortcoming of the organisations based on the logic of membership is that they usually represent the interests of platform workers at the local level, but they lack a national identity. In addition, the bargaining power of such organisations can be adversely affected by competition among workers within a union (Vandaele 2018).

Mainstream or longstanding trade unions function on the basis of the logic of influence, often operate in more than one sector (are multisectoral) and can fairly well represent the interests of platform workers, in particular, the interests of on-demand and crowdworkers. They are more effective in collective bargaining and social dialogue, compared to the organisations whose functioning is based on the logic of membership, and can even cooperate with employers' associations, federations (Ilsoe 2017), initiate agreement and code signing in the countries with strong traditions of social partnership. For instance, the Code of Conduct, which obliges platform organisers to start paying workers the wages that meet local standards by 2018, was signed by eight German digital platforms (Vandaele 2018). The Danish union 3F signed the agreement with platform *Hilfr.dk*. The agreement established the minimum wages, sick and holiday allowance, and pension contributions for platform workers. This agreement entered into force on 1 August 2018 and was the first collective agreement on platform work in Denmark. Trade unions supported food delivery bike couriers with setting up works councils in Austria and Germany, and initiated the protests and strikes to draw attention to the precarious working conditions on digital platforms in Belgium, the Netherlands, and the UK (European Foundation for the Improvement of Living and Working Conditions 2024). According to Piasna and Zwysen (2022), with similar bargaining power, two legitimate parties, sitting at the negotiating table, can easier conclude collective agreements and deals. Cooperation with employers' organisations can be useful in concluding multi-company and multi-sectoral agreements. The first steps have already been taken to conclude cross-border agreements (e.g. the agreement between German *Delivery Hero* and the European Federation of Food, Agriculture, and Tourism Trade Unions in 2018, which established the *Societas Europaea*) (Piasna and Zwysen 2022). Cross-border agreements can particularly serve to protect the interests of platform workers regardless of the country in which a worker operates since they represent a worker in the country where the platform operates. However, the main problems arising in the area of collective bargaining are anti-trust and competition regulation (for example, the minimum wage established in terms of service can be treated as fixing the price of the service). Another disadvantage of mainstream unions is that platform workers, who are members of these unions, have the legal status of an employee, which means that mainstream unions do not represent the interests of self-employed platform workers (Joyce and Stuart 2021).

Quasi-unions are established by the self-employed and freelancers who want to raise their empowerment and representation. They establish membership-based cooperatives which help to gain legitimacy and social protection (e.g. *Socíete Mutuelle d'Artistes (SMart)* in Belgium). These organisations resemble the associations of professionals and creative persons (e.g. translators' unions, lawyers' unions, associations of artists, associations of cultural workers), for whom it is both a form of collaboration and partnership, and a measure to strengthen their bargaining powers (Gherardini 2017). Quasi-unions help the self-employed and freelancers to gain legitimacy from employers' associations and political authorities and achieve that their professions/occupations have legally established and recognised wages, working time and similar standards. Nevertheless, as noted by Vandaele (2018), they are more attractive to part-time self-employed and workers who do platform work temporarily and are looking for salaried employment, because it is important for this group of platform workers to negotiate more flexible employment terms than to expect the additional services provided by a union (e.g. helping with assignments). However, looking at future prospects, it should be noted that self-employment promoted by the digital economy is one of the promising directions of labour market development. Thus, the representation of the self-employed through unions is an area which requires attention (Conaty et al. 2018).

Among the above-mentioned forms of collective representation of platform workers, traditional (mainstream) trade unions, which accept platform workers, undoubtedly have the greatest power. Although it can be assumed that the share of platform workers in various unions is relatively small (the data by the ILO (2024) indicate that union density in the platform economy stands at 13.4%), their main advantage is that they can represent the interests of platform workers beyond their actual member base. According to the "Syndicat European Trade Union" (2024), unions of platform workers not only help to set standards, such as the minimum wages, sick pay and other employment protection for the social protection of workers, but also serve in a legal sense by helping to include the presumption of employment with the reversal of the burden of proof when a worker tries to litigate his/her employment status. This means that if an individual worker has to go through a lengthy court process to have the status of an employee recognised, the burden of proof is reversed, and the digital platform has to prove that the worker is not an employee. Piasna and Zwysen (2022), however, note that although platform workers' unions win quite a lot of legal battles, legal leverage has its limits because application to different jurisdictions can yield different outcomes, which does not reduce platform workers' uncertainty about their working conditions. In this case, the adequate international labour standards and the adequate regulation of the platform economy can provide more certainty.

Anyway, as noted by the European Foundation for the Improvement of Living and Working Conditions (2024), despite the increasing activity of trade unions representing platform workers, the majority of platform workers are not represented by any trade union, and the self-employed and those for whom platform work is additional rather than the main one are extremely rarely represented. Piasna and Zwysen (2022) argue that in the absence of physical workplaces, geographical proximity, and opportunities for personal meetings, as well as in the absence of a clearly expressed identity of the company where employees work, the potential for the development of collective bargaining power is quite limited. The common experience of working for the same employer, in the same office or factory and having the usual working time of 8 or 9 h per day creates a sufficiently solid basis for collective unification. However, modern platform workers do not work directly for one employer, their workplace and working hours are not fixed, so it is more difficult for them to establish unions (Staunton 2018). Unionisation is easier when providing on-location services (e.g. transport, delivery), so trade union initiatives are more noticeable in these sectors (e.g. *Collectif des coursier-e-s* worker initiative in Belgium, *Collectif Coursiers Bordeaux* in France, *Liefern am Limit* in Germany). The European Foundation for the Improvement of Living and Working Conditions (2024) also notes that platform workers whose activities are highly visible in society (e.g. the "Deliveroo" riders) have greater potential to mobilise and negotiate working conditions, while cleaners or handy persons have less potential to negotiate. Remote platform work is also not clearly visible in society, so in this case online communication and charismatic leadership can contribute to creating online communities (e.g. *YouTubers Union*, *FairTube*) (Piasna and Zwysen 2022). In addition, the weight and power of platform worker unions is decreasing due to their conflicting interests and incompatible approaches (as, for example, in the cases of grass-root unions and mainstream trade unions), i.e. because of the clear fragmentation inherent in labour activism (Staunton 2018; Joyce and Stuart 2021). Therefore, in order to respond to the needs of platform workers as effectively as possible, trade unions will have to modernize their structures, unify approaches, fully understand the problems of platform workers, and become attractive to the young generation of workers (Heeger 2023).

Summarising, the establishment of digital platform worker unions shows that trade unions are becoming innovative and adapting to the realities in the labour market (Gebert 2021), and platform workers have stronger pro-union attitudes and are more receptive to union membership, compared to the general population (ILO 2024). Since platform organisers have greater bargaining power in relation to workers and do not want to negotiate with individual workers who are not formally organised, platform worker unions play a significant role in providing workers with the structured network support, financial and material resources, expertise, defending worker interests and leveraging power in relation to other stakeholders, which can facilitate the conclusion of collective agreements. The significant issues of collective bargaining which can be solved with participation of platform worker trade unions are fair pay, decent working time, social protection, and labour rights. Having gained more influence at the national level, unions can contribute to the revision of labour laws, and at the international level—to the conclusion of cross-border agreements which can especially serve in protecting the interests of platform workers regardless of the country in which a worker operates. No less important is the fact that digital platform worker unions can help mobilise non-standard workers and pave the way for union membership for solo self-employed workers, which is not characteristic of traditional trade unions. Nevertheless, as noted by Vandaele (2018), digital platform worker unions still need to get mature to gain more influence, to develop the relevant communication channels for workers, and more clearly formulate and declare their goals and objectives. In this way, the transparency of work through digital platforms will be increased, and the collective representation of workers in the digital labour market will be improved.

3.4 The Specificity of the Conditions for Digital Platform Work in Post-Soviet Economies

Historically, the labour market in post-Soviet Eastern European countries developed somewhat differently than the global labour market. As noted by Aleksynska (2021), national labour markets in these post-Soviet countries have several common features which make them unique and different from other national labour markets. These features are associated with the transition from the planned economy, which these countries followed while under the influence of the Soviet Union, to the market economy, the principles of which began to be implemented after the collapse of the Soviet Union.

The literature analysis revealed the main features of the transition which has affected the current economic and labour market situation in post-Soviet countries (see Table 3.2). The analysis of the features of the transition in post-Soviet Eastern European economies is important because some of the challenges and achievements of the transition period are still affecting national labour markets and shaping the work aspirations of the younger generation, which determines the specificity of the conditions for digital platform work.

Although free market-oriented economic reforms were started in 1987 under the *perestroika* policy initiated by the last General Secretary of the Soviet Union, Mikhail Gorbachev, these reforms were quite chaotic and caused many macroeconomic imbalances, and later the dramatic economic crisis of 1989–1991 (Dabrowski 2023). After 26 December 1991 when the Soviet Union ended its formal existence, the sovereign republics started their national economic reforms.

Table 3.2 shows that the transition of post-Soviet economies is characterised by rapid economic restructuring (Lehmann et al. 2012), but economic reforms are significantly correlated with political reforms, i.e. the direction of economic development largely depends on political decisions (Dabrowski 2023). Since the political and economic conditions varied from country to country, this led to the uneven pace of the reforms. Being pro-Western from the very beginning and having selected the strategy of the radical and comprehensive political and economic reforms, the Baltic States (Lithuania, Latvia, and Estonia) transformed rapidly, and in 2004 they accessed the European Union, who's funding further stimulated the economic development in these countries. Other post-Soviet economies had political debates on whether to select the cooperation with western or eastern countries, faced numerous institutional and structural distortions, which, in their turn, determined the slow market transition, unattractive environment for business and foreign investment, and continuous macroeconomic disequilibria (Dabrowski 2023).

Deregulation of prices and the elimination of subsidies for producers and benefits to consumers became the major factor leading to fiscal deficits and macroeconomic disequilibria (Dabrowski 2022). With no more subsidies to producers, many previously state-owned enterprises went bankrupt, the overall production volume decreased, which led to a physical shortage of goods in consumer markets. In response to this, some countries (e.g. Ukraine and Turkmenistan) delayed price deregulation for 2 years or even longer (e.g. Uzbekistan until 2016).

The creation of private property and private enterprises promoted market competition, helped to balance consumption demand with supply and to allocate resources more efficiently. Countries used different privatization methods (e.g. initial private offering (IPO), joint ventures with foreign firms, employee and management buyout, voucher privatization, etc.), depending on their political-economic expectations. Nevertheless, the process of privatization of previously state-owned enterprises was not simple, as stock markets did not exist or were infant. The obstacles to privatization delayed macroeconomic stabilization and led to inflation (International Monetary Fund 1998; Dabrowski 2023). This complex and uneven transition process has had lasting effects on labour market dynamics and regulatory frameworks in post-Soviet economies, influencing the current conditions for digital platform work, social protection coverage, and labour market inclusiveness, particularly

Table 3.2 The main features of the economic transition in post-Soviet countries of Eastern Europe

Feature	Result	Author(s), year
Significant correlation of economic reforms with political decisions	Uneven pace of reforms, economic reforms without quantitative objectives	Lehmann et al. (2012) and Dabrowski (2023)
Institutional and structural distortions	Slow transition to the market economy, unattractive environment for business and foreign investment	Dabrowski (2022, 2023)
Price deregulation	Fiscal deficit, macroeconomic disequilibria	International Monetary Fund (1998) and Dabrowski (2023)
Elimination of subsidies for producers	Bankruptcy of companies, reduced overall production volumes, lack of goods in consumer markets	Dabrowski (2022)
Creation of private property and private enterprises	Promotion of market competition, more efficient allocation of resources	International Monetary Fund (1998) and Dabrowski (2022, 2023)
Low efficiency of the financial sector	High capital reserve requirements, poor quality bank loan portfolios, nonperforming loans, lack of capital markets	International Monetary Fund (1998)
Different level of development of the labour markets	In post-Soviet non-EU countries—comparatively high poverty of working persons, low purchasing power of the population, labour force displacement, high level of informal work	Bruck et al. (2010), Lehmann et al. (2012), Lehmann (2015), Lehmann and Pignatti (2018), ILO (2018b) and International Monetary Fund (2019)
Heterogeneity of consumer markets	Countries with larger populations have larger consumer markets	Aleksynska (2021)
Changes in the share of individual sectors in the general structure of the economy	Increase in the share of the service sector in GDP; development of new forms of service provision, non-traditional forms of work using computer technologies	Benešova and Smutka (2016) and ILO (2016)
Differences in the development of social protection systems	In post-Soviet non-EU countries, social protection systems are not very efficient; a lack of social support provided by the state; poor enforcement of labour law	ILO (2019)
Mismatch between labour market demand and education	Overeducation, skills mismatch, attractiveness of tasks where workers are interchangeable (digital platform work)	Lamo and Messina (2010), Roberts (2014) and Kupets (2016)
Diminished influence of trade unions	Low bargaining power of workers	Crowley (2004), Ost (2009) and Kallaste and Woolfson (2009)

Source: compiled by the authors

highlighting challenges in adapting traditional labour regulations and social protection systems to new forms of work such as platform employment.

The development of a stable, market-oriented financial system was one of the biggest challenges in post-Soviet economies. Financial institutions did not play the role of financial intermediaries in the command economy, and there was a lack of capital markets. Many post-Soviet countries adopted the Basle Committee on Banking Supervision's guidelines on capital adequacy, but due to the high-risk environment, a capital requirement of 8% of risk-weighted assets was applied to banks. Many small banks went bankrupt, bank loan portfolios were of poor quality, the banking sector faced the problem of nonperforming loans inherited from the past (International Monetary Fund 1998).

Due to the turbulence of the economic reforms and low efficiency of the institutional and financial sectors, the economic growth in the post-Soviet countries which did not access the European Union has been slow, the labour markets have been underdeveloped, these countries are characterised by relatively high poverty of working persons (Bruck et al. 2010), the intense labour force displacement (Lehmann et al. 2012), high and constant level of informal work (Lehmann 2015; Lehmann and Pignatti 2018; ILO 2018b).

Post-Soviet countries also differ in the purchasing power of their populations and levels of economic development. In accordance with the ranks of the International Monetary Fund (2019), some post-Soviet countries, such as Estonia, Latvia, and Lithuania, are considered advanced economies and members of the European Union. Other post-Soviet countries, including Belarus, Moldova, Russia, and Ukraine, are non-EU members and developing economies. Table 3.3 depicts the purchasing power parity (PPP) of the population in these selected post-Soviet countries in 2022.

Table 3.3 reveals the significant difference between the purchasing power parity (PPP) of the population in developed and developing post-Soviet Eastern European countries. Sufficiently high wages can be earned in the domestic labour markets in the developed countries under consideration; their developed social protection systems make workers less socially vulnerable. Therefore, traditional work is considered acceptable and desirable, digital platforms are used to earn additional income or enter the labour market for young people who do not have previous work experience or skills, and thus cannot require high wages in traditional labour markets (Berg et al. 2018; Brancati et al. 2020; Rani and Dhir 2020, etc.). Meanwhile, the post-Soviet non-EU countries in Eastern Europe are developing economies with lower per capita income and less equal income distribution. This creates the situation when work with foreign customers (foreign customers are accessed through digital platforms) generates much higher income than work in the domestic market, so from this point of view, the conditions for digital platform work in the developing Eastern European countries are more favourable.

The post-Soviet economies are characterised by heterogeneity in consumer markets, meaning that different countries have different populations and numbers of potential customers in their domestic markets. This factor at least partly determines the situation that the development of digital platform work and mobile applications

Table 3.3 Purchasing power parity of the population in the selected post-Soviet Eastern European countries in 2022

Selected post-Soviet EU Member States	PPP (international dollars)	Selected post-Soviet non-EU Member States	PPP (international dollars)
Estonia	46,080	Russian Federation	35,770
Latvia	39,206	Moldova	15,310
Lithuania	46,790	Ukraine	13,360
		Belarus	21,800

Source: compiled by the authors, based on the data by the World Bank (2023)

is uneven in Eastern European countries: the greatest progress is observed in the countries with large populations and, therefore, large labour and consumer markets (Ukraine, Russia) (Aleksynska 2021). Digital platform work in these countries allows serving a relatively large part of the domestic market, so many digital labour platforms are being created. This type of work also tends to reduce the risk of unemployment.

Benešova and Smutka (2016) emphasize the significant changes in the share of individual economic sectors in the overall structure of the economy. For instance, an increase in the service sector's share of GDP was observed in Moldova and Ukraine in the period 2000–2014: the share of the service sector in GDP reached 68% in Moldova and 62% in Ukraine. According to the authors, the rapid development of the service sector in the countries mentioned above was determined by stronger ties with the EU. After the global economic crisis of 2008–2009, new forms of employment emerged, including the provision of services under contracts. This provided opportunities for the countries of the Eastern European region to expand the non-standard labour market by adopting digital technologies (ILO 2016). With the development of technology, a new generation of the workforce, characterised by IT skills, flexibility, creativity, self-confidence, and a developing entrepreneurial mindset, has grown up. These factors explain the fact that the diffusion of technology, as well as the search for work via the Internet in the Eastern European region has been much faster and more favourably received than in the old European countries, where the workforce is much more conservative and has the enrooted traditional methods of job search and communication; thus, the innovations in the developed economies have been adopted slowly.

Eastern European countries are characterised by different levels of development in their social protection systems. The countries that have successfully joined the European Union (Bulgaria, Croatia, the Czech Republic, Estonia, Hungary, Latvia, Lithuania, Poland, Romania, Slovakia, Slovenia) have undertaken significant reforms of their labour laws and social protection systems in line with EU requirements. While these reforms have generally made their labour and social protection systems more sustainable and inclusive, some challenges and gaps remain, particularly in ensuring full coverage and effectiveness. EU directives, regulations, and initiatives—such as the European Pillar of Social Rights—have become important legal frameworks guiding the regulation of digital work and platform economy practices across member states. Conversely, in countries such as Moldova and Ukraine, social protection systems remain less developed and labour law enforcement is often weak (ILO 2019). As a result, many workers in these countries must rely on multiple income sources, including digital platform work, to meet their employment and social needs. This has contributed to faster growth of digital labour markets in these countries, which cover a broader range of sectors and require diverse skills to generate income. Research by the European Training Foundation (2021) on digital platform work in Eastern Partnership countries (Ukraine, Armenia, Belarus, Moldova, Georgia, and Azerbaijan) found that Ukraine recorded the highest number of registered platform workers per capita. Common remote services in these countries include software development and technology, creative and multimedia, and sales and marketing support, while driving, delivery, and home services are predominant in on-location platform work.

Lamo and Messina (2010), Roberts (2014) and Kupets (2016) analyse the problem of post-Soviet economies when national education systems do not take into account the needs of the labour market, i.e. graduates do not have the skills needed in domestic labour markets, so the labour market demand is not satisfied. Only study-related work experience is useful when looking for a job by education (Roberts 2014). The labour force in general is characterised by overeducation (Roberts 2014; Kupets 2016). These features are characteristic not only of economically developing post-Soviet economies, such as Ukraine (Kupets 2016), but also of economically advanced countries (e.g. Lithuania, Estonia) (Lamo and Messina 2010; Roberts 2014). Uncertainty in the labour market further increases the probability of job mismatch, and the mismatch in one's first job has its effect 5 years after graduation (Roberts 2014). The aforementioned factors increase the attractiveness of digital platform work in post-Soviet Eastern European economies since this type of work does not require specific qualifications, and workers to perform the tasks are considered interchangeable (Schmidt 2017). Digital platform work is characterised by skill mismatch ('Cedefop' 2020), which is consistent with job mismatch tendencies in the labour markets in post-Soviet economies. The results presented by the European Training Foundation (2021) propose that digital skills and Internet literacy, technical skills, English and Russian language skills, as well as self-regulatory learning and independent working skills are most needed for digital platform work in Eastern Partnership countries.

The post-Soviet economies are characterised by a noticeably weakened image of trade unions and a reduced influence of collective bargaining (Crowley 2004; Ost 2009). When reshaping the landscape of industrial relations in the transition process, trade unions came to be treated as an aimless legacy of the Soviet Union since they previously used to be an institutional body which functioned only formally but did not actually protect workers' rights. Workers in post-Soviet economies have no previous direct experience of the value or benefits provided by the membership in a trade union. Therefore, trade unions are still facing challenges in proving their relevance to employees in post-Soviet economies. After conducting the research in three Baltic states (Lithuania, Latvia, and Estonia), Kallaste and Woolfson (2009) found that 26–28% of employees in the target countries are undecided, i.e. they would join a trade union if they could see the relevance of collective representation. In the presence of mistrust of trade unions and poor perception of their potential benefits, digital platform work which is characterised by the asymmetry of bargaining power (workers are in a weak bargaining position because the initial terms of a contract are already predetermined by platform organizers) and the disproportionate benefit which one party (platform organizers/managers) acquires to the disadvantage of the other party (workers) (Forde et al. 2017a, b; Benson 2017) has become an acceptable form of employment.

Summarising, the specificity of the conditions for digital platform work in Eastern European post-Soviet economies is determined to a significant extent by the factors related to the challenges of the transition period, which affected national labour markets and shaped the work aspirations of the younger generation. The significant correlation of the economic reforms with political decisions, primarily related to the integration into western or eastern political-economic blocs, led to the institutional and structural distortions, as well as the use of different mechanisms for price deregulation, formation of private property, and promotion of the efficiency of the financial sector. The former post-Soviet countries which joined the EU are characterised by their faster economic development, greater purchasing power of the population, and more developed labour law and social protection systems. However, these legal domains do not always evolve at the same pace, particularly in addressing the needs of platform workers. Workers in these countries feel more socially secure and can earn sufficiently high wages in the traditional labour market, so digital platform work is more often undertaken to earn additional income or enter the labour market for young people with no previous work experience. Meanwhile, the conditions for digital platform work are extremely favourable in the developing post-Soviet countries due to a relatively high unemployment rate, low purchasing power of the population, limited access to social protection for non-standard workers, and weak enforcement of labour-related rights in practice. Favourable conditions for digital platform work are created by the increasing share of the service sector in the overall economic structure, the spread of technology, job mismatch and overeducation, as well as low trust in trade unions and limited practical access to collective bargaining mechanisms in both developed and developing post-Soviet economies. Post-Soviet economies with larger populations have greater potential for the development of digital platform work because larger populations mean larger consumer markets.

References

Aleksynska M (2021) Digital Work in Eastern Europe: Overview of Trends, Outcomes, and Policy Responses. ILO Working Paper No. 32. Retrieved from: https://www.ilo.org/publications/digital-work-eastern-europe-overview-trends-outcomes-and-policy-responses-1

Aleksynska M, Bastrakova A, Kharchenko N (2019) Working Conditions on Digital Labour Platforms: Evidence from a Leading Labour Supply Economy. IZA Discussion Paper No. 12245. Retrieved from: https://docs.iza.org/dp12245.pdf

Amazon Mechanical Turk (2020) Participation Agreement as last updated 25 March 2020. Retrieved from: https://www.mturk.com/participation-agreement

Anwar MA, Graham M (2021) Between a rock and a hard place: freedom, flexibility, precarity and vulnerability in the gig economy in Africa. Compet Change 25:237–258. https://doi.org/10.1177/1024529420914473

Benešova I, Smutka L (2016) The post-soviet countries—development and structure of economy: is there any potential for future regional integration? Procedia Soc Behav Sci 220:30–39

Benson C (2017) Uber, UK Employment law and the gig economy. 2017 Midyear Meeting of the American Bar Association International Labor and Employment Law Committee, May 7–11, 2017, The Westbury Hotel Dublin. Available at: https://www.americanbar.org/content/dam/aba/events/labor_law/2017/05/INT/papers /uber_paper.authcheckdam.pdf

Berg J (2016) Income security in the on-demand economy: findings and policy lessons from a survey of Crowdworkers (March 1, 2016). Comp Labor Law Policy J 37(3):2016. Available at SSRN: https://ssrn.com/abstract=2740940

Berg J, Furrer M, Harmon E, Rani U, Silberman MS (2018) Digital labour platforms and the future of work: Towards decent work in the online world. International Labour Organization (September 20, 2018). (1) (PDF) Digital labour platforms and the future of work: Towards decent work in the online world. Retrieved from: https://www.ilo.org/publications/digital-labour-platforms-and-future-work-towards-decent-work-online-world

Brancati MCU, Pesole A, Macias F (2020) New evidence on platform workers in Europe: results from the second COLLEEM survey. JRC Science for Policy Report. Publications Office of the European Union, Luxembourg. Retrieved from: https://publications.jrc.ec.europa.eu/repository/handle/JRC118570

Bruck T, Danzer AM, Muravyev A, Weißhaar N (2010) Poverty during transition: household survey evidence from Ukraine. J Comp Econ 38(2):123–145

Cedefop (2020) Developing and matching skills in the online platform economy: findings on new forms of digital work and learning from Cedefop's CrowdLearn study. Retrieved from: https://www.cedefop.europa.eu/en/publications-and-resources/publications/3085

Christin A (2018) Counting clicks: quantification and variation in web journalism in the United States and France. Am J Sociol 123(5):1382–1415

Collective agreement between Hilfr ApS and 3F Private Service, Hotel and Restaurant from (2018) as translated by the Danish Confederation of Trade Unions. Retrieved from: https://www2.3f.dk/~/media/files/mainsite/forside/fagforening/privat%20service/overenskomster/hilfr%20collective%20agreement%202018.pd

Conaty P, Bird A, Ross C (2018) Working together. Trade union and co-operative innovations for precarious workers. Co-operatives UK, Manchester. Retrieved from: https://base.socioeco.org/docs/cuk_and_cc_-_working_together_final_print-quality.pdf

Crowley S (2004) Explaining labor weakness in post-communist Europe: historical legacies and comparative perspective. East Eur Politics Soc 18(3):394–429

Cruz SA, Gameiro A (2023) Digital work platform: understanding platforms, workers, clients in a service relation. Front Sociol 7(1075808). https://doi.org/10.3389/fsoc.2022.1075808

Dabrowski M (2022) Thirty years of economic transition in the former Soviet Union: macroeconomic dimension. Russ J Econ 8(2):95–121

Dabrowski M (2023) Thirty years of economic transition in the former Soviet Union: Microeconomic and institutional dimensions. Retrieved from: https://rujec.org/article/104761/

De Stefano V, Durri I, Stylogiannis Ch, Wouters M (2021) Platform work and the employment relationship. Working paper. International Labour Organization. https://webapps.ilo.org/static/english/intserv/working-papers/wp027/index.html

Dencik L, Wilkin P (2020) Digital Activism and the Political Culture of Trade Unionism. Retrieved from: MCS_DencikWilkin_full.pdf (cardiff.ac.uk)

Doordash (2020) Independent Contractor Agreement—Canada. Retrieved from: https://help.doordash.com/dashers/s/ica-ca?language=en_US

Drahokoupil J, Piasna A (2019) Work in the Platform Economy: Deliveroo Riders in Belgium and the SMart Arrangement. ETUI Research Paper - Working Paper 2019.01. Retrieved from: https://ssrn.com/abstract=3316133 or https://doi.org/10.2139/ssrn.3316133

Duffy BE (2017) (Not) getting paid to do what you love. Yale University Press, New Haven, CT

Dunn M (2020) Making gigs work: digital platforms, job quality and worker motivations. N Technol Work Employ 35:232–249. https://doi.org/10.1111/ntwe.12167

Eurofound (2018) Employment and working conditions of selected types of platform work. Retrieved from: https://www.eurofound.europa.eu/en/publications/2018/employment-and-working-conditions-selected-types-platform-work

European Commission (2017) Moving forward on the European pillar of social rights: commission continues work on fair and predictable employment contracts [press release]. European Commission, Brussels. Retrieved from: https://ec.europa.eu/social/main.jsp?langId=en&catId=89&newsId=2869&furtherNews

European Foundation for the Improvement of Living and Working Conditions (2024) Platform work: representation. Retrieved from: https://www.eurofound.europa.eu/en/platform-work-representation

European Parliament (2017) European Parliament resolution of 15 June 2017 on a European agenda for the collaborative economy (2017/2003(INI)). European Parliament, Brussels. Retrieved from: https://eur-lex.europa.eu/legal-content/EN/TXT/?uri=CELEX%3A52017IP0271

European Training Foundation (2021) Platform work in Eastern Partnership countries. Retrieved from: https://www.etf.europa.eu/sites/default/files/2021-06/platform_work_eastern_partnership_infographic.pdf

Forde C, Stuart M, Joyce S, Oliver L, Valizade D, Alberti G, Hardy K, Trappmann V, Umney C, Carson C (2017a) The Social Protection of Workers in the Platform Economy. Retrieved from: https://www.europarl.europa.eu/RegData/etudes/STUD/2017/614184/IPOL_STU(2017)614184_EN.pdf

Forde C, Stuart M, Joyce S, Oliver L, Valizade D, Alberti G, Hardy K, Trappmann V, Umney C, Carson C (2017b) The social protection of workers in the platform economy. European Parliament. The Social Protection of Workers in the Platform Economy. Retrieved from: https://www.europarl.europa.eu/thinktank/en/document/IPOL_STU(2017)614184

Gebert R (2021) The pitfalls and promises of successfully organizing Foodora couriers in Toronto. In: Drahokoupil J, Vandaele K (eds) A modern guide to labour and the platform economy. Edward Elgar Publishing, Cheltenham, pp 274–289

Geissinger A, Laurell C, Öberg C, Sandström C, Suseno Y (2021) The sharing economy and the transformation of work: evidence from Foodora. Personnel Review. Advance online publication. doi: https://doi.org/10.1108/PR-08-2019-0450

Gherardini A (2017) So many, so different! Industrial relations in creative sectors. Retrieved from: (PDF) So many, so different! Industrial relations in creative sectors (researchgate.net)

Handy (2020) Service Professional Agreement U.S. Retrieved from: https://www.handy.com/pro_terms [June 2020]

Heeger K (2023) Platform work and new roles for trade unions. Retrieved from: https://medium.com/@reshaping_work/platform-work-and-new-roles-for-trade-unions-d629397c66ad

Huws U, Spencer NH, Joyce S (2016) Crowd Work in Europe: Preliminary Results from a Survey in the UK, Sweden, Germany, Austria and the Netherlands. Foundation for European Progressive Studies. Retrieved from: https://uhra.herts.ac.uk/bitstream/handle/2299/21934/crowd_work_in_europe_draft_report_last_version.pdf?sequence=1&isAllowed=y

ILO (2016) Non-standard employment around the world: understanding challenges, shaping prospects. ILO, Geneva

ILO (2017) World Social Protection Report 2017–19: Universal Social Protection to Achieve the Sustainable Development Goals. Retrieved from: https://www.ilo.org/global/publications/books/WCMS_604882/lang%2D%2Den/index.htm

ILO (2018a) Women and men in the informal economy: a statistical picture, 3rd edn. Geneva, ILO

ILO (2018b) Job quality in the platform economy. Retrieved from: https://www.ilo.org/wcmsp5/groups/public/%2D%2D-dgreports/%2D%2D-cabinet/documents/publication/wcms_618167.pdf
ILO (2019) Universal social protection. Universal old-age, disability and survivors pensions in Ukraine. Geneva, ILO. Retrieved from: https://www.social-protection.org/gimi/gess/RessourcePDF.action?ressource.ressourceId=53966
ILO (2021) World employment and social outlook 2021: the role of digital labour platforms in transforming the world of work. International Labour Office. Retrieved from: World Employment and Social Outlook 2021: The role of digital labour platforms in transforming the world of work (ilo.org)
ILO (2024) Are platform workers willing to unionize? Exploring survey evidence from 14 European countries. Retrieved from: https://www.ilo.org/global/publications/working-papers/WCMS_910689/lang%2D%2Den/index.htm
ILO, ISSA and OECD (2023) Providing adequate and sustainable social protection for workers in the gig and platform economy. Retrieved from: https://www.ilo.org/wcmsp5/groups/public/%2D%2D-dgreports/%2D%2D-ddg_p/documents/publication/wcms_867535.pdf
Ilsoe A (2017) The digitalisation of service work: social partner responses in Denmark, Sweden and Germany. Transfer 23(3):333–348
Instacart (2020) Independent Contractor Agreement. Retrieved from: https://shoppers.instacart.com/contracts/2017
International Cooperative Alliance (2022) Platform cooperatives: an alternative model that empowers workers. Retrieved from: Platform cooperatives: an alternative model that empowers workers | ICA
International Monetary Fund (1998) The post-communist transition: patterns and prospects. Finance Dev 35(3) Retrieved from: https://www.imf.org/external/pubs/ft/fandd/1998/09/exeter.htm
International Monetary Fund (2019) World economic outlook: global manufacturing downturn, rising trade barriers. IMF, Washington
Jabagi N, Croteau A-M, Audebrand L, Marsan J (2019) Gig-workers' motivation: thinking beyond carrots and sticks. J Manag Psychol 34(4):192–213. https://doi.org/10.1108/JMP-06-2018-0255
Johnston H, Land-Kazlauskas C (2018) Organizing on-demand: representation, voice, and collective bargaining in the gig economy, ILO working paper no. 994981993502676. International Labour Office, Geneva
Joyce S, Stuart M (2021) Trade union responses to platform work: an evolving tension between mainstream and grassroots approaches. In: Drahokoupil J, Vandaele K (eds) A modern guide to labour and the platform economy, chapter 11. Edward Elgar Publishing, Cheltenham, pp 177–192
Kahancová M, Meszmann TT, Sedláková M (2020) Precarization via digitalization? Work arrangements in the on-demand platform economy in Hungary and Slovakia. Front Sociol 26(5):3. https://doi.org/10.3389/fsoc.2020.00003
Kallaste E, Woolfson C (2009) The paradox of post-communist trade unionism: 'you can't want what you can't imagine'. Econ Labour Relat Rev 20(1):93–110
Kelkar S (2018) Engineering a platform: the construction of interfaces, users, organizational roles, and the division of labor. New Media Soc 20(7):2629–2646
Kenney M, Zysman J (2016) The rise of the platform economy. Issues Sci Technol 32(3):61–69. https://www.researchgate.net/publication/309483265_The_Rise_of_the_Platform_Economy
Kupets O (2016) Skill mismatch and overeducation in transition economies. IZA World of Labor, No. 224
Lamo A, Messina J (2010) Formal education, mismatch and wages after transition. European Central Bank, Working Paper No. 1215. Retrieved from: https://www.ecb.europa.eu/pub/pdf/scpwps/ecbwp1215.pdf
Lehmann H (2015) Informal employment in transition countries: empirical evidence and research challenges. Comp Econ Stud 57(1):1–30

Lehmann H, Pignatti N (2018) Informal employment relationships and the labor market: is there segmentation in Ukraine? J Comp Econ 46(3):838–857

Lehmann H, Muravyev A, Pignatti N, Zaiceva A (2012) Worker displacement in Russia and Ukraine: a comparative analysis using micro data. In: Brück T, Lehmann H (eds) In the grip of transition: economic and social consequences of restructuring in Russia and Ukraine. Palgrave Macmillan, pp 7–46

Lieman R (2018) Uber voor alles. Hoe de on demand-economie ons leven beïnvloedt. Business Contact, Amsterdam

OECD (2023) Platform cooperatives and employment: an alternative for platform work. Retrieved from: 3eab339f-en.pdf (oecd-ilibrary.org)

OLA (2016) Subscription Agreement for India as effective from 1 November 2016. Retrieved from: https://partners.olacabs.com/public/terms_conditions/IN[June 2020]

Ost D (2009) The end of Postcommunism: trade unions in Eastern Europe's future. East Eur Politics Soc 23(1):13–33

Piasna A, Zwysen W (2022) New wine in old bottles: organizing and collective bargaining in the platform economy. Int J Lab Res 11(1/2):36–46

Rani U, Dhir RK (2020) Platform work and the COVID-19 pandemic. Indian J Labour Econ 63:163–171. https://doi.org/10.1007/s41027-020-00273-y

Rani U, Furrer M (2021) Digital labour platforms and new forms of flexible work in developing countries: algorithmic management of work and workers. Compet Chang 25:212–236. https://doi.org/10.1177/1024529420905187

Rivera VA, Lee DT (2021) I want to, but first I need to: understanding crowdworkers' career goals, challenges and tensions. ACM Human-Comp Interaction 5(CSCW1):1–22

Roberts P (2014) Job mismatch in early career of graduates under post-communism. Int J Manpow 35(4):500–513

Rosenblat A (2018) Uberland: how algorithms are re-writing the rules of work. University of California Press, Berkeley

Schmidt FA (2017) Digital labour market in the platform economy: mapping the political challenges of crowd work and gig work. Retrieved from: https://library.fes.de/pdf-files/wiso/13164.pdf

Scholz T (2016) Uberworked and underpaid: how workers are disrupting the digital economy. Polity Press, Cambridge. Retrieved from: treborscholz.pdf (free.fr)

Scholz T, Mannan M, Pentzien J, Plotkin H (2021) Policies for cooperative ownership in the digital economy. Retrieved from: https://platform.coop/blog/policies-for-cooperative-ownership-in-the-digital-economy/

Serrano MR (2014) Between accommodation and transformation: the two logics of union renewal. Eur J Ind Relat 20(3):219–235

Srnicek N (2016) Platform Capitalism. Polity, Cambridge. Retrieved from: https://mudancatecnologicaedinamicacapitalista.files.wordpress.com/2019/02/platform-capitalism.pdf

Staunton B (2018) Grassroots action prominent in the platform economy. Retrieved from: https://www.opendemocracy.net/en/can-europe-make-it/grassroots-action-prominent-in-platform-economy/

Stewart A, Stanford J (2017) Regulating work in the gig economy: what are the options? Econ Lab Relations Rev 28:420–437. https://doi.org/10.1177/1035304617722461

Syndicat European Trade Union (2024) Platform work: trade unions win for millions of workers. Retrieved from: Platform work: trade unions win for millions of workers | ETUC

Taskrabbit (2019) Terms of Service as update on 18 December 2019. Retrieved from: https://www.taskrabbit.com/terms

Torrent-Sellens J, Ficapal-Cusi P, Ertz M (2021) Motivations for labour provision on digital platforms in Europe. In: Handbook of research on the platform economy and the evolution of E-commerce, pp 81–103. https://doi.org/10.4018/978-1-7998-7545-1.ch004. Retrieved from: https://www.igi-global.com/viewtitle.aspx?titleid=288441

Tubaro P, Casilli A (2022) Who bears the burden of a pandemic? COVID-19 and the transfer of risk on digital platform workers. Am Behav Sci 15:1–22. https://doi.org/10.1177/00027642211066027

Umar M, Xu Y, Mirza SS (2021) The impact of Covid- 19 on gig economy. Economic Research - Ekonomska Istraživanja 34:2284–2296. https://doi.org/10.1080/1331677X.2020.1862688

Upwork (2018) Upwork Payroll Agreement. Retrieved from: https://www.upwork.com/legal#upwork-payroll-agreement

Vallas S, Schor JB (2020) What do platforms do? Understanding the gig economy. Annu Rev Sociol 46:273–294. Available at SSRN: https://ssrn.com/abstract=3670075 or http://dx.doi.org/10.1146/annurev-soc-121919-054857

Van Doorn N (2017) Platform labor: on the gendered and racialized exploitation of low-income service work in the "on-demand" economy. Inf Commun Soc 20(6):898–914

Vandaele K (2018) *Will trade unions survive in the platform economy?* European Trade Union Institute, Working Paper No. 2018.05. Retrieved from: https://eticasfoundation.org/wp-content/uploads/2019/03/WorkingPaper2018.05VandaeleTradeunionsPlatformeconomyWeb-1.pdf

Wonolo (2020) Frontline Payroll Services Agreement. Retrieved from: https://www.wonolo.com/frontline-payroll-services-agreement

Wood AJ, Graham M, Lehdonvirta V, Hjorth I (2019) Good gig, bad gig: autonomy and algorithmic control in the global gig economy. Work Employ Soc 33(1):56–75. https://doi.org/10.1177/0950017018785616

World Bank (2023) *Gross* national income per capita 2022, Atlas method and PPP. Retrieved from: https://databankfiles.worldbank.org/public/ddpext_download/GNIPC.pdf

World Economic Forum (2020) The promise of platform work: understanding the ecosystem. Retrieved from: https://www3.weforum.org/docs/WEF_The_Promise_of_Platform_Work.pdf

Chapter 4
European Union Initiatives for Sustainable Growth, Digital Transformation, and the Regulation of Platform Work

Deimilė Prapiestytė

Abstract This chapter provides a structured overview of the European Union's institutional efforts to implement the European Green Deal, with particular emphasis on strategies that foster a clean and circular economy. It is important to note that this document underscores the policy priorities delineated by the European Council and the concomitant European Commission initiatives, encompassing the European Green Deal Communication, the Circular Economy Action Plan, and the Industrial Strategy. Legislative instruments such as the Net-Zero Industry Act, the Critical Raw Materials Act, and directives supporting sustainable products and the "Right to Repair" are examined. The European Union's commitment to climate neutrality, industrial resilience, and sustainable consumption patterns is further underscored by advancements in specific sectors, including packaging, electronics, and ICT.

In parallel, the chapter addresses the EU's pursuit of a dual digital and green transition. It is widely acknowledged that a range of computing technologies have a pivotal role to play in facilitating sustainability objectives and serving as instruments for reducing the ecological impact of digital infrastructure. However, the 2024 assessments indicate that progress remains inadequate to achieve the 2030 targets, necessitating augmented investment and policy recalibration.

The chapter concludes with the presentation of the Platform Work Directive, a legislative response to the expansion of digital labour platforms across the EU. This directive has been developed with the intention of enhancing the social protection available to platform workers. It addresses critical challenges, including worker misclassification, the opacity of algorithmic management, and cross-border enforcement. The Platform Work Directive establishes also a presumption of employment status, mandates algorithmic transparency, safeguards personal data, and enhances enforcement capacities. This directive is indicative of the EU's broader commitment to ensuring fair, transparent, and accountable platform work.

D. Prapiestytė (✉)
Vilnius University, Law Faculty, Vilnius, Lithuania
e-mail: deimile.prapiestyte@tf.vu.lt

R. Remeikienė, L. Gasparėnienė (eds.), *Work and Legal Guidelines in the Age of Digitalisation and Green Transition*, European Union and its Neighbours in a Globalized World 25, https://doi.org/10.1007/978-3-032-03511-0_4

The European Union is implementing a cohesive strategy to navigate the interconnected transitions in environmental sustainability, digital innovation and the labor market. Recognising the growing interdependence of these areas, EU policies aim to promote a unified approach to transformation.

Central to this strategy is the 'twin transition', which combines the European Green Deal and the Digital Agenda. The Green Deal sets out a path towards achieving climate neutrality by 2050 and promotes sustainable practices in sectors such as energy, transport and industry. Meanwhile, the Digital Agenda—part of Europe's "Digital Decade" — focuses on driving economic and societal transformation through enhanced connectivity, digital skills, artificial intelligence, and cloud technologies. These two transitions are designed to reinforce each other: digital tools can improve energy efficiency and enable smart mobility, while achieving green goals requires innovative digital solutions to support sustainable development.

Effective regulation of platform work in the EU also supports broader social and environmental goals. Ensuring fair labour standards contributes to social justice in the digital economy. Thus, labour protections, digital fairness and environmental sustainability are jointly advanced as part of the EU's integrated transition strategy.

The main factors that led to the adoption of the EUs' "twin transition" strategy and the Platform Work Directive are outlined below.

4.1 European Union's Actions Aimed at Implementing the European Green Deal

The European Council plays an important role in the institutional framework of the European Union, as set out in Art. 13 TEU. Pursuant to Art. 15(1) TEU, this institution duly promotes the development of the European Union and establishes the general policy guidelines and priorities. It should be noted that the European Council does not have legislative powers. Attention should be drawn to the fact that the European Commission subsequently draws up the specific action plans necessary for the implementation of the European Union's policies and submits specific proposals to the Council of the European Union and the European Parliament. The Council of the European Union (the Council), when meeting in the various policy formations of the European Union, discusses proposed legislative and non-legislative actions and then, together with the European Parliament, during the legislative procedure, decides on the adoption of specific acts of European Union law.

On 20 June 2019, acting in the exercise of its powers to set policy guidelines and priorities for the European Union, the European Council adopted the EU strategic agenda for 2019–2024 (EU strategic agenda 2019), which sets out the priority areas on which the work of the European Council was to be focused and on which the work programmes of the other institutions of the European Union were to be based. The four priority areas included the following: protecting citizens and freedoms; developing a strong and vibrant economic base; building a climate-neutral, green, fair and social Europe; and promoting Europe's interests and values on the global stage.

As far as it regards the context of this research, two of the European Council's priorities should be distinguished. The first objective is to pursue the development of a strong and viable economic base, based, among other things, on the importance of a strong economic background for Europe's competitiveness, prosperity and role on the global stage, as well as for the creation of jobs. In the times where technological, security and sustainability challenges reshape the global landscape, the European Union needs to strengthen cohesion and to renew the basis for a long-term sustainable and inclusive economic growth. It also aims to ensure that Europe is digitally independent and can reap the benefits of this development in a fair way, and that European Union policies are shaped in a way that embodies societal values, promotes inclusiveness, and remains compatible with our lifestyle. It underlines the need for the European Union to work on all aspects of the digital revolution and artificial intelligence, such as infrastructure, connectivity, services, data, regulation and investment; these efforts should be complemented by the development of the service economy and the integration of digital services. The second objective is to build a climate-neutral, green, fair and social Europe which should be open to the changes brought about by the transition to the green economy, technological developments and globalisation. It should be emphasized that the European Union is able and must play a leading role in the profound transformation of its economy and society, and in counteracting climate impacts, taking into account national circumstances and social justice.

The European Council pointed out the fact that the adoption of the Strategic Agenda is the first step in a process that will be carried out by the institutions of the European Union and by the Member States, and that the Council will closely monitor the implementation of these priorities and, where appropriate, set further common policies and priorities.

On 19 December 2019, the European Commission published a Communication to the European Parliament, the European Council, the Council, the European Economic and Social Committee and the Committee of the Regions entitled "The European Green Deal" (hereinafter referred to as the "European Green Deal", the "EC Communication"), which sets out an initial roadmap of the key policies and measures needed to implement the Green Deal for Europe, with a view to updating it in line with evolving needs and the formulation of policy options (EC Communication 2019, p. 3).

The European Commission has indicated in the above-mentioned Communication that the implementation of the European Green Deal will require a review of the policies on the supply of clean energy to the economy as a whole, on industry, on production and consumption, on large-scale infrastructure, on transport, on food, on agriculture, on construction, as well as on taxation and social benefits. In addition, it has been envisaged that achieving these goals will require a greater consideration of the protection and restoration of natural ecosystems, the sustainable use of resources and the improvement of human health. It was noted that these are the fields where the changes that can bring the greatest benefits to the EU's economy, society and the natural environment are most needed. What is more, it has also been envisaged that the European Union should promote the necessary digital transformation; in addition, the tools that are the key drivers of change have been indicated. The European Commission pointed out that, although the above-mentioned fields of action are closely interlinked and complementary, considerable attention should be given to potential trade-offs between economic, environmental and social objectives. Finally, the implementation of the European Green Deal is intended to make a coherent use of all policy levers: regulation and standardisation, investment and innovation, national reforms, dialogue with social partners, and international cooperation. It is worth mentioning that the European Pillar of Social Rights will also be used to ensure that no one is left behind.

The EC Communication outlines a set of policies aimed at driving fundamental changes and transforming the European Union towards a sustainable future with the help of the key action lines, sometimes referred to as "individual European Green Deal Strategies": (1) Increasing the EU's Climate Ambition for 2030 and 2050[1]; (2) Supplying clean, affordable and secure energy; (3) Mobilising industry for a clean circular economy; (4) Building and renovating in an energy and resource efficient way; (5) Accelerating the shift to sustainable and smart mobility; (6) From Farm to Fork: a fair, healthy and environmentally friendly food system; (7) Preserving and restoring ecosystems and biodiversity; (8) A Zero Pollution ambition—for a toxic-free environment (EC Communication 2019, points 2.1.1 to 2.1.8.). The European Council, having taken note of the European Commission's Communication "The European Green Deal", recognised the need to put in place a framework that opens up opportunities to ensure a cost-effective as well as socially balanced and fair

[1] It should be noted that in each of the eight strategies outlined above for the implementation of the European Green Deal, the European Union has adopted both legislative measures and other specific actions. To give an example of such steps, in order to implement the "Fit for *55*" initiative, the European Union institutions have adopted completely new legislation or, in most cases, amended legislation to help the existing legislation to align with the targets set out in the European Green Deal. Another example is as follows: Regulation (EU) 2021/1119 of the European Parliament and of the Council of 30 June 2021 establishing the framework for achieving climate neutrality and amending Regulations (EC) No 401/2009 and (EU) 2018/1999 ("European Climate Law"), OJ 2021 L 243/1. In 2023, five pieces of legislation have been adopted in the EU, which will make up the "Fit for 55" related to this initiative: Directive (EU) 2023/958 of the European Parliament and of the Council of 10 May 2023 amending Directive 2003/87/EC as regards aviation's contribution to the Union's economy-wide emission reduction target and the appropriate implementation of a global market-based measure, OJ 2023 L 130/115, and Directive (EU) 2023/959 of the European Parliament and of the Council of 10 May 2023 amending Directive 2003/87/EC establishing a system for greenhouse gas emission allowance trading within the Union and Decision (EU) 2015/1814 concerning the establishment and operation of a market stability reserve for the Union greenhouse gas emission trading system, OJ 2023 L 130/134; Regulation (EU) 2023/1805 of the European Parliament and of the Council of 13 September 2023 on the use of renewable and low-carbon fuels in maritime transport, and amending Directive 2009/16/EC, OJ 2023 L 234/48; Regulation (EU) 2023/955 of the European Parliament and of the Council of 10 May 2023 establishing a Social Climate Fund and amending Regulation (EU) 2021/1060, OJ 2023 L 130/1; and Regulation (EU) 2023/956 of the European Parliament and of the Council of 10 May 2023 establishing a carbon border adjustment mechanism, OJ 2023 L 130/52.

transition to climate neutrality, taking into account the different national circumstances. In its conclusion adopted on 12 December 2019, the European Council noted that all relevant European Union legal acts and policies must be compatible with the achievement of the climate neutrality objective and contribute thereto, still respecting the principle of a level playing field (EUCO 29/19, 2019). Accordingly, the Council was invited to continue its work in this area.

As the European Commission identified these European Green Deal strategies 5 years ago, it is now possible to assess what concrete actions have been taken and what results have been achieved in the EU. In the context of this research, the hereby provided detailed overview will cover the measures the European Union had identified for 2019 and the actions that have already been taken to implement the strategy "Mobilising industry for a clean and circular economy". The wording of the title of this strategy should be taken into account in assessing the actions that the European Union had set out to take, specifically in the field of industry and, in particular, in the field of promoting the circular economy.

The 2019 EC Communication envisaged that a climate-neutral circular economy would require the full mobilisation of industry. In the view of the European Commission, it will take some 25 years (a lifespan of a generation) to transform the industrial sector as well as all value chains; in fact, to prepare for 2050, decisions and actions have to be taken within 5 years (starting with 2019). It was also noted that the transformation provides an opportunity to develop sustainable economic activities with high job creation; in addition, the European Green Deal will support and accelerate the transformation of the EU industry towards a sustainable and socially inclusive growth model.

The European Commission had envisaged that, in order to address the dual challenge of green and digital transformation, it would adopt the European Union's Industrial Strategy to help Europe seize the opportunities offered by the digital transformation, which will play a key role in achieving the objectives of the European Green Deal. The Industrial Strategy was accompanied by the modernisation of the European Union's economy and seizing the opportunities offered by the circular economy, both within the European Union and globally, through the adoption of an EU action plan for the Circular Economy.[2] The main objective of the new policy framework was supposed to foster the expansion of experimental markets for climate-neutral circular products inside and outside the EU. This will be followed by an overview of concrete European Union's actions related to the development and implementation of the European Industrial Strategy and the new Circular Economy Action Plan.

[2] The first step towards a circular economy in the EU was marked by the Communication from the Commission to the European Parliament, the Council, the European Economic and Social Committee and the Committee of the Regions "Closing the loop—An EU action plan for the Circular Economy" (COM/2015/0614 final) adopted by the European Commission on 2 December 2015). See Juškevičiūtė-Vilienė (2022).

Industrial Strategy of the European Union On 10 March 2020, the European Commission adopted a Communication to the European Parliament, the European Council, the Council, the European Economic and Social Committee and the Committee of the Regions on "A New Industrial Strategy for Europe" (COM/2020/102 final). On 5 May 2021, a re-launch of this strategy was presented in the European Commission's "Communication from the Commission to the European Parliament, the Council, the European Economic and Social Committee and the Committee of the Regions Updating the 2020 New Industrial Strategy: Building a stronger Single Market for Europe's recovery" (COM/2021/350 final). The update of the new European Industrial Strategy for 2020 was supposed to build on the lessons learnt from the COVID-19 crisis, to increase resilience and competitiveness of Europe, and to enable European industry to take a leading role in the green and digital transformation. The European Industrial Strategy focuses on the following key areas: strengthening the resilience of the Single Market, tackling the issue of the European Union's strategic dependence and accelerating the green and digital transformation.

On 1 February 2023, the European Commission presented the Communication from the Commission to the European Parliament, the European Council, the Council, the European Economic and Social Committee and the Committee of the Regions "A Green Deal Industrial Plan for the Net-Zero Age" (COM/2023/62 final), with the aim of speeding up the industrial transformation linked to climate neutrality and putting Europe on a pathway towards climate neutrality. In December 2023, the Council and the European Parliament reached a preliminary agreement to reform the design of the EU electricity market (Council, 2023). The EU legislative procedure ended with the adoption of the Regulation (EU) 2024/1735 of the European Parliament and of the Council of 13 June 2024 on establishing a framework of measures for strengthening Europe's net-zero technology manufacturing ecosystem and amending Regulation (EU) 2018/1724. The Regulation 2024/1735 aims to promote the industrial deployment of zero greenhouse gas ("GHG") balance technologies in industry which are necessary in order to meet the European Union's climate objectives; this would enable making use of the benefits of the Single Market and strengthening Europe's leadership in industrial green technologies. The Regulation 2024/1735 aims at facilitating conditions of investment in green technologies by simplifying authorisation procedures, supporting strategic projects on the basis of specific criteria that contribute to decarbonisation, facilitating access to markets for zero-emission products, introducing rules on public incentives, and improving the skills of Europe's workers. The Regulation 2024/1735 is also expected to accelerate progress towards achievement of the European Union's 2030 climate and energy targets and the transition to climate neutrality, while at the same time boosting the competitiveness of the European Union's industry, creating quality jobs, and supporting the European Union's efforts to become energy independent.

Regulation (EU) 2024/1252 of the European Parliament and of the Council establishing a framework for ensuring a secure and sustainable supply of critical raw materials and amending Regulations (EU) 168/2013, (EU) 2018/858, 2018/1724 and (EU) 2019/1020, the so-called Critical Raw Materials Act was adopted on 11 April 2024; this Regulation aims at increasing and diversifying the European Union's supply of critical raw materials; strengthening circularity, including recycling; supporting research and innovation in the field of resource efficiency and the development of substitutes; and reinforcing the EU's strategic self-reliance.

It is, therefore, clear that the European Union has not only adopted the new European Industrial Strategy as planned, but has also adopted new legislation to help ensure its implementation, and is continuing the legislative procedures necessary for its effective implementation.

Circular Economy in the European Union It should be noted that an overview will be provided hereby and will cover the steps taken by the European Union to implement the circular economy strategy of the European Green Deal. To start with, it is useful to briefly overview the main initiatives or actions related to the circular economy in the European Union that have been identified in the European Green Deal. First, it was stated that the Circular Economy Action Plan will formulate a policy on sustainable products, which will support the circular design of all products using a common methodology and principles. Priority will be given to reduction of amounts of materials and to the reuse before recycling. It was noted that the Circular Economy Action Plan will contain transformational roadmaps for all sectors, but will focus on resource-intensive sectors such as textiles, construction, electronics and plastics. In addition, the European Green Deal has foreseen that the Circular Economy Action Plan would include measures to encourage companies to offer reusable, durable and repairable products; and to enable consumers to choose those particular products. Among other things, the European Green Deal called for public authorities, including those in the European Union, to set a good example and ensure that their public procurement is green. The European Commission has committed itself to developing further legislation and guidelines on green public procurement (EC Communication 2019, p. 2.1.3.).

It should be noted that decoupling economic growth from resource use and moving towards circular systems of production and consumption is essential to achieve climate neutrality for the EU by 2050 (Council 2024).

On 11 March 2020, the European Commission published a Communication from the Commission to the European Parliament, the Council, the European Economic and Social Committee and the Committee of the Regions entitled "A new Circular Economy Action Plan For a cleaner and more competitive Europe" (COM/2020/98 final). This Communication presented a Circular Economy Action Plan consisting of more than 30 different actions in the following areas: ensuring circularity in sustainable product development and production processes; consumer empowerment; action in key sectors; and waste reduction. Targeted initiatives are foreseen for key product value chains such as electronics and ICT, batteries, packaging, plastics, textiles, construction and buildings, and food. In addition, a revision of waste legislation is foreseen. Besides, strengthening actions at the international and global level makes an important component of the Action Plan.

In December 2020, the Council adopted conclusions on "Making the Recovery Circular and Green" in response to the European Commission's Circular Economy Action Plan for a Cleaner and more Competitive Europe. Among other things, these conclusions emphasized the role of the circular economy in the post-COVID-19 recovery and established a link with digitalisation, underlining its importance in unlocking the full potential of the circular economy.

The above-mentioned EU legislation has already been adopted in order to contribute to ensuring the implementation of the circular economy strategy in the EU. Various measures have been adopted to ensure the development and production of sustainable products. The following example illustrates what has been mentioned above: the ordinary legislative procedure was launched, and on 23 April 2024 the European Parliament adopted the legislative resolution on the Proposal for a regulation of the European Parliament and of the Council establishing a framework for setting eco-design requirements for sustainable products and repealing Directive 2009/125/EC. The Regulation has the following aims: to introduce environmental sustainability requirements for almost all types of goods placed on the European Union market; to establish a digital product passport providing information on the environmental sustainability of products; and to prohibit the destruction of certain unsold consumer goods (textiles and footwear).

On 22 March 2023, the European Commission presented a Proposal for the Directive of the European Parliament and of the Council on common rules promoting the repair of goods and amending Regulation (EU) 2017/2394, Directives (EU) 2019/771 and (EU) 2020/1828 (COM/2023/155 final), i.e., what is called the "Right to Repair" Directive. The Proposal aims to encourage the repair rather than the replacement of defective or faulty goods. On 14 February 2024, the European Parliament and the Council reached a preliminary agreement on the draft Directive, providing that this new legislation will apply to all products subject to repair requirements under European Union law (i.e. washing machines, dishwashers, refrigerators or vacuum cleaners); obliging manufacturers of products subject to repair requirements to repair them; introducing a European information format to provide consumers with basic information on the repair service; and linking the national platforms on repair information to a European online platform. On 13 June 2024, the European Parliament and the Council adopted Directive (EU) 2024/1799 on common rules promoting the repair of goods and amending Regulation (EU) 2017/2394 and Directives (EU) 2019/771 and (EU) 2020/1828.

On 30 November 2022, the European Commission presented a Proposal for a revision of EU legislation on Packaging and Packaging Waste (COM/2022/677 final); Procedure 2022/0396/COD). On 24 April 2024, the European Parliament adopted a legislative resolution at first reading on the Proposal for a Regulation of the European Parliament and of the Council on packaging and packaging waste, amending Regulation (EU) 2019/1020 and Directive (EU) 2019/904, and repealing Directive 94/62/EC (Register Reference: P9_TA(2024)0318). The proposed new Regulation aims at reducing the increased amount of packaging waste generated in the EU, at the same time harmonising the rules in the internal market for packaging and promoting the circular economy.

Electronics as well as information and communication technologies (ICT), one of the most resource-intensive and circular sectors with the highest potential for circularity and the fastest-growing waste stream, is one of the sectors where the Circular Economy Action Plan includes measures to improve the durability and recyclability of electrical and electronic equipment. The European Union has taken a number of steps in this field, either by amending existing legislation or adopting completely new legislation. On 23 November 2022, the European Parliament and the Council adopted Directive (EU) 2022/2380 of the European Parliament and of the Council of 23 November 2022 amending Directive 2014/53/EU on the harmonisation of the laws of the Member States relating to the making available on the market of radio equipment (Directive (EU) 2022/2380, which is the legislation that will allow European Union's consumers to use a common USB Type-C charger for their electronic devices. In accordance with Art. 2 of Directive (EU) 2022/2380, Member States are obliged to adopt and publish, by 28 December 2023, the laws, regulations and administrative provisions necessary to comply with this Directive. It should be noted that certain categories or classes of radio equipment[3] will be subject to the provisions of Directive (EU) 2022/2380 as of 28 December 2024.

The European Union has also taken various actions in other areas where a circular economy strategy should be pursued and implemented, such as textiles,[4] batteries and battery waste,[5] etc.

To summarise, the European Union is implementing the European Green Deal with the aim of achieving climate neutrality, sustainable economic development and a circular economy. The 2019 strategic agenda set out the priorities that prompted the European Commission to launch the Green Deal, with the aim of transforming the energy sector, industry, transport, agriculture, and environmental protection. A key focus is transitioning industry to a clean, circular economy. The New Industrial Strategy for the EU, presented in 2020 and updated in 2021, emphasises the importance of green and digital transitions. In 2023, the Green Industry Roadmap was introduced, and the forthcoming Industrial Act for Climate Neutrality will promote green technologies and investment. The Critical Raw Materials Act, adopted in 2024, enhances supply security and strategic autonomy. Together, these actions demonstrate that the EU is taking concrete steps to implement its long-term sustainability strategies.

[3] See e.g. those listed in Annex Ia, Part I, points 1.1 to 1.12 of Directive (EU) 2022/2380, such as, but not limited to, portable mobile telephones, headsets, mice, cameras, keyboards, etc.

[4] Communication from the Commission to the European Parliament, the Council, the European Economic and Social Committee and the Committee of the Regions "EU Strategy for Sustainable and Circular Textiles" of March 30, 2022 (COM/2022/141 final).

[5] Regulation (EU) 2023/1542 of the European Parliament and of the Council of 12 July 2023 concerning batteries and waste batteries, amending Directive 2008/98/EC and Regulation (EU) 2019/1020 and repealing Directive 2006/66/EC (Regulation (EU) 2023/1542).

4.2 Digital Agenda for the European Union

The European Union has essentially set itself a dual challenge, i.e. the green transformation and the digital transformation; efforts to pursue the two objectives should, therefore, be made simultaneously.

Digital technologies will play a key role in achieving the sustainability objectives of the Green Deal in many different sectors. The European Commission will look for ways to ensure that digital technologies such as artificial intelligence, 5G, cloud and edge computing and the Internet of Things were able to accelerate and significantly increase the impact of policies in combating climate change and protecting the environment. In addition, digitalisation offers new opportunities of monitoring air and water pollution remotely or monitoring and optimising the use of energy and natural resources. At the same time, Europe needs a digital sector that carefully takes sustainability into account. The Commission will consider measures to improve the energy efficiency and performance of the sector—from broadband networks to data centres and ICT devices—in the context of the circular economy. The European Commission will assess whether there is a need for more transparency in disclosing the environmental impact of electronic communications services and stricter measures in the deployment of new networks; besides, the Commission will decide whether it is useful to support take-back schemes to encourage people to return unwanted devices, such as mobiles, tablets and chargers (EC Communication 2019, p. 2.1.3.).

In this respect, it should be recalled that as early as in March 2000, the Lisbon European Council set the target of "making the European Union the most competitive and dynamic knowledge-based economy in the world by 2010"; besides, the aim of enabling the implementation of the Lisbon Strategy has led to the adoption of, among other things, two Digital Agendas for Europe; one covered the period from 2010 to 2020 and the other one covered the period from 2020 to 2030, respectively. As the European Union has taken a number of actions between 2010 and now (before the end of the second period of implementation of the Digital Agenda for Europe) in order to realise the ambitions of the digital transformation, it is worth highlighting the most significant of them.

The Digital Agenda for Europe published by the European Commission on 19 May 2010 (EC Communication 2010) highlighted the key role of information and communication technologies (ICT) in achieving the objectives of the European Union, where the overall objective of the Digital Agenda is to ensure that the digital single market, based on high-speed and ultra-high-speed Internet access and interoperable applications, delivers sustainable economic and social benefits.[6] The

[6] It is important to note that the "Digital Agenda for Europe" was one of the priority issues identified in the Communication from the European Commission of 3 March 2010 on "Europe 2020". The Strategy for Smart, Sustainable and Inclusive Growth" (COM/2010/2020 final). In identifying this as a priority issue, the European Commission has set out the objective to accelerate the roll-out of high-speed internet and to ensure that households and businesses can benefit from the Digital Single Market.

implementation of this first Digital Agenda has achieved several key objectives, such as lowering the cost of electronic communications services,[7] abolishing roaming charges and strengthening consumer protection in telecoms through privacy[8] and general data protection measures (Regulation (EU) 2016/679).[9]

On 6 May 2015, the European Commission in its Communication to the European Parliament, the Council, the European Economic and Social Committee and the Committee of the Regions presented "The Digital Single Market Strategy for Europe" (EC Communication 2015) the aim of which was to ensure better access to digital goods and services across Europe, to foster an optimal environment for digital networks and services, and to increase the growth potential of the digital economy. The strategy stresses, among other things, that the completion of the implementation of the Digital Single Market will allow Europe to remain a global leader in the digital economy, helping European companies to expand their global presence.

"The White Paper on the Future of Europe. Reflections and Scenarios for the EU27 by 2025" (European Commission 2017) was published on 1 March 2017; in this publication the European Commission reiterated the need to strengthen the Single Market, especially in the digital sector, and to increase investment in the infrastructure of this sector. In addition, the European Commission's ongoing monitoring of the implementation of the adopted strategies helps to establish what actions should be taken to ensure an actual efficient implementation of the above-mentioned strategies. In its Communication to the European Parliament, the Council, the European Economic and Social Committee and the Committee of the Regions of 10 May 2017 titled "Mid-term Review on the Implementation of the Digital Single Market Strategy. A Connected Digital Single Market for All" (EC Communication 2017), the European Commission emphasized that a timely and effective Digital Single Market for the European Union requires a clear and stable legal environment which would help stimulate innovation, address market fragmentation and open up access to the new dynamic market to all market players under fair and balanced conditions. What is more, the document pointed out the need to take into account new trends and related challenges, such as those related to online platforms, and to

[7] Regulation (EU) 2022/612 of the European Parliament and of the Council of 6 April 2022 on roaming on public mobile networks within the Union, OJ 2022 L 115, pp. 1–37).

[8] Directive 2009/136/EC of the European Parliament and of the Council of 25 November 2009 amending Directive 2002/22/EC on universal service and users' rights relating to electronic communications networks and services, Directive 2002/58/EC concerning the processing of personal data and the protection of privacy in the electronic communications sector, and Regulation (EC) No 2006/2004 on co-operation between national authorities responsible for the enforcement of consumer protection laws, OJ 2009 L 337, pp. 11–36).

[9] Regulation (EU) 2016/679 and Directive (EU) 2016/680 of the European Parliament and of the Council of 27 April 2016 on the protection of natural persons with regard to the processing of personal data by competent authorities for the purposes of the prevention, investigation, detection or prosecution of criminal offences or the execution of criminal penalties, and on the free movement of such data, and repealing Council Framework Decision 2008/977/JHA (OJ 2016 L 119, p. 89).

provide for actions that will contribute to the development of fair and transparent trading practices on the above-mentioned platforms.

The second Digital Agenda for Europe covering the period from 2020 to 2030, essentially consisted of two Communications published by the European Commission: The Communication on Shaping Europe's Digital Future[10] of 19 February 2020, and the Communication on a Digital Agenda for Europe (2030 Digital Compass: the European way for the Digital Decade) of 9 March 2021.[11]

The European strategy for data,[12] published on 19 February 2020, focused on technology for people, promoted a competitive economy and supported an open, democratic society, with three main lines of action: technology for people; a fair and competitive economy; and an open, democratic and sustainable society. This strategy recalls that the dual challenge set by the European Union—the green transformation and the digital transformation—must be pursued simultaneously. It also highlights the digital component and digital solutions' importance for key sectors such as precision agriculture, transport and energy, in their efforts to achieve the ambitious sustainability goals under the Green Deal for Europe.

On 9 March 2021, the European Commission presented its vision and objectives for a successful digital transformation of Europe by 2030, where it highlighted four key axes that will give a concrete expression to the digital ambition: (1) a digitally-skilled population and highly-skilled digital professionals; (2) a secure, high-performance, and sustainable digital infrastructure; (3) the digital transformation of businesses; and (4) the digitalisation of public services. First, the document points out, among other things, that persons' use of digital technologies and services must comply with applicable legal standards and respect the rights and values inherent in the European model. Second, there is an indication that a safe, open and people-centred digital environment should not only respect the law, but also enable people to better assert their rights, such as the right to privacy and data protection, freedom of expression, children's rights and consumer rights. In addition, the European Commission, mindful of its role as guardian of the Treaties, recalled that digital principles are enshrined in the primary EU law, notably the Treaty on European Union, the Treaty on the Functioning of the European Union, the Charter of Fundamental Rights and the case-law of the Court of Justice of the European Union, as well as in the secondary legal acts.

---

[10] Communication from the European Commission to the European Parliament, the Council, the European Economic and Social Committee and the Committee of the Regions "Shaping Europe's Digital Future" of 19 February 2020 (COM/2020/67 final).

[11] Communication from the European Commission to the European Parliament, the Council, the European Economic and Social Committee and the Committee of the Regions of 9 March 2021, "2030 Digital Compass: The European Way for the Digital Decade" (COM/2021/118 final).

[12] At the same time (19 February 2020), the European Commission published two more documents of major importance for the European Union's digital sector: the White Paper "On Artificial Intelligence. A European approach to competence and trust" (COM/2020/65 final), and Communication to the European Parliament, the Council, the European Economic and Social Committee and the Committee of the Regions "A European Strategy for Data" (COM/2020/66 final).

The European Union takes specific legal measures to ensure adequate protection of fundamental rights in the digital sector. The European Declaration on Digital Rights and Principles (European Declaration 2022) for the Digital Decade of 26 January 2022 sets out commitments, in line with the European Union's fundamental values and rights, to ensure a safe, secure, sustainable and, what is of utmost importance, human-centred digital transformation. The above-mentioned declaration has been issued jointly by the European Parliament, the Council and the European Commission. It is important to note that this Declaration aims at explaining shared political intentions not only by recalling the most relevant rights in the context of the digital transformation but also by making the declaration serve as a reference point for businesses and other relevant actors when developing and deploying new technologies (Part 5 of the Recitals). For this reason, in the European Declaration on the Digital Decade where it refers to Digital Rights and Principles launched by the European Institutions, several key objectives and even concrete commitments have been identified with the aim to contribute to the achievement of the following goals: human-centeredness[13] of the digital transformation; solidarity and inclusion[14]; freedom of choice[15]; participation in the digital public sphere[16]; safety, security and empowerment,[17] as well as sustainability.[18]

On 2 July 2024, the European Commission published the second Report on the State of the Digital Decade (EC Second report, 2024), providing a comprehensive overview of the progress made in the quest to achieve the digital objectives and targets set for 2030 by the Digital Decade Policy Programme for the European Union. The report analyses, among other things, the national Digital Decade Strategic Roadmaps presented by the EU Member States which detail the planned national measures, actions and funding committed to contribute to the EU's digital transformation. The European Commission's analysis shows that the collective

[13] For example, a commitment has been made to take the necessary measures to ensure that the values of the Union and the rights of individuals recognised under the Union law are respected in real life and online, etc.

[14] A commitment is made to ensure that technological solutions respect people's rights, enable their access thereto and increase inclusiveness; to ensure that no one is left behind in the transformation process (elderly people, people with disabilities, etc.); to ensure that all Europeans have access to an accessible, safe and secure digital identity that allows them to use a wide range of online services; etc.

[15] A commitment is made to ensure transparency concerning the use of algorithms and artificial intelligence; to ensure that the online environment is safe, secure and fair and that fundamental rights are protected, etc.

[16] A commitment is made to further ensure the protection of fundamental rights on the internet; in particular, the freedom of expression and freedom of information; to create an online environment that protects people from misinformation and other forms of harmful content; etc.

[17] The aim is to ensure a safe and secure online environment, privacy and personal data control and the protection of children and young people online, etc.

[18] A commitment is made to help develop and deploy sustainable digital technologies that minimise their impact on the environment and society; to develop and deploy digital solutions that have a positive impact on the environment and the climate.

efforts of Member States fall short of the EU's level of ambition, therefore, the Commission calls for the reinforcement of joint European Union action and allocation of additional investment in digital skills, quality connectivity and the uptake of artificial intelligence.[19] It also recommends promoting the use of digital tools to ensure that many more people acquire both basic and specialised digital skills by 2030 (EC Strategy). The EU Member States will have to review and adjust their national roadmaps before 2 December 2024 to align them with the ambition of the Digital Decade Policy Programme; the Commission, in turn, will monitor and assess the implementation of these recommendations and report on the progress made in the next Digital Decade Report in 2025.

Mention should be made of the following most significant legislative measures adopted to date by the European Commission to implement the Digital Agenda for Europe: Digital Services Act (DSA) (Regulation (EU) 2022/2065) which ensures a safe and accountable online environment (the DSA regulates online intermediaries and platforms such as marketplaces, social networks, content sharing platforms, app stores as well as online travel and accommodation platforms); Digital Markets Act (DMA) (Regulation (EU) 2022/1925) which ensures the conditions for fair and open digital markets (introduces a narrowly defined set of objective criteria for a large internet platform to be considered to be an "access controller", which allows the DMA to continue to adequately address the problem of large, systemic internet platforms)[20]; the European Chip Act (Regulation (EU) 2023/1781) which strengthens Europe's competitiveness and resilience in semiconductor technology; the European Digital Identity (Regulation (EU) 2024/1183) which serves as a personal digital wallet for European Union citizens, residents or businesses (to be used for identification or authentication of certain personal information for access to public and private digital services across the European Union; users have full control and freedom of choice over the scope of sharing information); the Artificial Intelligence Act (Regulation (EU) 2024/1689) which aims to improve the functioning of the internal market and promote the uptake of human-centred and reliable artificial intelligence (AI), while ensuring a high level of protection of health, safety, fundamental rights enshrined in the Charter of Fundamental Rights of the European Union, including democracy, the rule of law and the protection of the environment from the detrimental effects of the AI systems in the Union, and by supporting

[19] The key figures are as follows: €250 billion have been allocated from the Next Generation EU Facility for digitisation; 80% of the EU population should have basic digital skills by 2030; in addition, €43 billion will be mobilised in total by 2030 for the implementation of the Chip Act.

[20] Legal doctrine considers that with the adoption of these legal acts, the European Union completed its digital services regulatory reform aimed at achieving two closely linked objectives: first, to create a safe digital space for all users of services, where human rights and fundamental freedoms are protected, and second, to ensure the functioning of open, competitive and fair markets for digital services. As the regulation adopted in the European Union will also apply to service providers established in third countries if they offer their services in the Union, it is likely that the application of the SPA and the SRA will also have an impact on the formulation of international regulatory standards for the operation of online platforms (Kalėda, S.L. 2023, pp. 26 and 40).

innovation; the European Data Strategy (Regulation (EU) 2023/2854)[21] which aims to put the European Union at the forefront of the data-driven society (creating a single market for data will allow data to move freely within the EU and across sectors, benefiting businesses, researchers and public administrations). Mention should be made of the Interoperable Europe Act (Regulation (EU) 2024/903),[22] adopted by the European Parliament and the Council on 13 March 2024, which sets out measures to promote the cross-border interoperability of trans-European digital public services, thus contributing to the interoperability of the underlying networks and information systems through the establishment of a common set of rules and a common governance framework (Art. 1(1) of the Interoperable Europe Act)[23] (it should be noted that interoperability is a key feature of a functioning digital single market, contributing to a more effective implementation of the digital dimensions (European Commission 2024b) of public policy; interoperability in the public sector has a significant impact on the right to free movement of goods, persons, services and capital as enshrined in the Treaties, as complex administrative procedures can create significant obstacles, in particular for small and medium sized enterprises[24]). Finally, the European Union, recognising that state-of-the-art digital network infrastructures are the backbone of a thriving digital economy and society, seeks to make a proper assessment of the needs of Europe's digital infrastructures as well as of the need to initiate the adoption of new legislation (European Commission 2024a).

In summary, the EU's Digital Agenda is a vital component of its twin green and digital transformation objectives. Digital technologies such as AI and the Internet of Things (IoT) are vital in achieving sustainability and climate targets. Since 2010, the EU has implemented major strategies, including the Digital Single Market Strategy, the Digital Compass 2030 and the European Data Strategy, with the aim of building a competitive, secure and inclusive digital economy. Key legislative acts include the Digital Services Act, the Digital Markets Act, the AI Act, the European Digital Identity Act and the European Chips Act. However, the 2024 State of the Digital Decade report highlights gaps in Member States' efforts, emphasising the need for increased investment and greater coordination to meet the 2030 targets.

[21] Regulation (EU) 2023/2854 of the European Parliament and of the Council of 13 December 2023 on harmonised rules on fair access to and use of data and amending Regulation (EU) 2017/2394 and Directive (EU) 2020/1828 (Data Act) (OJ L, 2023/2854, 22.12.2023).

[22] Article 23 of this Regulation provides that it shall apply from 12 July 2024; however, some provisions shall apply from 12 January 2025.

[23] Article 2 of the Regulation 2024/903 provides a definition of the term "cross-border interoperability" which means the ability of the Union entities and public sector bodies of Member States to interact with each other across borders by sharing data, information and knowledge through digital processes in line with the legal, organisational, semantic and technical requirements related to such cross-border interaction.

[24] Recital 1 of the Regulation 2024/903.

4.3 Platforms Work Regulation in the EU

The "road" to the Platform Work Directive. As it has already been mentioned, in its Communication "The European Green Deal" published on 11 December 2019, the European Commission set out a new growth strategy that aims at transforming the European Union into a fair and prosperous society, with a modern, resource-efficient and competitive economy with the level of net emissions of greenhouse gases (GHG) in 2050 equalled to zero and where economic growth is decoupled from resource use. In addition, the strategy aims to protect, conserve and enhance the EU's natural capital, and protect the health and well-being of citizens from environment-related risks and impacts. At the same time, this transition must be fair and inclusive, leaving no one behind (EC Communication (2019), p. 1.) In addition, it should also be kept in mind that the aspect of sustainability should be further embedded into all the fields of EU policy (EC Communication (2019), p. 2.2.). Eventually, the Just Transition Mechanism (Just Transition Mechanism) will target the regions and sectors most in need of transformation and will contribute, among other things, to the objective of protecting citizens and workers (who will be made particularly vulnerable due to the transformation), for example by providing them with access to re-skilling programmes. It should be noted that pro-active re-skilling and up-skilling are necessary to reap the benefits of the ecological transition[25] (EC Communication (2019), p 2.2.).In this context, it should be noted that Art. 3 TEU enshrines one of the objectives of the European Union, i.e., to promote the well-being of their peoples, to work for the sustainable development of Europe based on a highly competitive social market economy, aiming at full employment and social progress. In accordance with Art. 9 TFEU, in defining and implementing its policies and activities, the Union shall take into account the requirements linked to the promotion of a high level of employment, the guarantee of adequate social protection, the fight against social exclusion, and a high level of education, training and protection of human health. Articles 151 to 161 TFEU set out the Union's competence in the field of social policy. Art. 153 TFEU empowers the Union to support and complement the action of the Member States in certain areas (e.g. working conditions, social protection and social protection for workers, equality between women and men in terms of access to the labour market and treatment at work, etc.) in order to attain the objectives of Art. 151 TFEU.[26]

[25] To this end, the proposed "European Social Fund" will play an important role in helping Europe's workforce acquire the skills needed to move from declining to growing sectors and to adapt to new processes.

[26] Art. 151(1) TFEU provides that the Union and the Member States, having in mind fundamental social rights such as those set out in the European Social Charter signed in Turin on 18 October 1961 and in the 1989 Community Charter of the Fundamental Social Rights of Workers, shall have as their objectives the promotion of employment, improved living and working conditions, so as to make possible their harmonisation while the improvement is being maintained, proper social protection, dialogue between management and labour, the development of human resources with a view to lasting high employment and the combating of exclusion.

In addition, the Union may address specific issues, such as the adoption of measures to help ensuring social protection for the self-employed, on the basis of Art. 352 of the TFEU, which provides that where the Union needs to take action to achieve one of the objectives set out in the Treaties, in the areas defined by the Treaties, and where the Treaties do not provide for the requisite powers for that purpose, the Council may, unanimously and acting on a proposal from the European Commission, and subject to the consent of the European Parliament, adopt appropriate measures. In this context, it should be borne in mind that the European Union, in exercising the competences conferred on it by the Member States in the field of social policy and in the adoption of any new legislative measures, observes the principle of subsidiarity, and respects the right of every worker, as enshrined in the Charter of Fundamental Rights of the European Union (the "Charter"), to secure conditions of work in which he or she can work safely and in conditions which respect his or her health and dignity (Art. 31 of the Charter), as well as the workers' right to information and consultation (Art. 27 of the Charter). Finally, under the Inter-institutional Declaration of the European Parliament, the Council and the European Commission on the European Pillar of Social Rights ("the European Pillar of Social Rights"), issued in Gothenburg on 17 November 2017, a shared commitment and the responsibility were taken to provide for implementation at both Union level and Member State level within their respective competences, taking due account of different socioeconomic environments and the diversity of national systems, including the role of social partners, and in accordance with the principles of subsidiarity and proportionality (European Pillar of Social Rights, Recital 17). It should be noted that Recital 15 of the European Pillars of Social Rights states that the term "workers" used in this document concerns all persons in employment, regardless of their employment status, modality and duration; and Principle 5 of the European Pillar of Social rights provides that, regardless of the type and duration of the employment relationship, workers have the right to fair and equal treatment regarding working conditions, access to social protection and training; that, in accordance with legislation and collective agreements, the necessary flexibility for employers to adapt swiftly to changes in the economic context is to be ensured; and that innovative forms of work that ensure quality working conditions are to be fostered, that entrepreneurship and self-employment are to be encouraged and that occupational mobility is to be facilitated. In accordance with Principle 12 of the European Pillar of Social Rights, regardless of the type and duration of their employment relationship, workers, and, under comparable conditions, self-employed persons, have the right to adequate social protection (Interinstitutional Proclamation 2017).[27]

Finally, it has been repeatedly mentioned, that the digital transformation touches on various areas of activity in the European Union and has a major impact on the

[27] On 4 March 2021, the European Commission published a Communication to the European Parliament, the Council, the Economic and Social Committee and the Committee of the Regions on "An Action Plan for a European Pillar of Social Rights" (Brussels, 4.3.2021, COM (2021)102 final).

European Union's economy; and that its labour markets, and digital work platforms[28] are becoming an important element of this new emerging socio-economic environment, as they stimulate innovative services and new business models, and provide a wide range of opportunities for customers and businesses. However, more and more attention is given to the fact that introduction of new forms of work organisation on digital labour platforms may jeopardise existing rights and obligations in relation to labour law and social protection. In this context, the European Union has not only had to continue to pursue its most recent ambitions, such as sustainability and digital transformation, but at the same time strive for efficiency in other policy areas, including the field of social policy.

In the light of the above-mentioned facts, on 19 December 2021, the European Commission presented a Proposal for the Directive of the European Parliament and of the Council on Improving Working Conditions in Platform Work (the "Proposal for the Directive")[29] which aimed at improving the working conditions and the social rights of persons working through digital platforms. Among other aspects, the Proposal included an objective of supporting the conditions for the sustainable growth of the digital platforms in the Union (hereinafter referred to as "the Proposal for the Directive"). Alongside with this Proposal for the Directive, the European Commission published Communication "Better Working Conditions for a Stronger Social Europe. Harnessing the full Benefits of Digitalisation for the Future of Work" (EC Communication 2021). With this Communication, the European Commission called on Member States, social partners and all stakeholders to take concrete measures to improve the working conditions related to platform work, where the European Commission's main objective is to promote the benefits of the digital transformation, while safeguarding the European social market economy. In the above-mentioned Communication, the European Commission recalls that the Union has already set the tone on a global level in terms of addressing key issues such as personal data protection and the regulation of artificial intelligence systems; in addition, it indicated that setting global standards can improve legal clarity for digital labour platforms across the globe and, therefore, boost the sustainable growth of the platform economy (EC Communication 2021, part 7).

The submission of the European Commission's Proposal for the Directive, therefore, can be regarded as the final stage in a long process that has led to the recognition of the need to regulate platform work at the European Union level. The need to regulate platforms by adopting uniform regulatory rules was determined by the necessity to create a level playing field for all platforms operating in the EU. For a considerable period of time prior to the submission of the Proposal for the Directive, there had been a debate in the European Union, which was confirmed by various documents adopted by the European Union institutions. The following could serve as an example: in its Communication of 6 May 2015, the European Commission

---

[28] As defined in the Proposal for the Directive.

[29] European Commission's Proposal for the Directive of the European Parliament and of the Council on Improving Working Conditions in Platform Work (Brussels, 9.12.2021, COM (2021) 762 final, 2021/0414 (COD)).

presented "A Digital Single Market Strategy for Europe" (EC Communication 2015), setting out its ambition to complete the Digital Single Market as soon as possible and to play an active role in its implementation in close cooperation with all stakeholders. Part 3 of this Communication stated that „the market power of some online platforms potentially raises concerns, particularly in relation to the most powerful platforms whose importance for other market participants is becoming increasingly critical. In addition, the Communication highlighted the role of platforms where some platforms have proven to be innovators in the digital economy helping smaller businesses to move online and reach new markets; besides, the document drew attention to the probability that potentially new regulatory questions may appear (EC Communication 2015, Part 3). The European Commission's Communication of 25 May 2016 "Online Platforms and the Digital Single Market Opportunities and Challenges for Europe" (EC Communication 2016) reconfirmed that online platforms play a key role in innovation and growth in the Digital Single Market, and underlined the need to establish strong platform ecosystems in Europe that could complement or reinforce the existing legislation that governs certain activities of online platforms (EC Communication 2016, Part 6).

It should be noted that (prior to the submission of the Proposal for the Directive by the European Commission) previous European Union legislation in the field of social protection (mostly Directives) were making references to platform workers. Two trends can essentially be observed: the first is the adoption of the European Union legislation with binding force under Art. 288 TFEU, which also refers to platforms' employees, and the second one is the adoption of non-binding acts which may serve as a good incentive to initiate legislative procedures in the EU.

The first trend may be illustrated by the fact of the adoption on 20 June 2019 of Directive (EU) 2019/1152 on transparent and predictable working conditions (Directive (EU) 2019/1152)[30] in the European Union which includes measures to protect the working conditions of people in non-standard employment relationships, including digital platform workers. Recital 8 of Directive 2019/1152 states that in its case law,[31] the Court of Justice of the European Union (hereinafter referred to as "the Court of Justice", "the CJEU") has established criteria for determining the status of a worker. It has also been noted that the implementation of this Directive should take into account the interpretation of those criteria by the Court of Justice. In addition, it has been stated that domestic workers, on-demand workers, intermittent workers, voucher based-workers, platform workers, trainees and apprentices

[30] Art. 21 of the Directive provides that Member States have to take all the measures necessary to comply with this Directive by 1 August 2022, at the latest.

[31] See the case law of the Court of Justice referred to in Recital 8 of Directive 2009/1152: judgments of 3 July 1986, *Lawrie-Blum* (66/85, EU:C:1986:284); of 14 October 2010 *Union syndicale Solidaires Isère* (C-428/09, EU:C:2010:612); of 9 July 2015, *Balkaya* (C-229/14, EU:C:2015:455); of 4 December 2014, *FNV Kunsten Informatieen Media* (C-413/13, EU:C:2014:2411); and of 17 November 2016 *Betriebsrat der Ruhrlandklinik* (C-216/15, EU:C:2016:883). It should be noted that in these cases before the Court of Justice, the circumstances of the dispute did not concern persons performing platform work.

could fall within the scope of Directive 2019/1152, provided they fulfil the respective criteria. The document presents a clarification that genuinely self-employed persons should not fall within the scope of this Directive since they do not fulfil the Directive's criteria. It should be noted that both in the national implementation of this Directive and, where appropriate, in its direct application in practice, in cases where factual and legal circumstances so allow, it should be borne in mind that Art. 1 of Directive 2019/1152, which defines the purpose, subject-matter and scope of this Directive,[32] should be read in conjunction with Recital 8 of this Directive. Essentially the same wording on the scope of this Directive can be found in Directive (EU) 2022/2041 of 19 October 2022 on adequate minimum wages in the European Union (Directive (EU) 2022/2041) which envisages that the Directive could apply, inter alia, to platform workers (Directive 2022/2041, Recital 21). Directive 2022/2041 aims to improve the adequacy of minimum wages and increase workers' access to the protection in terms of minimum wages. Directive (EU) 2023/970 of 10 May 2023, which reinforces the application of the principle (Directive (EU) 2023/970) of equal pay for men and women for equal work or work of equal value by introducing pay transparency and enforcement mechanisms, also specifies that platform workers fall within the scope of this Directive (Directive 2023/970, Recital 18). Meanwhile, the aforementioned "European Declaration on Digital Rights and Principles for the Digital Decade", published by the European Commission on 26 January 2022, neither contains any specific provisions concerning digital (online) platforms workers, nor makes any specific reference to such workers. Chapter II "Solidarity and Inclusion" of the European Declaration states that everyone should have access to technologies that unite but not divide people, and that the digital transformation should contribute to creating a fair, inclusive society and the economy of the Union. Chapter II "Solidarity and Inclusion" of the Declaration, under the heading "Working Conditions", stipulates that everyone has the right to fair, just, healthy and safe working conditions and appropriate protection both in the digital environment and in the physical workplace, regardless of his or her employment status, modality or duration.

The second trend is reflected in the Council Recommendation of 8 November 2019 on access to social protection (Recommendation, 2019) for workers and the self-employed persons; the document, among other aspects, mention platform workers.[33] In particular, the Council Recommendation pointed out that the Union's labour markets are characterised by a wide range of forms of employment relationships as well as self-employment in addition to open-ended, full-time contracts,

---

[32] Art. 1(2) of Directive 2019/1152 stated that this Directive lays down minimum rights that apply to every worker in the Union who has an employment contract or employment relationship as defined by the law, collective agreements or practice in force in each Member State with consideration to the case-law of the Court of Justice.

[33] It should be noted that this Recommendation adopted by the Council is also referred to in Recital 11 of the Directive on the improvement of working conditions on digital platforms, which confirms the statement that acts adopted by the European Union institutions of a non-binding nature usually have an impact on the initiation of the adoption of European Union legislation.

some of which, such as on-demand work, voucher-based work and platform work, have developed more recently and increased in importance since the 2000s (Recital 11 of the Recommendation). Recital 18 of this Recommendation notes that in some Member States, certain categories of workers, such as short part-time workers, seasonal workers, on-demand workers, platform workers and those on temporary agency contracts or traineeships are excluded from social protection schemes. Moreover, it has been stated that workers who do not have full-time, open-ended contracts can encounter difficulties in being effectively covered by social protection measures, because they may not fulfil entitlement criteria for receiving benefits from contribution-based social protection schemes. Finally, in its Recommendation on access to social protection for workers and the self-employed persons, the Council recommended that in line with this Recommendation, Member States should ensure that both workers and self-employed persons have access to an effective and adequate social protection. It should be noted that this Recommendation covers unemployment, sickness and health, maternity and paternity, invalidity, old-age and survivors' benefits, and benefits in respect to accidents at work and occupational diseases. As part of performing its function of monitoring the application of this Recommendation, the European Commission submitted a Report (Report, 2023) to the Council on 31 January 2023 which presents the main conclusions on the application and implementation of this Recommendation in the Member States. It follows from the Report that reforms are needed to improve the participation of specific categories of people in social protection systems, in particular the self-employed persons or those working on non-standard contracts or in specific sectors (domestic services, culture) where non-standard forms of work are widespread; besides, groups of non-standard workers and the self-employed persons are covered by social protection measures to a lesser extent than others (e.g. by not being able to benefit from unemployment, sickness or other benefits). The European Commission also drew attention, among other things, to the need to regulate work on digital platforms thus ensuring better access to formal social protection; thereby in essence confirming the continued relevance of the need for the adoption of the proposed Directive on improving the conditions of work on digital platforms which had been proposed back in 2021. In addition, in the aforementioned report, the European Commission provided information on the level of social protection for digital platform workers in the Member States, indicating that over the past few years, the working conditions of platform workers have been at the centre of social policy debate with a particular focus on their employment status (self-employed or employees) and its impact on social protection coverage (Report 2023, p. 15).

It has been indicated that platform workers' access to social protection had been discussed in 11 NIPs (BE, DE, EE, FR, HR, IT, CY, LT, PT, RO and SI) with most of them considering it to be a challenge. Five Member States (BE, IT, CY, RO and SI) included concrete measures in their NIPs, while four Member States referred generally to the need to take action in this area in future (DE, EE, LT and PT). For instance, Cyprus counts platform workers among the group of people on non-standard contracts whose access to benefits (unemployment, accidents at work) should be extended through social insurance reform; Belgium and Romania announce legislative changes to ensure adequate social protection for platform workers, including those who are self-employed. Moreover, it has been stressed that since submitting their NIPs, some Member States (Greece, Spain, and France) have taken further action concerning platform workers, also by way of implementation of the Recovery and resilience plans. Portugal has announced about taking further measures, and other countries (Germany, Croatia, Luxembourg and the Netherlands) at the time of the preparation of the Report were discussing possible changes in their relevant legislation (Report 2023, p. 16).[34]

Finally, on 30 September 2022, the European Commission published its Communication "Guidelines on the application of Union competition law to collective agreements regarding the working conditions of solo self-employed persons" (the Guidelines) (EC Communication 2022). The Guidelines explain how the Commission will apply the Union competition law without prejudice to the application of other rules or principles of the Union law, i.e., the Guidelines do not create any social rights or obligations and do not affect the prerogatives of Member States in social policy or the autonomy of the social partners; besides, the Guidelines are without prejudice to the definitions of the terms 'worker' or 'self-employed person' under national law, or the possibility for solo self-employed persons to seek reclassification of their employment status (or the national authorities/courts to assess such cases) under Union or national law. Finally the Guidelines merely clarify the conditions under which certain solo self-employed persons and their counterparty/-ies can enter into collective negotiations and agreements without running the risk of infringing Art. 101 TFEU (EC Communication, 2022, point 10). It should be noted that the Guidelines contain the same definition of "digital labour platform" as the European Commission's Proposal for the Directive, and indicate a commitment to consider the need to update the definitions.

Guidelines if the definitions of the terms used in the adopted Platform Work Directive differ substantially. Part 3 of the Guidelines, "Solo self-employed persons working through digital labour platforms", provides examples and explanations of how digital labour platforms differ from other online platforms, and outlines the circumstances under which collective agreements between solo self-employed persons and digital labour platforms relating to working conditions fall outside the scope of Art. 101 TFEU (EC Communication, 2022, points 28–31).

Platform Work Directive On 23 October 2024 the European Parliament and the Council adopted the Directive (EU) 2024/2831 on improving working conditions in platform work (the "Platform Work Directive") (Directive (EU) 2024/2831). This directive will enter into force on 1 December 2024. Member States shall bring into

[34] In its Conclusion of 9 October 2023, which the Council presented after taking note of the European Commission's report, the Council stressed, inter alia, that the social protection of the self-employed persons is particularly relevant in the current process of the transformation of ways of working, and that nowadays, significant numbers of people combine dependent employment and self-employment or switch between them; therefore, cross-border mobility in case of platform work may pose challenges for the self-employed that need to be addressed (Brussels, 9.10.2023, 13,934/23, p. 26).

force the laws, regulations and administrative provisions necessary to complywith this directive by 2 December 2026.

Context and Objectives of the Platform Work Directive The revenues in the digital labour platform economy in the EU are estimated to have grown by around 500% during the past 5 years.[35] According to data from 2022, over 28 million people in the EU were working through Digital labour platforms; their number is expected to reach 43 million by 2025 (Council of the EU 2024).

It should be noted that digital labour platforms promote innovative services and new business models, and create many opportunities for consumers and businesses. Besides, digital platform workers (location-based platforms and online web-based platforms) are involved in various activities (Council of the EU 2024). It is, therefore, essential that the persons working through digital platforms have access to adequate working conditions and guarantees of social protection conditions.

It should be noted that, over time, it has had to be acknowledged that the new forms of work organisation introduced by digital labour platforms are putting at risk the existing rights and obligations in terms of labour law and social protection. The European Commission, in order to initiate procedures for the adoption of European Union legislation, has first of all to make a very good assessment of the need for any new legislation and of the major challenges in a given area, as later it helps to identify the most appropriate means of tackling these challenges. The European Commission was, therefore, able to draw on the results of the studies and, after consultation with the various stakeholder groups, to identify the following main problematic aspects of working through digital platforms which are as follows:

- most people working through digital platforms have been classified as self-employed; misclassification of employment status can lead to poor working conditions and inadequate social protection for people working through digital platforms, as well as denying them the rights and protections to which they are entitled as workers; these rights include the right to a minimum wage, working time rules, occupational safety and health, equal pay for men and women and the right to paid holidays, as well as better access to social protection against accidents at work, unemployment, sickness and old age;
- digital work platforms use automated systems to match labour supply and demand, allowing digital platforms to assign tasks, monitor, evaluate and make decisions about the people who work on them, this is the practice often referred to as algorithmic management; as algorithmic management is relatively new and, with the exception of the European Union's data protection rules, is a largely unregulated phenomenon in the digital platform economy, it poses challenges for both the employees of digital labour platforms and the self-employed persons working through such platforms;

[35] Paragraph 1 of the Explanatory Memorandum to the Proposal for a Directive.

- lack of traceability and transparency; the problem of traceability is particularly acute when digital platforms operate on a cross-border basis, making it unclear where and by whom digital platforms are operated; this makes it difficult for the relevant national authorities to enforce existing obligations, including in the area of social protection contributions.

The importance of these challenges identified by the European Commission is confirmed by statistics showing how many people can be directly affected by the inappropriate determination of the employment status of persons working through digital platforms (Council of the EU 2024).

Thus, having identified the emerging challenges in the area of social protection for persons working through digital platforms, in its Proposal for the Directive, the European Commission was able to formulate the general objective of improving the working conditions and social rights of persons working through digital platforms, including, among other things, efforts to foster the conditions for the sustained growth of digital platforms in the EU. The following specific objectives were identified to contribute to this overall objective:

1. to ensure that people working through digital platforms have (or can obtain) a fair employment status, based on their actual relationship with the digital labour platform, and have access to applicable employment and social protection rights (classification of work through digital platforms);
2. to ensure fairness, transparency and accountability of algorithmic management in the context of work through digital platforms; and
3. to increase transparency, traceability and awareness of changes in the way persons work through digital platforms, and improve enforcement of the applicable rules for all persons working through digital platforms, including those performing work in several countries.

As regards the legal basis of the Platform Work Directive and the principles of subsidiarity and proportionality, it should be noted that this Directive is based on Art. 153(1) (b), 153(2) (b) and 16(2) TFEU. Prior to the presentation of the Proposal for the Directive, an opinion prevailed that national action alone would not achieve the fundamental objectives of the European Union, based on the Treaty, of fostering sustainable economic growth and social progress, as Member States might be reluctant to adopt stricter rules or to strictly enforce compliance with the existing labour standards. Such a conclusion was based, inter alia, on an investigation whereby it was established that more than 100 court decisions and 15 administrative decisions dealing with the employment status of people working through platforms have been observed in the Member States, with varying outcomes but predominantly in favour of reclassifying people working through platforms as workers.[36] Moreover, taking

[36] It should be noted that Recital 7 of the Platform Work Directive also states that Court cases in several Member States have shown the persistence of misclassification of the employment status in certain types of platform work, in particular in sectors where digital labour platforms exert a certain degree of direction or control. While digital labour platforms frequently classify persons work-

into account the dual objective of the Platform Work Directive to improve the conditions for working on digital platforms and the protection of personal data, it has been assessed that this objective cannot be sufficiently achieved by the Member States and can, therefore, by reason of the need to lay down common minimum requirements, be better achieved at the level of the Union; where the Union may adopt measures in accordance with the principle of subsidiarity as set out in Art. 5 TEU. The Platform Work Directive also ensures compliance with the principle of proportionality by not going beyond what is necessary to achieve the objective (Platform Work Directive, Recital 67). It should be noted that the Platform Work Directive lays down minimum requirements, thus preserving the Member States' prerogative to introduce or maintain more favourable provisions for the persons working through digital platforms. The rights valid under the existing legal framework should continue to apply, including those regarding the mechanisms for establishing the existence of an employment relationship unless this Directive establishes more favourable provisions. The implementation of this Directive cannot be used to reduce the existing rights set out in existing Union or national law in this field, nor can it constitute valid grounds for reducing the general level of protection in the field covered by this Directive as well as existing prerogatives conferred on representatives. (Recital 68 of the Platform Work Directive).

Subject Matter and Scope The Platform Work Directive consists of VI chapters reflecting the objectives pursued by this Directive: general provisions (I); employment status (II); algorithmic management (III); transparency on platform work (IV); remedies and enforcement (V); final provisions (VI).

The purpose of this Directive is to improve the working conditions of persons performing platform work and the protection of personal data[37] (Art. 1(1) of the Platform Work Directive):

(a) by establishing measures to facilitate the correct determination of the employment status of persons performing digital platform work;
(b) by promoting transparency, fairness[38] and accountability in algorithmic management in platform work and by improving transparency in platform work, and
(c) by increasing transparency about working on digital platforms, including in cross-border situations.

ing through them as self-employed or "independent contractors", many courts have found that platforms exercise de facto direction and control over those persons, often integrating them in their main business activities. Those court cases have therefore reclassified purportedly self-employed persons as workers employed by the platforms.

[37] Recital 20 of the Platform Work Directive states that digital labour platforms differ from other online platforms as they use automated monitoring or decision-making systems to organise work performed by individuals at the request, one-off or repeated, of the recipient of a service provided by the platform.

[38] It should be noted that human supervision was foreseen after the discussion of the Proposal for the Directive in the European Parliament and the Council.

Art. 1(2) of the Platform Work Directive defines the subjective scope of application of the Directive, which covers all persons working on digital platforms in the Union under an employment contract or employment relationship within the meaning of the law in force in each Member State, in accordance with the applicable law or the collective agreements or the practice in force in each Member State, in the light of the case-law of the Court of Justice of the European Union.[39] As the European Commission pointed out in its Proposal for the Directive, such a reference to the case law of the Court of Justice is made in cases where the employment status of a person working on a digital platform is not clear (including in cases of fictitious self-employment) in order to allow for a correct determination of that status.

In accordance with Art. 1(1) of the Platform Work Directive, this Directive applies to digital labour platforms organising platform work performed in the Union, irrespective of their place of establishment and irrespective of the law otherwise applicable.

Definitions Art. 2(1) of the Platform Work Directive defines certain terms and concepts necessary for the application and interpretation of the provisions of this Directive, such as "digital labour platform", "platform work" and "person performing platform work. It should be noted that the list of terms defined in this Article of the Platform Work Directive has expanded considerably after the discussion on the Proposal for the Directive in the European Parliament and in the Council, with the addition of terms such as "intermediary",[40] "representatives", "platform workers'

[39] The same reference to the case law of the Court of Justice is made in Recital 18 of the Platform Work Directive, but in this context there is no reference to specific judgments of the Court of Justice, as this Court has not yet dealt with a case which has raised issues concerning the status of a platform worker (for example, the above-mentioned Directive 2019/1152, contains a reference to specific judgments of the Court of Justice that have established criteria for the status of workers). However, it should be noted that Recital 29 of the Directive on forms of employment refers to the case-law of the Court of Justice concerning the consequences of false declarations of self-employment and the impact of formal recognition as self-employed person under national law on the application of European Union law. In addition, in this context, a number of cases can be mentioned which dealt with digital platforms, but in these cases the Court of Justice dealt with the application of Union law on services to a wide range of activities based on the exchange economy carried out via digital platforms. For example, see Judgements of 20 December 2017, *Asociación Profesional Elite Taxi* (C-434/15, EU:C:2017:981); 10 April 2018, *Uber France* (C-320/16, EU:C:2018:221); 19 December 2019, *Airbnb Ireland* (C-390/18, EU:C:2019:1112); and of 22 September 2020, *Cali Apartments and HX* (C-724/18 and C-727/18, EU:C:2020:743). It is recognised in legal doctrine that the *Asociación Profesional Elite Taxi* and *Airbnb Ireland* judgments provided a "test" for the proper "legal qualification" of the activities carried out by digital platforms and subsequently for the determination of the applicable European Union law (see Grozdanovski, L. Les services fournis par les platforms numériques: quelle qualification juridique pour quell enjeux? Journal de tribunaux, 2020/22, n°6818, p. 449–455).

[40] "Intermediary" means a natural or legal person who, for the purpose of providing work on or through a digital work platform, (a) establishes a contractual relationship with that digital work platform and the person working on the digital platforms, or (b) is part of the subcontracting chain linking that digital work platform and the person working on the digital platform. It should be noted that, following deliberations at the European Parliament and the Council, the Platform Work

representatives", "automated monitoring systems", and "automated decision-making systems".

It should be noted that according to Art. 2 of the Platform Work Directive, a person performing platform work means any natural person performing platform work, irrespective of the contractual designation of the relationship between that individual and the digital labour platform by the parties involved.

In accordance with Art. 2 of the Platform Work Directive, platform worker means any person performing platform work who has an employment contract or employment relationship as defined by the law of a Member State, collective agreements or practice in force in the Member States with consideration to the case-law of the Court of Justice.

In addition, Art. 2(2) of the Platform Work Directive states that the definition of digital labour platforms laid down in paragraph 1, point (1) shall not include providers of a service whose primary purpose is to exploit or share assets or which allow non-professionals to resell goods.[41]

Employment Status The new Platform Work Directive establishes a presumption of an employment relationship (as opposed to self-employment) whenever the facts support it. Art. 4(1) of this Directive obliges Member States to establish appropriate and effective procedures to verify and ensure the proper determination of the employment status of persons working on digital platforms in order to establish the existence of an employment relationship within the meaning of the law in force in the Member States, of collective agreements or of the applicable practices, in the light of the case-law of the Court of Justice, including through the application of the presumption of the existence of an employment relationship as referred to in Art. 5 of this Directive. The European Commission based Art. 4(1) of the Proposal for the Directive on the need to ensure that the employment status of persons working on digital platforms is correctly identified and that persons who may have been misclassified can be reclassified.[42] The European Commission believes that this article

Directive includes a specific Art. 3 setting out the obligations of the intermediary in relation to persons working on digital platforms.

[41] This clarification has been included in the text of the Platform Work Directive following discussions at the European Parliament and the Council.

[42] For example, the French delegation's statement of 12 June 2023 on the Proposal for the Directive pointed out that the legal presumption mechanism aimed at facilitating a proper classification of the employment status of persons working on digital platforms would only be effective and relevant on condition that it did not apply to genuinely self-employed individuals. The need for this presumption to be based on clear, transparent and legally predictable conditions to be met was also underlined (10,107/23 ADD 3). The Belgian, Spanish, Luxembourg, Maltese, Dutch, Portuguese, Romanian, Slovenian and Spanish delegations took the same position, pointing out in their jointly adopted declaration of 12 June 2023, inter alia, that the rebuttable presumption of the legal presumption of the employment relationship provided for in the Proposal for the Directive should be applied in accordance with clear and transparent norms and mechanisms, which are generally applicable to all the Member States, and which are in line with the case-law of the Court of Justice of the European Union and the jurisprudence of national courts (10,107/23 ADD 2). The Lithuanian Delegation's statement of 12 June 2023 also stresses, inter alia, that the legal presumption, its cri-

will contribute to the possibility to allow persons that are possibly misclassified as self-employed workers (bogus self-employment) to have access to working conditions laid down in the Union or national law, taking into account their actual employment status. Art. 4(2) of the Platform Work Directive clarifies that the determination of the existence of an employment relationship should be based primarily on the facts relating to the actual performance of the work (the "preponderance of the facts" principle), and including the use of automated monitoring or decision-making systems in the organisation of work on the digital platforms.[43] However, it is also stated that it is irrelevant how the relationship is classified in any contractual arrangement that may have been agreed between the parties involved. Moreover, if the existence of an employment relationship is established, the party or parties assuming the employer's obligations shall be clearly identified in accordance with the legal systems of the Member States (Art. 4(3) of the Platform Work Directive[44]).

Legal Presumption The Platform Work Directive obliges the Member States to establish an efficient rebuttable legal presumption of employment at national level, aiming to correct the imbalance of power between the digital labour platform and the person performing platform work (Parlement européen; 20,240. The burden of proof lies with the platform, meaning that it is up to the platform to prove that there is no employment relationship (Art. 5(1-2) of the Platform Work Directive). According to Arti. 5(3) of the Platform Work Directive, the above-mentioned legal presumption applies in all relevant administrative or judicial proceedings where the question of the proper employment status of a digital platform worker arises. It also provides that the legal presumption does not apply to proceedings relating to tax, criminal and social protection matters, but leaves it open to Member States to apply the legal presumption in those proceedings in accordance with their national law. In addition, Art. 5(4) and (5) of the Platform Work Directive gives digital platform workers and their representatives, as well as the competent national authority, the right to initiate a process to determine the exact employment status of a digital platform worker. Art. 5(6) of the Platform Work Directive also provides that the legal presumption should apply to factual situations before the deadline for transposition of the Directive into national law. It should be noted that the wording of Art. 5 of the Platform Work Directive adopted by the European Parliament and the Council differs from the first version of the Article proposed by the European Commission, as it no longer contains the list[45] of criteria proposed by the European Commission to

---

teria, the requirements for the application of the legal presumption, the application of the legal presumption and the rebuttal of the legal presumption, should be proportionate and should not create an administrative burden for genuinely self-employed persons (10,107/23 ADD 1).

[43] This clarification has been included in the text of the Platform Work Directive following discussions at the European Parliament and the Council.

[44] Art. 4(3) of the Directive has been included in this version of the Platform Work Directive following discussions at the European Parliament and the Council.

[45] For example, effectively setting or defining wage ceilings; requiring a person working on a digital platform to comply with specific mandatory rules on arrival, treatment of the service recipient

show that a digital work platform is controlling the performance of the work, nor the requirement that at least two of the indicators must be met for the presumption to apply. However, the list of auxiliary measures proposed by the European Commission to be applied by the Member States to ensure an effective implementation of and compliance with the legal presumption is set out in a separate Art. 6 of the Platform Work Directive, entitled "Framework of supporting measures". It should be noted that this new provision[46] of the Platform Work Directive provides, inter alia, for the obligation to develop appropriate guidance, including in the form of concrete and practical recommendations, for digital labour platforms, persons performing platform work and the social partners (Art: 6(a) of the Platform Work Directive). In addition, Member States must develop guidance and establish appropriate procedures for competent national authorities to proactively identify, target and prosecute digital labour platforms which do not comply with the rules on correct determination of the employment status (Art. 6(b) of the Platform Work Directive). Member States must also provide for effective controls and inspections conducted by national authorities, in line with national law or practice, while ensuring that such controls and inspections are proportionate and non-discriminatory (Art. 6(c) of the Platform Work Directive). It should be noted that Art. 6(d) of the Platform Work Directive imposes a new obligation on Member States to provide for appropriate training[47] for competent national authorities and provide for the availability of technical expertise in the field of algorithmic management in order to enable those authorities to carry out the tasks envisaged under Art: 6(b) of the Platform Work Directive.

Algorithmic Management This is the first case in the EU where a Directive regulates the use of algorithms at work (Parlement européen 2024). The new Platform Work Directive aims to ensure that a person performing platform work cannot be fired or dismissed on the basis of a decision taken by an algorithm or an automated decision-making system. Instead, efforts are made to guarantee that digital labour platforms were supposed to ensure the prevalence of human oversight on important decisions directly affecting the persons performing platform work. The European Union legislator notes in the Platform Work Directive that algorithm-based technologies, including automated monitoring or decision-making systems (Recital 4 of the Platform Work Directive), are increasingly replacing the functions usually performed by managers in businesses, such as allocating tasks, the pricing of individual assignments, determining working schedules, giving instructions, evaluating the work performed, providing incentives or imposing sanctions. In addition, digital labour platforms in particular use such algorithmic systems as a standard way of organising and managing platform work through their infrastructure (Platform Work Directive, Recital 8). Thus, after defining which algorithm-based technologies

or performance of the work; supervising the performance of the work or checking the quality of the results of the work, including by electronic means; etc.

[46] Art. 6 of the Directive, entitled "Framework of supporting measures", was included in the Directive following discussions at the European Parliament and the Council.

[47] The European Commission's Proposal for the Directive did not include such an obligation.

are relevant for work on digital platforms, Art. 2 of the Platform Work Directive defines the terms "automated monitoring systems"[48] and "automated decision-making systems".[49]

With regard to algorithmic governance, it should be recalled, in particular, that according to Art. 1(1) of the Platform Work Directive, the main objective of this Directive, namely the improvement of working conditions and the protection of personal data in the context of work on digital platforms, will be pursued, inter alia, by promoting transparency, fairness, human oversight, safety and accountability in algorithmic management of platform work.

Recital 17 of the Platform Work Directive provides, inter alia, in relation to Art. 16 TEU,[50] that this Directive establishes rules to improve the protection of natural persons performing platform work regarding the processing of their personal data by increasing transparency, fairness and accountability of relevant algorithmic management procedures in platform work. In this respect, it is important to note that the final version of the Platform Work Directive has been supplemented by specific provisions to ensure data protection—Art. 7 "Limitations on processing of personal data by means of automated monitoring or decision-making systems" and Art. 8 "Data Protection Impact Assessment". Art. 7(1) and (2) of the Platform Work Directive thus establishes what personal data cannot be processed by digital work platforms using automated monitoring and decision-making systems and provides that this restriction applies to all persons working on digital platforms for all the duration of the procedure, i.e. from the start of the recruitment or selection procedure.[51] According to Art. 8(1) of the Platform Work Directive, processing of personal data by a digital labour platform by means of automated monitoring and decision-making systems is a type of processing likely to result in a high risk to the

[48] In accordance with Art. 2(1)(8) of the Platform Work Directive, these systems mean systems which are used for, or support monitoring, supervising or evaluating the work performance of persons performing platform work or the activities carried out within the work environment, including collecting personal data, through electronic means.

[49] In accordance with Art. 2(1)(9) of the Platform Work Directive, automated decision-making systems' means systems which are used to take or support, through electronic means, decisions that significantly affect persons performing platform work, including the working conditions of platform workers, in particular decisions affecting their recruitment, access to and organisation of work assignments, their earnings including the pricing of individual assignments, their safety and health, their working time, their access to training, promotion or its equivalent, their contractual status, including the restriction, suspension or termination of their account.

[50] Art. 16(1) TFEU provides that everyone has the right to the protection of his or her personal data.

[51] For example, it shall not process any personal data on the emotional or psychological state of the person performing platform work; shall not process any personal data in relation to private conversations, including exchanges with other persons performing platform work and their representatives; shall not process any biometric data of a person performing platform work, etc. See Recitals 40 and 41 of the Platform Work Directive for certain limitations on how digital work platforms may process personal data through automated monitoring and decision-making systems. The latter part provides for other categories of data that should not be processed by digital platforms, such as personal data that can be used to predict racial or ethnic origin, migration status, political opinions, trade union membership, etc.

rights and freedoms of natural persons within the meaning of Art. 35(1)[52] of Regulation (EU) 2016/679. It is also envisaged, in accordance with this provision of this Directive, that when carrying out, in accordance with Art. 35(1) of the Regulation (EU) 2016/679, an assessment of the impact of the processing of personal data by means of automated monitoring and decision-making systems on the protection of the personal data of individuals working on digital platforms, including the limitations on the processing of the personal data as set out in Art. 7 of the Platform Work Directive, it shall be intended to seek the views[53] of individuals working on digital platforms and of their representatives, when acting in the capacity of a controller, within the meaning of point 7 of Art. 4 of the Regulation (EU) 2016/679.

The objective of promoting transparency and fairness in algorithmic governance should be facilitated by proper implementation of Articles 9 to 11 of the Platform Work Directive in the domestic law of the Member States and the subsequent effective application and monitoring of these provisions in practice. Firstly, Art. 9[54] of the Platform Work Directive sets out the measures that Member States should take to ensure the transparency of automated monitoring or decision-making systems. In accordance with Art. 9(1) of this Directive, Member States shall require digital labour platforms to inform persons performing platform work, platform workers' representatives and, upon request, competent national authorities, of the use of automated monitoring or decision-making systems. In addition, the Platform Work Directive sets out what information Member States may require to be provided with and when, concerning separate automated decision-making systems and automated monitoring systems, including information on the use of these systems, as well as their implementation, monitoring, etc. What should be emphasized is, first, a strong focus on the information relating to personal data (e.g. recipients or categories of recipients of personal data processed by automated monitoring systems, the way how decisions taken by automated decision-making systems are affected by the personal data of the person working on the digital platform, etc.[55]). Second, Art.

[52] Under Art. 35 (1) ("Data protection impact assessment") of the Regulation (EU) 2016/679: Where a type of processing in particular using new technologies, and taking into account the nature, scope, context and purposes of the processing, is likely to result in a high risk to the rights and freedoms of natural persons, the controller shall, prior to the processing, carry out an assessment of the impact of the envisaged processing operations on the protection of personal data. A single assessment may address a set of similar processing operations that present similar high risks.

[53] See Recital 39 of the Platform Work Directive, which provides, inter alia, that this Directive lays down specific rules complementary to the Regulation (EU) 2016/679, in relation to the processing of personal data in the context of the processing of personal data through the use of automated systems in the context of the work on digital platforms, thus ensuring a higher level of protection of the personal data of individuals who perform platform work.

[54] This is a new and much more detailed version of Art. 9 of the Platform Work Directive, based on the former Art. 6 in the European Commission's Proposal for the Directive, and included in the text of the Directive after deliberations at the European Parliament and Council.

[55] As regards the protection of personal data, it should be noted that Art. 9(6) of the Platform Work Directive provides that persons performing platform work shall have the right to the portability of personal data generated through their performance of work in the context of a digital labour platform's automated monitoring and decision-making systems, including ratings and reviews without

10(1) of the Platform Work Directive envisages the requirement for Member States to ensure that digital labour platforms oversee and, with the involvement of workers' representatives, regularly, and at least every 2 years, carry out an evaluation of the impact of individual decisions taken or supported by automated monitoring and decision-making systems used by the digital labour platform on persons performing platform work, including, where applicable, on their working conditions and equal treatment at work. The wording of Art. 10(2) of the Platform Work Directive, as approved by the European Parliament and the Council, stipulates that Member States shall require digital labour platforms to ensure sufficient human resources for an effective oversight and evaluation of the impact of individual decisions taken or supported by automated monitoring or decision-making systems. In addition to the requirement that the persons charged by the digital labour platform with the function of oversight and evaluation shall have the necessary competence, training and authority to exercise that function, including for overriding automated decisions; the provision imposes an obligation to ensure that they are afforded a certain level of protection against adverse consequences resulting from the exercise of their functions (e.g. dismissal from their jobs, or equivalent disciplinary measures, etc.). Reference should be made to Article 10(3) and (5)[56] of the Platform Work Directive, which, respectively, oblige the digital work platform in cases where the oversight or the evaluation identifies a high risk of discrimination at work in the use of automated monitoring and decision-making systems or finds that individual decisions taken or supported by automated monitoring and decision-making systems have infringed the rights of a person performing platform work, the digital labour platform shall take the necessary steps, including, if appropriate, a modification of the automated monitoring and decision-making system or a discontinuance of its use, in order to avoid making such decisions in the future and provide that any decision to restrict, suspend or terminate the contractual relationship or the account of a person performing platform work or any other decision of equivalent detriment shall be taken by a human being.

Thirdly, Art. 11 of the Platform Work Directive aims at regulating human review of automated decision-making systems. This provision establishes that persons performing platform work shall have the right to obtain an explanation from the digital labour platform for any decision taken or supported by an automated decision-making system without undue delay.[57] The explanation, in oral or written form, shall

---

adversely affecting the rights of the recipient of the service under the Regulation (EU) 2016/679 . The digital labour platform shall provide persons performing platform work, free of charge, with tools to facilitate the effective exercise of their portability rights, referred to in Art. 20 of the Regulation (EU) 2016/679 R and in the first sentence of this paragraph. At the request of the person performing platform work, the digital labour platform shall transmit such personal data directly to a third party.

[56] Art. 10(3) of the Platform Work Directive (formerly Art. 7 of the European Commission's Proposal for the Directive, formerly Art. 7) has been re-worded and paragraphs 4 to 5 have been added thereto following the deliberations at the European Parliament and Council.

[57] It should be noted that the European Commission's proposed version of the Platform Work Directive included an additional requirement that the decision taken by the automated decision-

be presented in a transparent and intelligible manner, using clear and plain language. Besides, Member States shall ensure that digital labour platforms provide persons performing platform work with access to a contact person designated by the digital labour platform to discuss and to clarify the facts, circumstances and reasons having led to the decision (Art, 11(1), first subparagraph of the Platform Work Directive). In addition, Art. 11(1)(2) of the Platform Work Directive requires digital labour platforms to provide the person performing platform work with a written statement of the reasons for any decision supported or, where applicable, taken by an automated decision-making system to restrict, suspend or terminate the account of the person performing platform work, any decision to refuse the payment for work performed by the person performing platform work, any decision on the contractual status of the person performing platform work, any decision with similar effects or any other decision affecting the essential aspects of the employment or other contractual relationships. Persons performing platform work and, in accordance with national law or practice, representatives acting on behalf of the persons performing platform work shall have the right to request the digital labour platform to review all the above-mentioned decisions. It should be noted that the digital labour platform shall respond to such requests within 2 weeks by providing the person performing platform work with a sufficiently precise and adequately substantiated reply in the form of a written document which may be in electronic format (Art. 11(2) of the Platform Work Directive). Where the decision referred to in paragraph 1 infringes the rights of a person performing platform work, the digital labour platform shall rectify the decision without delay and in any case within 2 weeks of the adoption of the decision, or, where such rectification is not possible, the digital labour platform shall offer adequate compensation for the damage sustained (Art. 11(3) of the Platform Work Directive). In accordance with Art. 11(5) of the Platform Work Directive, this Article shall not apply to persons performing platform work who are business users as defined in Art. 2, point (1), of Regulation (EU) 2019/1150 (Regulation (EU) 2019/1150).[58]

Safety and Health Recital 2 of the Platform Work Directive recalls that Art. 31 of the Charter provides for the right of every worker to fair and just working conditions which respect his or her health, safety and dignity. Moreover, Recital 50 of this Directive states that Council Directive 89/391/EEC (Council Directive 89/391/EEC)[59] introduces measures to encourage improvements in the safety and health of

---

making system must have a significant impact on the working conditions of the employee working on the digital labour platform.

[58] "Business user" means any private individual acting in a commercial or professional capacity who, or any legal person which, through online intermediation services offers goods or services to consumers for purposes relating to its trade, business, craft or profession.

[59] The Directive 89/391 as modified by Regulation (EC) No 1137/2008 of the European Parliament and of the Council of 22 October 2008 adapting a number of instruments subject to the procedure laid down in Art. 251 of the Treaty to Council Decision 1999/468/EC, with regard to the regulatory procedure with scrutiny—Adaptation to the regulatory procedure with scrutiny—Part One. OJ L 311, 21.11.2008, p. 1–54.

workers at work, including the obligation for employers to assess the occupational health and safety risks and lays down general principles of prevention that employers are supposed to implement. Art. 12[60] of the Platform Work Directive is relevant to the implementation of the objectives set out in the Recitals of the Directive to ensure the safety and health of workers on digital platforms, which not only specifies the actions to be taken by digital platforms with regard to their workers, but also the obligation of the Member States to ensure that the digital platforms take preventive measures to ensure the health and safety of the platform's workers, including the cases of violence and harassment (Art. 12(5) of the Platform Work Directive). Digital labour platforms shall be obliged to ensure effective information, consultation and participation of platform workers and/or their representatives (Art. 12(2) of the Platform Work Directive). It can therefore be concluded that digital platforms will have to assess the potential risks of automated monitoring and decision-making systems to the safety of both physical and mental health of platform workers (in particular potential occupational accidents, psychosocial and ergonomic risks), to assess whether the safeguards for these systems are adequate to address these risks, taking into account the specific working conditions, and to take appropriate preventive and protective measures.

Information It should be noted that the Platform Work Directive provides for a number of recipients of the information, i.e., the employees of digital platforms and their representatives, the competent authorities of the Member States and the representatives of the persons performing platform work.

As regards the information to be provided by digital platforms to their employees or their representatives, it should be noted that Articles 13 and 14 of the Platform Work Directive provide that Member States shall ensure that the employees of digital platforms, or their representatives, are informed of decisions which may lead to the introduction of automated monitoring or decision-making systems or to substantial changes in the way they are used; besides, consultations with employees' representatives shall be carried out on the above-mentioned issues. The aim of this provision is to promote social dialogue on algorithmic management. Given the complexity of the subject matter, the representatives or the platform workers concerned can be assisted by an expert of their choice. It should be noted that there is a possibility for Member States to determine the frequency of requests for an expert, while at the same time ensuring the effectiveness of the assistance (Art. 13(3) of the Platform Work Directive).

As regards the relevant information to be provided by digital platforms to the competent authorities and to the representatives of the persons working on digital platforms, Art. 17(1) of the Platform Work Directive provides that the following information must be provided: the number of persons performing platform work

[60] A specific provision—Art. 12 of the Platform Work Directive - to ensure the safety and health of workers has been integrated into the text of the Directive following discussions at the European Parliament and the Council.

through the digital labour platform concerned, with a reference to the level of activity and their contractual or employment status; the general terms and conditions, determined by the digital labour platform and applicable to those contractual relationships; the average duration of activity, the average weekly number of working hours per person and the average income from the activity of persons performing platform work on a regular basis working through the digital labour platform concerned; and the intermediaries with whom the digital labour platform has a contractual relationship. It should be noted that Art. 17(2)-(5) of the Platform Work Directive stipulates, inter alia, that digital work platforms must provide the competent national authorities with information on the work carried out by the persons working on the digital platforms and their employment status. The articles stipulate that the information should be regularly updated, and that additional explanations or data should be provided on request.

Protection of Personal Data As already has been mentioned, according to Art. 1(1) of the Platform Work Directive, read in conjunction with Recital 17 of this Directive, the purpose of the Directive is to improve the working conditions of workers on digital platforms and to protect the personal data of the individuals who perform platform work. This dual nature of the two objectives is pursued simultaneously and, while they are mutually reinforcing and inextricably linked, neither of them is subordinate to the other. In accordance with Art. 1(2) (2) of the Platform Work Directive, this Directive lays down rules on how to improve the protection of natural persons in relation to the processing of their personal data by providing measures on algorithmic management (for more, see Chapter "Algorithmic management"), applicable to persons performing platform work in the Union, including those who do not have an employment contract or employment relationship (see Recital 18 of the Platform Work Directive). In this context, it should be noted that considerable efforts have been made to ensure the protection of personal data in Articles 7 to 9 of the Platform Work Directive, which regulate the processing of personal data through algorithmic control.

As regards the relationship between the Platform Work Directive and other European Union legislation aimed at ensuring adequate protection of personal data, it should be noted that Recital 39 of the Platform Work Directive establishes the relationship between the provisions of the Regulation (EU) 2016/679 and the provisions of this Directive in the context of the protection of personal data as far as it concerns the employment context. It is recalled that while the Regulation (EU) 2016/679 establishes a general framework for the protection of natural persons with regard to the processing of personal data, still it is necessary to lay down specific rules to address concerns relating to the processing of personal data as regards the use of automated monitoring or decision-making systems in the context of the work performed through platforms. Art. 88 of the Regulation (EU) 2016/679 stipulates that Member States may lay down more specific rules by law or collective agreements to ensure the protection of the rights and freedoms of employees with regard to the processing of their personal data in the employment context. Recital 64 of the Platform Work Directive sets out a number of measures that Member States should take in the context of platform work to ensure the protection of personal data of persons performing platform work. It has been pointed out that given that the above-mentioned Directive provides for more detailed rules and additional rules related to the Regulation (EU) 2016/679 concerning working on digital platforms in order to ensure the protection of personal data of persons working on digital platforms, the national supervisory authorities referred to in the Regulation (EU) 2016/679 should be competent to monitor the application of the above-mentioned safeguards. It has been noted that the enforcement of the more detailed and supplementary rules laid down in the Platform Work Directive should be governed by the Regulation (EU) 2016/679, in particular by the procedural framework set out in Chapters VI, VII and VIII thereof, in particular with regard to supervisory, cooperation and consistency mechanisms, remedies, liability and sanctions, including the power to impose administrative fines up to the amount referred to in Art. 83(5) of the Regulation (EU) 2016/679.[61] In addition, Recital 65 of the Platform Work Directive provides, inter alia, that data protection supervisory authorities and other competent authorities should cooperate, including on a cross-border basis, in the enforcement of this Directive.

Besides, according to Art. 9(6) of the Platform Work Directive, read in conjunction with Recital 46, persons performing platform work shall have the right to the portability of personal data generated through their performance of work in the context of a digital labour platform's automated monitoring and decision-making systems, including ratings and reviews without adversely affecting the rights of the recipient of the service under the GDPR. In addition, in accordance with this part of the Recitals of the Platform Work Directive, persons performing platform work should have the right to receive, without hindrance and in a structured commonly used and machine-readable format, any personal data generated through their performance of work in the context of a digital labour platform's automated monitoring and decision-making systems, including ratings and reviews.

Finally, Art. 28 of the Platform Work Directive leaves Member States the possibility to lay down more specific rules either by law or by collective agreements to ensure the protection of rights and freedoms in the processing of personal data

[61] Art. 83(5) of the Regulation (EU) 2016/679 provides that infringements of the following provisions shall, in accordance with paragraph 2, be subject to administrative fines up to 20,000,000 EUR, or in the case of an undertaking, up to 4% of the total worldwide annual turnover of the preceding financial year, whichever is higher: In addition, Art. 24(1) of the Platform Work Directive provides that the supervisory authority or authorities responsible for monitoring the application of Regulation (EU) 2016/679 shall also be responsible for monitoring and enforcing the application of Articles 7 to 11 of this Directive as far as data protection matters are concerned, in accordance with the relevant provisions in Chapters VI, VII and VIII of Regulation (EU) 2016/679, besides, the ceiling for administrative fines referred to in Art. 83(5) of that Regulation shall be applicable to infringements of Articles 7 to 11 of this Directive.

relating to persons working on digital platforms in accordance with Articles 9, 10 and 11, subject to Article 26(1).[62]

Art. 29 of the Platform Work Directive provides that Member States shall bring into force the laws, regulations and administrative provisions necessary to comply with this Directive by 2 December 2026. They shall immediately inform the Commission on the above-mentioned measures.

Thus, in the next few years, it will be possible to see in practice what are the real challenges faced by EU Member States in implementing the Platform Work Directive.

Summarising, the Platform Work Directive is a legislative response to the expansion of digital labour platforms across the EU. This Directive has been developed with the intention of enhancing the social protection available to platform workers. It addresses critical challenges, including worker misclassification, the opacity of algorithmic management, and cross-border enforcement. The Platform Work Directive establishes also a presumption of employment status, mandates algorithmic transparency, safeguards personal data, and enhances enforcement capacities. This Directive is indicative of the EU's broader commitment to ensuring fair, transparent, and accountable platform work.

Reference

Council (2024). https://www.consilium.europa.eu/en/policies/green-deal/ European Declaration (2022). European Commission "European Declaration on Digital Rights and Principles for the Digital Decade" of 26 January 2022. COM/2022/28 final.

Council of the EU (2024). https://www.consilium.europa.eu/en/infographics/digital-platform-workers/

EC Communication (2010). Communication from the Commission to the European Parliament, the Council, the European Economic and Social Committee and the Committee of the Regions A Digital Agenda for Europe. COM/2010/0245 final.

EC Communication (2015). Communication from the Commission to the European Parliament, the Council, the European Economic and Social Committee and the Committee of the Regions "A Digital Single Market Strategy for Europe". COM/2015/0192 final.

EC Communication (2016). Communication from the Commission to the European Parliament, the Council, the European Economic and Social Committee and the Committee of the Regions "Online Platforms and the Digital Single Market. Opportunities and Challenges for Europe". COM/2016/288 final.

EC Communication (2017). Communication from the Commission to the European Parliament, the Council, the European Economic and Social Committee and the Committee of the Regions

[62] Art. 26(1) of the Platform Work Directive stipulates that this Directive shall not constitute valid grounds for reducing the general level of protection already afforded to platform workers within Member States, including with regard to established procedures for the correct determination of the employment status of persons performing platform work as well as existing prerogatives of their representatives.

on "the Mid-Term Review on the implementation of the Digital Single Market Strategy A Connected Digital Single Market for All". COM/2017/0228 final.
EC Communication (2019). Communication to the European Parliament, the European Council, the Council, the European Economic and Social Committee and the Committee of the Regions "The European Green Deal". COM/2019/640 final.
EC Communication (2021). Communication from the European Commission to the European Parliament, the Council, the European Economic and Social Committee and the Committee of the Regions "Better working conditions for a stronger social Europe: harnessing the full benefits of digitalization for the future of work". COM/2021/761 final.
EC Communication (2022). Communication from the Commission "Guidelines on the application of Union competition law to collective agreements regarding the working conditions of solo self-employed persons". OJ 2022 C 374, pp. 2–13.
European Commission (2017) Moving forward on the European pillar of social rights: commission continues work on fair and predictable employment contracts [press release]. European Commission, Brussels. Retrieved from: https://ec.europa.eu/social/main.jsp?langId=en&catId=89&newsId=2869&furtherNews
European Commission (2024a). The White Paper published by the European Commission on 21 February 2024. "How to master Europe's digital infrastructure needs?". COM/2024/81 final.
European Commission (2024b). https://ec.europa.eu/commission/presscorner/detail/en/ip_24_1970
Interinstitutional Proclamation (2017). Interinstitutional Proclamation on the European Pillar of Social Rights. OJ 2017 C 428, pp. 10–15.
Juškevičiūtė-Vilienė, A. Žiedinės ekonomikos pagrindai Konstitucijoje? Teise. Pro, 2022-12-17 [https://www.teise.pro/index.php/2022/12/17/a-juskeviciute-viliene-ziedines-ekonomikos-pagrindai-konstitucijoje/].
Kalėda, S. L. (2023). New European Union's Regulatory Framework of the Digital Space: the Digital Markets. Teisė, 127, 25–42, https://doi.org/10.15388/Teise.2023.127.2
Parlement européen (2024). https://www.europarl.europa.eu/news/fr/press-room/20240419IPR20584/le-parlementadopte-la-directive-sur-le-travail-des-plateformes
Report (2023). Report from the Commission to the Council of 31 January 2023 on the implementation of the Council Recommendation on Access to Social Protection for Workers and the Self-employed. COM/2023/43 final.

Chapter 5
Problems of Labour Regulation on Digital Platforms in Eastern and Southeastern European Countries

Arnas Paliukėnas and Haroldas Šinkūnas

Abstract This chapter examines the legal and socio-economic challenges of regulating digital platform work in Eastern and Southeastern European countries. It focuses on Moldova, Ukraine, Bosnia and Herzegovina, Serbia, Montenegro, and Albania, offering comparative insights into national regulatory approaches, informal labour dynamics, and employment status misclassification. While digital platforms provide flexibility and new income opportunities, they also perpetuate undeclared work, legal ambiguity, and gaps in social protection. The analysis reveals that most countries in the region lack specific legal frameworks for platform workers, resulting in their widespread classification as self-employed and exclusion from labour rights and benefits. The chapter evaluates attempts at national and international reform, including the European Commission's directive negotiations and Ukraine's Diia City regime, highlighting divergent strategies and implementation barriers. Case studies reveal the prevalence of intermediary employment models, inconsistent contract types, and algorithmic control over work processes. The chapter emphasises the growing need for national legislative solutions that balance labour flexibility with adequate protection and legal clarity. It concludes that addressing informal work and legal misclassification is key to ensuring fair conditions in the platform economy, requiring political will, institutional capacity, and stronger worker representation.

Digital labour platforms promote innovative services and new business models, and offer many opportunities for customers and businesses. They can help to effectively match labour supply and demand and provide livelihood or additional income opportunities for various groups of people, including those who face barriers to access to the traditional labour market (e.g. young people, disabled people, migrants, members of racial and ethnic minorities or persons with care duties). Digital platform work expands the potential of building or expanding a customer base, sometimes cross-border. It helps business companies reach consumers, diversify revenue, create new lines of products/services, which contributes to business growth. For

A. Paliukėnas (✉) · H. Šinkūnas
Vilnius University, Law Faculty, Vilnius, Lithuania
e-mail: arnas.paliukenas@tf.vu.lt

R. Remeikienė, L. Gasparėnienė (eds.), *Work and Legal Guidelines in the Age of Digitalisation and Green Transition*, European Union and its Neighbours in a Globalized World 25, https://doi.org/10.1007/978-3-032-03511-0_5

consumers, digital platforms mean better access to products and services that would otherwise be difficult to access, as well as new and wider choices. For consumers, this means better access to products and services that would otherwise be difficult to access, as well as new and wider choices. Nevertheless, it is also the case that digital platforms are introducing new forms of work organisation and therefore endangering the existing rights and obligations related to labour law and social protection (Proposal for a Directive of the European Parliament and of the Council on improving working conditions in platform work, COM/2021/762 final).

Digital platforms are characterised by a different structure, services, work organisation methods, and control systems, so it is impossible to grant the status of an employee or a self-employed to all digital platform workers without reservations. Thus, there cannot be a uniform legal regulation applicable for all digital platforms and for all cases, especially since digital platform workers do not want to possess the same status. Although different countries and researchers offer different methods of categorising digital platform workers, they all agree that the legal status-related issues must be resolved through the adoption of relevant legislation.

It should be noted that the European Commission undertook the initiative to define the legal status of digital platform workers. On 11 March 2024, the Ministers of Employment and Social Affairs of the European Union approved the preliminary agreement reached by negotiators of the Council Presidency and the European Parliament on 8 February 2024 on the directive on work on digital platforms. This directive aims to improve the working conditions for digital platform workers and to regulate the use of algorithms on digital platforms.

The text of the directive, which would regulate the status of persons working on digital platforms, as well as other important issues of digital platform work, has been discussed by the European Commission since 2021. On 9 December 2021, a draft of the directive "On improving working conditions in platform work" was prepared. However, individual provisions of the directive were opposed by the EU member states—France, Germany, and Greece.

On 7 June 2023, the Committee of Permanent Representatives (COREPER I) adopted a proposal for the directive of the European Parliament and of the Council on improving working conditions in platform work, which established the criteria for identifying employment relationships, providing for at least three mandatory criteria for qualifying particular employment relationship. Although the European Parliament supported the position favourable to workers, when most of the work on digital platforms should be treated as salaried work, the Council did not approve the draft directive on 8 February 2024 since it was opposed by France, Germany, Greece, and Estonia.

However, the Member States reached a new preliminary agreement on the directive on 11 March 2024. One of the major points of disagreement in the negotiation of a new agreement was the establishment of criteria for identifying the employment status of platform workers. The section on the employment status of platform workers has been significantly amended in the new agreement, compared to the original draft of the directive. It no longer sets out the criteria for identifying one's employment status. The new agreement stipulates that the Member States will establish a legal presumption of employment in their legal systems, and this presumption will be applied after establishing factual circumstances proving the presence of control and management on digital platforms. These factual circumstances shall be determined with consideration of the national law and collective agreements, as well as the jurisprudence of the Court of Justice of the European Union. Digital platform workers, their representatives or national authorities will be able to rely on this legal presumption to claim that their employment status has been misjudged, and the onus of proving the absence of an employment relationship will be on a digital platform.

This agreement is the first step in regulating algorithm-based management in the workplace and setting the minimum EU standards to improve working conditions for millions of platform workers across the EU. It also aims to ensure that workers are adequately informed about the use of automated monitoring and decision-making systems, including in relation to their employment, working conditions and income.

After assessing the course of amendments to the previous draft directive and the new agreement, it can be concluded that the provisions of the new agreement mean maintaining the *status quo*, i.e. when the status of a platform worker will continue to be decided within the states through legal acts and court decisions. Nevertheless, the problems of regulating digital platform work will not be solved at the EU level. The directive no longer provides the criteria for identifying one's employment status, and the responsibility rests with each EU member state. The EU member states will establish a legal presumption of employment in their legal systems, which will come into play if facts which confirm the control of an employee and his/her subordination to an employer are confirmed. When identifying one's employment status, it is necessary to assess the relationship between a person providing services and a person controlling the former, i.e. to decide whether a person operates as employed or self-employed. These facts should be determined on the basis of the national law and collective agreements, including case law.

Eastern and Southeastern European countries—Serbia, Bosnia and Herzegovina, Albania, Moldova and Ukraine—are not EU member states, so the EU directive discussed above will not have any direct legal consequences on them, and the countries will be able to independently decide on the status of digital platform workers, at least in the nearest future.

This chapter focuses on the challenges of labour regulation on digital platforms in Eastern and Southeastern European countries, understood here as a diverse group of countries located in the geographical regions of Eastern and Southeastern Europe, which share a number of structural characteristics related to the development of digital labour markets. The selected countries—Serbia, Bosnia and Herzegovina, Albania, Moldova and Ukraine—are not members of the European Union and thus provide a relevant comparative field for analysing regulatory gaps, labour market fragmentation and institutional responses outside the EU legal framework. Although these countries differ in terms of historical legacy (e.g. former Yugoslav vs. post-Soviet), economic integration paths and institutional reforms, they are grouped together in this chapter because they face similar structural constraints in regulating non-standard forms of employment, including digital platform work. Moldova and Ukraine are discussed in more detail in separate subsections due to the availability of original empirical material collected in these countries and their role in earlier chapters of this book. Other countries—Serbia, Bosnia and Herzegovina, and Albania—are presented in a joint comparative subsection to highlight cross-country similarities in regulatory challenges. While Albania and other Western Balkan countries have distinctive social and legal development paths, they share common difficulties in addressing digital platform work due to weak institutional enforcement, fragmented labour laws, and high levels of informal employment.

Digital platforms in Eastern and Southeastern Europe rely less on algorithms than the similar digital platforms in the EU. As in the EU, most domestic platforms represent themselves as intermediaries between a worker and a customer, but not as employers. Unlike in the EU, digital platforms in Eastern and Southeastern European countries employ a relatively large proportion of workers illegally, and the basis of labour relations between workers and platforms, even within the same platforms, is very different, which causes several problems. The governments of these countries, however, pay little attention to digital platforms. The following subsections provide the more detailed analysis of the situation in different Eastern and Southeastern European countries.

5.1 Moldova

There is relatively little information in national sources about the prevailing form of employment on digital platforms in Moldova. The available sources allow to conclude that the forms of employment on digital platforms in Moldova are similar to those observed in international markets. Digital platform work and freelancing are not widespread in the Republic of Moldova. Relatively few Moldovans, especially those living outside Chisinau, use the Internet for economically productive purposes (Raja et al. 2018).

Moldova has several domestic platforms, such as *Freelancing.md* and *Rabota.md*, which are used to advertise services and find customers. However, these platforms should be treated as specialised job posting sites rather than digital labour platforms since they do not mediate between freelancers and customers (European Training Foundation 2021).

Moldovan workers use several types of digital platforms. First, these are ride-hailing services provided through an application for potential customers and drivers (*Yandex.Taxi* (www.taxi.yandex.md), *iTaxi* (www.itaxi.md) and *AlfaTaxi* (http://alfataxi.md)) Second, the country has several food delivery platforms, including Moldovan companies “StrausMD32” and “iFood”, as well as the international food delivery platform “Glovo”. It should be noted that they operate differently than similar ride-hailing platforms in other Eastern Partnership countries and the EU: in order to provide drivers or couriers with the necessary application on mobile phones and the access to online requests from customers, drivers/couriers must enter into an employment contract with platforms which are registered as limited liability companies in Moldova (European Training Foundation 2021).

In this regard, Moldova is an exception since most taxi and delivery service workers are considered employees. This is due to the lack of a legal framework for flexible independent work with several customers. Although the situation is criticised by digital platforms operating in Moldova, this approach provides greater protection for employees (European Training Foundation 2021).

The situation on digital platforms other than taxi and delivery service providers is much more complicated because neither platform work nor the activities of freelancers in general are recognised and regulated in Moldova. In the absence of specific legal provisions on the recognition of freelance work, potential employers/customers and workers in Moldova have several options for declaring their economic activities:

1. to conclude employment contracts (*contract individual de muncă*) regulated by the Labour Code. However, Moldova's labour code is considered one of the most worker-protective pieces of legislation in the region and does not favour flexible or casual employment arrangements.
2. to operate as an individual entrepreneur (*Intreprindere Invidivuala*) whose activities are regulated by the Civil Code. This option is not attractive for platform workers due to the high administrative burden of setting up an individual company and high business-related taxes (similar to the taxes paid by legal persons).
3. to establish a service contract (*Contract de prestări servicii*) regulated by the Civil Code. This comes with several drawbacks for both platforms and platform workers. Tax rates are very similar to those applicable to income from economic activities based on employment contracts (thus, there is no economic incentive to prioritise employment contracts as in most other countries) (European Training Foundation 2021).

Unlike in the case of an employment contract, a service provider is not entitled to social benefits, such as annual leave or pension which depends on one's wages and is paid to persons working under an employment contract. In addition, many Moldovan platform workers, especially those providing remote services, take the risk of operating in the "grey" economic zone and working informally. As a result, freelancers in Moldova are often punished for "illegal business activities" and tax evasion (European Training Foundation 2021).

In August 2020, the State Tax Service of Moldova issued a notice clarifying that freelancers, including those working on digital work platforms, fall within the definition of persons providing professional services, and taxes are levied on all their labour income, professional activity income, commissions, bonuses and other similar benefits at a personal income tax rate of 12% (Moldovan Tax Authorities 2020).

Tax requirements and administrative rules are not always optimal for the self-employed. Generally, employment under a civil contract in most states means that a contractor (a workers) is responsible for paying taxes. The approach to taxation may vary depending on the type of a contract or the legal status of a platform worker and specific agreements between platforms, workers and regulators.

This shows that there is a lack of appropriate legal regulation which would enable flexible self-employment activities with multiple customers and would create incentives for formal work on digital platforms in Moldova. Labour relations in Moldova are regulated by the Labour Code (Labour Code of the Republic of Moldova, 2003). The provisions of this code are not flexible, which may be an obstacle to its application to digital platform work. Flexibility in working hours, schedules and locations is one of the biggest advantages of digital platform work. It reduces market entry barriers, makes it easier to balance platform work with other commitments, and makes digital platform work a particularly attractive option for earning additional income. Nevertheless, worker safety becomes a major trade-off for those who select this occupation as their main job. Digital platform work is often highly competitive, tasks require a lot of unpaid time, and workers do not have access to the same social benefits as workers with employment contracts regulated the Labour Code. In Moldova, this compromise is not as clearly expressed as in the EU Member States, given the underdeveloped social support system. Thus, operating without an employment contract or without declaring a business activity is an acceptable option for many workers since the benefits of higher earnings are felt only in the short term. These factors should be taken into account when developing a new platform work regulation system in Moldova (Danish Trade Union Development Agency 2023).

One of the causes of limited employment contracts on digital platforms in Moldova is the lack of flexible labour regulations. To address this issue, the amendments to the Labour Code were approved in May 2020. The Labour Code was supplemented with a new chapter on remote work (Chapter IX1). The new provisions regulate remote work, the conclusion, amendment and termination of individual employment contracts allowing remote work, the specifics of organising remote work, and social protection in remote work. This is an important step which encourages employers to allow flexible working conditions in remote work. In addition to these provisions, the Labour Code was supplemented with certain clauses regarding flexible work schedules. Workplace flexibility refers to offering "flexible work arrangements" by introducing various options which change the time and/or place where work is usually performed (The 'Expanding Choices: Gender Responsive Family Policies for the Private Sector in the Western Balkans and Moldova' Project, the UN Population Fund (UNFPA), the Austrian Development Agency (ADA), the operational unit of the Austrian Development Cooperation, the Ministry of Labour and Social Protection and Chamber of Commerce and Industry of the Republic of Moldova 2022).

Although Moldovan national labour law allows for flexible working arrangements, including telework, various loopholes which discourage workers from taking advantage of work schedules that best suit their needs can be identified. Specifically, this refers to Article 100^1 of the Labour Code which stipulates that a flexible work schedule is set by an employer who has approved an employee's request, if this option is provided for in the collective labour agreement, the internal rules of the Labour Code, business establishment act or another normative act. When interpreted from an employee's perspective, this provision seems to deny the principle of respect for both parties' equal rights and interests in labour relations. Thus, as long as the implementation of flexible working arrangements remains at an employer's discretion, it is possible that flexible working practices will not be widespread in Moldova.

It should be noted that in some EU countries, such as Denmark, France, Sweden and others, many social problems of digital platform workers are resolved through collective bargaining. For instance, the first collective agreement with the *Hilfr* platform was signed in Denmark in April 2018. The 3F-*Hilfr* agreement regulates the working conditions of cleaners on the *Hilfr* cleaning service platform (Munkhom and Schjoler 2018). Under this agreement, cleaners automatically become employees after 100 h of work, unless they decide otherwise. By entering into this agreement, the parties clearly demonstrated the attempts to incorporate digital platforms into the Danish labour model are significant.

The contract does not prevent a cleaner from selecting "an employee's" status without providing 100 h of service or from maintaining "a freelancer's" status after providing 100 h of service. This is a major innovation in collective agreements. The agreement gives workers themselves a free choice whether or not to be covered by the agreement. The essence of this innovation is that the agreement gives a worker an unlimited choice of status (whether of an employee or a freelancer) in the relationship with a platform organiser. This is not in accordance with the principles of determining a worker's status in Danish labour and employment law. In addition, a platform may reject the application for the status of an employee by cleaners who have worked less than 100 h, if a fair and objective reason for such rejection is provided. Employed cleaners are entitled to a minimum hourly wage in line with the sectoral agreement. An employer has the right to apply higher hourly rates, but not lower. The agreement gives an employee several new rights: partial payment in case of delay in cancelling accepted cleaning work, pension contributions paid by *Hilfr*, vacation with pay, sick leave, protection against the removal of one's profile (or other unavailability of the profile) without a valid reason and only after receiving a written notification, and a clear right to daily breaks and daily and weekly rest periods (Marenko 2023). Later, some other collective agreements, such as the *Just Eat* agreement, according to which *Just Eat* food delivery couriers are considered employees, were established.

In the context of the situation in Moldova, it should be noted that labour relations and the social dialogue between employers and workers are regulated by Moldovan Law No. 1129 on Trade Unions (2000), Law No. 976 on Employer Organisations (2000), and Law no. 245 on Organising the National Consultation Commission and its activities. Thus, Moldova has a legal framework for the proper development of collective bargaining, but so far there has been no collective bargaining concerning the status of workers on digital platforms. This is due to the low trust of workers in trade unions, the illegal nature of work on digital platforms, and the frequent treatment of platform work as temporary. Taking this into account, it is necessary to change the attitude of digital platform workers towards trade unions because they can ensure better working conditions for digital platform workers through collective bargaining in the absence of the proper state legal regulation.

At the same time, it should be mentioned that digital platforms can alleviate the problems of unemployment and underemployment in Moldova. In addition, the employment opportunities offered by digital platforms, including the demand for high-skilled and well-paid work for international clients, can also help reduce emigration and brain drain from Moldova. Easy access to the global labour market can help to better match labour supply and demand and improve workers' skills (Ermsone 2019).

To improve the legal regulation of the activities of platform workers in Moldova, the first important step is to recognise platform work and the benefits it can deliver to the labour market, education and training development. However, the political debate in Moldova is at a very early stage compared to the EU Member States. Many initiatives launched at the EU level (in the case of Moldova, the European Pillar is worth mentioning) are aimed at improving work and skills development, and the right to social protection is recognised as one of the fundamental rights. Modernisation of the social protection system is a long-term process embedded in national development strategies, and some improvements can be observed in the public sector, especially in health care. The current tripartite discussions on amending Moldova's Labour Code aim to improve the regulation of temporary work with a view to expanding social protection.

5.2 Ukraine

Ukraine is a pioneer of the digital revolution, and is ranked first in Europe and fourth in the world in terms of the number of workers on digital platforms. At least 3% of the Ukrainian workforce works online on more than 40 different national and international labour platforms (Bertolini et al. 2022).

Unlike in Moldova, a very large proportion of persons employed on digital platforms in Ukraine are qualified professionals (IT experts, designers, programmers, translators, etc.). Their social protection situation is much better because they are often better educated, know their jobs well, have in-demand skills, earn higher wages, and are, therefore, less vulnerable. Nevertheless, there is another group of people, i.e. couriers, food delivery persons, transporters, whose situation due to their poorer education and the nature of the work they perform is completely different, much more complicated, and they obviously need better protection.

Digital platform workers are rarely employed under employment contracts in Ukraine. They mostly work under civil contracts as service providers. Therefore, platform workers do not enjoy the rights and privileges of traditional workers, such as paid holidays, social benefits and protection against immediate dismissal.

With the outbreak of the war with Russia, the situation of Ukrainian platform workers became even worse since they had to worry not only about the safety of their families, but also about how to earn a living under significantly more difficult working conditions. This is what happened to many workers in the food delivery sector: when the war broke out, a large number of platforms suddenly stopped operating, many of them owe their workers wages for the last week of work. Later, only food delivery platforms *Glovo* and *Bolt Food* resumed their operations to provide the essential services to the residents of the war-torn Ukrainian cities.

Ukrainian platform workers are facing not only financial problems. Their journeys have become unsafe, the Internet connection has been less stable, they have device charging disruptions, etc. However, digital platforms do not make any direct commitment to their workers, do not share the risk, do not compensate for lower wages. Digital platform workers are also responsible for their work equipment and inventory, such as cars for drivers, bicycles and bags for couriers (Bertolini et al. 2022).

Digital platform workers in Ukraine went on strike several times and required better working conditions, but it was of no use since platform managers did not agree to start any dialogue. After the protests of 72 platform workers in Ukraine (mainly from *Glovo*, *UberEats* and *Dominos Pizza*), about 30 digital platform workers decided to establish a union called the Independent Courier Union. They adopted a charter, but the union was not registered by the state, and eventually, due to the high turnover of platform workers, the activities of the union were terminated (Hadwiger 2022).

The Federation of Trade Unions of Ukraine (FTU), the largest federation of this type, expressed great concern about the platform economy, and set the objective of formalising digital platform work and giving workers the right to collective bargaining in its 2021–2026 strategy (Hadwiger 2022). However, this objective has not yet been achieved. It should also be noted that due to the martial law in Ukraine, strikes are prohibited, so digital platform workers must not defend their rights in this way.

Thus, the main problem that concerns the legal status of digital platform workers in Ukraine is the lack of legal regulation, which creates the conditions for illegal work and leads to the absence of any legal and social guarantees for platform workers.

The problems discussed above are not unknown to the politicians of the state. In recent years, there have been attempts to adopt amendments to legal acts, to introduce various initiatives. The Parliament has repeatedly tried to pass provisions which would enshrine zero-hours contracts, at-will employment and reduced overtime pay. Each time, such initiatives failed due to the opposition of the Federation of Trade Unions. Article 22 of the Constitution of Ukraine enshrines the principle of non-regression which stipulates that the rights already established cannot be limited or abolished, but only strengthened and expanded. Given this, it is very difficult to establish more flexible employment contracts and adopt any other changes which would help regulate the work on digital platforms and the status of digital platform workers.

Nevertheless, the Law "On promoting the development of the digital economy in Ukraine" entered into force on 14 August 2021 (Verkhovna Rada of Ukraine 2021). The Law on Amendments to the Tax Code of Ukraine was adopted in December 2021. The amendments provided the conditions for transforming the taxation framework and paved the way for the entry into force of the Law "On promoting the development of the digital economy in Ukraine". This law establishes a special legal regime for the development of the IT industry. The *Diia City* is the single economic and legal IT space. Companies which join this legal regime become residents of the *Diia City*. The *Diia City* is a special legal regime designed to create favourable conditions for IT business development in Ukraine. The major objective of the *Diia City* is to increase the investment attractiveness of the IT sector in the Ukrainian economy (President of Ukraine, Official website 2022).

The *Diia City* provides business-favourable tax conditions, where taxes are much lower than in the case of an employment relationship. Contracts established in *Diia City* are recognised as completely legal, and the residents of the *Diia City* can breathe easier without fearing that the relationship could be recognised as an employment relationship. The peculiarity of this regime is that not only companies operating on the territory of Ukraine can become residents of the *Diia City*. One of the requirements for a *Diia City* resident is registration on the territory of Ukraine, but the location of business does not necessarily have to be Ukraine. Only legal persons can become residents of the *Diia City* (DLF Attorneys-at-Law 2021).

Article 5, Paragraph 1 of the Law stipulates that a legal person registered in the territory of Ukraine in accordance with the procedure established by Ukrainian legislation, regardless of this person's residence and the location of business activity, can be a resident of the *Diia City* if meets all the following requirements: (1) performs one or more types of activities specified in Part 4 of this article (development, modification, testing and technical support of software, including computer games; other work in all stages of the software development life cycle, including domain business analysis, development of software specifications, user interface development, etc.); (2) the average monthly wages of the participating employees and other persons working on the platforms is at least the equivalent of EUR 1200 for each calendar month, counting from the next calendar month following the calendar month in which the status of a resident of the *Diia City* was acquired; (3) the average registered number of employees and specialists within a legal person is at least nine people; (4) the amount of qualified income of a legal person received during the first three calendar months following the calendar month in which the legal person acquired the status of a resident of the *Diia City* is not less than 90% of the amount of its total income for this period, and the amount of qualified income received for each calendar year when being a resident of the *Diia City* is at least 90% of the total income of the legal person for the same period (Verkhovna Rada of Ukraine 2021).

The law provides that a digital platform can employ individuals under both employment contracts and GIG contracts. Article 16 of the Law "On promoting the development of the digital economy in Ukraine" stipulates that when hiring an employee, a *Diia City* resident may enter into a special form of employment contract which is aimed at ensuring the conditions of initiative and independence with consideration of the employee's individual abilities and professional skills. The contracts increase the mutual responsibility of the parties. The term of the employment contract, the rights, duties and responsibilities of the parties (including material responsibilities), the terms of material support and work organising, termination of the contract (including before the end of the term) and other conditions may be determined by mutual agreement of the parties. If an employer loses the status of a

Diia City resident, the employment contract is not terminated, and the loss of the status of a *Diia City* resident does not affect the validity of the employment contract, including its individual provisions.

The Law also provides that a GIG contract can be concluded with an employee. A contract is not considered a contract within the scope of civil law if it does not clearly state that it is a GIG contract. The term of validity of a GIG contract, as well as the rights, duties and responsibilities of the parties to the contract, the wages of a GIG specialist, the terms of termination of the contract and other conditions are determined in a GIG contract. Services (work) provided (performed) under a GIG contract may include particular functions typical of certain positions, such as a chief engineer, a responsible person organising work related to personal data protection, etc. (Verkhovna Rada of Ukraine 2021). Pursuant to Article 17, Part 8 of the Law, in the absence of evidence that a resident of the *Diia City* has misled a person regarding the legal nature of the transaction, the conclusion and/or execution of a GIG contract cannot be considered as the conclusion and/or execution of an employment relationship. Disputes between GIG specialists and residents of the *Diia City* are settled in accordance with the civil procedure.

The analysis of the legal norms shows that the Ukrainian legislator allows the parties to freely decide which type of contract can legitimize their mutual relations. At the same time, it provides for a minimum wage regardless of the type of contract. This Law is assessed from two positions: supporters of labour law claim that it narrows the rights of digital platform workers and the latter become vulnerable since, for instance, pursuant to Article 18, paragraph 5 of the Law, any of the contract parties has the right to notify in writing (electronically) the other party about the cancellation of the contract no later than three calendar days before the termination of the contract during the first 3 months of the validity of a GIG contract; others argue that this provides flexible working conditions for both digital platforms and platform workers.

As already mentioned, the Law "On promoting the development of the digital economy in Ukraine" is intended for regulating the activities of companies and workers in the IT sector. Professionals in the IT sector are highly qualified and earn high wages, so they are not as vulnerable as digital platform workers in other sectors. They usually do not need special work tools, do not fall under algorithmic control. They usually perform specific, time-consuming tasks, less communicate with customers, have lower risks of accidents at work, etc. All this determines that ordinary legal regulation is appropriate for them.

However, the situation is completely different with other digital platform workers, such as couriers, transporters, food carriers, etc., because these persons usually do not receive the 1200 EUR remuneration provided for in the above-mentioned law. Moreover, their relationships with digital platforms are fundamentally different since their behaviour and workflow are largely controlled by digital platforms. i.e. digital platforms provide workers with orders, control the time of fulfilment of orders, set requirements for work tools and clothing, apply different control and monitoring algorithms, and the work itself is much more dangerous.

The emergence of an employment relationship (when an employee, defined by legal acts as a natural person who works in a company, institution, organization or for another natural person) is associated with the conclusion of an employment contract (Verkhovna Rada of Ukraine 2023).

A freelancer is a person who is self-employed or works under other conditions provided for by law (for example, under a civil law contract), as defined in Article 4 of the Law of Ukraine "On Employment of the Population" (Verkhovna Rada of Ukraine 2012).

The majority of digital platforms refer to their workers as freelancers, but this concept does not correspond to the above-mentioned legal norm since digital platforms provide their workers with work, rather than workers find tasks independently. Thus, work on digital platforms is currently regulated by the terms and conditions suggested by platforms which unilaterally apply legal terminology, but do not formally create any legal relationship (neither work nor civil) with users of their services. Cooperation with platform service users is disguised and presented as providing access to information or information services. Thus, digitalisation of labour relations is accompanied by an increase in the scale of the shadow economy in the labour market, and a decrease in the level of social protection for the working population (Sacharuk 2020). This is because digital platforms promote the growth of multitasking (performance of low-paid micro-tasks that do not require high professional qualifications and do not correspond to a worker's level of education) and overemployment (work) which goes well beyond normal working hours (Azmuk 2019).

Ukrainian labour law specialists Novikov and Lukianchikov (2019) offer several options for regulating work on digital platforms:

1. recognition of a new category of digital platform workers, inclusion of digital platform work into the scope of labour legislation, and development of target legal norms which would consider the nature of work;
2. introduction of a special normative legal regulation for excluding digital platform workers from the scope of the current labour legislation, but granting the certain level of legal protection for digital platform workers;
3. allowing digital platforms to create their own regulations based on the major principles of civil legislation for the use of hired labour.

The first option is considered to be optimal since the relationship between digital platforms and their workers usually has the features of an employment relationship, but their mutual relationship may also correspond to civil legal relationship in particular cases.

This position was supported by the courts of England, Italy and other countries where the courts explained the legal nature of the mutual relations between digital platforms and their workers. For instance, the London Employment Tribunal issued the decision of 12 November 2016 in the case of Aslam v. "Uber" (Employment Tribunals, Case Nos 2202550/2015), which stipulates that the "Uber" drivers shall not be considered the self-employed, but the employees. The court reached this decision taking into account the facts that: (a) the "Uber" drivers did not have the absolute right to accept and reject orders; (b) the "Uber" platform hired the drivers; (c) the "Uber" platform controlled the relevant information (a passenger's name, contact details and the intended destination) and did not provide it to drivers; (d) the "Uber" platform required drivers to accept orders and not cancel them, and applied penalties (for example, termination of contracts) to those who did not comply with the procedure; (e) the "Uber" platform determined the route of the trip, and the drivers had to follow it; (f) the "Uber" platform set the price of the drive, and a driver could not negotiate with a passenger; (g) the "Uber" platform imposed many requirements on drivers (e.g. a limited choice of acceptable vehicles), told the drivers how to do their job and controlled them in the process of the service provision; (h) the "Uber" platform applied the rating system to the rate the drivers; (i) the "Uber" platform imposed discounts, sometimes even excluding a driver, whose wages could be affected; (j) the "Uber" platform initially applied the guaranteed wage scheme, but later abandoned it; (k) the "Uber" platform handled passenger complaints about the driver performance; (l) the "Uber" platform reserved the right to unilaterally change the working conditions for drivers.

The decision of the Palermo Tribunal of 20 November 2020 is no less significant. In its decision, the Palermo Tribunal relied on the decision of the Court of Justice of the European Union (CJEU) of 20 December 2017, C-434/15, in which the activities of the "Glovo" platform were recognised as business activities aimed at transporting people and delivering food and drinks. The CJEU examined the intermediary services, provided by the "Uber" platform, and found that the services were provided by non-professional drivers who used their own vehicles for work. Nevertheless, the Court took into account the fact that the platform provided the drivers with the access to the application, without which they could not provide the services, and their services would not be used by potential customers. The Court also considered the influence of "Uber" on the terms of service which, for instance, cover setting a maximum price for the service, reception of payments from customers and subsequent transfers to drivers, driver control, and the requirements for the service and the quality of vehicles. Having examined the case, the Palermo Tribunal indicated that when hearing the cases of this type, it is extremely important to trace the digital nature of a platform, i.e. to find out whether it is a business activity. A platform can be considered a company, and the people working on its behalf can be considered workers. On the other hand, if we consider the activities of a platform only as intermediate activities between customers and service providers, the nature and conditions of a contract can be treated in a completely different way.

Thus, a contract may be qualified as an employment contract or a service contract, depending on the tests applied in each jurisdiction, particularly the intensity of the influence of a platform, the work performed, the economic dependence of the parties, and the permanence of an agreement. Considering the purpose and the nature of the service provided, the Tribunal decided that the "Glovo" platform should be recognised as a business activity.

The Palermo Tribunal found that the claimant carried out his activities for the delivery company for about 8 h a day, his activities were organised and fully controlled by the digital platform, through which he could provide the service. In addition, the delivery assignments were based on an algorithm that evaluated the location of a food hauler in relation to a restaurant and/or a delivery location. The platform controlled the performance of work by using a rating system, which included various parameters. The points were awarded with consideration of work efficiency, feedback from users or partners, and employee experience. Time reservation for delivery services depended on a hauler's rating: persons with higher rating had more freedom to reserve a more favourable shift time. In addition, several management-related working conditions were considered. For instance, to perform the work, a hauler was required to always have a mobile phone with a battery charge of at least 20% when he was logged into the platform application account. If a person did not meet these criteria, the algorithm did not assign any tasks. After examining the above circumstances, the Tribunal recognised that the person was subordinate to the platform as an employer.

The court practice discussed above suggests that there cannot be an unequivocal decision regarding the status of digital platform workers because digital platforms are very different not only in their activities, but also in work organising and control mechanisms, i.e. in some cases, platforms provide detailed requirements for service provision, control the process and demand appropriate behaviour from their workers, while in other cases they simply play the role of an intermediary and are minimally involved in the specifics of service provision. Thus, the activities of digital platforms cannot fall under the same regulation, especially because platform workers treat platform work from different positions: some treat it as their main job, while others use it as a secondary source of income generation and work only a few hours a week or a month. Therefore, it would not be appropriate to grant equal status to the different categories of platform workers.

Here we come to the conclusion that when solving the problems with the status of digital platform workers, recognition of a new category of digital platform workers, inclusion of digital platform work into the scope of labour legislation, and development of target legal norms which would consider the nature of work would be relevant. Unfortunately, no country has yet created an ideal legal mechanism for regulating work relations on digital platforms.

As already mentioned, the European Commission has been trying to define the status of digital platform workers for several years, but after assessing the course and direction of the amendments to the draft directive "On improving working conditions in platform work", as well as the new agreement, it can be concluded that the provisions of the new agreement mean the maintenance of the *status quo*, when the status of a platform worker will continue to be decided within a state both through legal regulation and judicial practice. It seems that the problems of regulating digital platform work are not going to be solved in a strictly unified manner at the EU level, at least in the near future. The directive will no longer set out any common and uniform criteria for identifying one's employment status, as this responsibility will now fall on each EU Member State. The EU Member States will establish a legal presumption of employment in their legal systems, and this presumption will come into play when the facts indicating the control and subordination of a worker are established. When identifying one's employment status, it is necessary to understand the essence of the relationship between a person who provides the services and a person who controls the former one, i.e. it is necessary to establish whether a person who provides the services is employed or self-employed. These facts should be established with consideration of national law, collective agreements and the emerging case law. This will undoubtedly lead to differences in Member States, with some of them considering digital platform work as self-employment and others—as employment.

In December 2023, the EU leaders decided to start accession negotiations with Ukraine, so Ukrainian legislation will have to comply with the EU law. In compliance with the EU legal regulation discussed above, Ukraine will have to establish a legal presumption of employment, which will come into force when the facts indicating the control and subordination of a worker are established.

While conducting literature analysis, we could not find the examples of the Ukrainian court practice on the issue under consideration. However, the Ukrainian government has recently proposed the amendments to the labour law with a view to reducing the scale of undeclared work. These proposals recognise any work as work performed under an employment contract regardless of the type of contract (even a civil law contract) established between the parties if the contract contains the following features:

1. a person performs work which requires a specific qualification or profession and is under the control of another person in whose interests the work is performed;
2. a company provides the person with means of production and/or work tools (e.g. vehicles, fuel);
3. a person is regularly paid in cash or in kind;
4. a company regulates a person's work and vacation time (*LigaZakon* 2019).

If the Parliament passed these amendments, they could have an impact on platform companies because civil law contracts with platform workers could be reclassified as employment contracts. In this case, platform workers would be entitled to the same rights and privileges as traditional workers, and platform companies would have to bear the additional burden of taxes and social protection.

In addition, various studies are being conducted in Ukraine to solve the problem of the status of platform workers. For instance, during the implementation of the IEP project of the National Academy of Sciences of Ukraine on the creation of a new quality of working life in the conditions of digital transformations, an expert survey, which involved 110 highly qualified specialists, was conducted between August and October 2021. The survey revealed that formalisation of the employment relations, prevention of the shadow economy and proper representation of workers' interests are the key determinants of the effective regulatory policy which could help ensure legal and social protection for digital platform workers in Ukraine. This is a fundamental point because the inclusion of platform workers in the national social and legal protection systems undoubtedly requires prevention of the shadow economy through business legalization and formalization. A separate task is the creation of the relevant forms and mechanisms for permanent defending of the collective interests of digital platform workers and the establishment of these forms and mechanisms in legal acts. Among the potential bodies which can act as effective defenders of the rights and interests of digital platform workers, trade unions have become the undisputed leader (as noted by 38.2% of the experts in the survey). 23.6% of the respondents believe that the process of ensuring the effective social and legal protection requires the establishment of state institutions with special competence. Among the potential bodies which can defend the rights and interests of platform workers, experts directly indicated platform workers themselves (14.6% of the experts), public human rights organisations in the area of digital technologies (12.7% of the experts) and insurance organisations with public legal status (10.9% of the experts). These results confirm, on the one hand, the perspective and relevance of creating the network trade unions; on the other hand, they reveal the relevance of expanding the range of activities of traditional trade unions into the area of the platform economy through creating and implementing the regulatory and organizational management policies which would ensure the social and legal protection for platform workers (Panjkova and Kasperovič 2022).

5.3 Bosnia and Herzegovina, Serbia, Montenegro and Albania

The platform economy in Bosnia and Herzegovina is at an early stage of development, although there are both international and domestic digital platforms such as *Fix.ba*, *Glovo*, *Korpa*, *mojTaxi*, *Šetnja.ba*, *StudenTime*, *Žuti Taksi*, and *Daibau.ba* (*Fairwork* 2023b). Platform work in Bosnia and Herzegovina became popular during the COVID-19 pandemic, although it was not a completely new phenomenon in the labour market. The most advanced and popular sector is food delivery. For many people who were laid off during the pandemic, it was an opportunity to find work. In addition to delivery platforms, Bosnia and Herzegovina has some other digital labour platforms. Workers can conclude contracts for providing various services, such as taxi, apartment cleaning, repairs, etc. Platforms mainly attract young people and workers with less opportunities to establish themselves in the labour market (*Fairwork* 2023c). Bosnia and Herzegovina, like many other countries, is facing the problem of reconciling traditional labour laws with the unique work dynamics on digital platforms. The traditional legal framework focuses on the labour relations based on long-established norms which may not adequately address the specific needs and vulnerabilities of platform workers.

Digital platforms operating in Bosnia and Herzegovina use various forms of employment: (a) "standard" open-ended, full-time employment contracts; (b) part-time work; (c) self-employment (including platform workers and freelancers, although BiH labour legislation does not recognize them as different categories); (d) temporary work (including fixed-term contracts, seasonal and casual work); (e) informal or undeclared work; (f) internships and student work (including volunteering) (Oruč et al. 2023).

Given the situation when platform work is still not recognised as a specific form of employment relationship by national legislation, platform workers are often categorised as independent contractors, which further increases their insecurity and vulnerability. Given the situation where platform work is still not recognized as a specific employment relationship by national legislation, platform workers are often categorized as independent contractors, which further increases their insecurity and vulnerability. In the case of contractual relations with a platform, workers often enter into service contracts; they are considered self-employed, which means that they themselves cover the costs of social insurance and labour protection. Thus, platform workers are in a less favourable position than other private sector workers.

Bosnia and Herzegovina's labour legislation cannot be considered state-wide legislation since legislation power (regulation of labour law) is held by three administrative units (the Federation of Bosnia and Herzegovina, Republika Srpska, and Brčko District), each of which has the autonomy to enact labour legislation in its territory. This leads to certain differences in the labour market policies. Nevertheless, labour laws in all three administrative units pass similar regulations, apart from some differences in their implementation (e.g. different participating institutions, different tax and benefit systems, etc.). In addition, the 10 cantons of the Federation of Bosnia and Herzegovina have legal systems which cannot revoke the rights granted to a person, but can introduce additional rights or provide more detailed regulations (e.g. the registers of self-employed persons). Thus, the absence of comprehensive and unified legislation leads to legal uncertainty. In view of this, labour relations, and thus the roles and responsibilities of employers and workers, are regulated by all labour laws (issued by three administrative units) (Labour Law for Federation of Bosnia and Herzegovina 2016; Labour Law for Republic of Srpska 2000; Employment Law of Brčko District 2019).

None of these laws recognises the specific status of platform workers. They cover only traditional forms of work where employment contracts are concluded. The laws allow regulating particular elements of labour relations through collective agreements and employment contracts. Self-employed persons, such as independent entrepreneurs, are treated in compliance with special craft regulations in two administrative units, while company law applies in the third unit (Zakon O obrtu i srodnim djelatnostima, 2009; Law on Craft-Entrepreneurial Activity for Republic of Srpska 2011; Law on Enterprises of Brcko District of Bosnia and Herzegovina. Law On Enterprises of Brcko District of Bosnia and Herzegovina 2011).

When it comes to digital platforms in Bosnia and Herzegovina, the most important things to analyse are part-time work and student employment. The current legal framework of the Federation of Bosnia and Herzegovina and Republika Srpska does not allow full-time employees to enter into additional part-time contracts, so full-time employees cannot earn additional income from working on digital platforms. Consequently, platforms are inclined to conclude contracts for temporary and casual work with full-time workers, or to avoid signing a contract altogether.

Furthermore, the labour laws in all three administrative units do not regulate or even recognise student work in Bosnia and Herzegovina. Both full-time and part-time students must comply with this regulation. Full-time students follow their curriculum, they have the status of a student, and the state usually covers or subsidizes their tuition costs. On the other hand, part-time students can be employed or unemployed and be registered with a local employment service. They follow a curriculum tailored to their work commitments. This means that part-time students are allowed to enter into part-time employment contracts, while full-time students must be registered with a student employment centre or service, but only to be able to do temporary or irregular work. The current regulation allows students to be employed temporarily and irregularly, but this right is limited by the short duration of the employment relationship which may last up to 60 days per year in the Federation of Bosnia and Herzegovina and 90 days per year in the Republic of Srpska (Law on Craft-Entrepreneurial Activity for Republic of Srpska 2011, Article 204).

Summarising, it can be stated that the full implementation of flexibility for platform workers in Bosnia and Herzegovina is hindered by the limitations in the country's labour law. As a consequence of these limitations, some platform workers work illegally.

The situation in Montenegro is similar. Digital platform workers are considered self-employed but not employees. The labour and social laws, which regulate such areas as the establishment of employment relationships, payment of social insurance contributions, sick leave, pregnancy, maternity/paternity and childcare leave, the right to join trade unions, working hours, safety and health protection at work, are hardly applied (Ivanovic 2022).

Self-employment in Montenegro is regulated by the Labour Law, in which remote platform workers are not unequivocally recognised as self-employed persons: although in theory they are subject to the Personal Income Tax Law, in practice they do not have a formal status of self-employed persons and are registered as unemployed (European Training Foundation 2023).

In addition, the Law on Foreigners of Montenegro, which regulates the conditions of entry, departure, movement, stay and work of foreigners in Montenegro, provides that a foreigner can work in Montenegro on the basis of a permit for temporary residence and work or must have a certificate of work registration; a foreigner can do only the works which a permit for temporary residence and work or a certificate of work registration has been issued for, and work only for an employer indicated in the documents mentioned above. In view of this, the Law on Foreigners does not give foreigners the right to do digital platform work in Montenegro, i.e. to operate in the so-called "gig" economy, and the Ministry of Foreign Affairs of Montenegro does not keep any official records of this category of foreigners, so basically these people operate on digital platforms illegally (Ivanovic 2022).

Albania's labour market is characterised by very low wages, but digital platform workers tend to earn more than those working in the construction or agricultural sectors. There were approximately 4447 digital platform workers per 100,000 inhabitants in Albania in 2023. Ensuring good working conditions on digital platforms is a challenge compounded by legal gaps, the lack of practices to exercise labour rights, and low expectations of workers.

Platform workers in Albania are mainly young people with primary and secondary education, and students who want to earn extra money while studying. Less in demand in a complicated labour market with many unemployed people in Albania, young people work on digital platforms for a short period of time (e.g. a few months), and want quick money rather than have long-term platform career aspirations. As a result, digital platforms constantly face the problems of a lack of consistent workforce and high worker turnover (European Training Foundation 2023).

The ILO estimates that nearly 56.7% of the total employment in Albania may be informal (Euronews Albania 2021). The term and concept of "a platform worker" is relatively new in the Albanian labour law system, and the companies operating in this sector are not yet properly represented in the market. This creates an uncertain environment for digital platform work. Although traditional work patterns are adequately defined in the Labour Code, they are often circumvented since the labour market is dominated by illegal work. Unstable social relations between employers and workers lead to the situation when employers do not fulfil their formal obligations, and workers are not entitled to social benefits. Although digital platforms were expected to improve the situation and promote sustainable work in Albania, it is still unclear whether this will be the case since most companies believe that formal work entails more costs than benefits, and if a platform has formal workers when other platforms do not, the former platform will be uncompetitive because platforms with informal workers (direct competitors) will incur lower costs (*Fairwork* 2023a).

Serbia is situated in the Central and Eastern European region, which is characterised by a high adoption of digital labour platforms, compared to the rest of the European continent. Serbia has 3.52 digital workers per 1000 population, compared to 1.72 in the United States (Kassi and Lehdonvirta 2016).

However, digital workers in Serbia cannot be salaried employees or operate on a service contract basis since digital platforms are not registered as employers in Serbia. The only option offered by the domestic legislation is the registration of a business entity or self-employment. Therefore, a third of digital platform workers obtain their legal status in this way. Those who select this option usually decide to operate as self-employed persons and only in rare cases establish companies. About two-thirds of digital platform workers in Serbia operate in the shadow economy because they have no option to act as independent workers and/or freelancers: although laws recognise these categories of persons, the status of an independent worker/a freelancer is only available to a limited number of professionals (e.g. artists, journalists, priests). Due to the lack of legal provisions, platform workers are often registered as unemployed at the State Employment Service or considered inactive residents, so their work is invisible (Andjelkovic et al. 2019).

Digital platforms in Serbia define themselves as intermediaries which facilitate exchanges between users and service providers who are treated as independent contractors. In addition, the operation of digital platforms in Serbia is based on several models. The first is that platforms allow restaurants or shops to offer their products through mobile or web applications without involving a platform in the delivery of products. This model is practiced in the food delivery sector. Tucker E. calls this model of work organising "the aggregator model" (Tucker 2020).

In Serbia, this model is used by *Glovo* and *Wolt* that offer advertising and marketing services to local restaurants and shops, handle payments for deliveries, but are not involved in work organising or monitoring the delivery. Restaurants or shops organise the delivery service themselves, customers can see that the delivery is organised by a product provider and can only receive information about the approximate time of delivery since an intermediary platform is not engaged in tracking deliveries. Platform workers who operate under this model have a contractual relationship with a restaurant or a shop, and have no contractual relationship with the intermediary platform. When a platform gets involved in providing delivery services, the work organising model becomes triangular. The essence of the triangular model is that digital platforms act as intermediaries between customers (clients and restaurants or shops) and service providers who are independent contractors. In fact, platform companies are more than intermediaries in the latter case since they exercise various levels of control over drivers and couriers: they control access to tasks, determine remuneration, require compliance with the rules of behaviour or appearance, check the quality of work, limit the choice of work, regulate working hours, and interfere in acceptance and rejection of assignments (Starcevic 2023).

The quadrilateral work organising model is the most common in Serbia. The model involves a new actor—a third-party contractor. The quadrilateral model is based on a commercial contract between a digital labour platform and a third-party contractor who acts as an employer that manages the workers on the platform. The role of third-party contractors in relation to workers is ambiguous. Formally, they are employers, but in practice they do not perform any employer functions: digital platforms organise work, determine remuneration, and control workers through algorithms. Even the decision to hire or fire a worker cannot be made by a third-party contractor without the consent of the platform since platforms are the only party that can activate or deactivate workers (i.e. worker accounts). A third-party contractor acts as a staffing agency and a payroll service that charges platform workers for the services. The fee varies from platform to platform, with some of them charging a flat 10% fee, others—3–10% fee, while food delivery platforms typically charge a scale of a certain percentage which depends on the amount of the revenue (Starcevic 2023).

Although the flexible forms of work enshrined in Serbian labour law are narrowly applied, the practice reveals that they are widely used by third-party contractors. For example, certain legal forms of business organisations are exempt from VAT up to a certain revenue threshold, so third-party contractors usually close their companies every 3 months and open new ones, re-employ the same persons, and thus evade tax paying.

It is worth noting that some Serbian platforms which receive complaints from workers handle, albeit reluctantly, these complaints, and in some cases terminate contracts, while others return all the money they owe workers. Despite individual cases, all digital labour platforms tend to insist that they are not a party to any relationship between a third-party and a worker, and are, therefore, not responsible for any wrongdoing by a third-party contractor (Starcevic 2023).

Considering this, it can be concluded that digital platforms have found a new way to prevent the establishment of labour relations by severing any contractual relationship with workers and using an intermediary employer. Therefore, Serbia needs the regulation of platform work which would cover the diversity of work organising and strategies that are currently used by digital platforms to evade their responsibilities as employers. This requires improving platform labour regulation to ensure that labour laws assign accountability and responsibility to digital platforms, regardless of their organisational model.

Illegal work on digital platforms undermines the sustainability of the existing social protection systems. Anticipating an increase in the number of freelancers, including digital workers, some European countries, such as France and Belgium, have reformed and adapted their social protection systems. Freelancers in these countries have the same protection as traditional employees. Meanwhile, the issue of the distribution of social protection costs between workers and platforms (as potential employers) requires greater involvement of the state. In the current circumstances, the state is expected to play a significant role and take over part of employers' responsibility in providing social insurance benefits. Digital platforms workers appreciate flexibility and the ability to adjust to other commitments. In this respect, they have an advantage over traditional workers who cannot plan their time in the same way. Judging by the flexibility of working hours and work-life balance, digital work in Serbia reflects European trends. The eight-hour workday, or the 40-hour work week, is one of the greatest achievements of the traditional regulation of labour relations. Work-life balance is another important aspect since it is a guarantee of meaningful and creative work which leaves time for leisure and relaxation.

The statistical data show that 83% of digital platform workers usually work 40 h a week or less. Thus, a workweek of most digital platform workers does not differ significantly from a workweek of traditional employees. This is in line with digital labour patterns in other European countries (Pesole et al. 2018).

Studies also show that digital platform workers who work more than 40 h a week tend to be entrepreneurs or have their own business, and digital work is their main source of income. Digital platforms work often involves non-standard work in the evening or at night. Nevertheless, digital platform workers value their freedom of choice when it comes to their working hours. The freedom to select the convenient working time allows most digital platform workers to combine work on the platforms with other commitments. An important feature of digital platform work is working from home, which makes it an attractive option for those who like working independently and away from the office. However, one must keep in mind that digital platform work can eventually worsen their work-life balance. An agreement which obliges a worker to work permanently "within four walls" blurs the line between work and leisure and opens space for fatigue, constant exhaustion and a lack of social contact, which digital platform workers often indicate as the negative aspects of their work. Despite its drawbacks, digital platform work in Serbia still retains the characteristics of traditional work with flexible working hours (Pesole et al. 2018).

Nevertheless, two-thirds of platform workers in Serbia do not pay taxes or social protection contributions, which they would have to pay as self-employed persons to be entitled to a retirement benefit and/or health insurance. This eventually attracted the attention of the tax authorities that began to investigate the payments received from abroad. In October 2020, the Serbian Tax Inspectorate began to require platform workers to retroactively pay taxes for the last 4 years. The "freedom" of the self-employed in Serbia comes at a price. Not only do they pay twice as much social insurance contributions as employees in the traditional employment relationships, but also must pay an employer's share of the contributions. They are also not entitled to sickness, maternity/paternity or unemployment benefits. In response, digital platform workers established an association which sent a demand to the government leaders to clarify the status of platform workers. However, the Ministry of Finance issued a statement to defaulters and explained that they will have to pay taxes and contributions regardless of their status in the future (*Deutsche Sozialversicherung Europavertretung* 2021).

Albania and Serbia want to attract so-called digital nomads, while Montenegro is considering following suit. Efforts are being made to find ways to bring freelancers, including platform workers, into the tax system. But the proposals for specific taxes for freelancers were rejected after the protests in both Montenegro and Serbia. In 2021, the Serbian government established a working group to examine the regulation of digital platform work, but it focuses on the problem of undeclared work rather than on working conditions and misclassification of digital platform workers (European Training Foundation 2023).

It should be mentioned that one of the first attempts to define the status of platform workers was the "Charter of Principles of Good Platform Work" approved by digital platforms in early 2020. This document was jointly approved by the largest Internet platforms (*Cabify*, *Deliveroo*, *Grab*, *MBO Partners*, *Postmates* and *Uber*) to establish the principles for improving the situation of platform workers and strengthen the cooperation between platforms and social partners. (*Mashina* 2024).

The charter consists of eight chapters, each dedicated to one corpus of platform worker rights. The Charter states that "The Government, platforms and users/customers share responsibility for ensuring adequate working conditions for platform workers with consideration of the domestic working practices. Platforms should have policies or guidelines consistent with domestic working practices to help protect workers from health and safety risks, and should strive to protect and promote the physical and mental well-being of workers." This legal construction, however, defines good intentions of digital labour platforms, but not their legal obligations. The charter defines the major concepts—a platform, a platform worker and a customer (an employer's customer). For example, next to the definition of the term "a platform worker", there is a footnote indicating that the term "a worker" (on a platform) is used as a general term and should not imply any form of employment relationship between a worker and a platform. This indicates that digital platforms do not recognise employment relationships with workers (*Mashina* 2024).

Platform work is much more intensive than salaried work. Self-employed platform workers tend to work longer and more intensively, which means that their workload is high. The algorithmic control allows couriers to reject orders, but this affects the quality of their subsequent tasks, so couriers practically have no choice but to accept orders from the platform almost non-stop, without having a rest, which means excessive work intensity. This is especially true for economically disadvantaged workers with more family responsibilities who are often online 24/7 to accomplish more tasks (Shevchuk et al. 2019).

A worker's rating provided by a platform's rating system determines the various rewards introduced by the platform, and those with high ratings have more privileges in addition to being able to receive higher wages. For instance, the higher is the rating of a worker, the more opportunities the worker must filter out low-quality, financially unattractive orders, so all workers strive to maintain the highest ratings, which they try to improve by increasing their working hours.

Flexible working hours and the "part-time" payment method, offered by platforms, create a relaxed and autonomous working atmosphere which attracts many new workers who seek freedom and good pay. But platforms have a built-in management model that rates and evaluates worker performance which in its turn, is tied to the payment workers receive. Therefore, workers must work hard to maintain the high performance on the platform. In the longer term, enjoying a free work schedule, workers find themselves in a never-ending "rush game", a vicious circle. Thus, the control of the work process on digital platforms leads to high intensity of work and high workload, which negatively affects workers' physical and mental health. This is especially true for full-time platformers who see platform work as their only job and main source of income, which makes them even more dependent on platform income and control over the work process (including longer working hours) conducted by a platform (Huang 2023).

Although platform workers have the option to plan their working hours, they commonly work unsocial hours (evenings, nights or even weekends) to optimise their income, or are forced to work unsocial working hours due to time differences with customers. Thus, high work autonomy and flexibility may lead to unsocial working hours. This may have negative effects on workers' work-life balance and well-being (Shevchuk et al. 2019).

Worker surveys confirm that work flexibility can either encourage workers to work and feel better or harm their health and well-being (Ojala et al. 2014). This is explained considering the fact that the work schedules set by workers themselves can appear unrealistic, which can lead to an increased workload and the negative effects on health, well-being and work-life balance. The importance of drawing boundaries between work and leisure for recovery and sleep must apply to all types of work, including platform work.

All this clearly shows that, as in the case of traditional labour relations, platform work must be rationed. However, none of the countries under consideration has the laws to regulate the maximum duration of the working time for digital platform workers. Working hours are not limited by digital platforms. For instance, the study conducted in Ukraine indicates that 7% of platform workers tend to work more than 85 h per week (Aleksynska et al. 2018). Employees working under an employment contract are not allowed to work that many hours because it is prohibited by law.

As for the legal status of digital platform workers in all the countries under consideration, it should be stated that the problem of illegal work should be solved first. This can be done through involving digital platforms. Platform technologies allow full recording of transactions and evaluating the degree of individual involvement of all market participants. In view of this, proper registration and taxation of platform work requires only political will and specific technological solutions which, for example, would link platform payment systems with tax authority systems. The further development of electronic systems, such as the Universal Income Declaration System for natural persons, is another step in reducing illegality. Policies to promote and regulate platform work must be comprehensive and cover the incentives and benefits for different economic actors. For instance, the attempts to requalify platform workers as employees may face resistance from both platforms and their workers since this would mean less flexibility for both parties. Therefore, the primary aim of the policies should be to ensure the protection for workers while maintaining the innovation potential and flexibility of digital platforms.

Summarising, it can be concluded that the employment relationships established on digital platforms are not stable since they can be broken after completing a specific task and do not guarantee constant income. This confirms the relevance of ensuring the legal and social protection for workers in this segment of the labour market. The problems are primarily related to the radical incompatibility between the social and legal protection systems and mechanisms applied to traditional salaried workers and workers in the platform economy. Protection of the self-employed on digital platforms against platform arbitrariness and/or non-fulfilment of obligations is necessary, but should not be equated with social protection for workers. Compared to the normative regulation of other forms of employment, labour law itself provides the wide complex of social guarantees and protection measures, but this is a feature of the social function of labour law that is not characteristic of civil or economic law since labour law considers the rights of employees but not of self-employed persons who work under civil contracts.

If employment on digital platforms has the features of an employment relationship, it should be regulated accordingly, and a digital platform worker should have the status of an employee and the corresponding social guarantees. If the work is performed under a civil contract, workers should not be entitled to social guarantees since their presence would eliminate the essential differences between labour and civil contracts. The entitlement to social insurance under an employment contract is related to a number of restrictions, such as subjection to internal regulations, work regime, disciplinary influence of an employer, etc., which are not present in civil contracts. A person can independently decide on the most suitable form of work.

The lack of consensus on the status of platform workers is due to the similarity of labour relations to civil legal relations. Labour relations have been regulated by the norms of civil law, and an employment contract has been considered one of the many types of civil contracts. Civil law was considered the main branch of the Roman law. Nevertheless, the Roman law also covered the rudiments of labour relations with its labour hire contracts when a free person used to sell his labour. Labour was considered a commodity, so the nature of a contract between a worker and an employer was no different from property contracts: one party sells labour, while the other buys it. Labour and the work process are treated as property, and civil law regulates legal relations related to property. An employment contract was considered a type of civil property contract, and there was no question of any independent labour law. Later they began to be separated, and currently labour and civil contracts are clearly demarcated and regulate different relationships.

The fact of the existence of labour relations between parties is disclosed by the following objective features: there is an agreement between the parties; a certain work function (i.e. the work which requires a certain profession, qualification, skills is performed or a certain position is held) defined by qualitative characteristics is carried out under the agreement; one of the parties works in obedience to the work order established by the other party; the work is paid. But laws do not prohibit concluding labour contracts regulated by civil law or carrying out independent activities to earn income or gain other economic benefits (The Supreme Court of Lithuania 2023).

After analysing the features of digital platform work in Moldova, Ukraine, Serbia, Albania, Bosnia and Herzegovina, and Montenegro, it can be stated that in addition to misclassification of digital platform workers and identification of their employment status, undeclared work is a serious problem. The lack of the statistical data makes it difficult to discuss the status of digital platform workers in these countries. There is no uniform, general employment status of platform workers either within individual countries or in the Eastern European region because domestic platforms can offer different types of contracts: some of them hire full-time or part-time workers by formalising their relationship in accordance with the Labour Code (by themselves or through temporary employment agencies), while others hire workers through third parties or offer service provision contracts.

If workers work for an intermediary, they benefit from social protection and employment rights, and their employer pays social contributions. Meanwhile, the self-employed must pay all taxes or social contributions themselves. The legal status of remote platform workers varies from country to country. For instance, the work of freelancers in Albania is regulated by the laws on social and health insurance, and income tax (European Training Foundation 2023). If freelance work is the main source of a worker's income, the worker is considered self-employed. To promote small businesses, governments introduce preferential tax regimes which also benefit people who work remotely through digital platforms. Serbia has no legal definition of the status of the self-employed and requires freelancers to register as entrepreneurs (Andjelkovic et al. 2019).

Freelancers who provide services to foreign companies in Bosnia and Herzegovina must report their income, but the lack of a regulatory framework leaves the employment status of freelancers unclear. (European Training Foundation 2023).

In general, the lack of monitoring and enforcement (and in some cases—proper regulation) of the new forms of employment (including platform work) leaves much room for illegality and manipulation which manifest in undeclared work and income across all types of platforms. Such manifestations can take many different forms.

Neither platforms nor authorities are inclined to verify the validity of the contracts of intermediary companies with platform workers. Thus, platform workers continue to work and get paid even after the termination of a contract, but they are no longer registered with authorities and are not entitled to any social or health care guarantees or benefits. Few platforms ensure that their contracts with intermediary agencies include mandatory social, health and retirement contributions to comply with applicable legal regulations. Serbia has frequent cases when several platform workers use the same account. In this case, one person registers the account with the platform and the tax inspectorate, but orders are executed by several persons to whom the account owner pays in cash. Persons working under service contracts tend to under-report their income. Due to the fact that platform work is hardly regulated (or regulations are not effective), the status of platform workers is unclear, the tax obligations and social protection rights are fragmented, and the working conditions are unstable (Andjelkovic et al. 2019).

It is obvious that many innovative forms of employment have disadvantages compared to the traditional forms of employment. First, given the lack of regulation in this area, new forms of work, including platform work, allow and sometimes even promote undeclared work and tax evasion. Given that the innovative forms of employment are often highly digitalised, online payments and open markets can be expected to provide more transparency and reliability than traditional cash payments in the shadow economy. However, appropriate political action is needed to implement the effective control.

The incentives for workers to formalise their work and income can also arise from the regulation of the areas which are not directly related to employment. Trust in government and social dialogue are the key components that are necessary for developing new policies. The political will and regulatory efforts should be accompanied by adequate institutional organisation, communication and clear information about the rights and responsibilities of all economic actors.

In addition, it must be recognised that many new forms of work, including platform work, in the EU Member States and the USA provide significantly worse social protection and labour rights for workers than traditional forms of work.

References

Aleksynska M, Bastrakova A, Kharchenko N (2018) Work on digital labour platforms in Ukraine: issues and policy perspectives. International Labour Office. Retrieved from: https://webapps.ilo.org/wcmsp5/groups/public/%2D%2D-ed_protect/%2D%2D-protrav/%2D%2D-travail/documents/publication/wcms_635370.pdf

Andjelkovic B, Sapic J, Skocajic M (2019) Digging into Gig Economy in Serbia: Who are the digital workers from Serbia and why do they work on global platforms? Retrieved from: https://www.researchgate.net/publication/332061375_Digging_into_Gig_Economy_in_Serbia_Who_are_digital_workers_from_Serbia_and_why_they_work_on_global_digital_platforms

Azmuk HA (2019) Зайнятість через цифрові платформи—нова реальність сучасної економіки: виклики та стратегії адаптації. Економічний простір, № 152. С. 74–75. Retrieved from: http://www.prostir.pdaba.dp.ua/index.php/journal/article/view/428

Bertolini A, Lopez F, Ustek-Spilda F, Graham M, Feuerstein P, Budu J (2022) What Does the War in Ukraine Mean for Platform Workers? Retrieved from: https://www.irs-blog.com/2022/05/06/what-does-the-war-in-ukraine-mean-for-platform-workers-a-bertolini-t-lopez-f-ustek-spilda-m-graham-p-feuerstein-and-j-budu%EF%BF%BC%EF%BF%BC/

Brcko District of Bosnia and Herzegovina (2011) *Law On Enterprises of Brcko District of Bosnia and Herzegovina.* Retrieved from: https://advokat-prnjavorac.com/legislation/Law-on-public-enterprises-of-Brcko-District-of-Bosnia-and-Herzegovina.pdf

Brcko District of Bosnia and Herzegovina (2019) *Employment Law of Brčko District.* Official Gazette of Brčko District, No. 34/19, 02/21, 06/21 and 15/22

Danish Trade Union Development Agency (2023) Labour market profile, Moldova 2023/2024. Retrieved from: https://www.ulandssekretariatet.dk/wp-content/uploads/2023/12/LMP-Moldova-2023-final-version.pdf

Deutsche Sozialversicherung Europavertretung (2021) *Spain prepares law to clarify status, whereas Serbia also demands retroactive taxes and contributions.* Retrieved from: https://dsv--europa.de/en/news/2021/03/plattformarbeiter-bald-arbeitnehmer.html

DLF Attorneys-at-Law (2021) Diia City legal framework in Ukraine. Retrieved from: https://dlf.ua/en/diia-city-legal-framework-in-ukraine/

Employment Tribunals (2015) Case Nos 2202550/2015. Reasons for the reserved judgement on preliminary hearing sent to the parties on 28 October 2016. Retrieved from: https://www.judiciary.uk/wp-content/uploads/2016/10/aslam-and-farrar-v-uber-reasons-20161028.pdf

Ermsone D (2019) Policies Supporting Youth Transition to Work in Armenia, Azerbaijan, Belarus, Georgia, Moldova and Ukraine. Retrieved from: https://www.etf.europa.eu/en/publications-and-resources/publications/policies-supporting-youth-transition-work

Euronews Albania (2021) *ILO recent report: 56.7% of all workers in Albania employed under informal arrangements.* Retrieved from: https://euronews.al/en/ilo-recent-report-56-7-of-all-workers-in-albania-employed-under-informal-arrangements/

European Training Foundation (2021) New forms of employment in the Eastern Partnership Countries: platform work—Moldova. Retrieved from: https://www.etf.europa.eu/en/publications-and-resources/publications/future-work-new-forms-employment-eastern-partnership

European Training Foundation (2023) Embracing the Digital Age. The future of work in the Western Balkans. New forms of employment and platform work. Retrieved from: https://www.etf.europa.eu/sites/default/files/2023-04/Embracing%20digital%20age_Western%20Balkans.pdf. p. 43

Expanding Choices: Gender Responsive Family Policies for the Private Sector in the Western Balkans and Moldova Project, the UN Population Fund (UNFPA), the Austrian Development Agency (ADA), the operational unit of the Austrian Development Cooperation, the Ministry of Labour and Social Protection and Chamber of Commerce and Industry of the Republic of Moldova (2022) *Expanding the working arrangements. Public policy recommendations for improved work-life balance.* Retrieved from: https://moldova.unfpa.org/sites/default/files/pub-pdf/expanding_the_working_arrangements.pdf

Fairwork (2023a) Assessing work in the Albanian platform economy. Albania Ratings 2023. Retrieved from: https://fair.work/wp-content/uploads/sites/17/2023/11/Fairwork_Albania_Report_2023.pdf

Fairwork (2023b) Bosnia and Herzegovina. Retrieved from: https://fair.work/en/ratings/bosnia-and-herzegovina/

Fairwork (2023c) Labour standards in the platform economy. Bosnia and Herzegovina Ratings 2023. Retrieved from: https://fair.work/wp-content/uploads/sites/17/2023/09/Fairwork-BiH-Ratings-2023-EN-red.pdf

Federation of Bosnia and Herzegovina (2016) Labour Law for Federation of Bosnia and Herzegovina. Retrieved from: http://fipa.gov.ba/publikacije_materijali/zakoni/05.08.2016.Labour%20Law%20FBIH_ENG_2016.pdf

Hadwiger F (2022) Realizing the opportunities of the platform economy through freedom of association and collective bargaining. International Labour Organization, Working Paper No. 995203991802676. Retrieved from: https://ideas.repec.org/p/ilo/ilowps/995203991802676.html

Huang H (2023) Algorithmic management in food-delivery platform economy in China. N Technol Work Employ 2023:5. https://onlinelibrary.wiley.com/doi/10.1111/ntwe.12228

Ivanovic I (2022) No one is responsible for "gig" workers. Retrieved from: https://en.vijesti.me/news/economy/629563/no-one-is-in-charge-of-gig-workers

Kassi O, Lehdonvirta V (2016) Online labour index: measuring the online gig economy for policy and research. In: The internet, policy and politics conferences proceedings. Oxford Internet Institute, University of Oxford, Oxford. Retrieved from: https://www.sciencedirect.com/science/article/abs/pii/S0040162518301331

LigaZakon (2019) *Новий Трудовий кодекс конкретизує ознаки трудових відносин.* Retrieved from: https://buh.ligazakon.net/news/191910_noviy-trudoviy-kodeks-konkretizu-oznaki-trudovikh-vdnosin

Marenco M (2023) Imagined Futures of Work in the Making: The Politics of Platform Workers' Contract Classification in Denmark, France, Italy, and the Netherlands. Dissertation. Scientific-disciplinary sector: SPS/09. Scuola Normale Superiore, 2023

Mashina (2024) Safety and Health at Work for Platform Workers. Retrieved from: https://www.masina.rs/eng/safety-and-health-at-work-for-platform-workers/

Moldovan Tax Authorities (2020) Tax Monitor. Official gazette. August, 2020

Munkholm NV, Schjoler CH (2018) Platform work and the Danish model - legal perspectives. Nordic J Commerc Law 1:117–144

Novikov DO, Lukianchikov OM (2019) *Про перспективи трудового права в гіг-економіці.* Проблеми реалізації прав громадян у сфері праці та соціального забезпечення: тези доповідей та наукових повідомлень учасників IX Міжнародної наукової практичної конференції, яка при свячена 50-річчю створення кафедри трудового права Національного юридичного університету ім. Ярослава Мудрого, м. Харків, 11 жовтня 2019 р. / за ред. О.М. Ярошенка. Харків: Право, С. 223. Retrieved from: https://dspace.hnpu.edu.ua/items/a799f390-3123-4da5-a3b5-c9bfda44ad18

Ojala S, Natti J, Anttila T (2014) Informal overtime at home instead of telework: increase in negative work-family Interface. Int J Sociol Soc Policy 34(1/2):69–87

Oruč N, Kurta A, Kurtović I (2023) Platform work in Bosnia and Herzegovina: solution for unemployment or deepening precarity. Retrieved from: https://fair.work/en/fw/blog/platform-work-in-bosnia-and-herzegovina-solution-for-unemployment-or-deepening-precarity/

Panjkova OB, Kasperovič OJ (2022) *Проблеми соціальної та правової захищеності платформних зайнятих і пріоритети регуляторної політики України в умовах воєнного стану.* С. 101–102. Retrieved from: https://doi.org/10.15407/econindustry2022.02.091

Pesole A, Urzi Brancati MC, Fernandez-Macias E, Biagi F, Gonzalez Vazquez I (2018) Platform workers in Europe. Evidence from the COLLEEM survey. EUR 29275 EN. Publications Office of the European Union, Luxembourg. https://doi.org/10.2760/742789. Retrieved from: https://publications.jrc.ec.europa.eu/repository/handle/JRC112157

President of Ukraine. Official website (2022) The launch of "Diia City" will allow Ukraine to become the largest IT hub in Europe—President. Retrieved from: https://www.president.gov.ua/en/news/zapusk-diya-city-dast-ukrayini-zmogu-stati-najbilshim-it-hab-72753

Raja S, Midari V, Khan B, Leuca S (2018) Digital Jobs in Moldova. The World Bank Group, Working Paper No. 134079, pp. 1–50. Retrieved from: https://documents1.worldbank.org/curated/en/165681548705998410/pdf/Final-version-of-report-on-digital-jobs-in-Moldova.pdf

Republic of Srpska (2000) Labour Law for Republic of Srpska. Retrieved from: https://advokat--prnjavorac.com/legislation/Labour-Law-of-RS.pdf

Republic of Srpska (2011) Law On Craft-Entrepreneurial Activity for Republic of Srpska. Official Gazette of RS 117/2011, 121/2012, 67/2013, 44/2016 and 84/2019

Sacharuk IC (2020) *Перспективи правового регулювання трудової діяльності працівників цифрових платформ.* Науковий вісник публічного та приватного права, випуск 6, том 2, 2020. С. 75. Retrieved from: https://doi.org/10.32844/2618-1258.2020.6-2.13

Shevchuk A, Strebkov D, Davis SN (2019) The autonomy paradox: how night work undermines subjective Well-being of internet-based freelancers. ILR Rev 72:75–100. https://doi.org/10.1177/0019793918767114

Starcevic J (2023) Platform work in Croatia and Serbia: varieties of organizational models and work arrangements. Retrieved from: https://www.researchgate.net/publication/376204635

The Supreme Court of Lithuania (2023) The ruling of the Civil Cases Division of the Supreme Court of Lithuania on 4 April 2023 in civil case No. e3K-3-109-684/2023

Tucker E (2020) Towards a political economy of platform-mediated work. Stud Political Econ 101(3) No. 185 207

Verkhovna Rada of Ukraine (2012) *Про зайнятість населення: Закон України від 5 липня 2012 р. зі змінами.* Retrieved from: https://zakon.rada.gov.ua/laws/show/5067-17#Text

Verkhovna Rada of Ukraine (2021) *Про стимулювання цифрової економіки: Закон України від 15.07.2021. Офіційний веб-сайт Верховної ради України.* Retrieved from: https://zakon.rada.gov.ua/laws/show/1667-20#Text

Verkhovna Rada of Ukraine (2023) *Кодекс законів про працю України зі змінами та доповненнями.* Retrieved from: https://zakon.rada.gov.ua/laws/show/322-08#Text

Chapter 6
Empirical Results from a Survay of Digital Platform Workers in Moldova

Liliana Staver, Grigore Belostecinic, Larisa Dodu-Gugea, and Larisa Mistrean

Abstract This chapter provides an in-depth analysis of digital platform work in the Republic of Moldova, based on a comprehensive national survey conducted between June and August 2024. The study examines the demographic composition, educational attainment, occupational diversity, and geographic distribution of platform workers, while also assessing their motivations, working conditions, and perceived vulnerabilities in the emerging platform economy. Using a mixed-methods approach with CATI and CAWI instruments, the survey collected responses from 846 individuals in urban and rural regions. The findings reveal a complex interplay between flexibility, autonomy, and income supplementation, juxtaposed with widespread informality, lack of legal protection, and precarious working conditions. Particular attention is paid to gender and age disparities, the role of platform work as a primary and supplementary source of income, and the implications for social justice and labor market inclusion. Comparative references to global literature contextualize Moldova's position within broader platform work dynamics, highlighting both convergences and local specificities. The chapter concludes with policy-oriented reflections on the regulation of platform-mediated work, highlighting the urgent need to reconcile digital innovation with fair labor standards and comprehensive social protection frameworks.

This chapter presents the results of a comprehensive survey conducted between June and August 2024 on the topic of digital platform work in the Republic of Moldova. The purpose of the survey was to understand the demographics, education levels, and professional occupations of platform workers and their perspectives on working conditions, challenges, and potential improvements. The survey was conducted across more than 90 localities in Moldova, covering both urban and rural environments.

The digital economy has grown significantly over the past decade, reshaping traditional labor markets and creating new opportunities for work. Moldova is no

L. Staver (✉) · G. Belostecinic · L. Dodu-Gugea · L. Mistrean
Academy of Economic Studies of Moldova (ASEM), Chişinău, Moldova
e-mail: liliana.condratchi@ase.md; belostecinic@ase.md; dodu-gugea.larisa@ase.md; mistrean_larisa@ase.md

R. Remeikienė, L. Gasparėnienė (eds.), *Work and Legal Guidelines in the Age of Digitalisation and Green Transition*, European Union and its Neighbours in a Globalized World 25, https://doi.org/10.1007/978-3-032-03511-0_6

exception, as digital platforms increasingly play a role in providing flexible employment options. However, these opportunities come with challenges, particularly concerning labor conditions, legal definitions of workers' status, and social protection.

Moldova was selected as a case study due to its uniquely illustrative regulatory, economic and social context, the scarcity of existing research and the quality and significance of our original empirical data. It is both methodologically justified and crucially enhances the scholarly coherence and practical value of the entire work to maintain this Chapter as a distinct section within the book.

As a non-EU post-Soviet country, Moldova does not apply EU labour directives, which results in a high level of legal ambiguity regarding platform work. At the same time, the country is undergoing rapid alignment with EU standards, which makes the current transitional stage especially relevant for empirical analysis. Furthermore, the lack of existing national research and data on digital platform work highlights the added value of this original survey. The nationally representative data collected using a robust methodology allows for an in-depth exploration of how digitalisation is shaping labour market dynamics in a country with limited institutional capacity and growing integration ambitions. The Moldovan case offers insights not only into national specificities but also into broader regional trends and methodological pathways for future studies in similar non-EU contexts.

6.1 Methodology and Data Collection

Data for this study were collected through a comprehensive questionnaire using both the CATI (Computer-Assisted Telephone Interviewing) and CAWI (Computer-Assisted Web Interviewing) methods. The questionnaire was developed in both Romanian and Russian, utilizing the data collection software provided by Imaps Expert Ltd. And IDATA Ltd. It underwent thorough testing, including technical assessments, to ensure proper functionality, including skip logic (routing), filters, and other programmed checks.

The survey targeted a sample of 1,000 platform workers across both urban and rural settings in Moldova. Of these, 846 respondents provided valid interviews, yielding a valid completion rate of 84.6% relative to the targeted sample. The participants included employees, freelancers, and independent contractors across different age groups and gender categories. The survey questions covered various topics, such as working conditions, social protection, legal status, and the balance between professional and personal life.

Data analysis was conducted using descriptive statistics to identify trends and significant areas of concern within the platform labor market. The results of the questionnaire are available in percentage form, presented in tables, and disaggregated by larger respondent categories (e.g., employment status, gender, age group, urban vs. rural) for more detailed analysis.

6.2 Sample Description

In the annexes at the end of the study, the data collected through the questionnaire is presented in detail. Comprehensive tables display the percentage outcomes, along with disaggregated data, allowing for an in-depth examination of the findings across different respondent categories. The annexes provide a clear and accessible structure for further reference, ensuring transparency in both the methodology and the results. This structure facilitates a deeper understanding of the study's conclusions and offers clarity on the specific trends related to platform work in Moldova, particularly in terms of working conditions and the social and legal challenges faced by workers.

6.2.1 Demographic Distribution

Age Distribution The age distribution of the respondents reveals a significant presence of middle-aged workers, with the majority falling between 25 and 54 years old (see Fig. 6.1).

This indicates that digital platform work attracts a broad range of participants, with the highest concentration in the mid-career group (35–54 years). Younger workers also represent a significant portion, demonstrating that platform work is appealing to early-career professionals as well.

Gender Distribution The gender distribution among respondents shows a relatively balanced participation, though there is a slight male predominance (see Fig. 6.2).

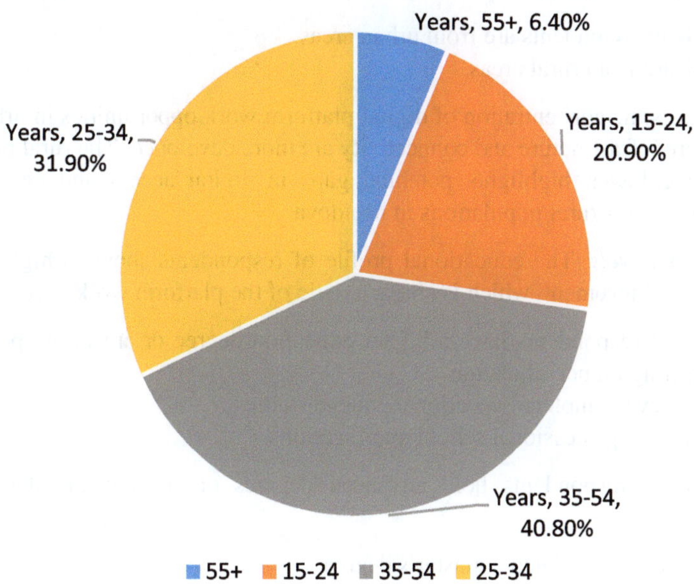

Fig. 6.1 Age distribution of respondents. *Source*: compiled by the authors

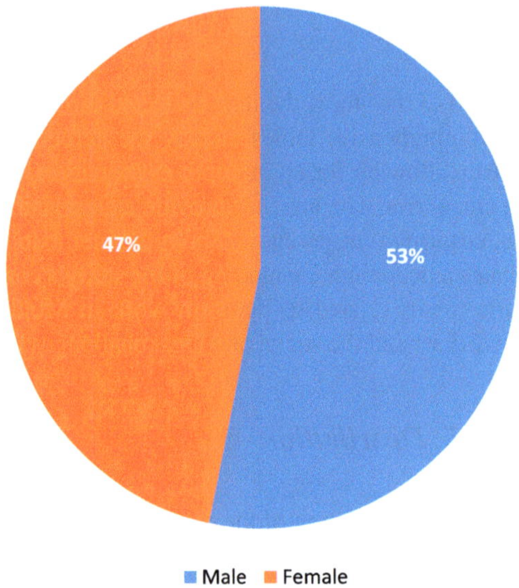

Fig. 6.2 Gender distribution of respondents. *Source*: compiled by the authors

This highlights the inclusivity of platform work across genders, though the slightly higher male participation may reflect sector-specific trends, particularly in fields traditionally dominated by male workers, such as logistics and transport.

Geographical Distribution (Urban vs. Rural) There is a clear skew towards urban respondents:

- 83.9% of respondents are from urban areas,
- 16.1% are from rural areas.

This reflects the concentration of digital platform work opportunities in urban centers, where infrastructure and connectivity are more developed. The rural participation, while lower, highlights potential gaps in digital access and employment opportunities for rural populations in Moldova.

Education Levels The educational profile of respondents shows a high level of academic achievement, which is characteristic of the platform workforce:

- 39.7% of respondents have a higher education degree or are in the process of completing higher education,
- 13.8% have completed vocational college studies,
- 11.7% have professional school qualifications.

Additionally, respondents hold advanced degrees or specialized education as follows:

- 11.5% have completed a master's degree,
- 10.4% have some incomplete secondary education,

- 9% have completed high school,
- 2.1% have obtained a Ph.D. or equivalent.

This diverse educational background highlights that digital platform work in Moldova attracts individuals with varying levels of formal education, including both entry-level workers and highly educated professionals. The significant share of respondents with higher education suggests that platform work can serve as a flexible or supplementary income source for those with academic qualifications.

Occupational Distribution The occupational data reveals the diversity of professional involvement among platform workers in Moldova:

- 37.5% of respondents are salaried employees,
- 20.8% identify as freelancers,
- 14.5% are managers or entrepreneurs.

Other notable occupational categories include:

- 11.7% are students,
- 6.6% are unemployed,
- 5.4% are homemakers.

This distribution suggests that platform work serves different functions depending on the respondent's primary occupation. For salaried employees and freelancers, it may provide additional income or flexibility, while for students and unemployed individuals, platform work may represent a primary or transitional source of income.

6.3 Results and Discussion

Question 1

Which of the following definitions do you believe best explains what digital labor platforms are? (please check one or more answers that reflect your point of view)

The perception of digital labor platforms in Moldova aligns with global trends, where platforms are predominantly seen as intermediaries that connect clients with service providers, a role extensively documented in existing literature (see Fig. 6.3). This intermediary role is well-documented in the literature, with Chin and Yean Chin and Yean (2021) emphasizing how digital platforms facilitate transactions in labor markets, effectively reducing transaction costs and enhancing flexibility for both workers and clients. In Moldova, survey result indicates that 49.4% of respondents view these platforms as intermediaries, particularly in urban settings, which reflects the broader global understanding of the platforms' primary function in linking labor supply with demand (Au-Yeung and Qiu 2022).

However, as in many other countries, there is also a substantial group (35.9%) that views platforms primarily as tools for executing transactions and managing payments, mirroring global research on the transactional and economic nature of platforms as seen in work by Daramola and Etim (Daramola and Etim 2022), who discuss the transactional dominance in platform-mediated work. Furthermore, the

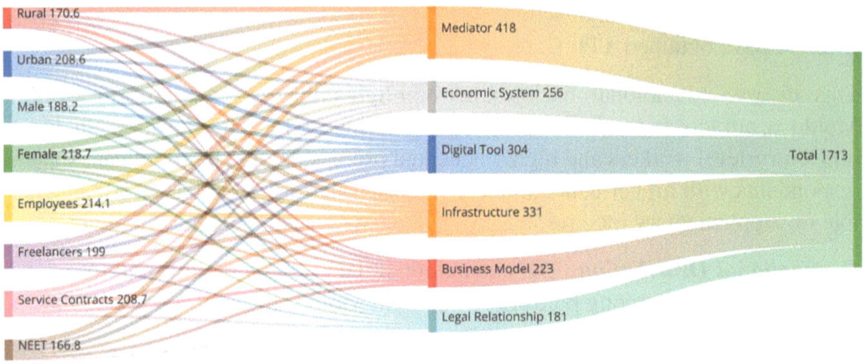

Fig. 6.3 Distribution of perception of definition of digital platforms by demographics and professional status of respondents. *Source*: compiled by the authors

notion of platforms as part of a broader economic system for distributing tasks among freelancers (30.3%) parallels findings in De Stefano's (2016) research, which highlights platforms' role in facilitating gig work and freelancing across different sectors globally.

Interestingly, the lower emphasis on platforms as business models (26.4%) or legal frameworks (21.4%) in Moldova contrasts with findings from more developed economies. For instance, Berg et al. Daramola and Etim (2022) highlight that in developed contexts, there is a heightened concern regarding worker classification and legal protections. This suggests that Moldova's platform economy may still be in an earlier stage of formalization, where issues of legal frameworks and worker protections are not yet as pronounced. This comparison underscores the shared characteristics of Moldova's platform economy with global trends while revealing unique local nuances, particularly the lesser focus on legal structures and protections for workers.

Question 2

What types of activities do you carry out on digital platforms? (please check one or more answers relevant to you)

Republic of Moldova, like many countries, is seeing a significant shift in the way labor markets function, with digital platforms facilitating diverse forms of employment, particularly in low- and middle-skilled sectors. The most prominent activity on these platforms, delivery services/food delivery, engages a substantial portion of the population, especially men, which reflects global tendencies observed in gig economies around the world. For instance, studies from Europe and North America have consistently shown that food delivery and courier services dominate the gig economy landscape, where men are overrepresented due to the physically demanding nature of the work (De Stefano 2015; Balaram et al. 2017). Moldova's data reinforces this trend, with 28.6% of male respondents reporting engagement in food delivery compared to just 11.6% of women, illustrating how traditional gender roles may still influence labor market participation in this sector (see Fig. 6.4).

Moreover, home improvement and renovation services rank second in popularity, with a notable male dominance, as expected given the nature of the work. Globally, similar patterns have been observed, with platform-based services like TaskRabbit seeing higher male participation in jobs involving physical labor (Rosenblat and Stark 2016). In contrast, sectors like tutoring, translation, and other knowledge-based services have higher female participation, which is again consistent with global findings where women tend to dominate freelance work in education, translation, and content creation (Hunt et al. 2019). In Moldova, 15.9% of women participate in tutoring and 13.9% in translation services, indicating that digital platforms are providing women with avenues to monetize intellectual and service-based work, particularly in urban areas where access to these platforms is more prevalent.

However, the overall participation in higher-paying sectors such as IT and information services remains low across both genders. This points to a broader issue that Moldova faces regarding digital infrastructure and tech-sector development. While globally, IT services form a significant part of the gig economy, particularly in developed countries, Moldova's lower engagement in this sector (3.3% overall, with men slightly outpacing women) highlights the country's nascent tech ecosystem,

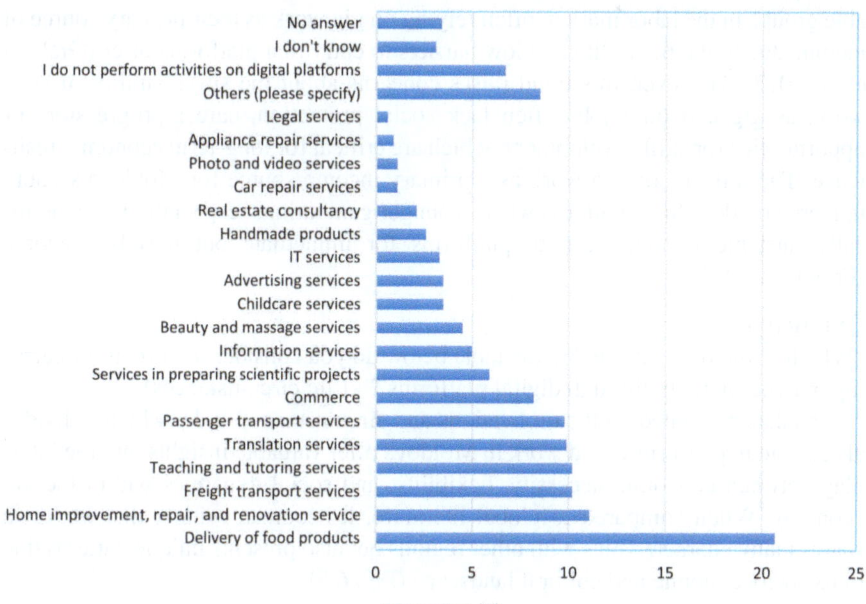

Fig. 6.4 Distribution of activities performed on digital platforms by respondents (%)
Source: **compiled by the authors.**

which still lacks the scale and maturity seen in places like India or the United States, where freelance tech work is a major contributor to the gig economy (Berg et al. 2018). This trend suggests that Moldova has yet to fully harness the potential of digital platforms to foster high-skill, high-pay employment, leaving its digital workforce predominantly engaged in lower-skill sectors.

The gender disparity observed across sectors further emphasizes global inequalities reflected in Moldova's platform economy. Women, while finding opportunities in caregiving, translation, and tutoring, remain largely underrepresented in technical fields such as IT, which globally offers higher wages and more significant growth potential (ILO 2021b). This mirrors findings from studies on platform economies in the Global South, where gender norms and unequal access to education continue to limit women's participation in high-tech fields (Wood et al. 2019). In Moldova, this division is stark, with only 5.1% of women engaging in handmade product sales compared to 0.4% of men, and similarly high gender divides in fields like childcare, where women dominate. This reflects both the opportunities and constraints that digital platforms offer for women in the region. While platforms create income opportunities in traditionally unpaid or informal sectors like care work, they also perpetuate existing gender divisions, limiting women's access to higher-skilled and better-paying jobs.

The reliance on platforms for low-wage, low-skill work in Moldova is particularly evident in the high engagement rates among NEET individuals, with 45.5% participating in food delivery services. Globally, NEETs are one of the most vulnerable groups in the labor market, often relying on gig work as their primary source of income due to the flexibility and low barriers to entry that platforms offer (Graham et al. 2017). However, this trend raises concerns about the sustainability of such work, as gig economy jobs often lack social protection, career progression, or opportunities for skill development, which are critical for long-term economic resilience. The reliance on gig work as a primary income source for Moldova's youth mirrors broader global patterns where younger generations, especially in economically unstable regions, turn to platforms for immediate but unstable income (Friedman 2014).

Question 3

"Which of the reasons listed in the table below do you consider important for carrying out your activity through digital platforms?" (Life circumstances)

The data presented on the motivations and circumstances under which individuals engage in platform-based work in Moldova offer valuable insights into the interplay between economic necessity, flexibility, and social dynamics within the gig economy. When compared to global literature, it becomes evident that Moldova shares many characteristics with other regions but also presents unique patterns due to its socioeconomic and cultural landscape (Fig. 6.5).

Additional Questions

Question 3.1. Working through digital platforms is the main source of income

Question 3.2. Work through digital platforms is an additional source of income

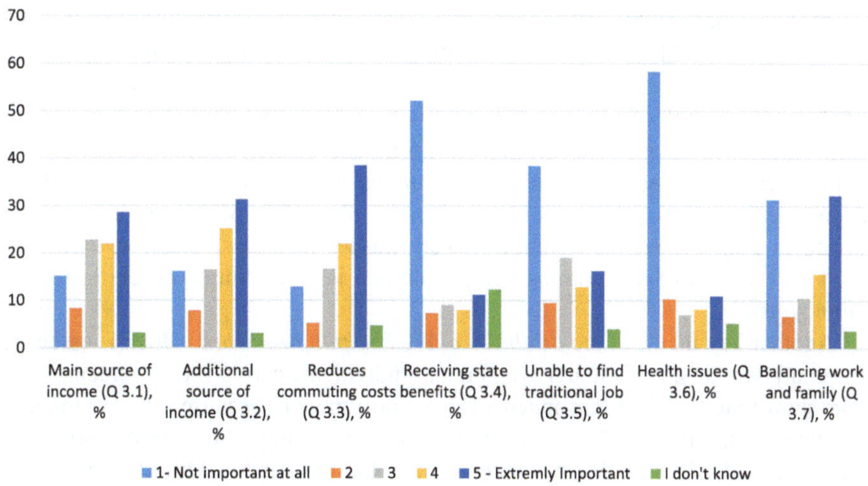

Fig. 6.5 Overview of responses for working through digital platforms. *Source*: compiled by the authors

Question 3.3. Work through digital platforms contributes to reducing commuting costs, lunch expenses, renting an apartment near the workplace, etc.

Question 3.4. I work on the digital platform unofficially to receive state benefits at the same time (e.g., unemployment benefits, etc.)

Question 3.5. I cannot find a job in the traditional labor market

Question 3.6. I have health issues that make it difficult to find another type of job

Question 3.7. Working on a digital platform allows me to balance my work time with caring for a family member (for example, children, elderly parents, or family members with disabilities)

One of the main findings of the data is the extent to which platform work serves as a *primary or supplementary source of income*. Approximately 28.6% of respondents indicate that platform work is their primary source of income, while 31.3% consider it a supplementary income. This dual role of platform work aligns with global trends, particularly in low- and middle-income countries where platform work offers immediate but often insufficient income. Studies from the International Labour Organization (ILO 2021b) have highlighted that platform work is increasingly becoming a primary income source for people in vulnerable economic conditions, especially for those who are unable to find traditional full-time jobs. The Moldovan case mirrors these findings, where 16.2% of respondents say they cannot find traditional employment, a reflection of both the limitations of the formal labor market and the accessibility of gig work. This finding is consistent with research in other Eastern European countries and globally, where gig work provides income to those marginalized from traditional labor markets, including NEETs (Not in Education, Employment, or Training) and freelancers (Berg et al. 2018).

A closer look at the data reveals that *rural workers* and those in specific age brackets are more likely to depend on platform work as their primary income source. For example, younger workers (15–24 years old) and those in rural areas are more likely to view platform work as a primary or supplementary income compared to their urban counterparts. This may indicate a greater reliance on platforms in regions with fewer traditional employment opportunities, as also observed in studies of gig economies in developing regions (Graham et al. 2017). Moldova's rural-urban divide in employment opportunities likely pushes rural individuals towards gig work as a means of overcoming geographic and infrastructural barriers to formal employment.

Another key theme is the *flexibility offered by platform work*, which is essential for many workers, particularly women and individuals caring for dependents. The data show that 32.2% of respondents value platform work because it allows them to balance work with family care responsibilities, including childcare or caring for elderly parents. This finding resonates with global literature that highlights the role of platform work in providing flexibility, especially for women who often bear the brunt of caregiving responsibilities (Hunt et al. 2019). Globally, gig work is frequently cited for allowing workers to dictate their schedules, making it a popular choice for those needing to balance paid labor with unpaid care work. In Moldova, as in many parts of the world, this flexibility is crucial for workers in the informal economy, which lacks protections such as paid leave or maternity benefits.

The *lack of social protection* for platform workers is another area of concern reflected in the data. A significant portion of respondents (30.6%) strongly agree that platform work is associated with a lack of social protection benefits, such as unemployment insurance, paid leave, and health benefits. This is consistent with global literature that points to the precarious nature of platform work, where workers are typically classified as independent contractors, thus excluded from traditional labor protections (De Stefano 2016; Forde et al. 2017a, b). The Moldovan gig workers' experience mirrors that of workers across Europe and North America, where platforms like Uber and Deliveroo have been criticized for exploiting legal loopholes to avoid providing employee benefits (Wood et al. 2019). This absence of protection further marginalizes already vulnerable workers, especially NEETs and those without access to formal employment.

Additionally, the *circumstantial nature of platform work*—where individuals are forced into the gig economy due to a lack of alternatives—plays a significant role. A substantial percentage (38.4%) of respondents indicated that they engage in platform work because they cannot find a job in the traditional labor market. This underscores the role of platforms as a fallback option in Moldova's constrained labor market. Similar findings have been observed in regions experiencing economic hardship or high unemployment, where platform work serves as a last resort for many workers (Friedman 2014). For instance, in countries such as South Africa and Brazil, platform work often fills gaps left by inadequate formal employment, and workers turn to platforms not by choice but by necessity (Hunt et al. 2019).

Moreover, a notable percentage (37.5%) of respondents agree that the *lack of job flexibility* in traditional employment drives them towards platform work. The ability to avoid daily commuting costs, lunch expenses, and rent in urban centers is also a significant factor, with 38.5% of respondents acknowledging these savings as a motivation for their participation in platform work. This aligns with global observations where workers opt for remote or platform-based work to reduce the financial burdens associated with traditional employment settings.

Question 4

Which of the reasons listed in the table below do you consider important for carrying out your activity through digital platforms? (Personal priorities)

Figure 6.6 shows the most important personal priorities for working through digital platforms.

Additional Questions

Question 4.1. Flexibility—I can freely choose the time, duration, location, and tools for my work.

Question 4.2. Autonomy—I can manage my own work activities, the process, and my career progression.

Question 4.3. I prefer to work outside the traditional environment, such as the typical office setting.

Question 4.4. Higher work efficiency—I can use my working time more efficiently and take fewer unproductive breaks.

Question 4.5. Anonymity—Working through a digital platform provides me with enhanced security, as I do not disclose my full personal details when registering on the platform (clients only see my registration number, country, and system rating).

The motivations for engaging in digital platform work in Moldova reflect broader global trends, which can be analyzed in the context of existing literature

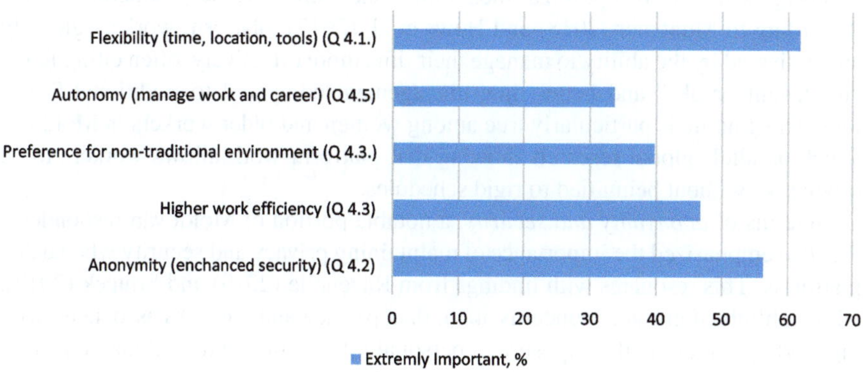

Fig. 6.6 Most important personal priorities for working through digital platforms (extremely important—5). *Source*: compiled by the authors

on the gig economy. Flexibility, autonomy, and efficiency are key drivers of platform work both in Moldova and globally, as evidenced by research from scholars such as De Stefano (2016) and Ravenelle (2019), who found that workers are often drawn to gig platforms because of the ability to choose when, where, and how they work. In Moldova, 61.9% of respondents emphasized flexibility as "extremely important", particularly younger workers and women, which aligns with global findings that younger generations, especially Millennials and Gen Z, prioritize flexibility and work-life balance in choosing gig work over traditional employment.

Moreover, autonomy is another critical motivator. In Moldova, 56.2% of respondents ranked autonomy as "extremely important", with younger individuals (15–24 years) showing an even higher preference (61.1%). This mirrors global research by Kalleberg (2009) and Schmidt (2017), which highlights how platform workers often seek independence from traditional hierarchical employment structures, allowing them to manage their own workloads, progression, and career trajectories. Freelancers and independent workers globally, as in Moldova, value this autonomy, seeing platform work as a means of bypassing rigid corporate environments.

The preference for *working outside traditional environments* was also strongly reflected in the Moldovan data, with 39.7% of respondents finding this "extremely important". This is consistent with findings by Schor (2020) *and* Wood et al. (2019), who argue that platform work has redefined the work environment, offering an alternative to the traditional office setup. Particularly since the COVID-19 pandemic, remote work and non-office-based roles have become more desirable globally, with many workers opting for the flexibility that digital platforms offer, as indicated by the high percentage of women and older workers in Moldova seeking these alternatives.

Efficiency was another major factor, with 46.8% of Moldovan respondents citing it as "extremely important". This motivation is aligned with global literature that discusses how gig platforms are perceived to offer more efficient ways of working, allowing workers to optimize their time and minimize unproductive hours. According to Muntaner (2018) and Huws et al. (2017), platform workers globally are motivated by the ability to manage their time more effectively, often citing fewer "inefficient breaks" and better time management compared to traditional 9-to-5 jobs. This finding is particularly true among women and older workers in Moldova, which parallels global research showing that platform work allows workers to be productive without being tied to rigid schedules.

In terms of *anonymity and security*, a notable portion of Moldovan respondents (33.7%) emphasized the importance of maintaining privacy and security when using platforms. This resonates with findings from Ravenelle (2019) and Srnicek (2017), who highlighted growing concerns about data privacy and the risks associated with gig work, particularly the exposure of personal information in digital marketplaces. Globally, workers are increasingly aware of the need for security, with platforms offering partial anonymity, such as using registration numbers or ratings instead of full names.

Figure 6.7 highlights gender differences in the "extremely important – 5" ratings for various personal priorities when working through digital platforms.

Key observations:

- *Flexibility* is slightly more important for women (63.8%) than men (60.3%).
- *Autonomy* is also valued more by women (57.3%) than men (55.2%).
- Women place greater emphasis on *preferring non-traditional work environments* (43.4% vs. 36.7% for men).
- *Higher work efficiency* is considered extremely important by a larger percentage of women (50.4%) compared to men (43.6%).
- *Anonymity* is more important to women (36.0%) than men (32.0%).

These differences indicate that flexibility, autonomy, and efficiency are slightly more critical for women compared to men.

Question 5

Which of the reasons listed in the table below do you consider important for carrying out your activity through digital platforms? (Social needs).

Figure 6.8 summarises the most important social needs for working through digital platforms.

Aditional Questions:

Question 5.1. Competence—when working through digital platforms, I feel professional and skilled, and the tasks are more interesting

Question 5.2. I communicate with clients; I feel useful to society

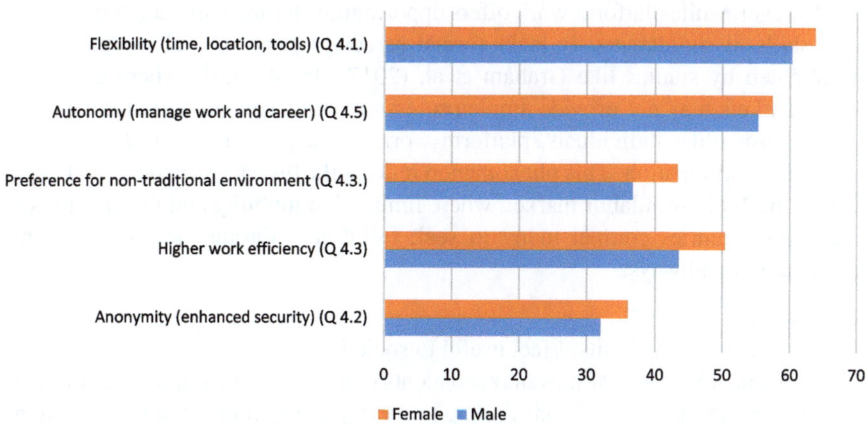

Fig. 6.7 Gender differences in personal priorities for working through digital platforms (extremely important—5). *Source*: compiled by the authors.

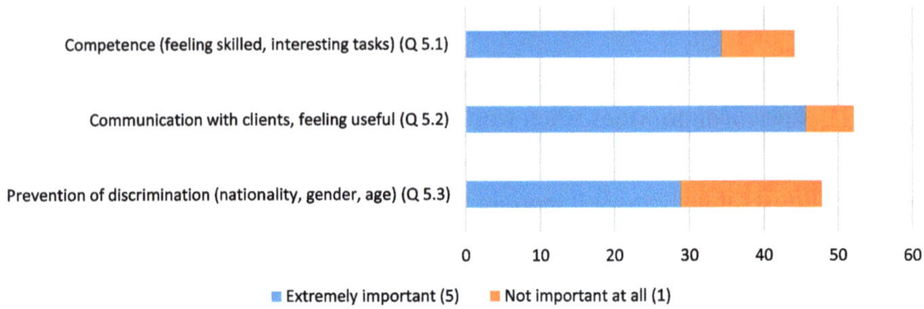

Fig. 6.8 Summary of social needs for working through digital platforms. (extremely important—5 vs. not important—1) (%). *Source*: compiled by the authors

Question 5.3. Prevention of discrimination—working through digital platforms helps prevent discrimination based on nationality, gender, age, etc., because I can remain anonymous

Question 5.1

Competence—when working through digital platforms, I feel professional and skilled, and the tasks are more interesting.

In Moldova, 34.3% of respondents reported that working on digital platforms enhances their sense of professionalism, skill development, and task engagement. This sentiment is particularly pronounced among older workers, with 42.4% of respondents aged 55+ and above expressing strong professional satisfaction from platform work. These findings resonate with global research, where gig workers in higher-skilled sectors, such as digital marketing, information technology, and consultancy, often report a sense of competence and autonomy (Wood et al. 2019).

However, while platform work offers opportunities for the application of specialized skills, it simultaneously lacks formal career progression and recognition, as highlighted by studies like Graham et al. (2017). In Moldova, where traditional labor markets may not provide ample professional engagement opportunities, particularly for older individuals, platform work fills a gap, allowing for continued economic participation. This phenomenon reflects the broader structural challenges within the Moldovan labor market, where limited job mobility and formal employment opportunities compel many to seek fulfillment through less conventional employment pathways.

Question 5.2

I communicate with clients; I feel useful to society

A notable 45.7% of Moldovan respondents emphasized the importance of client interaction and the sense of contributing to society as key motivations for engaging in platform work. This finding is particularly significant among women (47.9%) and older individuals (66.6% of respondents aged 55 and above). The social dimension of platform work, often overlooked in economic analyses, has been explored in global studies by scholars like Schor (2020), who argue that gig work can provide a sense of purpose, particularly in service-oriented sectors such as education, personal care, and consulting.

In Moldova, where traditional employment avenues may offer limited opportunities for meaningful social engagement, platform work serves as a conduit for personal connection and societal contribution. This dynamic is consistent with findings in other emerging economies, where workers derive satisfaction not only from the financial benefits of gig work but also from the relational aspects of interacting with clients and communities (Friedman 2014). This is especially pertinent for women and older adults, who may find traditional jobs less accommodating to these social needs.

Question 5.3

Prevention of discrimination—working through digital platforms helps prevent discrimination based on nationality, gender, age, etc., because I can remain anonymous

A significant proportion of Moldovan respondents (28.9%) indicated that the anonymity provided by digital platforms helps mitigate discrimination based on nationality, gender, or age. This motivation was particularly emphasized by women (34%) and older workers (33.3%). Globally, research on platform work, such as that by Barratt (2019), has identified the potential of digital platforms to reduce discrimination by allowing workers to conceal personal characteristics that might otherwise subject them to bias in traditional employment settings.

In Moldova, where discrimination based on age and gender remains a persistent issue, the anonymity afforded by platform work offers an opportunity for marginalized groups to participate in the labor market on more equitable terms. While this potential benefit is acknowledged in global discourse, it is important to note that anonymity alone does not eliminate structural inequalities. Workers may still face challenges such as wage disparities and biased treatment by clients, even if their personal details are concealed (Hunt et al. 2019).

Global studies, such as those by Schmidt (2017) and De Stefano (2016), highlight flexibility and autonomy as primary motivators for platform work. Moldova reflects these trends, with respondents consistently prioritizing the ability to control working hours, location, and workload. In line with global research, platform work in Moldova functions as a critical alternative to traditional employment, particularly for those encountering barriers to accessing the formal labor market.

However, Moldovan respondents exhibit heightened motivations regarding social interaction, societal contribution, and the prevention of discrimination, which appear more pronounced than in higher-income Western economies. This suggests that platform work in Moldova serves not only as an economic lifeline but also as a means of addressing broader social and professional needs. The differences between Moldova and wealthier nations may stem from the more constrained structure of the Moldovan labor market, where traditional employment opportunities are fewer, particularly for women, older workers, and individuals facing discrimination.

Question 6
In your opinion, which of the factors listed in the table below contribute to the exploitation of workers through digital labor platforms?

Figure 6.9 summarizes the key factors contributing to the exploitation of workers on digital platforms, based on the percentage of respondents who "strongly agree" with each factor.

Additional Questions:
Question 6.1. When working through digital platforms, I do not have social protection, and I cannot receive insurance or social assistance (such as sickness benefits, maternity leave, unemployment benefits, etc.)

Question 6.2. I work more unofficially through digital platforms.

Question 6.3. I am not guaranteed the minimum wage.

Question 6.4. When I work through digital platforms, I do not have the right to paid leave, vacation time, or other types of leave.

Question 6.5. Lack of flexibility—I have to constantly monitor the internet or mobile applications because tasks do not come regularly.

Question 6.6. Lack of autonomy—I cannot significantly influence the nature and variety of tasks, and I am not free to select working methods.

Question 6.7. Irregular working hours, unequal workload, and spending unpaid time waiting for tasks.

Question 6.8. There is no communication between workers, clients, and the organizers/owners of the platforms, and workers' activities are essentially self-managed.

Question 6.9. Limited opportunities for skills development and career progression - repetitive tasks requiring minimal training.

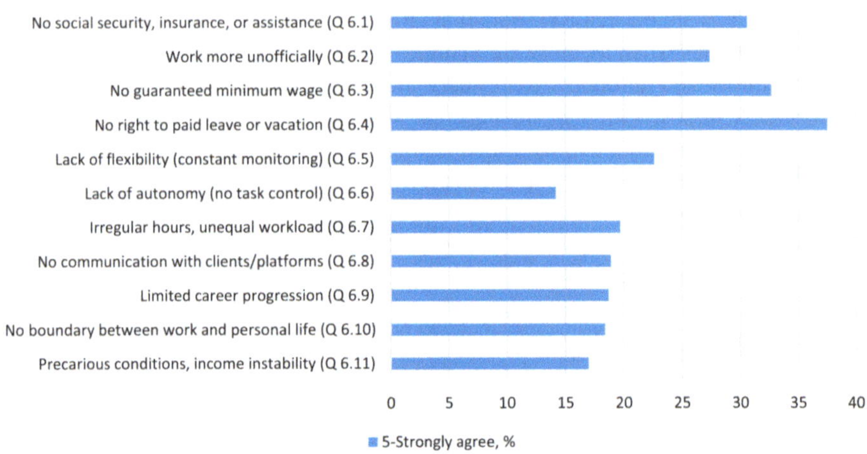

Fig. 6.9 Factors contributing to exploitation on digital labor platforms (strongly agree—5) (%). *Source*: compiled by the authors

Question 6.1
When working through digital platforms, I do not have social protection, and I cannot receive insurance or social assistance (such as sickness benefits, maternity leave, unemployment benefits, etc.)

A significant portion (30.6%) of respondents strongly agree that workers on digital platforms face exploitation due to the lack of social protection protections, with the sentiment being particularly strong among older age groups (35–54 years) and among those classified as freelancers or contract workers (31.8% and 37%, respectively).

Globally, this concern mirrors findings from research on the gig economy. For instance, Schmidt (2017) and De Stefano (2016) argue that platform workers worldwide often face precarious working conditions, where the lack of social protection, health benefits, and job stability is a primary issue. Studies in the United States, Europe, and emerging markets alike reveal that workers in the gig economy are frequently denied benefits typically provided to traditional employees, such as unemployment insurance, paid sick leave, and maternity benefits. This contributes to a growing divide between "standard" and "non-standard" employment.

The Moldovan data reflects these global trends, with 29.8% of male respondents and 31.6% of female respondents agreeing that this is a serious issue. This can be explained by the fact that, as in many parts of the world, Moldovan labor laws were designed for traditional employment structures and struggle to accommodate the evolving dynamics of the digital economy. Freelancers and contract workers, who make up a large part of the platform workforce, are particularly vulnerable in this respect, as highlighted by Huws et al. (2017), who emphasize that self-employed workers in the gig economy often fall outside the protections offered by national labor laws.

Interestingly, the younger respondents (aged 15–24) are less likely to strongly agree that a lack of social protection constitutes exploitation, possibly reflecting a short-term view of platform work as a means of earning supplementary income. Conversely, older respondents (particularly those aged 35–54) express higher levels of concern, possibly due to their greater reliance on these protections as they balance work with personal responsibilities such as health and family care.

This trend aligns with findings from Muntaner (2018), which suggest that younger workers are often more tolerant of precarious conditions, viewing gig work as flexible and temporary, while older workers may see it as a necessary source of stable income, especially when they struggle to find traditional employment.

In Moldova, the lack of adequate social protection for gig workers is exacerbated by a relatively underdeveloped welfare state compared to Western countries. Moldova's labor market, much like that of other Eastern European countries, has been slow to adapt to the gig economy, and the gap between traditional employment benefits and platform work is widening. This contrasts with countries like Germany or the Netherlands, where discussions around extending social protections to gig workers are more advanced, with proposals for platform-specific regulations being discussed.

However, Moldova is not alone in this struggle. Many emerging economies, particularly in Southeast Asia and Latin America, face similar challenges in updating labor laws to cover non-standard workers. In these regions, gig workers often operate in legal grey zones, which leaves them without access to labor rights, as explored by Kalleberg (2009) and Schor (2020).

Question 6.2

I work more unofficially through digital platforms

The survey shows that 27.4% of respondents strongly agree that they work more unofficially through digital platforms. This trend is particularly strong among freelancers, individuals aged 25–34 years, and workers without formal employment contracts, such as those classified as NEET (Not in Education, Employment, or Training). This aligns with global observations that platform work often exists in a legally grey area, where workers are not fully integrated into formal employment frameworks (De Stefano 2016).

Globally, gig work is often categorized as informal or unofficial, particularly in regions with less robust labor regulations. For example, in countries like India or Brazil, platform workers frequently operate outside of formal labor protections and without official contracts, making it difficult for authorities to track their employment status or ensure fair labor conditions (Graham et al. 2017). This unofficial status may be a result of both workers' desire to avoid formal employment taxes or restrictions and platforms' reluctance to provide the benefits typically associated with formal employment.

The data reveals that urban respondents are more likely to agree that they work unofficially on platforms than rural respondents. This urban bias may be attributed to higher internet penetration, access to technology, and the availability of digital platforms in cities compared to rural areas. Rural workers may face additional barriers to accessing platform work, such as poor infrastructure, but they may also engage in traditional, non-digital forms of informal work (ILO 2021a, b).

The finding that urban areas see a higher prevalence of unofficial work also mirrors global trends. In high-income countries like the United States, gig workers in urban centers often take on platform work to supplement their income or as their primary job, but without formal recognition or benefits (Ravenelle 2019). This urban concentration of gig work is seen worldwide, where access to gig platforms is predominantly concentrated in areas with better technological infrastructure.

Female respondents reported engaging in unofficial work through digital platforms slightly more than their male counterparts (29.4% vs. 25.7%). This difference highlights the role digital platforms play in offering flexible work options for women, who may face traditional labor market barriers or prefer gig work to balance other responsibilities, such as childcare or household duties.

This pattern is consistent with global findings that women often use platform work to reconcile paid employment with unpaid care responsibilities (Hunt et al. 2019).

In many countries, women are overrepresented in platform work, particularly in sectors like freelancing, domestic work, and online tutoring, where flexibility is key. However, because many women engage in this work unofficially, they lack access to social protection, job stability, or formal labor protections, deepening gender disparities in the workforce.

The data shows that workers aged 25–34 years and freelancers are among the most likely to agree that they work unofficially on platforms, at 28.5% and 30.3%, respectively. This suggests that younger workers, especially freelancers, are more willing to engage in unofficial platform work to navigate the current labor market. Freelancers, in particular, may choose platform work due to the flexibility and autonomy it offers, but this often comes at the cost of lacking formal contracts and social protections.

Younger workers globally, particularly *Millennials* and *Gen Z*, have shown a strong preference for gig and freelance work over traditional employment. This is often due to the flexibility it provides, even though it typically comes with less stability (Schor 2020). These workers may be less concerned about traditional employment benefits like pensions or health insurance but more focused on flexibility and income generation. However, the trade-off is often precarious employment, as shown in the Moldovan data.

Freelancers (30.3%) and NEET respondents (47.6%) are significantly more likely to engage in unofficial work on platforms. Freelancers are typically hired on a per-task basis, without formal contracts or employment protections, which places them in a vulnerable position. NEETs, meanwhile, may resort to platform work as a stopgap solution in the absence of traditional employment opportunities, further reinforcing their exclusion from the formal labor market. This mirrors trends observed in studies by the ILO, which show that digital platform work can offer short-term income solutions for those marginalized from the labor market, such as NEETs, but often without the stability or long-term prospects that formal employment provides. In countries like Spain and Italy, platform work has been shown to be a significant source of income for NEETs, but it does little to improve their long-term employment outcomes (Friedman 2014).

Question 6.3

I am not guaranteed the minimum wage

In Moldova, 32.7% of respondents strongly agreed that they are not guaranteed a minimum wage when working through digital platforms. This concern is particularly pronounced among freelancers (34.4%) and rural workers (21.3%). This aligns with global trends where workers in the gig economy often operate without the protections typically afforded by traditional employment, including minimum wage guarantees. Globally, platform work has been criticized for its lack of wage security. Research by De Stefano (2016) shows that gig workers are often paid per task, meaning their earnings fluctuate based on demand, task availability, and platform algorithms. In the U.S., for instance, Uber and Lyft drivers have reported earning below minimum wage after deducting expenses such as fuel and vehicle maintenance.

In Moldova, rural workers may be especially vulnerable due to fewer employment opportunities outside of platform work. The digital platform's promise of flexibility and earnings potential is undermined by this lack of wage security. Europe has taken some steps toward addressing these issues, as seen in countries like Spain, where recent regulations now classify some platform workers as employees, ensuring access to minimum wage and other benefits (European Commission 2021a, b, c). However, in countries like Moldova, such protections are still largely absent, leaving workers to fend for themselves in an uncertain labor market.

Question 6.4

When I work through digital platforms, I do not have the right to paid leave, vacation time, or other types of leave

The absence of paid leave is a major concern for platform workers in Moldova, with 37.5% of respondents strongly agreeing that they do not have access to paid vacation, sick leave, or other types of leave. This finding is consistent with *global research*, where platform workers frequently lack the basic employment benefits that are provided in traditional jobs (Huws et al. 2017). For example, in Canada and Germany, gig workers have raised similar concerns, noting that the flexibility of gig work comes at the expense of job security and benefits like paid leave and healthcare. Women and older workers in Moldova are particularly affected by this issue, which is not surprising given that these groups are often more reliant on consistent benefits like paid leave due to caregiving responsibilities or health concerns. Globally, studies have shown that the lack of paid leave in the gig economy exacerbates inequalities, particularly for workers from lower-income backgrounds who are less able to afford time off without pay (Ravenelle 2019). In Moldova, this issue is compounded by the country's weaker social safety net, making it difficult for platform workers to access paid leave or government assistance when needed.

Question 6.5

Lack of flexibility—I have to constantly monitor the internet or mobile applications because tasks do not come regularly

Contrary to the perception that platform work offers unparalleled flexibility, 22.6% of Moldovan respondents reported that they must constantly monitor the internet or mobile applications because tasks do not come regularly. This reflects a *global issue* in platform work, where "algorithmic control" reduces the actual flexibility available to workers (Wood et al. 2019). While platforms like *Uber*, *Deliveroo*, or *TaskRabbit* market themselves as providing flexibility, in practice, workers often have to remain available for long periods to ensure they receive tasks.

In Moldova, younger workers (15–24 years) are particularly affected by this issue, as their lack of job experience may push them into platform work, where they feel compelled to constantly monitor platforms for new assignments. Globally, the literature shows that gig workers frequently experience stress and burnout due to the unpredictability of task allocation, which leads to extended periods of unpaid waiting time (Schor 2020). In countries like India and Brazil, where platform work has become a significant source of income for millions, workers have reported similar frustrations, stating that they are forced to be "always on" to secure enough tasks to earn a livable income (Graham et al. 2017).

Question 6.6

Lack of autonomy—I cannot significantly influence the nature and variety of tasks, and I am not free to select working methods

In the Moldovan survey, 14.2% of respondents strongly agreed that they lack autonomy in their work, unable to influence the nature and variety of tasks or select their working methods. This reflects a *common issue in the gig economy*: despite being marketed as offering freedom and autonomy, platform work often operates under significant algorithmic control. Workers on platforms such as *Amazon Mechanical Turk*, *Upwork,* or *Uber* are subject to algorithmic systems that determine task allocation, worker ratings, and compensation (Rosenblat and Stark 2016).

In *Western economies*, autonomy has been a key selling point for platform work, but global research shows that this autonomy is often illusory. For example, workers in *ride-hailing* and *food delivery* services frequently find themselves with little control over the hours they work or the types of jobs they perform (Graham et al. 2017). In Moldova, the lack of autonomy may be exacerbated by the limited availability of traditional employment, forcing workers to accept platform work despite its constraints. This is particularly concerning for younger workers and those in rural areas, where job opportunities outside of digital platforms are scarce.

Question 6.7

Irregular working hours, unequal workload, and spending unpaid time waiting for tasks

About 19.7% of Moldovan respondents strongly agreed that irregular work hours and unpaid waiting time are major issues. This mirrors global concerns about the "gig economy trap", where workers face unpredictable schedules and are not compensated for the time spent waiting between tasks (Schor 2020). For instance, *delivery workers* in urban areas, such as those working for *DoorDash* or *Postmates* in the United States, often report long periods of unpaid time while waiting for orders, leading to significant undercompensation when compared to traditional hourly employment. In Moldova, this issue is particularly problematic for women and older workers, who may have caregiving responsibilities that make irregular work hours especially challenging. The unpredictability of platform work can disrupt family life and create stress, which is not compensated by the flexibility that platforms claim to offer. Globally, this issue is not limited to gig workers in high-income countries; platform workers in Africa and Southeast Asia also report similar concerns, particularly regarding the lack of paid waiting time and the stress of managing irregular workloads.

Question 6.8

There is no communication between workers, clients, and the organizers/owners of the platforms, and workers' activities are essentially self-managed

Moldovan respondents (18.9%) indicated a lack of communication between workers, clients, and platform organizers, leading to self-managed activities. This reflects a broader trend in platform work, where workers often feel isolated due to the lack of interaction with supervisors or peers (Srnicek 2017). In *ride-hailing* or *gig delivery services*, for instance, workers are often left to manage their own schedules and deal with customer issues independently, with little to no support from platform operators. This lack of communication can lead to feelings of isolation and disempowerment, especially in jobs that require direct interaction with customers but offer little managerial oversight (Barratt, 2019). In Moldova, the isolation experienced by platform workers may be exacerbated by the country's smaller and less-developed digital economy, which provides fewer opportunities for networking or collaboration. This isolation is also seen globally in platform-based sectors such as *domestic work*, where workers report feeling disconnected from both clients and platform operators, leading to a lack of accountability and support (Graham et al. 2017).

Question 6.9

Limited opportunities for skills development and career progression - repetitive tasks requiring minimal training

A notable 18.7% of Moldovan workers strongly agreed that there are limited opportunities for skill development and career progression on digital platforms. Globally, this is a key issue in low-skill sectors of the gig economy, where platform jobs tend to be repetitive and require minimal training. For instance, workers in *cleaning services* or *ride-hailing* often find themselves stuck in entry-level positions with no opportunities for advancement, regardless of how long they have been working for the platform (Graham et al. 2017). In Moldova, the lack of career progression is particularly concerning for younger workers and freelancers, who may enter platform work hoping for professional growth but find that their tasks are limited to low-skill, repetitive jobs. This issue is compounded in countries like Moldova, where the overall job market offers few opportunities for advancement, making platform work one of the only available options for many workers. In high-income countries, such as the UK or Germany, similar concerns have been raised by platform workers who feel that they are trapped in "dead-end" jobs with no clear path to career development (Huws et al. 2017).

Question 6.10

There is no clear boundary between work and personal life, with technology invading personal time

With 18.4% of respondents agreeing that there is no clear boundary between work and personal life due to technology, the issue of "techno-stress" emerges as a significant concern. Globally, gig workers report that the constant connectivity required by digital platforms invades their personal lives, making it difficult to disconnect from work (Ravenelle 2019). For instance, workers on platforms like *Uber* or *Lyft* often feel compelled to remain online and available for tasks, even during their personal time, to maximize their earnings (Schor 2020). In Moldova, younger workers are particularly affected by this issue, likely due to their greater reliance on smartphones and digital platforms for work. Globally, this blurring of the lines between work and personal life is a well-documented issue in platform work, with workers in India and Brazil reporting similar challenges. The constant availability required by gig platforms contributes to high levels of stress and anxiety, particularly for workers who are juggling multiple jobs or caregiving responsibilities (Graham et al. 2017).

Question 6.11

Precarious working conditions and income instability reduce motivation and job satisfaction

Precarious working conditions and income instability significantly impact job satisfaction, with 17% of Moldovan respondents strongly agreeing that these factors reduce their motivation. This aligns with global research, which shows that platform workers are often subject to fluctuating income levels and insecure working conditions (Huws et al. 2017). For instance, workers on *Amazon Mechanical Turk* or *TaskRabbit* often report inconsistent pay and limited job security, which makes it difficult to plan for the future (Graham et al. 2017). In Moldova, this issue is particularly acute for freelancers and workers with service contracts, who are more likely to face income instability due to the project-based nature of their work. Globally, precariousness is a defining feature of the gig economy, with workers in Europe, North America, and Asia reporting similar dissatisfaction due to the volatile nature of their work. This instability is particularly damaging for workers in low-income countries like Moldova, where the social safety net is weaker, leaving platform workers vulnerable to financial insecurity (Srnicek 2017).

Question 7

In your opinion, which of the factors listed in the table below contribute to the exploitation of workers through digital labor platforms?

Figure 6.10 summarizes the key factors related to work on digital platforms, based on the percentage of respondents who "strongly agree".

Additional Questions:

Question 7.1. Precarious working conditions and income instability reduce motivation and job satisfaction.

Question 7.2. Social protection is sufficient, and I have access to social benefits.

Question 7.3. Technologies enhance the transparency of activities; everything is official.

Question 7.4. My income from working through digital platforms is quite high.

Question 7.5. I have a lot of flexibility in selecting tasks, working hours, intensity, and methods.

Question 7.6. I have a lot of freedom of action, and I can manage my career.

Question 7.7. My workweek is shorter than the usual 40-hour workweek; I have more time for family obligations and leisure.

Question 7.8. I am not subordinate to managers in traditional companies; I can create my own reputation.

Question 7.9. Working on digital platforms helps me learn foreign languages (e.g., English), master digital technologies, and acquire other skills.

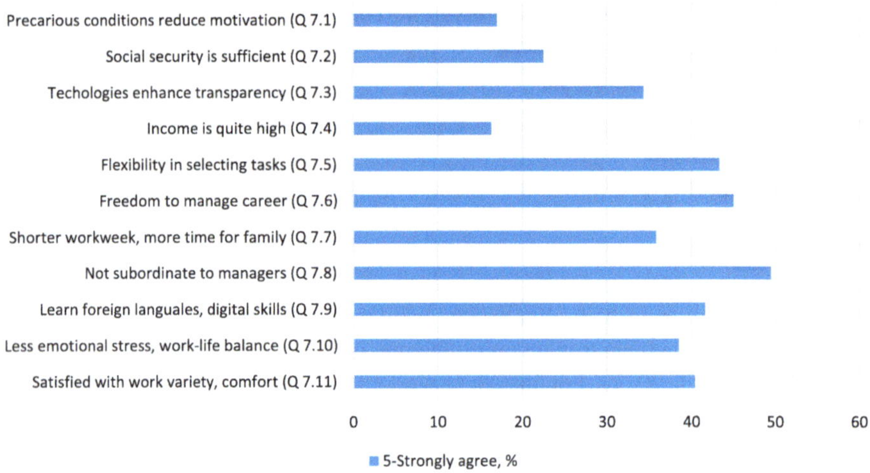

Fig. 6.10 Summary of factors related to work on digital labor platforms (strongly agree—5) (%). *Source*: compiled by the authors

Question 7.10. I feel less emotional stress; I experience a balance between professional and personal life.

Question 7.11. I feel satisfied.

Key Observations:

- Not being subordinate to managers and freedom to manage career are the most agreed-upon benefits, with 49.5% and 45.0%, respectively.
- Flexibility in selecting tasks and learning new skills (such as foreign languages and digital technologies) are also highly rated, with 43.3% and 41.6% agreement.
- Work variety and comfort and less emotional stress are also important, showing high levels of satisfaction with the work-life balance.

Figure 6.11 highlights the gender differences in perceptions of various factors related to working on digital platforms. Key observations include:

- Men rate technologies enhancing transparency and not being subordinate to managers higher than women, with 38.6% of men and 50.7% of men strongly agreeing, compared to 29.4% and 48.3% of women, respectively.
- Women place greater emphasis on less emotional stress and work variety, comfort, with 40.3% and 45.3% strongly agreeing, compared to 36.8% and 36.2% of men.
- Both genders strongly agree on flexibility in selecting tasks and freedom to manage career, though men slightly edge out women in these categories.

Question 7.1

Precarious working conditions and income instability reduce motivation and job satisfaction

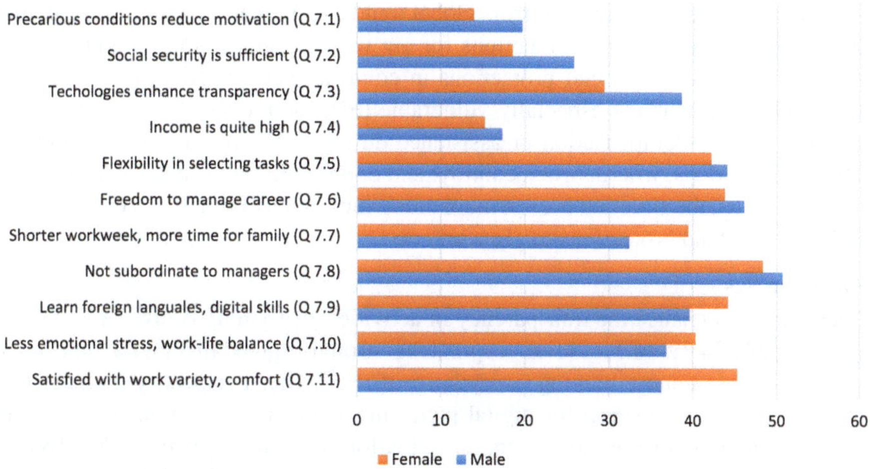

Fig. 6.11 Gender differences in benefits of working on digital labor platforms (strongly agree—5) (%). *Source*: compiled by the authors

A significant 17% of respondents in Moldova strongly agreed that precarious working conditions and income instability lead to a reduction in motivation and job satisfaction. This finding is consistent with *global research* that identifies precariousness as a core issue for platform workers. Studies by Huws et al. (2017) and Schor (2020) demonstrate that irregular pay and lack of benefits, which are typical in platform-based work, contribute to heightened worker dissatisfaction, especially in low-income settings.

In a global context, research shows that platform workers—especially those engaged in low-wage sectors such as food delivery and ride-hailing—often struggle with unpredictable incomes and insufficient social protections (De Stefano 2016). For instance, platform workers in countries like India or Brazil face instability similar to that described by Moldovan respondents, as they must navigate irregular demand and opaque pay structures. Moldovan workers, like their counterparts globally, face challenges related to financial unpredictability, which fundamentally affects job satisfaction and personal well-being.

Question 7.2

Social protection is sufficient, and I have access to social benefits

With only 22.5% of respondents strongly agreeing that they have sufficient social protection, this result reflects a broader issue seen across gig economies worldwide. *In* most gig work settings, workers are classified as independent contractors, which excludes them from access to benefits like health insurance, unemployment insurance, and pension plans. This lack of security was a key issue raised in the European Parliament's resolution on working conditions for digital platform workers (European Commission 2021a, b, c).

The challenge in Moldova mirrors global trends, particularly in developing countries where labor laws and protections for gig workers are even more underdeveloped. The absence of social protections in countries such as Nigeria or Pakistan leaves platform workers especially vulnerable to economic shocks, with very few avenues to seek compensation or assistance during times of need (Graham et al. 2017). In Moldova, where formal employment opportunities may also lack adequate social benefits, the situation is even more precarious, intensifying the need for social reforms to extend protections to gig workers.

Question 7.3

Technologies enhance the transparency of activities; everything is official

A notable 34.3% of Moldovan respondents strongly agreed that digital platforms enhance transparency, making everything official. This perspective reflects the broader *global enthusiasm* for digital platforms as tools for formalizing informal labor, particularly in emerging economies. Platforms such as *Upwork* or *Freelancer* enable workers to track hours, payments, and client feedback, adding a layer of transparency to otherwise informal or freelance work.

However, despite the perceived transparency, there is a growing body of *critical research* questioning the genuine openness of these systems. For example, Barratt (2019) argues that while platforms create an appearance of fairness and transparency, the algorithmic management of work distribution and compensation often lacks real accountability. Workers may not have visibility into how tasks are allocated or why their earnings fluctuate, leading to frustration and a sense of powerlessness. In Moldova, this technological transparency may be a double-edged sword: while it increases formality, it also amplifies the *algorithmic control* that limits worker autonomy.

Question 7.4

My income from working through digital platforms is quite high

Only 16.3% of Moldovan respondents strongly agreed that their income from digital platforms is high, suggesting a disconnect between the promise of platform work and its economic reality. This finding resonates with global reports of low earnings for platform workers, particularly in developing economies. Research by Schor (2020) and De Stefano (2016) reveals that gig work, while flexible, often results in lower earnings than traditional employment, especially when accounting for work-related expenses such as internet access, equipment, or transportation.

For instance, platform drivers in countries like South Africa and Mexico often report that after covering their expenses, their effective hourly wage is well below the minimum wage. This pattern holds in Moldova, where gig workers likely struggle to achieve a sustainable income, particularly in sectors like ride-hailing or delivery, which have thin profit margins and intense competition.

Question 7.5

I have a lot of flexibility in selecting tasks, working hours, intensity, and methods

Flexibility is often cited as one of the key advantages of gig work, and in Moldova, 43.3% of respondents strongly agreed that they have significant flexibility in choosing tasks, hours, and working methods. This echoes findings from global studies which show that workers are drawn to the flexibility offered by platforms, especially when compared to the rigid structures of traditional employment (Wood et al. 2019). For workers in countries like Germany or the United States, the ability to control one's work schedule is particularly valued by those balancing multiple jobs, education, or caregiving responsibilities.

However, the illusion of flexibility has been a subject of criticism in academic literature. Although workers have nominal control over them when they work, platform algorithms often nudge them towards working at peak hours or accepting lower-paying tasks to maintain their ratings (Rosenblat and Stark 2016). In Moldova, this flexibility may be particularly attractive to young workers (15–24 years), but it also comes with trade-offs, such as inconsistent income and the pressure to be available whenever tasks are offered.

Question 7.6

I have a lot of freedom of action, and I can manage my career

The survey results show that 45% of respondents strongly agreed that they have the freedom to manage their career and reputation, a figure that aligns with global perceptions of autonomy in gig work. Platforms like *Fiverr* or *Upwork* empower workers to build personal brands and attract clients without the need for traditional gatekeepers (Wood et al. 2019). In countries like Indonesia and Philippines, digital platforms have provided unprecedented opportunities for freelancers to access international markets and grow their careers.

However, Graham et al. (2017) warn that this autonomy is often curtailed by the design of platform systems, which exert significant control through ratings, task allocation, and pay scales. In Moldova, where the formal labor market may offer fewer opportunities for career advancement, platform work might seem like a liberating alternative. But like workers globally, Moldovans are still subject to the same invisible forces of algorithmic control, which limit their actual career management and earning potential.

Question 7.7

My workweek is shorter than the usual 40-hour workweek; I have more time for family obligations and leisure

The idea that platform work offers more personal time is supported by 35.8% of respondents in Moldova who agree that their workweek is shorter than the traditional 40-hour week. This mirrors the global perception that gig work can offer a better work-life balance, particularly for those who prioritize family time or personal interests (Schor 2020). In countries like France or Italy, many platform workers engage in part-time gigs to supplement their primary income or to accommodate other commitments.

However, research from Ravenelle (2019) and others has shown that this shorter workweek often comes at the expense of financial stability. Workers who reduce their hours typically earn less and may find it difficult to make ends meet. In

Moldova, the lower cost of living might make shorter hours more feasible, but for many workers, especially those with family obligations, the lack of a reliable income may overshadow the perceived benefits of reduced working hours.

Question 7.8
I am not subordinate to managers in traditional companies; I can create my own reputation

A strong sense of independence is evident in the 49.5% of Moldovan respondents who agreed that they are not subordinate to traditional managers. This desire for autonomy is consistent with global trends, where workers seek to escape the hierarchies and rigid structures of traditional employment. Platforms like *TaskRabbit* or *Etsy* are popular in countries like the United States for precisely this reason, allowing workers to operate outside of traditional management systems.

Nevertheless, Barratt (2019) and De Stefano (2016) caution that this independence is often illusory. While workers may not have a boss in the traditional sense, they are still subject to the dictates of platform algorithms, which control access to work, determine pay, and enforce rules. In Moldova, this sense of independence might be more pronounced due to the lack of opportunities in the formal job market, making platform work appear more attractive despite its inherent limitations.

Question 8
Did you enter into a legal agreement (e.g., employment contract, etc.) or sign another type of document for work through the digital platform? (Please select a relevant response).

The data you have presented provides a comprehensive overview of the engagement with legal agreements among workers in Moldova's gig economy. The majority of respondents (65.7%) have not entered into formal legal agreements, a trend that aligns with the global state of digital platform work, where informality is a persistent issue. However, this dataset reveals key insights into the specific demographic, geographic, and gender differences that further complicate the labor landscape in Moldova.

Overall Trends in Informality
65.7% of respondents report not having formal legal agreements (e.g., employment contracts) when working through digital platforms, highlighting the informal nature of this sector. The high prevalence of informal work agreements is consistent with global patterns. In countries with nascent digital economies, like Moldova, gig work often bypasses traditional regulatory frameworks (Fig. 6.12).

The International Labour Organization (ILO) and researchers such as Berg et al. (2018) have pointed out that the majority of platform workers globally lack formal employment contracts, leaving them without access to fundamental labor rights like social protection, paid leave, and minimum wage protections.

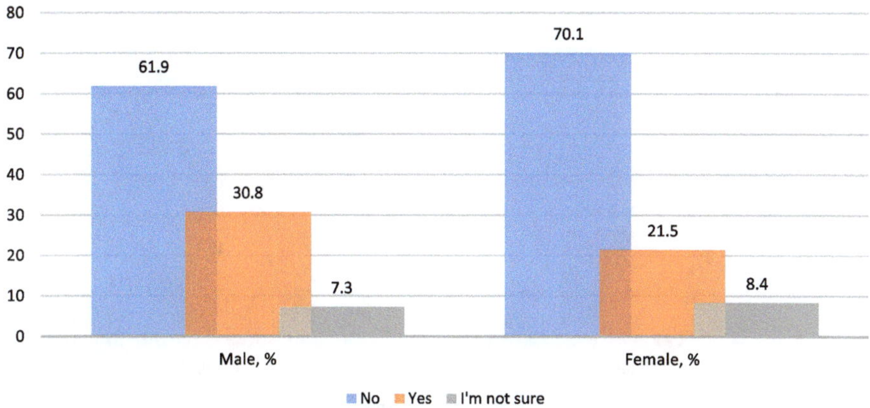

Fig. 6.12 Responses to entering a legal agreement for work on digital platforms (%). *Source*: compiled by the authors

Men (30.8%) are more likely than women (21.5%) to have formal legal agreements. This significant gender gap is concerning as it mirrors global trends in the gig economy, where women often occupy roles that are lower-paying and less formalized.

Research by De Stefano (2016) has shown that women in the gig economy are often confined to roles with lower barriers to entry, such as care work or micro-tasks, which offer fewer opportunities for formal contracts. This reflects the same gendered inequalities found in Moldova's platform economy, suggesting that women's roles in the gig economy need closer regulatory attention to ensure equality in legal protections.

Urban vs. Rural Differences

A key distinction in the data is the difference between urban and rural workers, with rural workers being more likely (69.9%) to lack formal legal agreements compared to urban workers (64.9%). This rural-urban divide suggests that geographical access to formal work arrangements and legal awareness may be contributing factors to the disparity (Fig. 6.13).

In rural areas, access to legal support and awareness of workers' rights may be lower, leading to higher levels of informality. Similar trends are seen in countries like South Africa where rural gig workers are less protected compared to their urban counterparts (Graham et al. 2017). This highlights a need for targeted interventions in Moldova to educate rural workers about their rights and formalize their employment status.

Age Group Dynamics

Figure 6.14 gives an overview of age-based responses to entering a legal agreement for work. Workers in the 25–34 and 35–54 age groups are the most likely to have formal agreements (27.4% and 27.8%, respectively), while both the

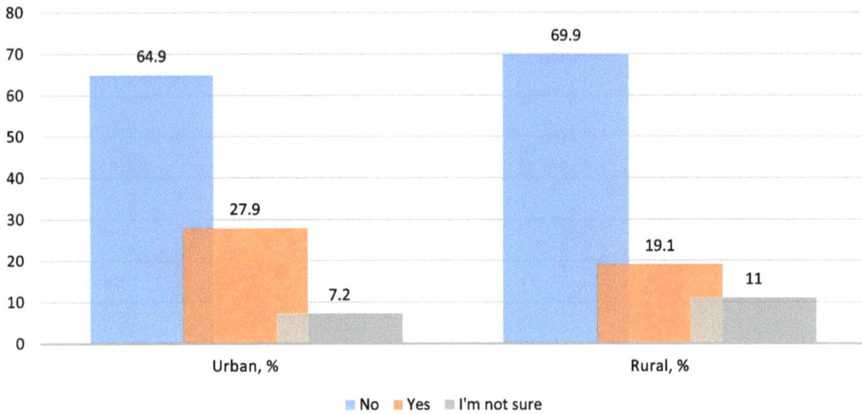

Fig. 6.13 Regional responses to entering a legal agreement for work on digital platforms (%). *Source*: compiled by the authors

youngest (15–24) and oldest (55+) workers are more likely to lack formal agreements. This pattern is consistent with global trends where younger workers, particularly those in entry-level positions, are less likely to seek or receive formal contracts.

In the case of younger workers (64.4% lacking agreements), they often enter platform work as a steppingstone to more traditional forms of employment, a pattern observed globally (Wood et al. 2019). Meanwhile, older workers (66.1% without agreements) may engage in platform work as supplementary income, reflecting the casualization of work for this age group.

Employment Status and Legal Clarity

Formal employees and freelancers have a higher likelihood of having legal agreements (28.2% and 27%, respectively). This suggests that individuals who rely more on structured and continuous forms of digital work, or those who view it as their primary employment, are more aware of the need for legal formalization.

NEET (Not in Employment, Education, or Training) individuals are the least likely to have formal agreements (only 9.5%), indicating extreme vulnerability in this demographic. Globally, NEET individuals are among the most marginalized in the labor market, and in Moldova, their lack of formal agreements places them at even greater risk of exploitation.

Uncertainty in Legal Status

7.8% of respondents were unsure of whether they had a formal agreement, with rural respondents (11%) and younger workers (11.3%) being the most uncertain. This reflects a significant gap in understanding legal obligations and rights, which is a common issue in the platform economy.

This uncertainty is reflected globally, where workers often unknowingly accept terms and conditions without understanding their legal implications. Barratt (2019)

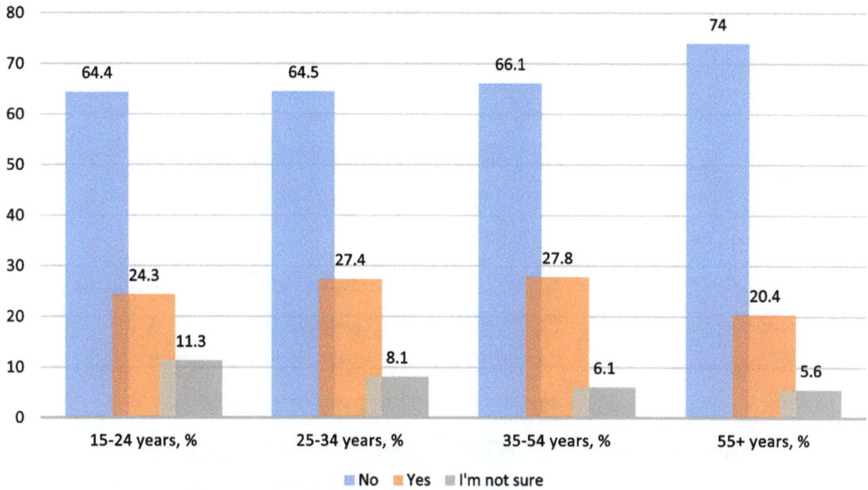

Fig. 6.14 Age—based responses to entering a legal agreement for work. *Source*: compiled by the authors

highlights how platform companies use complex legal language that makes it difficult for workers to fully comprehend the nature of their agreement, exacerbating legal uncertainty.

Moldova's gig economy reflects many of the global challenges facing platform workers. Studies by Berg et al. (2018) and Wood et al. (2019) demonstrate that gig workers globally often work without formal legal protection. This lack of legal status results in precarious working conditions, lower job security, and exclusion from benefits typically afforded to formal employees.

The gender gap observed in Moldova is consistent with global data, where women in the gig economy are often underpaid and under-protected. Moreover, the informality in rural areas is reflective of broader global issues where rural workers are typically more vulnerable and less likely to benefit from the protections available to their urban counterparts.

Question 9

What major issues have you noticed regarding the terms of the legal agreement (e.g., employment contract) proposed through the digital platform? (Please select one or more relevant responses).

The data provided offers critical insights into the nature of legal agreements for digital platform workers in Moldova, reflecting broader challenges observed globally in the platform economy. The issues identified in this dataset—ranging from unclear legal frameworks to imbalanced contracts—underscore the need for legal reform and worker protection measures in this rapidly growing sector (Fig. 6.15).

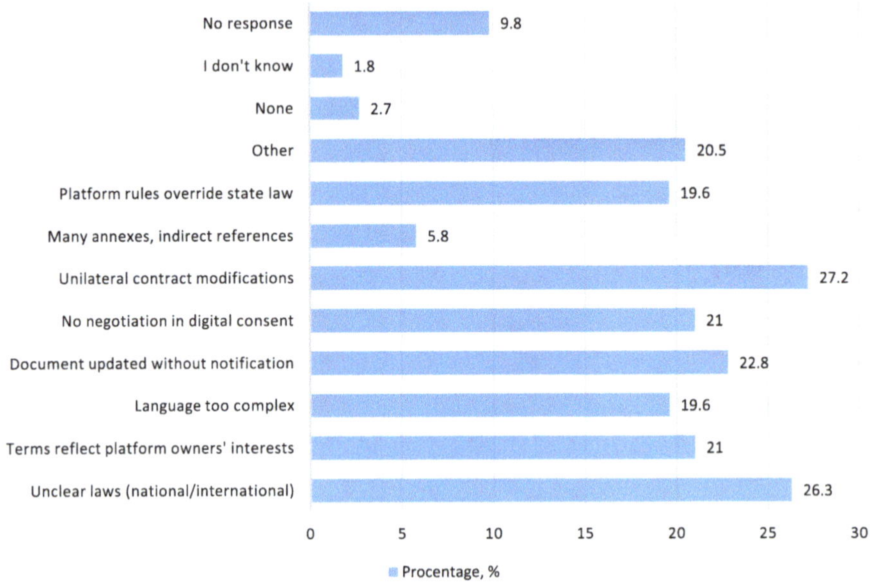

Fig. 6.15 Major issues in legal agreements proposed by digital platforms (%). *Source*: compiled by the authors

Lack of Clarity in Applicable Laws

A significant 26.3% of respondents indicate uncertainty regarding which laws—national or international—apply when working through digital platforms. This uncertainty is particularly pronounced among men (28.1%) and the 55+ age group (36.4%), suggesting that older and more experienced workers might face heightened confusion when navigating these complex legal frameworks.

This finding is consistent with global observations, where cross-border digital labor often leads to jurisdictional ambiguities. As noted by Vallas and Schor (2020), digital platforms blur the lines of employment law, creating confusion about which national legal frameworks apply. This trend is even more relevant in Moldova, where national labor laws may not yet be fully adapted to the realities of platform work, further complicating workers' understanding of their rights.

Imbalance in Legal Terms Favoring Platform Owners

The data shows that 21% of respondents feel that the legal terms primarily favor platform owners, leaving freelancers and independent workers at a disadvantage. This perception is stronger among urban respondents (20.7%), freelancers (27.4%), and workers aged 55+ (18.2%).

This imbalance reflects the broader dynamics of power in the platform economy, where platforms often hold the upper hand in dictating contractual terms. Adams-Prassl (2018) highlights that platforms frequently impose one-sided contracts, limiting workers' ability to negotiate fairer terms. In Moldova, this imbalance may be exacerbated by the lack of robust legal protections for platform workers, leaving them vulnerable to exploitation.

Complexity of Legal Language

A notable 19.6% of respondents report that the language of legal agreements is too complex and difficult to understand, with this issue being particularly prevalent among older respondents (45.5%) and freelancers. The use of overly technical or legalistic language in contracts can lead to misunderstandings or, worse, uninformed consent to terms that are not in the workers' favor.

Aloisi (2019) points out that such complexity is a deliberate strategy used by platforms to obscure the rights and obligations of workers. The lack of legal clarity in these agreements places Moldovan workers at a disadvantage, especially those with limited access to legal support or expertise, such as rural workers or freelancers.

Unilateral Updates to Agreements

The fact that 27.2% of respondents highlight the ability of platforms to unilaterally modify contract terms without notifying workers is deeply concerning. This practice erodes trust between workers and platforms and reinforces the power imbalance inherent in the gig economy. Freelancers (30.5%) and older workers (27.3%) are particularly vulnerable to these unilateral changes.

Globally, this issue has prompted regulatory responses, particularly in the European Union, where directives are being introduced to ensure that workers are notified and consulted before any changes are made to their contracts. Aloisi and De Stefano (2020) argue that such measures are essential to protect workers from the arbitrary exercise of power by platforms.

Lack of Negotiation Opportunities

Twenty-one percent of respondents express concern that the digital acceptance of work offers (via "click-to-accept" buttons) eliminates the possibility of negotiation or expressing opinions. This issue is particularly significant for those aged 55+ (45.5%) and workers on service contracts (23.1%). This trend points to the increasing automation of labor relations in the platform economy, where human negotiation is replaced by algorithmic decision-making.

The lack of negotiation opportunities for Moldovan workers reflects a broader trend in the global gig economy, where platforms dictate terms and limit worker input. Wood et al. (2019) have highlighted the rise of algorithmic control in the gig economy, where workers are subjected to the terms and conditions set by platforms without any room for negotiation.

Document Complexity

Although only 5.8% of respondents mentioned the complexity of legal documents with numerous annexes and indirect references, this issue remains significant. Legal agreements that are difficult to navigate can further alienate workers from understanding their rights and responsibilities, particularly in situations where annexes contain key legal details.

Such complexity is often used to obfuscate the true nature of the agreement and the obligations imposed on workers, as highlighted by Adams-Prassl (2018). Ensuring that contracts are straightforward and easy to understand is crucial to promoting transparency and fairness in platform work.

Platform Rules vs. National Laws

A concerning 19.6% of respondents feel that platform rules sometimes override national legislation. This sentiment is particularly prevalent in urban areas (21.2%) and among *freelancers* (21.4%), indicating that platform workers in Moldova feel increasingly disconnected from the protections offered by national labor laws.

Globally, platforms often operate in a legal gray area, where the transnational nature of their operations allows them to bypass local labor laws. As noted by Kenney and Zysman (2016), platforms frequently create their own regulatory frameworks, leading to conflicts with national labor regulations. This trend is particularly problematic in Moldova, where labor laws are still evolving to accommodate the realities of platform work.

Figure 6.16 compares how different employment groups (Employees, Freelancers, Workers with service contracts, and NEETs) perceive key issues in legal agreements proposed by digital platforms:

- Freelancers and workers with service contracts are most concerned about unilateral contract modifications (30.5% and 30.8%, respectively).
- Freelancers also face significant issues with document updates without notification (28.8%) and lack of negotiation in digital consent (25.4%).
- Employees primarily highlight unclear laws (25%) and terms reflecting platform owners' interests (27.4%).

NEETs focus on terms favoring platform owners and lack of negotiation, with 50% noting these as major issues. These issues are not unique to Moldova but are reflective of global challenges in the platform economy. Studies by Berg et al. (2018) and De Stefano (2016) highlight the precarity of platform work, where workers often lack formal legal protection and are subject to unilateral changes in contractual terms. The power imbalance between platforms and workers is a consistent theme, with platforms holding most of the bargaining power.

The EU has recognized these challenges and is moving towards implementing regulations that protect gig economy workers by ensuring *greater transparency*, *legal clarity*, and *worker rights*. Moldova can draw lessons from these initiatives to better protect its platform workers, ensuring that national labor laws are enforced and that platform rules do not override state legislation.

Question 10

In your opinion, which of the factors listed in the table below determine or hinder sustainable development in the European Union? (Economic Factors).

Figure 6.17 summarizes the economic factors influencing sustainable development in the European Union, based on respondents' perceptions:

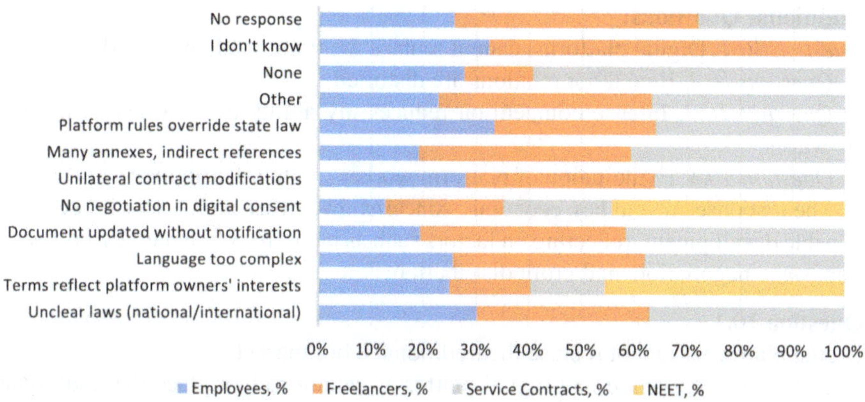

Fig. 6.16 Legal issues in agreements by employment tatus (%). *Source*: compiled by the authors

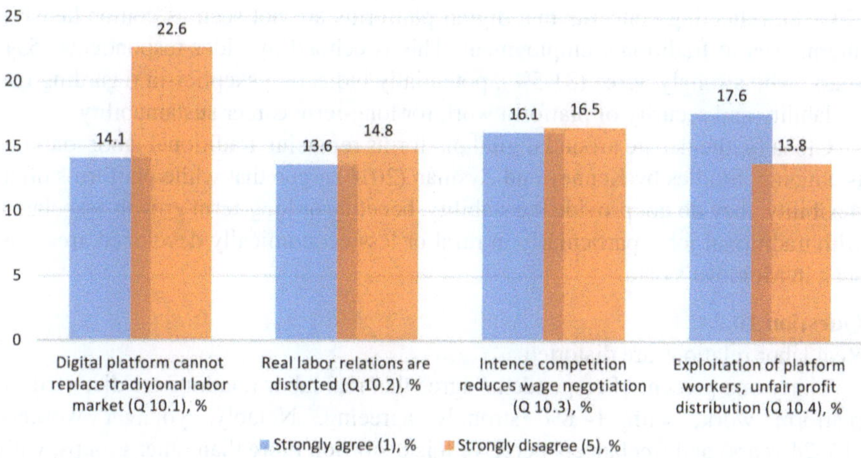

Fig. 6.17 Economic factors impacting sustainable development in the EU (%). *Source*: compiled by the authors

- 22.6% strongly agree that digital platforms cannot replace the traditional labor market, while 14.1% strongly disagree.
- 14.8% strongly agree that real labor relations are distorted, with a similar 13.6% strongly disagreeing.
- 16.5% strongly agree that intense competition reduces workers' ability to negotiate wages, while 16.1% strongly disagree.
- 13.8% strongly agree that there is exploitation of platform workers and unfair profit distribution, with a higher 17.6% strongly disagreeing.

This comparison highlights the mixed views on how digital platforms impact labor markets and workers' conditions in the EU.

Additional Questions:

Question 10.1. Digital platforms cannot replace the traditional labor market.

Question 10.2. Real labor relations are distorted.

Question 10.3. Intense competition reduces my ability as a worker to negotiate wages.

Question 10.4. Exploitation of platform workers, unfair distribution of profits.

The responses reveal key economic concerns that either promote or hinder sustainable development, reflecting on factors such as labor market dynamics, competition, wage negotiation, and profit distribution.

Question 10.1

Digital platforms cannot replace the traditional labor market

22.6% strongly agree that digital platforms cannot fully replace the traditional labor market, while 26.5% are neutral, suggesting a significant divide in perceptions.

This sentiment is more pronounced among rural workers (33.1%) and men (24.8%), reflecting concerns that digital platforms are not seen as comprehensive alternatives to traditional employment. This is echoed by older respondents (55+ years) who strongly agree (31.5%), potentially indicating skepticism regarding the scalability and security of platform work for long-term career sustainability.

Globally, the debate around digital platforms replacing traditional labor markets is ongoing. Studies by Kenney and Zysman (2016) argue that while platforms offer flexibility, they do not provide the stability, benefits, or long-term growth associated with traditional jobs, particularly in rural or less economically developed areas, as seen in Moldova's data.

Question 10.2

Real labor relations are distorted

Thirty one percent of respondents agree that real labor relations are distorted by platform work, with 14.8% strongly agreeing. Notably, younger workers (15–24 years) and freelancers perceive this distortion more than other groups, with 36.1% of the younger demographic agreeing. This reflects growing concerns about the lack of traditional labor protections—such as collective bargaining rights and job security—within digital platform work. The EU has recognized these distortions, with the European Commission exploring policy frameworks to address the labor rights of gig workers. Wood et al. (2019) suggest that platform work often blurs the lines between employer and worker, leading to uncertain labor relations and precarious working conditions.

Question 10.3

Intense competition reduces my ability as a worker to negotiate wages

24.5% of respondents agree that intense competition in the platform economy reduces their ability to negotiate wages, with 16.5% strongly agreeing.

Figure 6.18 illustrates how different age groups perceive the impact of intense competition on their ability to negotiate wages:

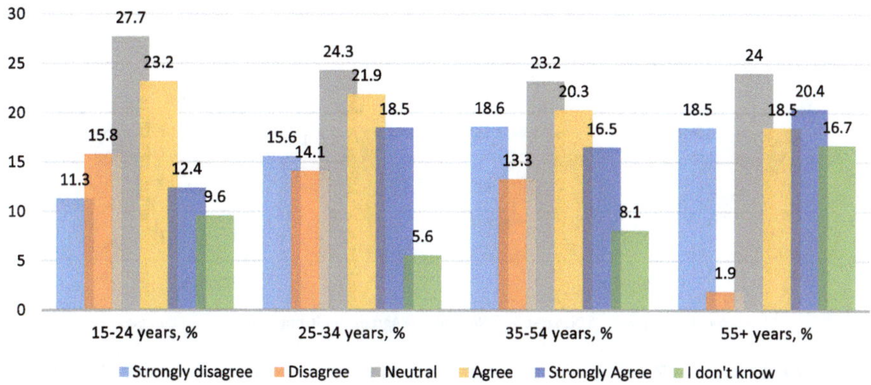

Fig. 6.18 Age-based responses to intense competition reducing wage negociation (%). *Source*: compiled by the authors

- *Younger respondents* (15–24 years) are more likely to feel neutral or uncertain, with 27.7% choosing "Neutral" and 9.6% responding "I don't know".
- *Older respondents* (55+ years) show a stronger belief that competition reduces wage negotiation, with 20.4% strongly agreeing and a relatively high percentage (16.7%) uncertain.
- *Middle-aged respondents* (25–34 and 35–54 years) tend to agree more with the statement, particularly in the 25–34 age group, where 18.5% strongly agree.

This analysis shows that perceptions of competition affecting wage negotiation vary across age groups, with younger respondents expressing more uncertainty and older respondents leaning more toward agreement.

Figure 6.19 compares how urban and rural respondents perceive the impact of intense competition on wage negotiation:

- Both urban and rural respondents have similar perceptions, with around 16% strongly agreeing that competition reduces their ability to negotiate wages.
- Rural respondents show more uncertainty, with 16.2% responding "I don't know", compared to just 6.6% of urban respondents.
- Urban respondents tend to express more neutrality, with 25.3% selecting "Neutral", compared to 20.6% of rural respondents.

This shows that while the overall perception is quite similar, rural respondents are more uncertain about the impact of competition on wage negotiation. Freelancers and service contract workers report the highest levels of concern, as platform models inherently promote competition among workers, which drives down wages. This sentiment is reflected globally, where platforms operate under algorithmic management, often leading to wage suppression as workers are pitted against each other for tasks. Aloisi and De Stefano (2020) argue that the lack of collective bargaining in platform work exacerbates wage inequality, a trend that is clearly reflected in

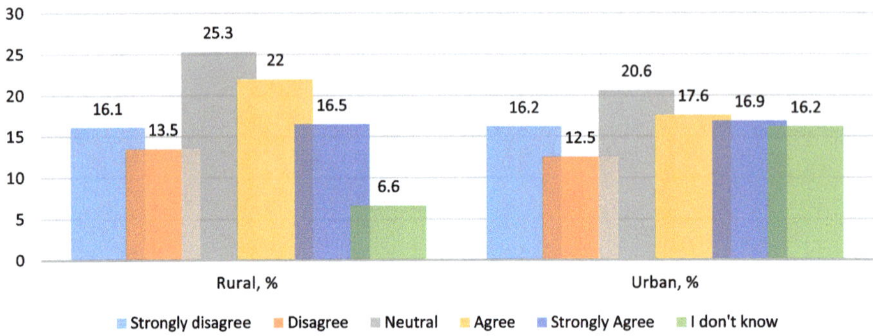

Fig. 6.19 Urban vs. Rural responses to intense competition reducing wage negociation (%). *Source*: compiled by the authors

Moldova's data. This competitive pressure threatens sustainable economic development by creating a race to the bottom for wages.

Question 10.4

Exploitation of platform workers, unfair distribution of profits

24.2% of respondents agree that there is an exploitation of platform workers, with 13.8% strongly agreeing. Interestingly, 26.2% of women and younger workers (25–34 years) are more likely to perceive this issue, highlighting concerns that profits generated by platform work disproportionately benefit platform owners rather than workers. This aligns with global research that shows how platforms extract surplus value from workers, keeping the majority of profits while providing minimal protection or benefits to their labor force (Adams-Prassl 2018). This dynamic has led to calls for the redistribution of profits and better wage protections for platform workers, as seen in movements for fairer pay in the *gig economy* in countries like the UK and USA.

Question 11

In your opinion, which of the factors listed in the table determine or hinder sustainable development in the European Union? (Social factors).

Figure 6.20 provides an all-in-one overview of the responses to *Question 11*, which covers various social factors that determine or hinder sustainable development in the European Union. It compares perceptions of platform workers on issues like:

- *Automated algorithms imposing control*
- *Inadequate social protection*
- *Exploitative or abusive working conditions*
- *Flexibility leading to uncertainty*
- *Irregular working hours*
- *Intense competition increasing vulnerability*
- *Salary instability*
- *Anonymity and discrimination*

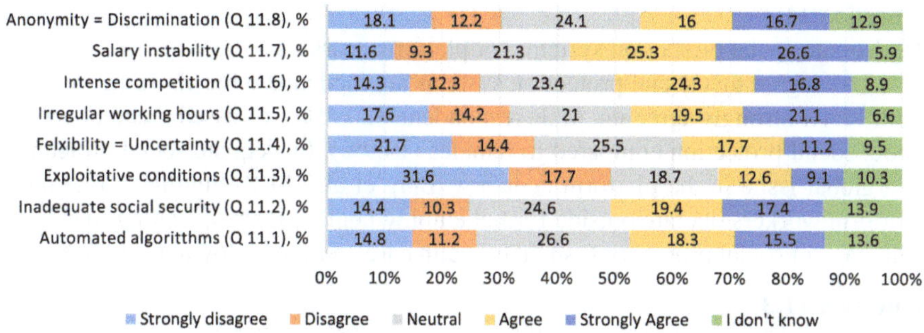

Fig. 6.20 Overview of question 11: factors affecting sustainable development of the EU (Social Factors) (%). *Source*: compiled by the authors

Each response category (strongly disagree to I don't know) is represented for all the listed factors, allowing for a comprehensive view of how respondents feel about each social issue.

Additional Questions:

Question 11.1. Automated algorithms impose too much control over platform workers.

Question 11.2. Inadequate social protection systems for platform workers.

Question 11.3. Exploitative/abusive working conditions.

Question 11.4. Flexibility and autonomy actually mean uncertainty and insecure working conditions.

Question 11.5. Irregular and long working hours generate overtime and pose health risks for platform workers.

Question 11.6. Intense competition increases the psychological and social vulnerability of platform workers

Question 11.7. Salary instability generates financial insecurity for platform workers.

Question 11.8. Anonymity when working through digital platforms does not protect against discrimination.

The results highlight key challenges that platform workers face, particularly in relation to autonomy, social protection, and fairness.

Question 11.1

Automated algorithms impose too much control over platform workers

18.3% of respondents agree that automated algorithms control platform workers too heavily, while 15.5% strongly agree. This concern is more pronounced among workers (25–34 years) and employees, reflecting their vulnerability to algorithmic control. Algorithms dictate work availability, which can lead to over-monitoring and limit worker autonomy. Research by Wood et al. (2019) also indicates that algorithmic control in the platform economy reduces workers' ability to exercise choice, contributing to psychological strain and reducing job satisfaction.

Question 11.2

Inadequate social protection systems for platform workers

19.4% agree that social protection systems are inadequate for platform workers, with 17.4% strongly agreeing. Male respondents (20.4%) expressed greater concern about social protection compared to females (13.9%). Inadequate social protection is a global issue in the platform economy. Berg et al. (2018) highlights that most platform workers operate outside formal employment structures, leading to significant gaps in social protections, such as health care and unemployment insurance.

Question 11.3

Exploitative/abusive working conditions

31.6% of respondents strongly disagreed that their working conditions were exploitative, while 12.6% agreed with this statement. Urban workers seem more divided, with 13.1% agreeing that exploitative conditions exist, while a substantial portion (31%) disagreed. This highlights a split in perception, likely driven by differences in how platform work is structured between urban and rural settings. This issue aligns with global observations of platform economies, where workers often report exploitative conditions due to the lack of formal employment protections. Kenney and Zysman (2016) argue that platforms have normalized precarious labor, particularly by shifting risks (e.g., job insecurity, lack of benefits) onto workers.

Question 11.4

Flexibility and autonomy actually mean uncertainty and insecure working conditions

17.7% of respondents agreed that flexibility in platform work actually results in insecurity, with 21.7% strongly disagree. Interestingly, freelancers (16.0%) and those working under service contracts (26.1%) were more likely to agree, reflecting their firsthand experience with the downside of flexible arrangements, which can translate into irregular hours and income instability. While flexibility is marketed as a benefit of platform work, Aloisi (2019) points out that it often results in insecure conditions, where workers bear the full burden of financial risk and unpredictable schedules.

Question 11.5

Irregular and long working hours generate overtime and pose health risks for platform workers

21.1% strongly agree that long hours of platform work led to overtime and health risks, with 19.5% agreeing. Older workers (55+ years) were particularly concerned about this, with 27.7% strongly agreeing, indicating that the physical toll of long hours may disproportionately affect older workers. The EU has acknowledged the health risks associated with platform work and is working on policies aimed at reducing these risks. The Moldovan data reflects the broader trend of health concerns caused by overwork and irregular hours, which are common in the gig economy.

Question 11.6

Intense competition increases the psychological and social vulnerability of platform workers

24.3% agree that competition in the platform economy increases psychological and social vulnerability, with 16.8% strongly agreeing. Freelancers (24.5% agree) and NEET individuals (28.7% agree) are particularly vulnerable to this competitive pressure, as they lack the protection and bargaining power that formal employees might have. Younger workers (23.2%) also reported heightened vulnerability, as they often enter the platform economy with fewer resources and networks. This finding echoes Vallas and Schor (2020), who argue that competition in the gig economy exacerbates worker insecurity, as the oversupply of labor on platforms creates downward pressure on wages and job stability.

Question 11.7

Salary instability generates financial insecurity for platform workers

26.6% of respondents strongly agree that salary instability creates financial insecurity, with 25.3% agreeing. Financial insecurity is more prominent among freelancers (27.5%) and NEET individuals (54.5%), groups that typically face more precarious working conditions. De Stefano (2016) highlights that wage instability is one of the biggest challenges facing gig workers globally. In Moldova, platform workers are similarly affected by the lack of consistent income, which hinders their ability to plan for the future and secure their financial wellbeing.

Question 11.8

Anonymity when working through digital platforms does not protect against discrimination

16.7% strongly agree that anonymity in platform work does not protect against discrimination, while 16.0% agree. Interestingly, older respondents (55+ years) are more likely to express concern about discrimination, with 24.0% strongly agreeing that anonymity fails to offer protection. Kenney and Zysman (2016) argue that while platforms often promote themselves as meritocratic, they can also perpetuate discrimination through algorithms that inadvertently reflect biases. This aligns with Moldova's data, where discrimination continues to be a concern despite the anonymity provided by digital platforms.

Question 11

In your opinion, which of the factors listed in the table below determine or hinder sustainable development in the European Union? (Environmental factors).

Figure 6.21 displays the responses to *Question 12* across different environmental factors, broken down by gender. Each subplot represents one of the factors, with the responses grouped into categories such as "Strongly Disagree", "Disagree", "Neutral", "Agree", "Strongly Agree" and "Don't Know".

The four environmental factors covered are:

1. Lower prices promote excessive consumption
2. Phones and computers consume a lot of electricity
3. Electronic devices have a short lifespan
4. Internet traffic and servers require a lot of energy

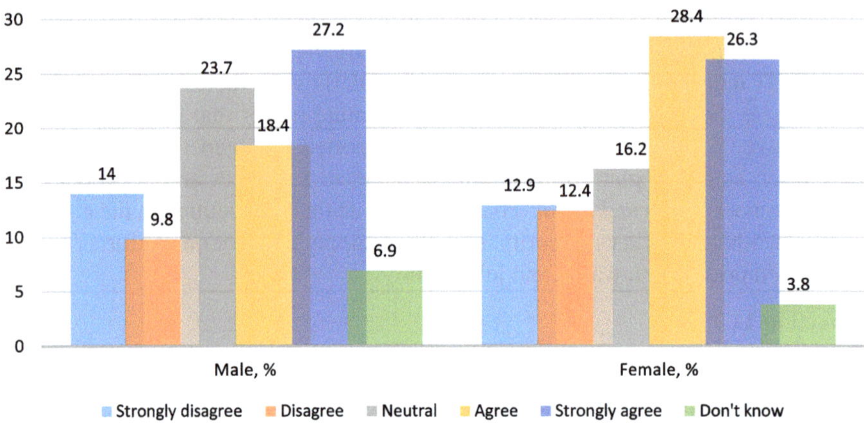

Lower price promote excessive consumtion (Q 12.1)

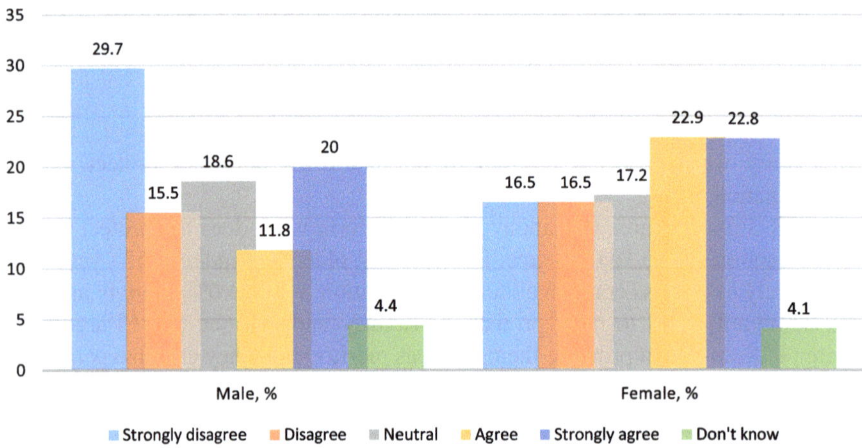

Phones and computers consume a lot of electricity (Q 12.2)

Fig. 6.21 Responses by gender (Environmental factors) (%). *Source*: compiled by the authors

Additional Questions:

Question 12.1. Lower prices for goods and services promote excessive consumption.

Question 12.2. Phones and computers consume a large amount of electricity.

Question 12.3. Electronic devices have a relatively short lifespan (life cycle)

Question 12.4. Internet traffic and servers require a lot of energy.

The European Union (EU) has long been at the forefront of global efforts to achieve sustainable development, with policies such as the *European Green Deal* aimed at making Europe climate-neutral by 2050. However, the success of such initiatives depends not only on top-down policies but also on public attitudes and

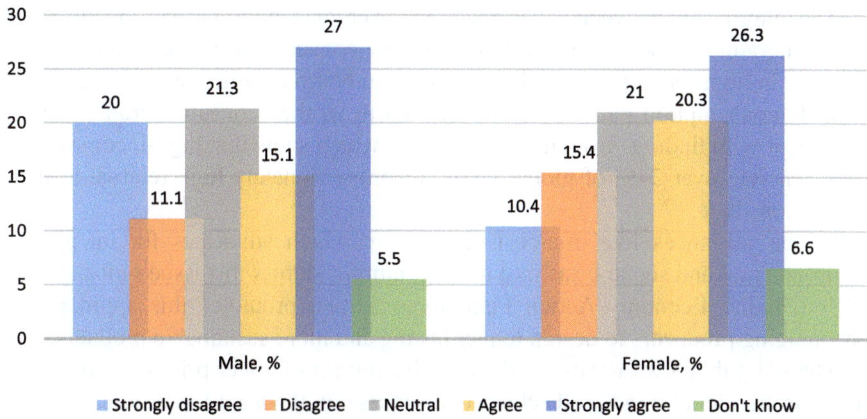

Electroni devices have a short lifespan (Q 12.3)

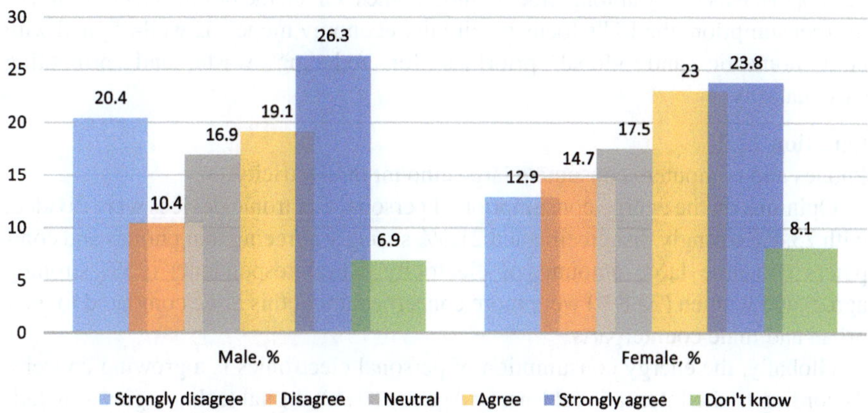

Internet traffic and servers require a lot of energy (Q 12.4)

Fig. 6.21 (continued)

behaviors. Understanding how various demographic groups perceive environmental challenges is essential to implementing effective solutions. This chapter explores the attitudes of EU citizens toward four key environmental issues—consumption, electronic waste, energy use in digital technologies, and the environmental footprint of internet infrastructure—and compares these findings with global trends and scholarly research.

Question 12.1

Lower prices for goods and services promote excessive consumption

A substantial proportion of respondents (26.9%) strongly agree that lower prices for goods and services promote excessive consumption, with 23% moderately agreeing. This concern is more prevalent among older respondents (25–34 years, 29.6% strongly agree) and women (26.3%).

The relationship between lower prices and overconsumption is well-documented in the literature. Jackson (2016) describes how consumer-driven economies, particularly in high-income regions like Europe and North America, encourage unsustainable consumption patterns, often referred to as the "consumer trap". This is consistent with findings from the *World Bank*, which show that high-income countries generate over 34% of global waste, disproportionately high relative to their population share.

Recent initiatives like true-cost accounting, which advocates for integrating environmental and social costs into pricing, aim to address this issue globally. The EU's Circular Economy Action Plan, for example, promotes this approach by encouraging producers to design longer lasting and more sustainable products.

The EU public's awareness of the negative impact of lower prices on consumption mirrors global trends and scholarly discourse on the need for sustainable consumption practices. The findings suggest that policies promoting sustainable pricing strategies, such as eco-taxes or incentives for buying durable goods, could find public support, especially among older demographics. Given the public's recognition of overconsumption, the EU's focus on circular economy models is well-aligned with both domestic and global priorities for reducing waste and promoting sustainability.

Question 12.2

Phones and computers consume a large amount of electricity

Opinions on the energy consumption of personal electronic devices were divided, with 23.4% strongly disagreeing and 21.3% strongly agreeing that phones and computers consume large amounts of electricity. Rural respondents (25% strongly agree) and women (22.8%) were more concerned about this issue compared to their urban and male counterparts.

Globally, the energy consumption of personal electronics is a growing concern. According to the International Energy Agency (IEA), digital technologies—including phones, computers, and data centers—currently consume around 1% of the world's electricity, but this is expected to rise significantly with the expansion of cloud services, 5G, and artificial intelligence. A study by Andrae and Edler (2015) projects that global energy use by information and communications technology (ICT) could account for as much as 8% of total electricity demand by 2030 if current trends continue.

The public's concern about the energy consumption of personal devices reflects broader awareness of this issue, yet there remains a knowledge gap, particularly in urban areas where the effects of energy use may be less visible. This is consistent with findings by Bieser and Hilty (2018), who argue that urban populations are often less aware of the energy implications of their digital consumption due to the indirect nature of cloud services.

The results highlight an opportunity to raise awareness, especially in urban areas, about the environmental impact of digital technologies. Public education campaigns could focus on promoting energy-efficient devices and encouraging behavioral changes, such as reducing screen time and opting for low-energy modes.

Additionally, the EU's push for green digital infrastructure, as outlined in the European Green Deal, could help mitigate these concerns by promoting energy-efficient data centers and devices.

Question 12.3

Electronic devices have a relatively short lifespan (life cycle)

A majority of respondents (26.7% strongly agree, 17.5% agree) believe that electronic devices have short lifespans. This concern is particularly pronounced among older respondents, with 31.3% of those aged 35–54 and above strongly agreeing.

The issue of planned obsolescence, where manufacturers deliberately limit the lifespan of products to encourage frequent replacements, has been widely criticized for contributing to the global e-waste crisis. According to the Global E-waste Monitor (2020), the world generated 53.6 million metric tons of e-waste in 2019, with Europe having one of the highest per capita generation rates. The short lifespan of consumer electronics is a major driver of this crisis.

The Right to Repair movement has gained traction globally, advocating for policies that allow consumers to repair their own devices and reduce the environmental impact of frequent replacements. In response, the EU introduced the Circular Electronics Initiative as part of its Circular Economy Action Plan, which encourages the design of longer lasting and repairable electronics.

The widespread concern about the short lifespan of electronics in the EU echoes global trends. Public support for policies promoting repairability and extended warranties suggests a potential pathway for reducing e-waste and promoting sustainable consumption. Given the alignment with EU policy initiatives, this presents a unique opportunity to lead in the global effort to curb electronic waste.

Question 12.4

Internet traffic and servers require a lot of energy

A significant portion of respondents (25.3%) strongly agree that internet traffic and server infrastructure require substantial amounts of energy. Older individuals (33.3% of those aged 55+ and above) expressed the highest levels of concern.

The energy demands of the digital economy are expected to rise as internet traffic and data storage needs increase. According to the IEA, data centers and digital infrastructure could account for up to 10% of global electricity use by 2030 if efficiency measures are not adopted. Initiatives like green data centers, which use renewable energy to power cloud services, have been proposed as solutions to this challenge.

Globally, large technology companies like *Google* and *Microsoft* have committed to powering their data centers entirely with renewable energy by the mid-2030s. In Europe, the *European Green Deal* and *Digital Strategy* include specific provisions aimed at reducing the carbon footprint of the digital sector through efficiency improvements and the promotion of clean energy.

The concern expressed by older EU citizens about the energy demands of the internet reflects growing awareness of the environmental impact of the digital economy. The EU's leadership in promoting *green digital infrastructure*, including energy-efficient data centers, is well-positioned to address this issue. Public support for these initiatives may encourage further investments in renewable-powered digital technologies.

Question 13
In your opinion, which of the measures listed below would be the most useful to improve working conditions through digital platforms? (Please select one or more relevant responses.)

Approximately 45.7% of respondents identified increasing social protection for digital platform workers as the most effective measure. Women (51.4%) were more likely to select this option compared to men (40.8%), and urban respondents (47.3%) showed more support than those in rural areas (37.5%). Older respondents (55+ years) showed the highest level of concern (50%).

This finding aligns with existing literature, which emphasizes that digital platform workers often lack adequate social protection, such as health insurance, pensions, and paid leave. The International Labour Organization (ILO) has highlighted similar challenges regarding access to social protection for platform workers as a global concern (ILO 2021b).

Improving work-life balance was identified by 41.5% of respondents as a critical measure. Both men and women supported this measure in nearly equal proportions, and respondents across all age groups expressed concern for this issue. However, temporary contract workers and those in the NEET (Not in Education, Employment, or Training) category showed heightened interest in improving work-life balance.

This perception is reinforced by research showing that platform workers often struggle with fragmented work hours and the lack of clear boundaries between work and personal time. The flexibility offered by platforms frequently leads to irregular work patterns and overwork, as highlighted by Berg (2016) and Schmidt (2017), who propose that regulating working hours and rest periods could be essential for these workers.

A clear legal definition of the status of platform workers was selected by 36.8% of respondents as a priority measure. Female respondents (41.8%) and younger respondents (15–24 years, 39%) particularly emphasized the need for clarification on this issue. Many platform workers are classified as freelancers, which limits their access to benefits and labor rights.

This result is consistent with global debates on the ambiguous legal status of platform workers. In many countries, they are categorized as independent contractors, which reduces their protection. De Stefano (2016) emphasizes that clear legal definitions are crucial for ensuring equal rights and access to social protections for all workers.

Improving the representation of workers' interests was selected by 35.5% of respondents, with higher support among younger respondents (40.1%). The lack of unions or other forms of worker organization represents a significant challenge for platform workers, leaving them vulnerable to exploitation and poor working conditions.

Research supports this finding, noting that weak representation makes platform workers more susceptible to precarious employment conditions. Heeks (2017) and other scholars argue that the formation of worker unions or associations could significantly improve platform workers' ability to defend their rights and negotiate better working conditions.

About 35.5% of respondents also emphasized the need for greater control over data and algorithms as a key measure for improving working conditions. This concern was particularly prominent among respondents aged 35–54 and female workers. The control over the algorithms that allocate tasks and determine income is a critical issue in the digital economy, where platform algorithms are often opaque and may lead to inequalities.

This issue has been well-documented in academic literature, with algorithms identified as a key factor in shaping the working conditions of platform workers. Studies suggest the need for greater transparency and accountability in the way algorithms are designed and used to manage labor. The concept of "algorithmic accountability" is emerging as an important discussion point in research on platform economies (Binns 2018).

References

Adams-Prassl J (2018) Humans as a service: the promise and perils of work in the gig economy (introduction). Oxford University Press, Oxford. https://ssrn.com/abstract=3167329

Aloisi A (2019) Negotiating the digital transformation of work: Non-standard workers' voice, collective rights and mobilisation practices in the platform economy (EUI Working Paper MWP 2019/03). SSRN. https://doi.org/10.2139/ssrn.3404990

Aloisi A, De Stefano V (2020). Regulation and the future of work: the employment relationship as an innovation facilitator. International Labour Review. Special Issue: Future of work (Part II). *Rethinking Institutions for Social Justice, 159*(1), 47–69. https://doi.org/10.1111/ilr.12160

Andrae ASG, Edler T (2015) On global electricity usage of communication technology: trends to 2030. Challenges 6(1):117–157. https://doi.org/10.3390/challe6010117

Au-Yeung TC, Qiu JL (2022) Institutions, occupations and connectivity: the embeddedness of gig work and platform-mediated labour market in Hong Kong. Crit Sociol 48(7–8):1169–1187. https://doi.org/10.1177/08969205221090581

Balaram B, Warden J, Wallace-Stephens F (2017) Good gigs: a fairer future for the UK'S gig economy. RSA. https://doi.org/10.1007/978-3-030-29010-8_32

Barratt T (2019). Alex Rosenblat, Uberland: How algorithms are rewriting the rules of work. *Journal of Industrial Relations, 62*(1), 157–159. https://doi.org/10.1177/0022185619875363

Berg J (2016) Income security in the on-demand economy: findings and policy lessons from a survey of Crowdworkers (March 1, 2016). Comp Labor Law Policy J 37(3):2016. Available at SSRN: https://ssrn.com/abstract=2740940

Berg J, Furrer M, Harmon E, Rani U, Silberman MS (2018) Digital labour platforms and the future of work: Towards decent work in the online world. International Labour Organization (September 20, 2018). (1) (PDF) Digital labour platforms and the future of work: Towards decent work in the online world. Retrieved from: https://www.ilo.org/publications/digital-labour-platforms-and-future-work-towards-decent-work-online-world

Bieser JCT, Hilty LM (2018) Assessing indirect environmental effects of information and communication technology (ICT): a systematic literature review. Sustainability 10(8):2662. https://doi.org/10.3390/su10082662

Binns R (2018) Algorithmic accountability and public reason. Philos Technol 31:543–556. https://doi.org/10.1007/s13347-017-0263-5

Chin TL, Yean TF (2021) Digital platform workers: setting the hrm research agenda. Proceedings of the Ninth International Conference on Entrepreneurship and Business Management (ICEBM 2020). https://doi.org/10.2991/aebmr.k.210507.013

Daramola O, Etim E (2022) Affordances of digital platforms insub-saharanafrica: an analytical review. Electronic J Information Syst Developing Countries 88(4). https://doi.org/10.1002/isd2.12213

De Stefano V (2015) The Rise of the 'Just-in-Time Workforce': On-Demand Work, Crowd Work and Labour Protection in the 'Gig-Economy' (October 28, 2015). Comparative Labor Law & Policy Journal, Forthcoming, Bocconi Legal Studies Research Paper No. 2682602, Available at SSRN: https://ssrn.com/abstract=2682602 or https://doi.org/10.2139/ssrn.2682602

De Stefano V (2016) The rise of the "just-in-time workforce": on-demand work, crowdwork, and labour protection in the "gig-economy.". Comp Labor Law Policy J 37(3):471–504

European Commission (2021a) Platform work and the future of employment in Europe. The future of work—European Commission (europa.eu)

European Commission (2021b) Proposal for a Directive of the European Parliament and of the Council on improving working conditions in platform work. COM/2021/762 final. Retrieved from: https://eur-lex.europa.eu/legal-content/EN/ALL/?uri=CELEX%3A52021PC0762

European Commission (2021c) Zero pollution action plan. Retrieved from: https://environment.ec.europa.eu/strategy/zero-pollution-action-plan_en

Forde C, Stuart M, Joyce S, Oliver L, Valizade D, Alberti G, Hardy K, Trappmann V, Umney C, Carson C (2017a) The Social Protection of Workers in the Platform Economy. Retrieved from: https://www.europarl.europa.eu/RegData/etudes/STUD/2017/614184/IPOL_STU(2017)614184_EN.pdf

Forde C, Stuart M, Joyce S, Oliver L, Valizade D, Alberti G, Hardy K, Trappmann V, Umney C, Carson C (2017b) The social protection of workers in the platform economy. European Parliament. The Social Protection of Workers in the Platform Economy. Retrieved from: https://www.europarl.europa.eu/thinktank/en/document/IPOL_STU(2017)614184

Friedman G (2014) Workers without employers: shadow corporations and the rise of the gig economy. Review of Keynesian. Economics 2(2):171–188. Retrieved Sep 29, 2024, from https://doi.org/10.4337/roke.2014.02.03

Graham M, Hjorth I, Lehdonvirta V (2017) Digital labour and development: impacts of global digital labour platforms and the gig economy on worker livelihoods. Transfer Eur Rev Labour Res 23(2). https://doi.org/10.1177/1024258916687250. Retrieved from: https://journals.sagepub.com/doi/10.1177/1024258916687250#bibr14-1024258916687250

Heeks R (2017) Decent Work and the Digital Gig Economy: A Developing Country Perspective on Employment Impacts and Standards in Online Outsourcing, Crowdwork, Etc (August 2, 2017). Development Informatics Working Paper no. 71, 2017, Available at SSRN: https://ssrn.com/abstract=3431033 or https://doi.org/10.2139/ssrn.3431033

Hunt A, Samman E, Mansour-Ille D, Olan F (2019) Women in the gig economy: Paid work, care and flexibility in Kenya and South Africa (November 2019). Overseas Development Institute. Women in the gig economy: paid work, care and flexibility in Kenya and South Africa | ODI: Think change. https://odi.org/en/publications/women-in-the-gig-economy-paid-work-care-and-flexibility-in-kenya-and-south-africa/

Huws U, Spencer NH, Joyce S (2017) Work in the European gig economy: Research results from the UK, Sweden, Germany, Austria, the Netherlands, Switzerland, and Italy. Foundation for European Progressive Studies. Retrieved from: https://feps-europe.eu/publication/555-work-in-the-european-gig-economy-research-results-from-the-uk-sweden-germany-austria-the-netherlands-switzerland-and-italy/

ILO (2021a) Non-standard forms of employment. Retrieved from: https://www.ilo.org/global/topics/non-standard-employment/lang%2D%2Den/index.htm

ILO (2021b) World employment and social outlook 2021: the role of digital labour platforms in transforming the world of work. International Labour Office. Retrieved from: World Employment and Social Outlook 2021: The role of digital labour platforms in transforming the world of work (ilo.org)

Jackson T (2016) Prosperity without growth: foundations for the economy of tomorrow, 2nd edn. Routledge. https://doi.org/10.4324/9781315677453

Kalleberg AL (2009) Precarious work, insecure workers: employment relations in transition. Am Sociol Rev 74(1):1–22. https://doi.org/10.1177/000312240907400101

Kenney M, Zysman J (2016) The rise of the platform economy. Issues Sci Technol 32(3):61–69. https://www.researchgate.net/publication/309483265_The_Rise_of_the_Platform_Economy

Muntaner C (2018) Digital platforms, gig economy, precarious employment, and the invisible hand of social class. Int J Health Serv 48(4):597–600. https://doi.org/10.1177/0020731418801413. PMID: 30213247

Ravenelle AJ (2019) Hustle and gig: struggling and surviving in the sharing economy (1st ed.). (PDF) hustle and gig: struggling and surviving in the sharing economy. By Alexandrea J. Ravenelle. University of California Press, Oakland. https://doi.org/10.2307/j.ctvcwp0kc

Rosenblat A, Stark L (2016) Algorithmic labor and information asymmetries: a case study of Uber's drivers (July 30, 2016). Int J Commun 10:27. Available at SSRN: https://ssrn.com/abstract=2686227 or http://dx.doi.org/10.2139/ssrn.2686227

Schmidt FA (2017) Digital labour market in the platform economy: mapping the political challenges of crowd work and gig work. Retrieved from: https://library.fes.de/pdf-files/wiso/13164.pdf

Schor JB (2020) After the gig: how the sharing economy got hijacked and how to win it back. University of California Press, Oakland. ISBN: 9780520385672

Srnicek N (2017) Platform capitalism. Polity Press, Cambridge. ISBN: 1509504907

Vallas S, Schor JB (2020) What do platforms do? Understanding the gig economy. Annu Rev Sociol 46:273–294. Available at SSRN: https://ssrn.com/abstract=3670075 or http://dx.doi.org/10.1146/annurev-soc-121919-054857

Wood AJ, Graham M, Lehdonvirta V, Hjorth I (2019) Good gig, bad gig: autonomy and algorithmic control in the global gig economy. Work Employ Soc 33(1):56–75. https://doi.org/10.1177/0950017018785616

Chapter 7
Conclusions

Ligita Gasparėnienė and Rita Remeikienė

1. While digitalisation-driven automation and robotisation pose a risk to employment, particularly for low-skilled workers, they also present opportunities for economic growth and job creation in the long term. The replacement of human labour with smart devices may initially lead to job displacement, but the resulting increase in labour and business productivity can drive demand across other sectors, potentially raising overall employment levels. Furthermore, automation can foster the creation of higher-quality jobs with better wages, contributing to an improved labour market. To mitigate the negative effects on vulnerable workers, it is crucial to focus on reskilling and upskilling initiatives, ensuring that the workforce can adapt to the changing economic landscape and benefit from the opportunities presented by technological advancements.
2. The rise of digital platform work is significantly transforming the labour market by promoting flexibility and creating new models of work, such as freelance, service contracts, and multiple job arrangements. While digital platforms offer potential for better matching of labour supply and demand, especially in regions like Europe, the share of platform workers remains relatively small compared to Asia, indicating substantial growth opportunities. However, this shift also brings challenges, including low wages, shorter paid working hours, and intense competition among workers. Moreover, the lack of formal qualification verification on digital platforms may discourage workers from improving their skills, leading to inefficiencies in workforce qualifications and skill mismatches. To fully harness the potential of digital platform work while addressing its downsides, it is essential to implement policies that ensure fair wages, encourage skill development, and foster efficient matching of qualifications to job tasks.

L. Gasparėnienė · R. Remeikienė (✉)
Faculty of Law, Vilnius University, Vilnius, Lithuania
e-mail: ligita.gaspareniene@tf.vu.lt; rita.remeikiene@tf.vu.lt

R. Remeikienė, L. Gasparėnienė (eds.), *Work and Legal Guidelines in the Age of Digitalisation and Green Transition*, European Union and its Neighbours in a Globalized World 25, https://doi.org/10.1007/978-3-032-03511-0_7

3. Digital labour platforms are characterized by minimal external regulation, which results in disruptive and unclear relationships between workers and employers. The lack of subordination and institutional visibility at the organizational level creates a power imbalance, with workers often misclassified as self-employed or independent contractors, leading to violations of their rights and increased social vulnerability. The terms of service on these platforms typically prioritize the commercial interests of platform owners, sidelining the concerns and welfare of workers. This reflects the significant power advantage held by platform owners. However, as digital platforms evolve and as understanding of their operations deepens, there are growing opportunities for workers to gain greater autonomy and influence over their working conditions. To address the challenges posed by this new labour model, it is essential to establish clearer regulations that protect workers' rights, ensure fair treatment, and promote a more balanced relationship between workers and platform owners.
4. Digitalisation-driven changes in the labour market are creating a divide between manual workers, whose jobs are increasingly at risk due to automation, and educated workers with creative and decision-making abilities, who face less risk of job displacement. As competition between human labour and technology intensifies, wages are expected to stagnate, and workers' bargaining power may decrease, especially with the growing trend of limited attachment to specific workplaces. The impact of digitalisation also varies by country, with lower labour costs leading to greater positive effects and higher labour costs experiencing milder consequences. However, the polarisation in the labour market can be mitigated through rising worker qualifications and the integration of machines and software for routine and non-routine tasks. To address the disruptive effects of digitalisation, welfare state protections must be adapted to support workers, ensuring that innovation is promoted while balancing its benefits and challenges for the workforce.
5. The shift from a "brown" economy, characterized by the misallocation of capital, to a "green" economy offers significant potential for long-term economic growth, job creation, and sustainability. The green transition is expected to enhance resource and innovation efficiency, transform production processes, and reshape demand structures, leading to increased aggregate income and improved macroeconomic conditions. The growth of green innovation is closely tied to broader innovation, as it often requires complementary advancements. Although gaps in green investments remain, particularly in sectors like energy, agriculture, and infrastructure, increased investments in these areas are likely to stimulate job creation. The adoption of efficiency-enhancing and disruptive technologies, along with the demand for low-carbon products, such as electric vehicles and renewable energy, will further drive growth. These changes, supported by knowledge spillovers and R&D advancements, will bolster competitiveness, especially in sectors with existing comparative advantages. Ultimately, the green transition not only offers economic benefits but also strengthens national competitiveness and employment, positioning these sectors as key drivers of future growth.

6. The green transformation policies will bring significant changes to the labour market, creating both new opportunities and risks. The positive effects are likely to include the creation of green and green-collar jobs in industries such as construction, transportation, energy, agriculture, and forestry, as well as in technologically advanced sectors like waste management and environmental research. These changes will lead to an overall increase in employment, particularly for low- and medium-skilled workers, and offer more geographically dispersed and online job opportunities. However, the transition may also have negative consequences, including job losses in high-environmental footprint industries, reduced demand in less productive companies, and rising inequality and polarisation in the labour market. Despite these challenges, the overall impact on employment is expected to be moderate, as the affected industries form a relatively small portion of total employment, and many jobs will shift across sectors rather than be lost. The pace at which workers' skills can be adapted to meet new demands will depend on the speed of green technology development, with local labour markets experiencing greater mismatches in areas where reorientation is slower.
7. The conditions for digital platform work in Eastern European post-Soviet economies are heavily influenced by the legacy of the transition period and the political-economic decisions made during this time. The integration into Western or Eastern blocs has led to significant institutional and structural distortions, shaping labour market dynamics and work aspirations, particularly among the younger generation. In post-Soviet countries that joined the EU, faster economic development, greater purchasing power, and more efficient social protection systems have created a more secure traditional labour market, making digital platform work a secondary income source or entry point for youth. In contrast, developing post-Soviet countries, characterized by high unemployment, low purchasing power, and inefficient social systems, provide more favourable conditions for digital platform work as workers seek alternative income sources. Additionally, the increasing share of the service sector, technological advances, job mismatches, and a lack of trust in trade unions further contribute to the expansion of digital platform work, especially in larger post-Soviet economies with greater consumer market potential.
8. On 23 October 2024 the European Parliament and the Council adopted the directive (EU) 2024/2831 on improving working conditions in platform work. This Directive will come into force on 1 December 2024. Member states will then have 2 years to incorporate the provisions of the directive into their national legislation. These new EU law's rules aim to improve working conditions for the more than 28 million people working on digital job platforms across the EU. This is the first-ever piece of EU legislation to regulate algorithmic management in the workplace and to set EU minimum standards to improve working conditions for millions of platform workers across the EU. The Platform Work Directive will make the use of algorithms in human resources management more transparent, ensuring that automated systems are monitored by qualified staff and that workers have the right to contest automated decisions. It will also help correctly determine the employment status of people working for platforms, enabling

them to benefit from any labour rights they are entitled to. Member states will establish a legal presumption of employment in their legal systems that will be triggered when certain facts indicating control and direction are found. The main compromise elements revolve around a legal presumption which will help determine the correct employment status of persons working in digital platforms:— member states will establish a legal presumption of employment in their legal systems, to be triggered when facts indicating control and direction are found; – those facts will be determined according to national law and collective agreements, while taking into account the case-law of the Court of Justice of the European Union; – persons working in digital platforms, their representatives or national authorities may invoke this legal presumption and claim they are misclassified; – it is up to the digital platform to prove that there is no employment relationship. Moreover, member states will provide guidance to digital platforms and national authorities when the new measures are being put in place for the effective implementation of and respect for the legal presumption. The Platform Work Directive introduces rules that protect platform workers' data more robustly. Digital labour platforms will be forbidden from processing certain types of personal data, such as data on someone's emotional or psychological state and personal beliefs.

9. The survey data on digital platform work in Moldova reveals a complex interplay of financial, social, and professional motivations. While Moldovan workers value the flexibility, autonomy, and skill development opportunities provided by platform work, the precarious nature of this type of employment also exposes them to vulnerabilities, such as income instability and a lack of social protections. These challenges, compounded by Moldova's economic instability and rural-urban divide, underscore the dual-edged nature of platform work in the country.

    9.1 Moldovan platform workers, like their global counterparts, experience significant gaps in *social protection coverage*. This issue is particularly concerning for older workers and those in freelance or temporary contract positions. The lack of a clear legal status for platform workers contributes to this vulnerability, as many are categorized as independent contractors, which excludes them from essential social protection. This situation mirrors global trends, where platform workers face similar challenges in securing labor rights and benefits.
    9.2 *Flexibility* remains one of the most attractive features of platform work, with many Moldovan workers appreciating the autonomy it offers. However, the unregulated nature of platform work can blur the boundaries between personal and professional life, leading to difficulties in maintaining a healthy *work-life balance*. Younger workers may tolerate these conditions for short-term benefits, but older workers, especially those dependent on platform work for primary income, are more affected by its precariousness.
    9.3 Moldovan workers face *income instability* due to the intense competition on platforms and the *control exercised by algorithms* that determine task

distribution and compensation. This lack of transparency and control over earnings reflects broader global concerns about the fairness of algorithmic management in the gig economy. Addressing these issues through better regulatory oversight of platforms is critical for ensuring that workers are fairly compensated.

Moldova's experience with platform work aligns closely with international patterns. Across the world, platform workers face similar challenges—precarious working conditions, income insecurity, and a lack of social protections. These vulnerabilities highlight the need for legislative reforms that extend labor protections to non-standard forms of employment, a conversation that is gaining traction both in Moldova and globally.

The findings also resonate with ongoing discussions in the European Union about the need to formalize platform work and integrate it into existing labor market frameworks. The EU's push for sustainable development and the protection of workers' rights aligns with Moldova's efforts to secure fair treatment and protections for its growing platform workforce.

To address the challenges faced by platform workers in Moldova, *policymakers must prioritize the following:*

1. *Legal clarity and social protection.* Introducing clear legal frameworks that define the status of platform workers is essential. Moldova should consider adopting policies that align with international best practices, ensuring that all workers, regardless of their employment classification, have access to social protections such as health insurance, pensions, and fair wages.
2. *Formalization of platform work.* Encouraging the formalization of platform work by extending traditional labor market protections to gig workers will help reduce the vulnerabilities they face. This could involve implementing minimum wage standards, enforcing fair contract terms, and ensuring workers have the right to organize and negotiate collectively.
3. *Balancing flexibility with fairness.* While platform work offers flexibility, it should not come at the cost of workers' well-being. Policymakers must find a balance between preserving the autonomy that attracts many to platform work and ensuring that these workers are not exploited. This includes regulating algorithmic management to ensure transparency and fairness in how tasks and compensation are allocated.
4. *Support for vulnerable groups.* Particular attention should be paid to women, younger workers, and those in rural areas, who are more likely to engage in platform work due to limited alternative employment opportunities. Gender disparities and geographic divides in platform work must be addressed through targeted policies that promote inclusion and provide additional support for these groups.

The Moldovan gig economy, much like its global counterparts, presents both opportunities and challenges. While platform work offers immediate income opportunities, especially in the country's constrained labor market, it also exacerbates vulnerabilities for those who rely on it as their primary source of income. As

Moldova continues to integrate into the global digital economy, proactive policy interventions focusing on social protections, legal clarity, and equitable opportunities will be essential to creating a more resilient and inclusive gig economy. By addressing these critical issues, Moldova can ensure that its platform economy contributes positively to both economic development and social justice, aligning with broader global efforts to formalize and protect platform work.

Annexes

Question 1 Which of the following definitions do you believe best explains what digital labor platforms are? (please check one or more answers that reflect your point of view)

R. Remeikienė, L. Gasparėnienė (eds.), *Work and Legal Guidelines in the Age of Digitalisation and Green Transition*, European Union and its Neighbours in a Globalized World 25, https://doi.org/10.1007/978-3-032-03511-0

Answer	N	Total	Urban	Rural	Male	Female	15–24 years	25–34 years	35–54 years	55+	Employees	Freelancers	Workers with service contracts	NEET[a]	Others	None
A mediator that connects a client with a service provider	418	49.4	49.9	47.1	46.1	53.2	48.6	50	51.3	37	52.7	49	39.1	42.9	36.4	48.5
An economic system designed to contribute to the standardization of work activities and the distribution of tasks among freelancers	256	30.3	30.7	27.9	28.4	32.4	27.1	29.6	30.7	40.7	33.6	29.1	26.1	28.6	0	33.3
A digital tool for placing orders, executing transactions, and making payment	304	35.9	37.3	28.7	33	39.2	31.6	37.4	37.4	33.3	41.9	30.9	45.7	33.3	27.3	39.4
A technical infrastructure (internet, mobile apps, websites) that enables the reception and acceptance of information in any geographic location	331	39.1	40.1	33.8	34.6	44.3	33.3	40	40.3	46.3	40.6	39.4	39.1	28.6	36.4	30.3
A business model through which digital platforms generate profit by using freelancers	223	26.4	27.9	18.4	25.7	27.1	26	31.9	22.6	24.1	23.8	27.9	30.4	28.6	9.1	27.3
A legal relationship (e.g., employment contracts) between a digital platform and workers registered on the platform regarding the performance of specific tasks or services.	181	21.4	22.7	14.7	20.4	22.5	18.1	19.6	23.8	25.9	21.5	22.7	28.3	4.8	0	12.1
Others (please specify)	4	0.5	0.6	0	0.2	0.8	0.6	0.4	0.6	0	0	0.7	0	0	0	3
I don't know	37	4.4	3.7	8.1	4.4	4.3	5.6	2.6	5.2	3.7	3.4	5	2.2	0	0	12.1
No answer	9	1.1	1	1.5	1.1	1	0.6	0.4	1.7	1.9	1.3	0.7	0	9.5	0	0
Total	1763	208.5	213.9	180.2	193.9	224.8	191.5	211.9	213.6	212.9	218.8	205.4	210.9	176.3	109.2	206

[a]Not in Education, Employment, or Training

Question 2 What types of activities do you carry out on digital platforms? (please check one or more answers relevant to You)

Answer	N	Total	Urban	Rural	Male	Female	15–24 years	25–34 years	35–54 years	55+	Employees	Freelancers	Workers with service contracts	"NEET"	Others	None
Delivery of food products	175	20.7	20.6	21.3	28.6	11.6	32.8	19.6	17.1	9.3	22.5	19.9	17.4	14.3	45.5	15.2
Home improvement, repair, and renovation service	95	11.2	11.1	11.8	16.9	4.8	4.5	10.7	14.5	14.8	9.7	13.3	10.9	4.8	9.1	3
Freight transport services	86	10.2	10.8	6.6	13.7	6.1	7.9	12.6	10.1	5.6	11.4	9.4	8.7	9.5	0	15.2
Teaching and tutoring services	86	10.2	10.4	8.1	4.9	15.9	12.4	6.7	11.6	9.3	8.7	10.5	13	9.5	27.3	6.1
Translation services	84	9.9	10.6	6.6	6.4	13.9	11.3	7.4	11	11.1	10.7	9.4	15.2	4.8	0	9.1
Passenger transport services	83	9.8	10.3	7.4	12.9	6.3	9	8.9	11.6	5.6	9.1	11	10.9	4.8	9.1	3
Commerce	69	8.2	7.5	11.8	6.2	10.4	5.1	12.2	7.2	3.7	9.1	7.3	6.5	4.8	18.2	12.1
Services in preparing scientific projects	50	5.9	6.3	3.7	3.8	8.4	8.5	3	7.2	3.7	7.7	4.3	8.7	0	0	12.1
Information services	42	5	5.8	0.7	4.9	5.1	5.1	4.8	4.9	5.6	5.4	5.5	4.3	0	0	0
Beauty and massage services	38	4.5	3.9	7.4	0.2	9.4	6.2	4.4	3.5	5.6	3.7	5	4.3	9.5	0	3
Childcare services	30	3.5	3.8	2.2	1.3	6.1	4	3.3	3.2	5.6	2.7	3.4	6.5	19	0	0
Advertising services	30	3.5	4.1	0.7	3.8	3.3	1.7	6.3	2	5.6	3.4	3.9	6.5	0	0	0
IT services	28	3.3	3.8	0.7	4.2	2.3	5.1	3.7	2.3	1.9	3.4	4.1	0	0	0	0
Handmade products	22	2.6	2.7	2.2	0.4	5.1	0.6	3.7	2.9	1.9	1	3.7	0	9.5	0	3
Real estate consultancy	18	2.1	2.3	1.5	2	2.3	0.6	1.1	3.2	5.6	2	2.3	2.2	0	9.1	0
Car repair services	9	1.1	1.1	0.7	1.6	0.5	0	1.5	1.2	1.9	0.7	1.6	0	0	0	0

Answer	N	Total	Urban	Rural	Male	Female	15–24 years	25–34 years	35–54 years	55+	Employees	Freelancers	Workers with service contracts	"NEET"	Others	None
Photo and video services	9	1.1	1.1	0.7	1.3	0.8	0.6	1.9	0.9	0	0.7	1.4	0	0	0	3
Appliance repair services	8	0.9	1	0.7	1.8	0	0	0.7	1.4	1.9	0.7	1.4	0	0	0	0
Legal services	5	0.6	0.7	0	0.2	1	0	0.4	0.6	3.7	0.7	0.7	0	0	0	0
Others (please specify)	72	8.5	8.9	6.6	8.2	8.9	6.8	7.8	9.3	13	7.7	10.1	6.5	0	0	6.1
I do not perform activities on digital platforms	57	6.7	5.9	11	4.4	9.4	9	6.7	5.8	5.6	6.7	4.3	13	19	0	24.2
I don't know	26	3.1	2.3	7.4	3.5	2.5	4	3.7	2.6	0	3	3.7	0	0	0	3
No answer	29	3.4	3	5.9	2.7	4.3	5.1	1.9	3.8	3.7	3.7	3.7	0	0	0	6.1
Total	1151	136	138	125.7	133.9	138.4	140.3	133	137.9	124.7	134.4	139.9	134.6	109.5	118.3	124.2

Question 3 Which of the reasons listed in the table below do you consider important for carrying out your activity through digital platforms? (Life circumstances)

Question 3.1. Working through digital platforms is the main source of income

Answer	N	Total	Urban	Rural	Male	Female	15–24 years	25–34 years	35–54 years	55+	Employees	Freelancers	Workers with service contracts	"NEET"	Others	None
1—not important at all	128	15.1	15.9	11	15.1	15.2	7.3	15.2	18	22.2	16.8	13.7	15.2	14.3	36.4	12.1
2	70	8.3	7.5	12.5	8.2	8.4	9.6	6.3	9	9.3	9.4	8.5	4.3	4.8	0	6.1
3	193	22.8	21.1	31.7	22.2	23.5	28.2	21.1	22	18.5	22.1	21.7	30.5	28.6	18.2	30.3
4	186	22	22.8	17.6	20.8	23.3	30	21.9	18.6	18.5	24.5	20.1	28.3	14.3	36.3	15.2
5—extremely important	242	28.6	30	21.3	30.4	26.6	21.5	31.4	30.4	25.9	24.2	32.8	17.4	38	9.1	30.2
I don't know	27	3.2	2.7	5.9	3.3	3	3.4	4.1	2	5.6	3	3.2	4.3	0	0	6.1
Total	846	100	100	100	100	100	100	100	100	100	100	100	100	100	100	100

Question 3.2. The work through digital platforms is an additional source of income

Answer	N	Total	Urban	Rural	Male	Female	15–24 years	25–34 years	35–54 years	55+	Employees	Freelancers	Workers with service contracts	"NEET"	Others	None
1—not important at all	136	16.1	17	11	13.5	19	7.9	16.7	19.4	18.5	13.8	17.6	13	19	36.3	12.1
2	66	7.8	8.5	4.4	9.3	6.1	13	6.3	6.7	5.6	8.4	7.8	8.7	0	9.1	6.1
3	140	16.5	16.1	19.1	17.7	15.2	18.6	18.9	13.9	14.8	16.8	15.1	28.3	14.3	18.2	18.2
4	213	25.2	23.8	32.4	23.3	27.3	32.8	25.2	21.2	25.9	26.2	24.9	23.9	23.8	18.2	24.2
5—extremely important	265	31.3	31.8	28.7	33.1	29.4	24.3	29.6	36.2	31.5	32.5	31.4	26.1	33.4	18.2	30.3
I don't know	26	3.1	2.8	4.4	3.1	3	3.4	3.3	2.6	3.7	2.3	3.2	0	9.5	0	9.1
Total	846	100	100	100	100	100	100	100	100	100	100	100	100	100	100	100

Question 3.3. Work through digital platforms contributes to reducing commuting costs, lunch expenses, renting an apartment near the workplace, etc.

Answer	N	Total	Urban	Rural	Male	Female	15–24 years	25–34 years	35–54 years	55+	Employees	Freelancers	Workers with service contracts	"NEET"	Others	None
1—not important at all	109	12.9	13	12.5	15.3	10.1	12.4	11.1	13.3	20.4	11.4	12.8	21.7	14.3	36.3	6.1
2	44	5.2	4.5	8.8	4.9	5.6	5.1	7.8	3.8	1.9	4	5.5	6.5	9.5	18.2	3
3	141	16.7	16.6	16.9	21.1	11.6	15.8	19.3	16.2	9.3	19.8	14.9	19.6	4.8	0	21.2
4	186	22	20.8	27.9	18	26.6	26	21.1	21.7	14.8	21.1	23.3	19.6	23.8	18.2	15.2
5—extremely important	326	38.5	40.9	26.5	35.6	41.8	35.1	34.8	41.2	51.7	38.7	38.7	30.4	47.6	18.2	48.4
I don't know	40	4.7	4.2	7.4	5.1	4.3	5.6	5.9	3.8	1.9	5	4.8	2.2	0	9.1	6.1
Total	846	100	100	100	100	100	100	100	100	100	100	100	100	100	100	100

Question 3.4. I work on the digital platform unofficially to receive state benefits at the same time (e.g., unemployment benefits, etc.)

Answer	N	Total	Urban	Rural	Male	Female	15–24 years	25–34 years	35–54 years	55+	Employees	Freelancers	Workers with service contracts	"NEET"	Others	None
1—not important at all	440	52.1	52.1	51.5	55.2	48.3	41.4	53.8	55.6	55.5	55.3	50.9	52.1	42.8	45.4	42.4
2	62	7.3	7.9	4.4	7.8	6.8	9	6.3	7.2	7.4	6.4	8	6.5	4.8	0	12.1
3	77	9.1	8.9	10.3	9.5	8.6	13	9.6	7	7.4	9.4	8.5	8.7	14.3	27.3	6.1
4	68	8	7.5	11	6	10.4	12.4	4.4	9.9	0	10.1	6.9	10.9	4.8	9.1	3
5—extremely important	95	11.2	12.1	6.6	10	12.7	7.3	15.2	9.9	13	8.4	12.4	10.9	23.8	0	18.2
I don't know	104	12.3	11.5	16.2	11.5	13.2	16.9	10.7	10.4	16.7	10.4	13.3	10.9	9.5	18.2	18.2
Total	846	100	100	100	100	100	100	100	100	100	100	100	100	100	100	100

Question 3.5. I cannot find a job in the traditional labor market

Answer	N	Total	Urban	Rural	Male	Female	15–24 years	25–34 years	35–54 years	55+	Employees	Freelancers	Workers with service contracts	"NEET"	Others	None
1—not important at all	325	38.4	38.1	39.8	38.4	38.5	31.1	41.2	40.9	33.3	41	38.7	36.9	28.6	36.3	21.2
2	80	9.5	10	6.6	9.3	9.6	10.2	9.6	8.7	11.1	7.4	10.8	8.7	9.5	18.2	9.1
3	162	19.1	20	14.7	20.4	17.7	22	20	17.4	16.7	17.4	19.7	19.6	19	27.3	24.3
4	108	12.8	12.3	15.4	12.6	12.9	15.3	13.3	11.9	7.4	16.1	9.8	17.4	4.8	0	24.2
5—extremely important	137	16.2	16.1	16.9	15.3	17.2	16.9	13.7	15.9	27.8	15.1	16.2	15.2	38.1	0	18.2
I don't know	34	4	3.5	6.6	4	4.1	4.5	2.2	5.2	3.7	3	4.8	2.2	0	18.2	3
Total	846	100	100	100	100	100	100	100	100	100	100	100	100	100	100	100

Question 3.6. I have health issues that make it difficult to find another type of job

Answer	N	Total	Urban	Rural	Male	Female	15–24 years	25–34 years	35–54 years	55+	Employees	Freelancers	Workers with service contracts	"NEET"	Others	None
1—not important at all	494	58.3	58.7	57.3	58.7	57.9	57.1	64.6	58.2	33.4	62.2	57.9	50	47.6	54.5	51.4
2	87	10.3	10.8	7.4	10.9	9.6	11.3	8.5	10.4	14.8	7.7	12.1	19.6	0	0	6.1
3	59	7	7.3	5.1	8.2	5.6	10.2	4.8	7	7.4	7	6.2	10.9	9.5	18.2	6.1
4	69	8.2	8.3	7.4	7.1	9.4	6.2	7	9.6	11.1	7	7.8	6.5	23.8	9.1	15.2
5—extremely important	93	11	10.3	14.7	9.3	12.9	9.6	10.7	9	29.6	9.7	11.4	8.7	14.3	9.1	18.2
I don't know	44	5.2	4.6	8.1	5.8	4.6	5.6	4.4	5.8	3.7	6.4	4.6	4.3	4.8	9.1	3
Total	846	100	100	100	100	100	100	100	100	100	100	100	100	100	100	100

Question 3.7. Working on a digital platform allows me to balance my work time with caring for a family member (for example, children, *elderly* parents, or family members with disabilities)

Answer	N	Total	Urban	Rural	Male	Female	15–24 years	25–34 years	35–54 years	55+	Employees	Freelancers	Workers with service contracts	"NEET"	Others	None
1—not important at all	265	31.3	31.5	30.1	33.6	28.9	31.1	30	32.8	29.6	34.8	28.8	43.4	33.3	27.3	15.2
2	57	6.7	6.8	6.6	6.4	7.1	9.6	7	5.5	3.7	5	7.6	2.2	14.3	18.2	9.1
3	89	10.5	10.3	11.8	10.2	10.9	11.9	10.7	9.9	9.3	11.4	10.3	10.9	9.5	9.1	6.1
4	132	15.6	15.1	18.4	14.6	16.7	16.4	16.3	15.1	13	12.8	17.2	10.9	14.3	18.2	27.3
5—extremely important	272	32.2	33.3	25.7	31.7	32.6	25.4	33	33.5	40.7	32.6	32	30.4	28.6	27.2	36.2
I don't know	31	3.7	3	7.4	3.5	3.8	5.6	3	3.2	3.7	3.4	4.1	2.2	0	0	6.1
Total	846	100	100	100	100	100	100	100	100	100	100	100	100	100	100	100

Question 4 Which of the reasons listed in the table below do you consider important for carrying out your activity through digital platforms? (Personal priorities)

Question 4.1. Flexibility—I can freely choose the time, duration, location, and tools for my work.

Answer	N	Total	Urban	Rural	Male	Female	15–24 years	25–34 years	35–54 years	55+	Employees	Freelancers	Workers with service contracts	"NEET"	Others	None
1—not important at all	33	3.9	3.4	6.6	4.4	3.3	3.4	3.7	4.9	0	4.7	3.2	6.5	4.8	0	3
2	21	2.5	2.5	2.2	2.7	2.3	1.7	2.6	2.9	1.9	2.7	1.4	8.7	4.8	0	6.1
3	65	7.7	7.9	6.6	8.4	6.8	6.2	8.9	7.2	9.3	8.7	6.2	10.9	9.5	18.2	9.1
4	191	22.6	21.7	27.2	22.4	22.8	20.9	23.7	22.3	24.1	18.5	23.3	26.1	19	54.5	36.4
5—extremely important	524	61.9	63.1	55.9	60.3	63.8	66.7	59.6	61	64.7	64.4	63.8	47.8	61.9	27.3	45.4
I don't know	12	1.4	1.4	1.5	1.8	1	1.1	1.5	1.7	0	1	2.1	0	0	0	0
Total	846	100	100	100	100	100	100	100	100	100	100	100	100	100	100	100

Question 4.2. Autonomy—I can manage my own work activities, the process, and my career progression

Answer	N	Total	Urban	Rural	Male	Female	15–24 years	25–34 years	35–54 years	55+	Employees	Freelancers	Workers with service contracts	"NEET"	Others	None
1—not important at all	42	5	4.6	6.6	6.2	3.5	2.8	4.4	6.4	5.6	3.7	4.6	10.9	4.8	27.3	6.1
2	24	2.8	3	2.2	3.1	2.5	3.4	2.6	2.6	3.7	3.7	2.1	6.5	0	9.1	0
3	79	9.3	9.2	10.3	9.5	9.1	9	10	9.3	7.4	10.7	7.6	15.2	4.8	9.1	15.2
4	204	24.1	24.1	24.3	23.3	25.1	20.9	26.7	23.5	25.9	23.8	23.6	26.1	23.8	27.3	30.3
5—extremely important	475	56.2	56.7	52.9	55.2	57.3	61.1	55.2	54.4	55.5	55.8	58.9	41.3	66.6	27.2	45.4
I don't know	22	2.6	2.4	3.7	2.7	2.5	2.8	1.1	3.8	1.9	2.3	3.2	0	0	0	3
Total	846	100	100	100	100	100	100	100	100	100	100	100	100	100	100	100

Question 4.3. I prefer to work outside the traditional environment, such as the typical office setting

Answer	N	Total	Urban	Rural	Male	Female	15–24 years	25–34 years	35–54 years	55+	Employees	Freelancers	Workers with service contracts	"NEET"	Others	None
1—not important at all	115	13.6	12	22.1	16.6	10.1	11.9	15.9	12.8	13	15.8	12.1	10.9	19	36.3	6.1
2	50	5.9	6.2	4.4	6.9	4.8	7.3	5.6	6.1	1.9	5.4	5.7	10.9	9.5	9.1	3
3	161	19	20.3	12.5	18.8	19.2	18.6	20	20	9.3	17.8	19.9	10.9	4.8	27.3	36.4
4	158	18.7	18.2	21.3	17.5	20	24.3	17.4	16.2	22.2	19.8	17.8	19.6	14.3	27.3	18.2
5—extremely important	336	39.7	40.6	34.6	36.7	43.4	35.6	38.9	40.3	53.6	38.5	41.1	43.4	52.4	0	33.3
I don't know	26	3.1	2.7	5.1	3.5	2.5	2.3	2.2	4.6	0	2.7	3.4	4.3	0	0	3
Total	846	100	100	100	100	100	100	100	100	100	100	100	100	100	100	100

Question 4.4. Higher work efficiency—I can use my working time more efficiently and take fewer unproductive breaks

Answer	N	Total	Urban	Rural	Male	Female	15–24 years	25–34 years	35–54 years	55+	Employees	Freelancers	Workers with service contracts	"NEET"	Others	None
1—not important at all	45	5.3	4.8	8.1	7.8	2.5	3.4	5.6	5.8	7.4	6.7	4.1	6.5	4.8	18.2	3
2	36	4.3	3.7	7.4	4	4.6	5.1	3.3	4.6	3.7	3.4	3.7	8.7	14.3	9.1	6.1
3	136	16.1	16.1	16.2	17.3	14.7	16.4	18.9	14.2	13	16.8	16.2	15.2	4.8	9.1	18.2
4	206	24.3	23.9	26.5	24.4	24.3	27.1	24.1	24.3	16.7	23.2	23.3	37	28.6	27.3	27.3
5—extremely important	396	46.8	48.7	36.7	43.6	50.4	46.3	45.1	46.8	57.3	46.5	49.5	30.4	42.7	36.3	42.4
I don't know	27	3.2	2.8	5.1	2.9	3.5	1.7	3	4.3	1.9	3.4	3.2	2.2	4.8	0	3
Total	846	100	100	100	100	100	100	100	100	100	100	100	100	100	100	100

Question 4.5. Anonymity—Working through a digital platform provides me with enhanced security, as I do not disclose my full personal details when registering on the platform (clients only see my registration number, country, and system rating)

Answer	N	Total	Urban	Rural	Male	Female	15–24 years	25–34 years	35–54 years	55+	Employees	Freelancers	Workers with service contracts	"NEET"	Others	None
1—not important at all	120	14.2	13.2	19.1	14.4	13.9	10.7	18.1	13	13	12.4	16	15.2	9.5	9.1	9.1
2	75	8.9	9.6	5.1	9.1	8.6	12.4	11.1	5.8	5.6	10.4	7.1	17.4	9.5	0	9.1
3	142	16.8	16.6	17.6	16.4	17.2	18.1	14.4	18	16.7	16.4	14.6	19.6	28.6	27.3	33.2
4	179	21.2	20.8	22.8	22.8	19.2	24.9	22.6	19.1	14.8	21.5	21.7	17.4	14.3	36.3	15.2
5—extremely important	286	33.7	35	28	32	36	29.9	29.7	37.7	42.5	34.6	35.1	30.4	33.3	0	27.3
I don't know	44	5.2	4.8	7.4	5.3	5.1	4	4.1	6.4	7.4	4.7	5.5	0	4.8	27.3	6.1
Total	846	100	100	100	100	100	100	100	100	100	100	100	100	100	100	100

Question 5 Which of the reasons listed in the table below do you consider important for carrying out your activity through digital platforms? (Social needs)

Question 5.1. Competence—when working through digital platforms, I feel professional and skilled, and the tasks are more interesting

Answer	N	Total	Urban	Rural	Male	Female	15–24 years	25–34 years	35–54 years	55+	Employees	Freelancers	Workers with service contracts	"NEET"	Others	None
1—not important at all	84	9.9	10.1	8.8	12.2	7.3	9.6	12.2	8.4	9.3	8.4	9.8	17.4	14.3	27.3	6.1
2	56	6.6	5.8	11	6.7	6.6	7.3	7.4	6.4	1.9	8.1	5.9	6.5	0	0	9.1
3	181	21.4	21.7	19.9	23.1	19.5	21.5	20.4	22.3	20.4	20.8	20.8	26.1	23.8	36.3	21.2
4	210	24.8	25.5	21.3	22	28.1	28.2	24.1	24.3	20.4	26.5	23.8	19.6	28.6	27.3	27.3
5—extremely important	290	34.3	34.5	33.1	33.1	35.5	30	33.7	35.7	42.4	34.2	36	30.4	33.3	9.1	27.2
I don't know	25	3	2.4	5.9	2.9	3	3.4	2.2	2.9	5.6	2	3.7	0	0	0	9.1
Total	846	100	100	100	100	100	100	100	100	100	100	100	100	100	100	100

Question 5.2. I communicate with clients; I feel useful to society

Answer	N	Total	Urban	Rural	Male	Female	15–24 years	25–34 years	35–54 years	55+	Employees	Freelancers	Workers with service contracts	"NEET"	Others	None
1—not important at all	54	6.4	6.5	5.9	9.3	3	7.3	7.4	4.6	9.3	5.7	5.9	8.7	4.8	18.2	12.1
2	43	5.1	5.2	4.4	6.2	3.8	6.8	4.1	5.5	1.9	5	4.6	10.9	9.5	9.1	0
3	134	15.8	15.4	18.4	17.1	14.4	21.5	14.1	15.7	7.4	16.1	15.8	15.2	0	18.2	24.2
4	219	25.9	24.2	34.6	22.4	29.9	28.2	29.6	23.5	14.8	28.9	23.6	26.1	23.8	27.3	30.3
5—extremely important	387	45.7	47.7	35.2	43.9	47.9	35.1	44.1	49.3	66.6	44.3	48	39.1	61.9	27.2	33.4
I don't know	9	1.1	1	1.5	1.1	1	1.1	0.7	1.4	0	0	2.1	0	0	0	0
Total	846	100	100	100	100	100	100	100	100	100	100	100	100	100	100	100

Question 5.3. Prevention of discrimination—working through digital platforms helps prevent discrimination based on nationality, gender, age, etc., because I can remain anonymous

Answer	N	Total	Urban	Rural	Male	Female	15–24 years	25–34 years	35–54 years	55+	Employees	Freelancers	Workers with service contracts	"NEET"	Others	None
1—not important at all	160	18.9	18.7	19.9	23.3	13.9	13	24.1	17.1	24.1	18.1	18.3	17.4	42.8	27.3	18.2
2	84	9.9	10.6	6.6	11.1	8.6	11.9	8.5	9.9	11.1	11.7	7.8	13	14.3	9.1	15.2
3	147	17.4	17.6	16.2	17.1	17.7	18.6	18.5	16.8	11.1	17.1	17.8	26.1	19	0	6.1
4	146	17.3	17	18.4	16	18.7	24.3	14.8	17.1	7.4	16.4	17.8	19.6	4.8	18.2	21.2
5—extremely important	245	28.9	29.5	26.4	24.5	34	27.7	26.3	31	33.3	30.7	28.9	23.9	14.3	27.2	33.2
I don't know	64	7.6	6.6	12.5	8	7.1	4.5	7.8	8.1	13	6	9.4	0	4.8	18.2	6.1
Total	846	100	100	100	100	100	100	100	100	100	100	100	100	100	100	100

Question 6 In Your opinion, which of the factors listed in the table below contribute to the exploitation of workers through digital labor platforms?

Question 6.1. When working through digital platforms, I do not have social security, and I cannot receive insurance or social assistance (such as sickness benefits, maternity leave, unemployment benefits, etc.)

Answer	N	Total	Urban	Rural	Male	Female	15–24 years	25–34 years	35–54 years	55+	Employees	Freelancers	Workers with service contracts	“NEET”	Others	None
1—strongly disagree	151	17.8	17.9	17.6	18.4	17.2	13	20	18.8	16.7	15.8	19.5	15.2	23.8	27.2	12.1
2	87	10.3	10.8	7.4	11.3	9.1	14.7	9.6	9.6	3.7	10.1	9.6	8.7	23.8	18.2	12.1
3	142	16.8	16.1	20.6	15.7	18	26.5	15.9	12.8	14.8	19.1	15.3	17.4	0	9.1	27.3
4	138	16.3	15.8	19.1	15.7	17	15.3	18.1	15.7	14.8	18.5	14	21.7	14.3	18.2	21.2
5—strongly agree	259	30.6	32.6	19.9	29.8	31.6	20.3	30.1	35.9	33.3	29.1	31.8	37	33.3	18.2	21.2
I don’t know	69	8.2	6.8	15.4	9.1	7.1	10.2	6.3	7.2	16.7	7.4	9.8	0	4.8	9.1	6.1
Total	846	100	100	100	100	100	100	100	100	100	100	100	100	100	100	100

Question 6.2. I work more unofficially through digital platforms

Answer	N	Total	Urban	Rural	Male	Female	15–24 years	25–34 years	35–54 years	55+	Employees	Freelancers	Workers with service contracts	"NEET"	Others	None
1—strongly disagree	227	26.8	26.9	26.5	30.3	22.8	19.2	32.3	26.4	27.8	28.8	26.5	26.1	14.3	18.2	24.2
2	92	10.9	10.1	14.7	10.2	11.6	16.4	7.4	10.1	14.8	8.4	11.2	17.4	14.3	27.2	12.1
3	134	15.8	16.5	12.5	16.9	14.7	20.4	14.8	15.1	11.1	20.1	13	15.2	9.5	18.2	18.2
4	114	13.5	12.7	17.6	11.1	16.2	18.6	12.2	12.2	11.1	14.8	12.6	15.2	4.8	18.2	15.2
5—strongly agree	232	27.4	29	19.1	25.7	29.4	19.2	28.5	30.4	29.6	23.2	30.3	23.9	47.6	9.1	27.3
I don't know	47	5.6	4.8	9.6	5.8	5.3	6.2	4.8	5.8	5.6	4.7	6.4	2.2	9.5	9.1	3
Total	846	100	100	100	100	100	100	100	100	100	100	100	100	100	100	100

Question 6.3. I am not guaranteed the minimum wage

Answer	N	Total	Urban	Rural	Male	Female	15–24 years	25–34 years	35–54 years	55+	Employees	Freelancers	Workers with service contracts	"NEET"	Others	None
1—strongly disagree	178	21	21.5	18.4	22.8	19	19.2	24.1	20	18.5	24.2	21.1	17.4	4.8	9.1	12.1
2	87	10.3	10	11.8	8.9	11.9	13.6	8.1	10.1	11.1	10.7	8.5	13	23.8	18.2	15.2
3	134	15.8	14.8	21.3	14.9	17	21.4	14.4	15.7	5.6	17.8	14.9	17.4	9.5	9.1	15.2
4	126	14.9	14.2	18.4	12.6	17.5	18.1	14.1	13.6	16.7	14.4	14.9	17.4	4.8	36.3	15.2
5—strongly agree	276	32.7	34.9	21.3	34.1	30.8	20.9	35.2	35.1	42.5	28.2	34.4	28.3	52.3	27.3	42.3
I don't know	45	5.3	4.6	8.8	6.7	3.8	6.8	4.1	5.5	5.6	4.7	6.2	6.5	4.8	0	0
Total	846	100	100	100	100	100	100	100	100	100	100	100	100	100	100	100

Question 6.4. When I work through digital platforms, I do not have the right to paid leave, vacation time, or other types of leave

Answer	N	Total	Urban	Rural	Male	Female	15–24 years	25–34 years	35–54 years	55+	Employees	Freelancers	Workers with service contracts	"NEET"	Others	None
1—strongly disagree	193	22.8	22.5	24.3	24.4	21	25.4	24.1	22.3	11.1	23.8	22.9	17.4	19	18.2	24.2
2	83	9.8	9.3	12.5	9.8	9.9	10.7	9.3	9.9	9.3	9.7	7.8	23.9	19	9.1	12.1
3	100	11.8	12.3	9.6	12	11.6	17.5	12.2	9.6	5.6	13.1	11.7	4.3	0	18.2	18.2
4	110	13	12.8	14	9.5	17	13	11.5	13.3	18.5	12.4	12.6	19.6	14.3	18.2	12.1
5—strongly agree	317	37.5	38.6	31.5	39.9	34.7	26.1	39.6	39.7	49.9	37.3	38.8	32.6	42.9	27.2	27.3
I don't know	43	5.1	4.5	8.1	4.4	5.8	7.3	3.3	5.2	5.6	3.7	6.2	2.2	4.8	9.1	6.1
Total	846	100	100	100	100	100	100	100	100	100	100	100	100	100	100	100

Question 6.5. Lack of flexibility—I have to constantly monitor the internet or mobile applications because tasks do not come regularly

Answer	N	Total	Urban	Rural	Male	Female	15–24 years	25–34 years	35–54 years	55+	Employees	Freelancers	Workers with service contracts	"NEET"	Others	None
1—strongly disagree	150	17.7	18.2	15.4	19.7	15.4	22	16.3	18.3	7.4	18.1	18.1	10.9	19	9.1	21.2
2	95	11.2	11	12.5	9.8	12.9	15.3	8.5	11.3	11.1	8.4	12.6	10.9	9.5	18.2	18.2
3	204	24.2	24.2	23.6	22.6	25.9	23.7	24.1	23.8	27.8	24.5	22	32.6	28.7	54.5	24.2
4	176	20.8	20.3	23.5	19.3	22.5	20.3	23	20	16.7	23.8	19	30.4	9.5	9.1	15.2
5—strongly agree	191	22.6	22.8	21.3	25.5	19.2	16.4	25.9	21.4	33.3	22.5	24.2	13	23.8	9.1	18.2
I don't know	30	3.5	3.5	3.7	3.1	4.1	2.3	2.2	5.2	3.7	2.7	4.1	2.2	9.5	0	3
Total	846	100	100	100	100	100	100	100	100	100	100	100	100	100	100	100

Question 6.6. Lack of autonomy—I cannot significantly influence the nature and variety of tasks, and I am not free to select working methods.

Answer	N	Total	Urban	Rural	Male	Female	15–24 years	25–34 years	35–54 years	55+	Employees	Freelancers	Workers with service contracts	"NEET"	Others	None
1—strongly disagree	210	24.8	25.8	19.1	25.8	23.8	18.1	27	26.6	24.1	24.9	26.2	13	23.8	9.1	27.1
2	137	16.2	15.5	20	13.5	19.2	26.5	13	14.5	9.3	15.4	15.1	28.3	9.5	36.4	18.2
3	187	22.1	23	17.6	20.8	23.5	21.5	23	21.2	25.9	21.1	22.7	21.7	28.7	36.3	15.2
4	146	17.3	17.2	17.6	17.5	17	17.5	18.5	15.4	22.2	19.1	14	28.3	19	18.2	27.3
5—strongly agree	120	14.2	14.1	14.7	17.5	10.4	11.3	14.4	14.8	18.5	14.1	15.8	6.5	19	0	6.1
I don't know	46	5.4	4.4	11	4.9	6.1	5.1	4.1	7.5	0	5.4	6.2	2.2	0	0	6.1
Total	846	100	100	100	100	100	100	100	100	100	100	100	100	100	100	100

Question 6.7. Irregular working hours, unequal workload, and spending unpaid time waiting for tasks.

Answer	N	Total	Urban	Rural	Male	Female	15–24 years	25–34 years	35–54 years	55+	Employees	Freelancers	Workers with service contracts	"NEET"	Others	None
1—strongly disagree	189	22.4	22.9	19.7	23.5	21	19.2	21.9	25.5	14.8	22.5	23.2	10.9	14.3	27.2	27.2
2	122	14.4	14.5	14	13.1	15.9	19.8	13.7	11.9	16.7	15.1	12.4	26.1	14.3	27.3	15.2
3	180	21.3	21.8	18.4	18.6	24.3	21.5	21.1	21.2	22.2	19.8	22	30.4	14.3	0	24.2
4	147	17.4	16.9	19.9	16	19	16.4	18.1	17.7	14.8	19.5	15.8	17.4	19	27.3	15.2
5—strongly agree	167	19.7	19.7	19.9	24.6	14.2	16.9	21.5	19.1	24.1	19.1	21.3	10.9	28.6	18.2	12.1
I don't know	41	4.8	4.2	8.1	4.2	5.6	6.2	3.7	4.6	7.4	4	5.3	4.3	9.5	0	6.1
Total	846	100	100	100	100	100	100	100	100	100	100	100	100	100	100	100

Question 6.8. There is no communication between workers, clients, and the organizers/owners of the platforms, and workers' activities are *essentially* self-managed

Answer	N	Total	Urban	Rural	Male	Female	15–24 years	25–34 years	35–54 years	55+	Employees	Freelancers	Workers with service contracts	"NEET"	Others	None
1—strongly disagree	172	20.3	20.4	19.9	21.9	18.5	22	21.1	19.7	14.8	21.8	19.9	13	14.3	54.5	15.2
2	100	11.8	12	11	11.3	12.4	16.9	11.1	10.4	7.4	10.4	13	13	14.3	0	9.1
3	190	22.5	22.8	20.6	20	25.4	25	22.3	23	13	24.2	21.3	30.5	14.3	9.1	21.2
4	176	20.8	20.4	22.8	20.6	21	16.9	20.7	21.4	29.6	23.5	19.5	26.1	9.5	27.3	12.1
5—strongly agree	160	18.9	18.9	19.1	22	15.4	12.4	21.1	19.7	24.1	15.4	20.4	15.2	33.3	9.1	30.3
I don't know	48	5.7	5.5	6.6	4.2	7.3	6.8	3.7	5.8	11.1	4.7	5.9	2.2	14.3	0	12.1
Total	846	100	100	100	100	100	100	100	100	100	100	100	100	100	100	100

Question 6.9. Limited opportunities for skills development and career progression—repetitive tasks requiring minimal training

Answer	N	Total	Urban	Rural	Male	Female	15–24 years	25–34 years	35–54 years	55+	Employees	Freelancers	Workers with service contracts	"NEET"	Others	None
1—strongly disagree	176	20.8	20.8	20.6	19.5	22.3	21.5	19.6	21.4	20.4	19.1	22.6	17.4	14.3	18.2	21.2
2	113	13.4	13.5	12.5	11.8	15.2	16.9	12.6	12.2	13	13.8	13.5	19.6	9.5	9.1	3
3	196	23.1	23.3	22.8	23.3	23	24.2	21.9	24.7	16.7	23.5	22	21.7	14.3	45.4	36.4
4	149	17.6	18.2	14.7	16	19.5	15.3	16.7	18.8	22.2	18.8	17.4	21.7	9.5	9.1	12.1
5—strongly agree	158	18.7	19.3	15.4	24.7	11.6	15.3	22.2	17.1	22.1	18.1	18.1	17.4	38.1	18.2	21.2
I don't know	54	6.4	4.9	14	4.7	8.4	6.8	7	5.8	5.6	6.7	6.4	2.2	14.3	0	6.1
Total	846	100	100	100	100	100	100	100	100	100	100	100	100	100	100	100

Question 6.10. There is no clear boundary between work and personal life, with technology invading personal time

Answer	N	Total	Urban	Rural	Male	Female	15–24 years	25–34 years	35–54 years	55+	Employees	Freelancers	Workers with service contracts	"NEET"	Others	None
1—strongly disagree	180	21.3	21.5	19.9	21.7	20.8	17.5	23.3	22.6	14.8	20.8	22.4	13	33.4	18.2	15.2
2	118	13.9	13.7	15.4	13.1	14.9	20.3	12.6	12.5	9.3	15.1	13.5	10.9	4.8	27.3	15.2
3	196	23.3	22.3	27.9	24.3	22	26.6	24.2	20.3	25.9	21.7	22.9	32.6	19	9.1	33.3
4	161	19	19.4	16.9	17.7	20.5	19.8	18.1	18	27.7	20.5	17.8	28.3	9.5	27.2	12.1
5—strongly agree	156	18.4	19.3	14	19.7	17	11.3	19.6	22	13	18.5	18.8	10.9	23.8	18.2	21.2
I don't know	35	4.1	3.8	5.9	3.5	4.8	4.5	2.2	4.6	9.3	3.4	4.6	4.3	9.5	0	3
Total	846	100	100	100	100	100	100	100	100	100	100	100	100	100	100	100

Question 6.11. Precarious working conditions and income instability reduce motivation and job satisfaction

Answer	N	Total	Urban	Rural	Male	Female	15–24 years	25–34 years	35–54 years	55+	Employees	Freelancers	Workers with service contracts	"NEET"	Others	None
1—strongly disagree	203	24.1	25.1	18.4	22	26.4	19.8	20.7	28	27.8	21.1	26.1	21.7	19	36.3	24.2
2	107	12.6	12.4	14	10.9	14.7	18.1	10.7	11.9	9.3	13.4	12.1	13	14.3	9.1	12.1
3	192	22.7	22.8	22	23.6	21.5	27	26.1	18	22.2	25.9	21.1	26.2	14.3	18.2	18.2
4	140	16.5	16.6	16.2	17.1	15.9	13	17	17.7	18.5	15.8	16.9	15.2	4.8	18.2	27.3
5—strongly agree	144	17	17	16.9	19.7	13.9	15.3	20.7	14.8	18.5	17.1	16.5	21.7	38.1	9.1	6.1
I don't know	60	7.1	6.1	12.5	6.7	7.6	6.8	4.8	9.6	3.7	6.7	7.3	2.2	9.5	9.1	12.1
Total	846	100	100	100	100	100	100	100	100	100	100	100	100	100	100	100

Question 7 In Your opinion, Which of the factors listed in the table Below contribute to the exploitation of workers Through digital labor platforms?

Question 7.1. Precarious working conditions and income instability reduce motivation and job satisfaction

Answer	N	Total	Urban	Rural	Male	Female	15–24 years	25–34 years	35–54 years	55+	Employees	Freelancers	Workers with service contracts	"NEET"	Others	None
1—strongly disagree	203	24.1	25.1	18.4	22	26.4	19.8	20.7	28	27.8	21.1	26.1	21.7	19	36.3	24.2
2	107	12.6	12.4	14	10.9	14.7	18.1	10.7	11.9	9.3	13.4	12.1	13	14.3	9.1	12.1
3	192	22.7	22.8	22	23.6	21.5	27	26.1	18	22.2	25.9	21.1	26.2	14.3	18.2	18.2
4	140	16.5	16.6	16.2	17.1	15.9	13	17	17.7	18.5	15.8	16.9	15.2	4.8	18.2	27.3
5—strongly agree	144	17	17	16.9	19.7	13.9	15.3	20.7	14.8	18.5	17.1	16.5	21.7	38.1	9.1	6.1
I don't know	60	7.1	6.1	12.5	6.7	7.6	6.8	4.8	9.6	3.7	6.7	7.3	2.2	9.5	9.1	12.1
Total	846	100	100	100	100	100	100	100	100	100	100	100	100	100	100	100

Question 7.2. Social security is sufficient, and I have access to social benefits

Answer	N	Total	Urban	Rural	Male	Female	15–24 years	25–34 years	35–54 years	55+	Employees	Freelancers	Workers with service contracts	"NEET"	Others	None
1—strongly disagree	141	16.7	15.1	25	18	15.2	9	19.3	18.3	18.5	16.4	15.8	15.2	28.6	18.2	24.2
2	63	7.4	7.9	5.1	8.2	6.6	8.5	7	7.2	7.4	6.4	8	10.9	9.5	9.1	3
3	207	24.4	25.6	18.4	22	27.3	23.7	26	25.3	14.8	28.2	20.6	37	33.3	27.2	18.2
4	179	21.2	21.7	18.4	16.9	26.1	26.1	18.1	20	27.8	19.1	22.7	21.7	9.5	27.3	24.2
5—strongly agree	190	22.5	22.5	22.1	25.8	18.5	22	22.2	22	27.8	21.8	24	13	14.3	18.2	27.4
I don't know	66	7.8	7.2	11	9.1	6.3	10.7	7.4	7.2	3.7	8.1	8.9	2.2	4.8	0	3
Total	846	100	100	100	100	100	100	100	100	100	100	100	100	100	100	100

Question 7.3. Technologies enhance the transparency of activities; everything is official

Answer	N	Total	Urban	Rural	Male	Female	15–24 years	25–34 years	35–54 years	55+	Employees	Freelancers	Workers with service contracts	"NEET"	Others	None
1—strongly disagree	76	9	8.5	11.8	10	7.8	5.1	10.4	10.7	3.7	6	10.5	10.9	19	0	9.1
2	65	7.7	7.7	7.4	6.7	8.9	8.5	10.7	5.5	3.7	6.4	8.2	4.3	9.5	18.2	12.1
3	165	19.5	19.4	19.9	18.8	20.3	22	17.8	19.7	18.5	23.2	17.4	23.9	9.5	9.1	18.2
4	222	26.2	26.8	23.5	22.4	30.6	29.9	20.4	28.4	29.6	28.2	24.3	30.4	23.8	36.4	27.3
5—strongly agree	290	34.3	34.4	33.7	38.6	29.4	31.7	37	32.2	42.6	34.5	35.3	28.3	33.4	36.3	27.2
I don't know	28	3.3	3.2	3.7	3.5	3	2.8	3.7	3.5	1.9	1.7	4.3	2.2	4.8	0	6.1
Total	846	100	100	100	100	100	100	100	100	100	100	100	100	100	100	100

Question 7.4. My income from working through digital platforms is quite high

Answer	N	Total	Urban	Rural	Male	Female	15–24 years	25–34 years	35–54 years	55+	Employees	Freelancers	Workers with service contracts	"NEET"	Others	None
1—strongly disagree	157	18.6	17	26.5	20	17	11.3	23.3	19.1	14.8	16.4	17.8	23.9	28.6	36.3	27.3
2	95	11.2	10.6	14.7	10.2	12.4	15.8	7.4	10.7	18.5	9.4	12.8	10.9	0	18.2	12.1
3	238	28.2	28	28.7	30.8	25.1	26	28.9	28.2	31.4	29.2	27.5	26.1	33.4	18.2	30.3
4	177	20.9	22.4	13.2	16.6	25.7	21.5	20.4	21.7	16.7	22.8	20.1	23.9	19	18.2	12.1
5—strongly agree	138	16.3	17.2	11.8	17.3	15.2	20.3	15.2	15.7	13	16.8	17.2	13	9.5	0	15.2
I don't know	41	4.8	4.8	5.1	5.1	4.6	5.1	4.8	4.6	5.6	5.4	4.6	2.2	9.5	9.1	3
Total	846	100	100	100	100	100	100	100	100	100	100	100	100	100	100	100

Question 7.5. I have a lot of flexibility in selecting tasks, working hours, intensity, and methods

Answer	N	Total	Urban	Rural	Male	Female	15–24 years	25–34 years	35–54 years	55+	Employees	Freelancers	Workers with service contracts	"NEET"	Others	None
1—strongly disagree	43	5.1	5.4	3.7	5.1	5.1	4	8.5	3.8	0	6	4.3	8.7	0	9.1	3
2	39	4.6	4.6	4.4	4.2	5.1	5.6	4.8	3.8	5.6	5.7	3.2	6.5	4.8	9.1	9.1
3	151	17.8	17.3	20.6	21.1	14.2	21.5	15.6	17.4	20.4	16.4	17.4	23.9	23.8	18.2	24.2
4	221	26.1	24.6	33.8	22.6	30.1	27.1	27.4	25.2	22.2	27.9	24.3	30.4	19	36.3	30.3
5—strongly agree	366	43.3	44.9	35.3	44.1	42.2	37.8	41.5	46.6	48.1	40.6	47.8	30.5	47.6	18.2	30.4
I don't know	26	3.1	3.2	2.2	2.9	3.3	4	2.2	3.2	3.7	3.4	3	0	4.8	9.1	3
Total	846	100	100	100	100	100	100	100	100	100	100	100	100	100	100	100

Question 7.6. I have a lot of freedom of action, and I can manage my career

Answer	N	Total	Urban	Rural	Male	Female	15–24 years	25–34 years	35–54 years	55+	Employees	Freelancers	Workers with service contracts	"NEET"	Others	None
1—strongly disagree	50	5.9	5.6	7.4	7.5	4.1	4.5	8.5	4.3	7.4	7.7	4.3	8.7	4.8	9.1	6.1
2	36	4.3	4.6	2.2	3.8	4.8	6.2	4.1	3.8	1.9	3.7	5	0	4.8	9.1	3
3	126	14.9	14.1	19.1	15.3	14.4	18.6	14.8	13.3	13	16.1	12.8	23.9	9.5	45.4	12.1
4	218	25.8	25.5	27.2	22.6	29.4	30.5	25.9	23.2	25.9	26.8	24.9	30.4	14.3	27.3	27.3
5—strongly agree	381	45.0	46.7	36.7	46.1	43.8	35.1	43.7	50.8	48.1	41	49.1	37	61.8	9.1	42.4
I don't know	35	4.1	3.5	7.4	4.7	3.5	5.1	3	4.6	3.7	4.7	3.9	0	4.8	0	9.1
Total	846	100	100	100	100	100	100	100	100	100	100	100	100	100	100	100

Question 7.7. My workweek is shorter than the usual 40-hour workweek; I have more time for family obligations and leisure

Answer	N	Total	Urban	Rural	Male	Female	15–24 years	25–34 years	35–54 years	55+	Employees	Freelancers	Workers with service contracts	"NEET"	Others	None
1—strongly disagree	134	15.8	15.9	15.4	18.8	12.4	6.2	21.1	16.8	14.8	14.1	16.5	26.1	4.8	27.3	12.1
2	61	7.2	7.2	7.4	8.2	6.1	10.7	5.9	5.8	11.1	9.1	6.2	8.7	0	9.1	6.1
3	159	18.8	18.3	21.3	20	17.5	18.6	17.4	19.7	20.4	22.1	17.6	15.2	9.5	27.2	12.1
4	160	18.9	18.6	20.6	17.3	20.8	23.2	18.9	16.5	20.4	17.8	20.6	10.9	19	18.2	18.2
5—strongly agree	302	35.8	37	28.7	32.4	39.4	36.2	34.5	37.1	31.4	32.9	35.9	36.9	61.9	18.2	45.4
I don't know	30	3.5	3	6.6	3.3	3.8	5.1	2.2	4.1	1.9	4	3.2	2.2	4.8	0	6.1
Total	846	100	100	100	100	100	100	100	100	100	100	100	100	100	100	100

Question 7.8. I am not subordinate to managers in traditional companies; I can create my own reputation

Answer	N	Total	Urban	Rural	Male	Female	15–24 years	25–34 years	35–54 years	55+	Employees	Freelancers	Workers with service contracts	"NEET"	Others	None
1—strongly disagree	58	6.9	6.8	7.4	8	5.6	3.4	9.3	7	5.6	8.4	5	13	4.8	18.2	6.1
2	31	3.7	3.9	2.2	3.8	3.5	6.2	4.4	2.3	0	4	3	8.7	0	9.1	3
3	114	13.5	13.9	11	14.9	11.9	16.9	11.9	13.6	9.3	16.4	9.6	26.1	9.5	45.4	12.1
4	185	21.9	20	31.6	18.2	26.1	29.4	21.5	17.7	25.9	19.5	22.7	19.6	23.8	18.2	36.4
5—strongly agree	420	49.5	51.7	39	50.7	48.3	38.5	49.6	54.2	57.3	46.3	55.4	28.3	57.1	9.1	42.4
I don't know	38	4.5	3.7	8.8	4.4	4.6	5.6	3.3	5.2	1.9	5.4	4.3	4.3	4.8	0	0
Total	846	100	100	100	100	100	100	100	100	100	100	100	100	100	100	100

Question 7.9. Working on digital platforms helps me learn foreign languages (e.g., English), master digital technologies, and acquire other skills

Answer	N	Total	Urban	Rural	Male	Female	15–24 years	25–34 years	35–54 years	55+	Employees	Freelancers	Workers with service contracts	"NEET"	Others	None
1—strongly disagree	122	14.4	13.8	17.6	16.2	12.4	5.6	17.4	15.4	22.2	14.1	14.2	15.2	23.8	9.1	15.2
2	45	5.3	5.6	3.7	7.3	3	4.5	6.7	5.2	1.9	4.7	5.9	6.5	0	0	6.1
3	125	14.8	14.8	14.7	13.7	15.9	18.1	14.4	13.9	11.1	14.8	14	10.9	19	18.2	27.3
4	170	20.1	19.6	22.8	18.8	21.5	23.2	20	19.7	13	22.1	19.2	23.9	4.8	27.3	15.2
5—strongly agree	352	41.6	42.5	36.8	39.6	44.2	45.2	37.4	42.3	46.2	40.6	42.6	39.2	47.6	45.4	36.2
I don't know	32	3.8	3.7	4.4	4.4	3	3.4	4.1	3.5	5.6	3.7	4.1	4.3	4.8	0	0
Total	846	100	100	100	100	100	100	100	100	100	100	100	100	100	100	100

Question 7.10. I feel less emotional stress; I experience a balance between professional and personal life

Answer	N	Total	Urban	Rural	Male	Female	15–24 years	25–34 years	35–54 years	55+	Employees	Freelancers	Workers with service contracts	"NEET"	Others	None
1—strongly disagree	64	7.6	6.5	13.2	8.2	6.8	5.6	10	7.5	1.9	9.4	6.6	6.5	0	0	12.1
2	46	5.4	5.9	2.9	5.5	5.3	8.5	5.2	4.6	1.9	3.7	5.3	15.2	4.8	27.3	3
3	178	21	21	21.3	25.1	16.5	23.2	24.4	17.1	22.2	23.2	19.2	26.1	14.3	27.3	21.2
4	194	22.9	23.5	19.9	19.1	27.3	26	17	26.1	22.2	22.5	23.1	30.5	19	45.4	9.1
5—strongly agree	325	38.5	39.4	33.1	36.8	40.3	29.9	38.2	41.2	49.9	35.5	41.7	21.7	57.1	0	45.5
I don't know	39	4.6	3.7	9.6	5.3	3.8	6.8	5.2	3.5	1.9	5.7	4.1	0	4.8	0	9.1
Total	846	100	100	100	100	100	100	100	100	100	100	100	100	100	100	100

Question 7.11. I feel satisfied with the work, the variety of tasks, flexibility, and comfort when working from home

Answer	N	Total	Urban	Rural	Male	Female	15–24 years	25–34 years	35–54 years	55+	Employees	Freelancers	Workers with service contracts	"NEET"	Others	None
1—strongly disagree	64	7.6	6.9	11	10.6	4.1	2.3	9.3	8.7	9.3	8.4	7.6	0	0	9.1	15.2
2	44	5.2	5.5	3.7	6.4	3.8	4.5	5.2	5.8	3.7	5.4	4.8	10.9	0	9.1	3
3	152	18	18	17.6	20	15.7	21.5	19.6	15.9	11.1	20.1	14.6	34.8	9.5	54.5	12.1
4	204	24.1	23.4	27.9	21.3	27.3	26.6	23	24.1	22.2	21.8	26.5	17.4	23.8	18.2	24.2
5—strongly agree	342	40.4	41.8	33.2	36.2	45.3	38.9	39.6	40.3	50	40.3	41.7	30.4	57.2	9.1	39.4
I don't know	40	4.7	4.4	6.6	5.5	3.8	6.2	3.3	5.2	3.7	4	4.8	6.5	9.5	0	6.1
Total	846	100	100	100	100	100	100	100	100	100	100	100	100	100	100	100

Question 8 Did You enter into a legal agreement (e.g., employment contract, etc.) or sign Another type of document for work Through the digital platform? (Please select a relevant response)

Answer	N	Total	Urban	Rural	Male	Female	15–24 years	25–34 years	35–54 years	55+	Employees	Freelancers	Workers with service contracts	"NEET"	Others	None
No	556	65.7	64.9	69.9	61.9	70.1	64.4	64.5	66.1	74	62.7	65.4	71.7	85.7	54.5	78.8
Yes	224	26.5	27.9	19.1	30.8	21.5	24.3	27.4	27.8	20.4	28.2	27	28.3	9.5	27.3	12.1
I'm not sure, it's hard to specify	66	7.8	7.2	11	7.3	8.4	11.3	8.1	6.1	5.6	9.1	7.6	0	4.8	18.2	9.1
Total	846	100	100	100	100	100	100	100	100	100	100	100	100	100	100	100

Question 9 What major issues have you noticed regarding the terms of the legal agreement (e.g., employment contract) proposed through the digital platform? (Please select one or more relevant responses)

Answer	N	Total	Urban	Rural	Male	Female	15–24 years	25–34 years	35–54 years	55+	Employees	Freelancers	Workers with service contracts	"NEET"	Others	None
It is unclear which laws—National or international—Need to be followed when working on international digital platforms	61	26.3	27.3	19.2	28.1	23.5	27.9	28.4	22.9	36.4	25	27.1	30.8	0	33.3	25
The terms of the legal relationship (e.g., the contract) primarily reflect the interests of the platform owners, rather than the interests of freelancers	59	21	20.7	23.1	21.6	20	23.3	18.9	21.9	18.2	27.4	16.9	15.4	50	33.3	0

The terms of the legal relationship (e.g., the contract) are presented in language that is too complex and difficult for freelancers to understand	51	19.6	19.2	23.1	19.4	20	16.3	25.7	13.5	45.5	15.5	22	23.1	0	33.3	25
The legal relationship (e.g., the contract) allows platform organizers to update the document's content without prior notification to freelancers	47	22.8	24.7	7.7	19.4	28.2	14	25.7	20.8	54.5	14.3	28.8	30.8	0	0	25

Answer	N	Total	Urban	Rural	Male	Female	15–24 years	25–34 years	35–54 years	55+	Employees	Freelancers	Workers with service contracts	"NEET"	Others	None
The submission and acceptance of a work offer are done digitally (by clicking the consent button), which does not allow for negotiations or the expression of opinions	46	21	22.2	11.5	20.1	22.4	14	21.6	20.8	45.5	14.3	25.4	23.1	50	0	25
The legal relationship (e.g., the contract) allows platform organizers to unilaterally modify the terms of the contract without notifying freelancers	44	27.2	28.3	19.2	22.3	35.3	23.3	32.4	25	27.3	23.8	30.5	30.8	0	0	25
The main document contains many annexes and indirect references	44	5.8	5.6	7.7	6.5	4.7	11.6	8.1	2.1	0	3.6	7.6	7.7	0	0	0

It seems to me that the rules of the digital work platform override even state legislation	22	19.6	21.2	7.7	20.9	17.6	14	20.3	21.9	18.2	21.4	19.5	23.1	0	0	0
Other	4	20.5	21.2	15.4	20.1	21.2	9.3	21.6	22.9	36.4	14.3	25.4	23.1	0	0	25
None	47	2.7	3	0	2.9	2.4	2.3	2.7	3.1	0	3.6	1.7	7.7	0	0	0
I don't know	13	1.8	1.5	3.8	2.2	1.2	0	1.4	2.1	9.1	1.2	2.5	0	0	0	0
No response	6	9.8	10.1	7.7	11.5	7.1	0	14.9	11.5	0	7.1	12.7	7.7	0	0	0
Total	444	198.2	205.1	146.2	195	203.5	155.8	221.6	188.5	290.9	171.4	220.3	223.1	100	100	150

Question 10 In Your opinion, Which of the factors listed in the table Below determine or hinder sustainable development in the European Union? (Economic Factors)

Question 10.1. Digital platforms cannot replace the traditional labor market

Answer	N	Total	Urban	Rural	Male	Female	15–24 years	25–34 years	35–54 years	55+	Employees	Freelancers	Workers with service contracts	"NEET" (Not in Education, Employment, or Training)	Others	None
1—strongly disagree	119	14.1	14.8	10.3	18.4	9.1	11.3	18.1	13.9	3.7	15.4	14.6	6.5	23.8	0	3
2	106	12.5	13.7	6.6	10.2	15.2	17.5	11.1	12.5	3.7	12.8	12.1	10.9	14.3	9.1	18.2
3	225	26.5	26.8	25	25.6	27.9	26.1	25.2	29.3	18.5	27.6	25.5	39.2	28.5	27.3	15.2
4	157	18.6	19	16.2	15.5	22	20.3	16.7	15.9	38.9	17.4	17.8	23.9	14.3	36.3	27.2
5—strongly agree	191	22.6	20.6	33.1	24.8	20	19.2	24.1	21.7	31.5	22.1	24.3	13	14.3	27.3	21.2
I don't know	48	5.7	5.1	8.8	5.5	5.8	5.6	4.8	6.7	3.7	4.7	5.7	6.5	4.8	0	15.2
Total	846	100	100	100	100	100	100	100	100	100	100	100	100	100	100	100

Question 10.2. Real labor relations are distorted

Answer	N	Total	Urban	Rural	Male	Female	15–24 years	25–34 years	35–54 years	55+	Employees	Freelancers	Workers with service contracts	"NEET"	Others	None
1—strongly disagree	115	13.6	13.8	12.5	15.3	11.6	8.5	14.8	15.9	9.3	15.1	14	4.3	19	9.1	6.1
2	117	13.8	15.4	5.9	12.4	15.4	16.4	11.9	15.1	7.4	10.1	15.8	17.4	9.5	9.1	21.2
3	262	31	30.9	30.9	29.9	32.3	36.1	31.5	28.7	25.9	32.2	27.7	43.6	23.8	45.4	45.4
4	145	17.1	16.8	19.1	16.9	17.5	17.5	18.5	15.1	22.2	17.1	16.7	21.7	33.4	18.2	6.1
5—strongly agree	125	14.8	15.1	13.2	17.5	11.6	11.9	14.8	14.2	27.8	14.1	16.9	8.7	4.8	9.1	9.1
I don't know	82	9.7	8	18.4	8	11.6	9.6	8.5	11	7.4	11.4	8.9	4.3	9.5	9.1	12.1
Total	846	100	100	100	100	100	100	100	100	100	100	100	100	100	100	100

Question 10.3. Intense competition reduces my ability as a worker to negotiate wages

Answer	N	Total	Urban	Rural	Male	Female	15–24 years	25–34 years	35–54 years	55+	Employees	Freelancers	Workers with service contracts	"NEET"	Others	None
1—strongly disagree	136	16.1	16.1	16.2	16.2	15.9	11.3	15.6	18.6	18.5	15.8	18.3	6.5	9.5	18.2	6.1
2	113	13.4	13.5	12.5	11.3	15.7	15.8	14.1	13.3	1.9	11.7	14	19.6	4.8	27.3	12.1
3	208	24.5	25.3	20.6	25.2	23.8	27.7	24.3	23.2	24	25.6	23.1	23.9	28.5	27.2	33.3
4	180	21.3	22	17.6	20.2	22.5	23.2	21.9	20.3	18.5	24.8	18.1	28.3	28.6	18.2	18.2
5—strongly agree	140	16.5	16.5	16.9	19.1	13.7	12.4	18.5	16.5	20.4	13.4	18.5	17.4	14.3	0	24.2
I don't know	69	8.2	6.6	16.2	8	8.4	9.6	5.6	8.1	16.7	8.7	8	4.3	14.3	9.1	6.1
Total	846	100	100	100	100	100	100	100	100	100	100	100	100	100	100	100

Question 10.4. Exploitation of platform workers, unfair distribution of profits

Answer	N	Total	Urban	Rural	Male	Female	15–24 years	25–34 years	35–54 years	55+	Employees	Freelancers	Workers with service contracts	"NEET"	Others	None
1—strongly disagree	149	17.6	17.2	19.9	20.4	14.4	13	20.4	17.1	22.2	16.1	19.7	15.2	14.3	18.2	9.1
2	98	11.6	12	9.6	12	11.1	14.7	8.5	12.8	9.3	12.4	10.5	6.5	9.5	9.1	27.3
3	204	24.2	24.8	20.6	22.4	26.2	25.9	25.6	22.8	18.5	24.4	23.5	21.7	38.1	18.2	24.2
4	172	20.3	21.5	14	16.9	24.3	19.8	18.1	22.9	16.7	24.2	17.2	32.7	9.5	36.3	12.1
5—strongly agree	117	13.8	13.9	13.2	15.7	11.6	13	18.1	11.6	9.3	10.1	15.6	19.6	14.3	9.1	18.2
I don't know	106	12.5	10.6	22.7	12.6	12.4	13.6	9.3	12.8	24	12.8	13.5	4.3	14.3	9.1	9.1
Total	846	100	100	100	100	100	100	100	100	100	100	100	100	100	100	100

Question 11 In Your opinion, which of the factors listed in the table determine or hinder sustainable development in the European Union? (Social factors)

Question 11.1. Automated algorithms impose too much control over platform workers

Answer	N	Total	Urban	Rural	Male	Female	15–24 years	25–34 years	35–54 years	55+	Employees	Freelancers	Workers with service contracts	"NEET"	Others	None
1—strongly disagree	125	14.8	14.5	16.2	17.3	11.9	10.2	17.4	15.4	13	13.4	16.5	6.5	19	9.1	15.2
2	95	11.2	11.5	9.6	9.3	13.4	20.3	10.7	8.4	1.9	10.1	11.4	19.6	0	9.1	15.2
3	225	26.6	27.7	21.3	24.1	29.4	28.2	29	24	25.8	24.5	27.5	19.6	23.8	36.3	42.3
4	155	18.3	19	14.7	18.2	18.5	15.8	15.2	21.7	20.4	21.1	14.9	32.6	28.6	18.2	12.1
5—strongly agree	131	15.5	15.2	16.9	20.2	10.1	11.9	18.1	15.1	16.7	17.1	15.1	13	14.3	27.3	6.1
I don't know	115	13.6	12.1	21.3	10.9	16.7	13.6	9.6	15.4	22.2	13.8	14.6	8.7	14.3	0	9.1
Total	846	100	100	100	100	100	100	100	100	100	100	100	100	100	100	100

Question 11.2. Inadequate social security systems for platform workers

Answer	N	Total	Urban	Rural	Male	Female	15–24 years	25–34 years	35–54 years	55+	Employees	Freelancers	Workers with service contracts	"NEET"	Others	None
1—strongly disagree	122	14.4	14.1	16.2	13.7	15.2	11.9	17.4	13.3	14.8	15.8	14.9	2.2	19	18.2	9.1
2	87	10.3	10	11.8	10	10.6	18.6	7	9.9	1.9	9.4	10.5	10.9	4.8	18.2	15.2
3	208	24.6	24.5	25	25.1	24.1	25.9	26.4	24	14.8	26.1	22.1	32.5	23.9	27.2	33.2
4	164	19.4	20.1	15.4	16.6	22.5	21.5	18.1	18.3	25.9	17.1	21.7	15.2	23.8	18.2	12.1
5—strongly agree	147	17.4	18.3	12.5	20.4	13.9	11.9	18.9	19.1	16.7	17.8	16.2	28.3	19	9.1	15.2
I don't know	118	13.9	13	19.1	14.2	13.7	10.2	12.2	15.4	25.9	13.8	14.6	10.9	9.5	9.1	15.2
Total	846	100	100	100	100	100	100	100	100	100	100	100	100	100	100	100

Question 11.3. Exploitative/abusive working conditions

Answer	N	Total	Urban	Rural	Male	Female	15–24 years	25–34 years	35–54 years	55+	Employees	Freelancers	Workers with service contracts	"NEET"	Others	None
1—strongly disagree	267	31.6	31.0	34.6	27.9	35.7	26.7	34.1	32.8	27.8	30.3	33.5	26.2	23.8	27.2	30.3
2	150	17.7	17.9	16.9	17.3	18.2	20.9	17.8	16.2	16.7	20.1	15.3	15.2	23.8	9.1	30.3
3	158	18.7	19.4	14.7	18.8	18.5	15.8	21.1	19.4	11.1	18.1	18.8	23.9	23.8	18.2	12.1
4	107	12.6	13.1	10.3	12.9	12.4	18.6	10	11.3	14.8	11.1	12.4	21.7	14.3	9.1	18.2
5—strongly agree	77	9.1	8.9	10.3	11.1	6.8	9	9.6	7.8	14.8	9.7	9.2	8.7	9.5	9.1	3
I don't know	87	10.3	9.7	13.2	12	8.4	9	7.4	12.5	14.8	10.7	10.8	4.3	4.8	27.3	6.1
Total	846	100	100	100	100	100	100	100	100	100	100	100	100	100	100	100

Question 11.4. Flexibility and autonomy actually mean uncertainty and insecure working conditions

Answer	N	Total	Urban	Rural	Male	Female	15–24 years	25–34 years	35–54 years	55+	Employees	Freelancers	Workers with service contracts	"NEET"	Others	None
1—strongly disagree	184	21.7	22.3	19.1	21.7	21.8	21.5	23.3	20.3	24.1	20.1	25.2	10.9	9.5	27.2	12.1
2	122	14.4	13.5	19.1	13.1	15.9	24.8	13	11.3	7.4	17.8	11.9	19.6	9.5	18.2	12.1
3	215	25.5	26	22.1	22.8	28.5	23.7	26.7	25.8	22.2	25.8	24.5	32.6	33.3	18.2	21.2
4	150	17.7	17.6	18.4	17.3	18.2	15.3	19.3	17.1	22.2	16.8	16	26.1	38.1	18.2	24.3
5—strongly agree	95	11.2	12.4	5.1	14.2	7.8	6.8	10.7	13.3	14.8	9.4	12.6	6.5	4.8	0	24.2
I don't know	80	9.5	8.2	16.2	10.9	7.8	7.9	7	12.2	9.3	10.1	9.8	4.3	4.8	18.2	6.1
Total	846	100	100	100	100	100	100	100	100	100	100	100	100	100	100	100

Question 11.5. Irregular and long working hours generate overtime and pose health risks for platform workers

Answer	N	Total	Urban	Rural	Male	Female	15–24 years	25–34 years	35–54 years	55+	Employees	Freelancers	Workers with service contracts	"NEET"	Others	None
1—strongly disagree	149	17.6	17.9	16.2	17.7	17.5	14.1	20.7	17.1	16.7	16.8	19.7	13	14.3	9.1	9.1
2	120	14.2	13.1	19.9	14.2	14.2	20.3	12.6	13.3	7.4	13.1	14.6	10.9	9.5	18.2	24.2
3	178	21	20.8	22	21.5	20.5	19.8	21.9	21.2	20.4	22.1	19.9	28.3	19	18.2	18.2
4	165	19.5	20	16.9	14.9	24.7	22.1	18.1	19.1	20.4	19.1	20.2	17.4	19	18.2	18.2
5—strongly agree	178	21.1	21.7	17.6	24.2	17.5	18.6	21.1	21.2	27.7	20.8	19.7	26.1	33.4	36.3	21.2
I don't know	56	6.6	6.5	7.4	7.5	5.6	5.1	5.6	8.1	7.4	8.1	5.9	4.3	4.8	0	9.1
Total	846	100	100	100	100	100	100	100	100	100	100	100	100	100	100	100

Question 11.6. Intense competition increases the psychological and social vulnerability of platform workers

Answer	N	Total	Urban	Rural	Male	Female	15–24 years	25–34 years	35–54 years	55+	Employees	Freelancers	Workers with service contracts	"NEET"	Others	None
1—strongly disagree	121	14.3	14.8	11.8	14.6	13.9	11.3	14.4	15.9	13	15.1	15.1	6.5	19	9.1	6.1
2	104	12.3	12.7	10.3	11.5	13.2	19.2	12.6	9.9	3.7	10.7	11.9	17.4	19	18.2	18.2
3	198	23.4	23.5	22.8	23	24.1	22	24.4	23.5	22.2	25.9	22.7	19.6	19	18.2	21.2
4	206	24.3	24.1	25.7	20.8	28.3	23.2	24.5	24.9	24	22.1	24.5	37	28.7	18.2	24.2
5—strongly agree	142	16.8	17	15.4	19.7	13.4	13.6	17.4	16.8	24.1	15.8	17.8	13	9.5	27.2	18.2
I don't know	75	8.9	7.9	14	10.4	7.1	10.7	6.7	9	13	10.4	8	6.5	4.8	9.1	12.1
Total	846	100	100	100	100	100	100	100	100	100	100	100	100	100	100	100

Question 11.7. Salary instability generates financial insecurity for platform workers

Answer	N	Total	Urban	Rural	Male	Female	15–24 years	25–34 years	35–54 years	55+	Employees	Freelancers	Workers with service contracts	"NEET"	Others	None
1—strongly disagree	98	11.6	11.8	10.3	11.5	11.6	9	14.4	11.9	3.7	10.1	13	2.2	23.8	18.2	9.1
2	79	9.3	9.6	8.1	8.2	10.6	9.6	10.4	8.4	9.3	9.4	10.1	8.7	4.8	0	6.1
3	180	21.3	20.8	23.5	22.2	20.3	27.7	21.9	18.8	13	22.1	20.1	28.3	14.3	18.2	24.2
4	214	25.3	24.9	27.2	19.7	31.7	27.1	22.2	27.2	22.2	25.8	24.5	28.2	28.5	9.1	30.3
5—strongly agree	225	26.6	27.3	23.5	31.5	21	22.6	25.9	26.7	42.5	25.9	27.5	26.1	14.3	54.5	21.2
I don't know	50	5.9	5.6	7.4	6.9	4.8	4	5.2	7	9.3	6.7	4.8	6.5	14.3	0	9.1
Total	846	100	100	100	100	100	100	100	100	100	100	100	100	100	100	100

Question 11.8. Anonymity when working through digital platforms does not protect against discrimination

Answer	N	Total	Urban	Rural	Male	Female	15–24 years	25–34 years	35–54 years	55+	Employees	Freelancers	Workers with service contracts	"NEET"	Others	None
1—strongly disagree	153	18.1	19.3	11.8	18.2	18	10.7	22.2	19.4	13	18.5	19.7	6.5	19	0	15.2
2	103	12.2	12.7	9.6	12	12.4	16.9	10.4	11.6	9.3	10.4	13.3	10.9	4.8	27.3	15.2
3	205	24.1	25.1	19.9	23.3	25.3	25.5	26.7	22.9	16.7	25.2	24	34.8	14.3	9.1	15.2
4	135	16	15.6	17.6	13.5	18.7	18.1	14.8	15.4	18.5	15.4	14.6	23.9	19	27.3	21.2
5—strongly agree	141	16.7	16.6	16.9	20.8	11.9	15.8	15.2	17.1	24	16.1	15.8	17.4	23.9	27.2	24.1
I don't know	109	12.9	10.7	24.2	12.2	13.7	13	10.7	13.6	18.5	14.4	12.6	6.5	19	9.1	9.1
Total	846	100	100	100	100	100	100	100	100	100	100	100	100	100	100	100

Question 12 In your opinion, which of the factors listed in the table below determine or hinder sustainable development in the European Union? (Environmental factors)

Question 12.1. Lower prices for goods and services promote excessive consumption

Answer	N	Total	Urban	Rural	Male	Female	15–24 years	25–34 years	35–54 years	55+	Employees	Freelancers	Workers with service contracts	"NEET"	Others	None
1—strongly disagree	114	13.5	13.4	14	14	12.9	14.1	14.1	12.5	14.8	12.1	14.6	10.9	4.8	27.3	15.2
2	93	11	11.1	10.3	9.8	12.4	14.7	10	9.9	11.1	9.7	12.6	8.7	14.3	0	6.1
3	171	20.2	19.9	22.1	23.7	16.2	22.6	20.4	19.7	14.8	23.5	18.3	19.6	14.3	18.2	21.2
4	195	23	22.7	24.9	18.4	28.4	23.7	22.2	22.3	29.6	20.1	23.8	30.4	23.8	18.2	30.2
5—strongly agree	227	26.9	27.5	22.8	27.2	26.3	18.1	29.6	30.1	20.4	29.2	25.9	23.9	33.3	27.2	18.2
I don't know	46	5.4	5.4	5.9	6.9	3.8	6.8	3.7	5.5	9.3	5.4	4.8	6.5	9.5	9.1	9.1
Total	846	100	100	100	100	100	100	100	100	100	100	100	100	100	100	100

Question 12.2. Phones and computers consume a large amount of electricity

Answer	N	Total	Urban	Rural	Male	Female	15–24 years	25–34 years	35–54 years	55+	Employees	Freelancers	Workers with service contracts	“NEET”	Others	None
1—strongly disagree	199	23.4	24.4	18.4	29.7	16.5	19.2	26.8	24.5	16.7	24.2	23.3	26.1	19	27.3	18.2
2	135	16	15.8	16.9	15.5	16.5	20.3	15.9	14.2	13	15.8	16.7	19.6	9.5	0	12.1
3	152	18	17.5	20.6	18.6	17.2	22	18.1	16.2	14.8	21.1	17.4	10.9	14.3	0	15.2
4	144	17	17.2	16.2	11.8	22.9	16.4	14.4	18.8	20.4	14.8	18.8	10.9	14.3	18.2	24.2
5—strongly agree	180	21.3	20.6	25	20	22.8	19.8	19.6	22	29.5	21.1	18.8	30.3	28.6	54.5	27.3
I don’t know	36	4.3	4.5	2.9	4.4	4.1	2.3	5.2	4.3	5.6	3	5	2.2	14.3	0	3
Total	846	100	100	100	100	100	100	100	100	100	100	100	100	100	100	100

Question 12.3. Electronic devices have a relatively short lifespan (life cycle)

Answer	N	Total	Urban	Rural	Male	Female	15–24 years	25–34 years	35–54 years	55+	Employees	Freelancers	Workers with service contracts	"NEET"	Others	None
1—strongly disagree	131	15.5	16.2	11.8	20	10.4	15.3	17.8	15.4	5.6	15.1	17.2	8.7	4.8	9.1	15.2
2	111	13.1	13.7	10.3	11.1	15.4	19.2	12.6	11.6	5.6	11.7	14	21.7	4.8	9.1	9.1
3	179	21.2	20.7	23.5	21.3	21	24.3	25.2	15.9	24.1	23.8	20.4	19.6	9.5	18.2	18.2
4	148	17.5	17	19.9	15.1	20.3	18.6	13.7	19.1	22.2	15.8	17.8	17.4	14.3	9.1	33.3
5—strongly agree	226	26.7	25.9	30.8	27	26.3	18.1	26.3	31.3	27.7	27.9	24.7	28.3	42.8	54.5	21.2
I don't know	51	6	6.5	3.7	5.5	6.6	4.5	4.4	6.7	14.8	5.7	5.9	4.3	23.8	0	3
Total	846	100	100	100	100	100	100	100	100	100	100	100	100	100	100	100

Question 12.4. Internet traffic and servers require a lot of energy

Answer	N	Total	Urban	Rural	Male	Female	15–24 years	25–34 years	35–54 years	55+	Employees	Freelancers	Workers with service contracts	"NEET"	Others	None
1—strongly disagree	143	16.9	17.2	15.4	20.4	12.9	16.4	18.1	16.2	16.7	16.8	17.6	23.9	4.8	9.1	9.1
2	105	12.4	12.3	13.2	10.4	14.7	15.8	12.6	11	9.3	12.4	13.7	6.5	4.8	0	12.1
3	145	17.1	17.5	15.4	16.9	17.5	24.8	17.8	13.6	11.1	19.8	16.2	17.4	9.5	18.2	9.1
4	177	20.9	21.1	19.9	19.1	23	19.8	23.7	19.7	18.5	20.5	20.1	21.7	19	27.3	33.3
5—strongly agree	213	25.3	24.4	28.7	26.3	23.8	18.1	21.1	30.8	33.3	24.8	23.9	26.2	38.1	45.4	30.3
I don't know	63	7.4	7.5	7.4	6.9	8.1	5.1	6.7	8.7	11.1	5.7	8.5	4.3	23.8	0	6.1
Total	846	100	100	100	100	100	100	100	100	100	100	100	100	100	100	100

Question 13 In Your opinion, which of the measures listed Below would be the most useful to improve working conditions Through digital platforms? (Please select one or more relevant resp onses.)

Answer	N	Total	Urban	Rural	Male	Female	15–24 years	25–34 years	35–54 years	55+	Employees	Freelancers	Workers with service contracts	"NEET"	Others	None
Increasing social security for digital platform workers	387	45.7	47.3	37.5	40.8	51.4	42.4	44.4	47.8	50	45.6	48.1	41.3	52.4	18.2	27.3
Improving the work-life balance of digital platform workers	351	41.5	41.4	41.9	41.2	41.8	38.4	41.9	42.3	44.4	40.3	43	43.5	33.3	9.1	45.5
A specific and clear definition of the legal status of platform workers (clearly stating whether they are employees or independent workers/freelancers)	311	36.8	37.9	30.9	32.4	41.8	39	38.1	35.7	29.6	36.2	36.6	37	33.3	45.5	42.4
Improving the representation of workers' interests (e.g., organizing congresses of platform workers, establishing workers' unions, etc.)	300	35.5	36.1	32.4	34.8	36.2	40.1	35.9	32.2	38.9	32.9	38.7	37	14.3	36.4	27.3

Greater control over data and control of automated systems (algorithms) on digital platforms	300	35.5	35.8	33.8	32.8	38.5	31.1	34.1	38.6	37	36.6	36.6	26.1	23.8	18.2	36.4
Other (please specify)	14	1.7	2	0	1.1	2.3	0	1.9	2.6	0	1.3	2.1	0	0	0	3
I don't know	68	8	6.1	18.4	8.2	7.8	9.6	6.3	8.4	9.3	8.4	7.8	8.7	9.5	9.1	6.1
No response	16	1.9	1.8	2.2	2.2	1.5	1.1	1.9	2.3	1.9	2.7	1.1	2.2	4.8	0	3
Total	1747	206.6	208.4	197.1	193.5	221.3	201.7	204.5	209.9	211.1	204	214	195.8	171.4	136.5	191

MIX
Papier aus verantwortungsvollen Quellen
Paper from responsible sources
FSC® C105338

If you have any concerns about our products,
you can contact us on
ProductSafety@springernature.com

In case Publisher is established outside the EU,
the EU authorized representative is:
Springer Nature Customer Service Center GmbH
Europaplatz 3, 69115 Heidelberg, Germany

Printed by Libri Plureos GmbH
in Hamburg, Germany